# ISN'T ONE WIFE ENOUGH?

*Books by the Same Author*

Social Psychology
Sociology, A Study of Society and Culture
Personality and Problems of Adjustment

# ISN'T ONE

## by Kimball Young

*Illustrated with Photographs*

Henry Holt and Company  ·  New York

# WIFE

# ENOUGH?

IN MEMORIAM BRIGHAM YOUNG.

"And the Place which knew him once shall know him no more."

First Edition

Library of Congress Catalog Card Number: 54-5461

Printed in the United States of America

The cartoon reproduced on the title page
is taken from *Puck,* September, 1877.

To Lillian

who says the Mormons are highly
overrated

# ACKNOWLEDGMENTS

With respect to the many individuals who have contributed to this book in the way of personal accounts, I have,
except in the cases of public record, altered the names of my
informants. Materials from about seventy-five families were
secured through interviews conducted by Mr. and Mrs. J. E.
Hulett, Miss Fay Ollerton, and myself. My debt to these informants is heavy indeed. These family stories form the basis
of the discussion of the psychology of personality under the
plural system. I also want to thank Mr. and Mrs. Hulett and
Miss Ollerton for many suggestions regarding the interpretation of these data.

With regard to the historical materials, I appreciate the
efforts of the librarians who helped to locate and examine the
rich data on this phase of Mormonism. These include not
only material on the public controversy but many personal
documents such as diaries, journals, and autobiographies as
well. In particular I want to thank the Wisconsin Historical
Society Library, the New York Public Library, the Library
of Congress, the Presbyterian Historical Library in Philadel-

phia, the Chicago Historical Library and the Newberry Library in Chicago, the State Historical Library in Springfield, Illinois, the State Historical Library, the Public Library, and the University of Utah Library—all three in Salt Lake City, Utah—and the Brigham Young University Library in Provo, Utah. And most especially I have a heavy debt to the Henry E. Huntington Library in San Marino, California, at which place I was able finally to finish this long-promised work.

In addition to the above, I wish to thank various institutions for their generous grants-in-aid. These include the University of Wisconsin, the Carnegie Corporation of New York, the Social Science Research Council, the Wenner-Gren Foundation for Anthropological Research (formerly the Viking Fund), Northwestern University, and last but not least the John Simon Guggenheim Memorial Foundation for a fellowship for 1952.

The author wishes to thank the following for permission to quote certain materials: Dodd, Mead & Company from *Man and Superman* by Bernard Shaw, copyright, 1903, by George Bernard Shaw; Alfred A. Knopf, Inc. from *No Man Knows My History, the Life of Joseph Smith, the Mormon Prophet*, 1945, by Fawn M. Brodie; and *The New Yorker*, August 17, 1946, a drawing entitled, "Footnotes to American History. An enterprising salesman interests Brigham Young in the first group-insurance policy" by Carl Rose.

# PREFACE

This book aims to tell an honest story of one of the most interesting and informative episodes in American history. A practice as deviant and emotionally loaded as plural marriage was certain to arouse in some persons strong negative feelings, while to the faithful Mormon it was regarded as a divine command. In telling and analyzing the views and actions of individuals who participated in the system or of those who opposed it, I have tried to steer as objective a course as possible.

This book is a contribution to social science as well as to Americana. Among other things it shows how individuals learn to accept radical changes in their habits and values. It still astounds us that thousands of pious Christians brought up on the sacredness of monogamy could be quickly converted to polygamy as the most desirable form of marriage and family life. Yet, as will be amply demonstrated, the shift from earlier to newer patterns of family life was easier to adopt in theory than in practice. Many women and their husbands as well experienced severe personal trauma in bringing themselves to live in polygamy.

A student of systematic social science may well ask if any generalization may be drawn from this story. Here within three quarters of a century we see the emergence, fruition, and death of a basic institution, that of marriage and family. Certainly it is apparent to me that to introduce such radical and divergent patterns of life in so short a time, there is needed some strong motivation supported by intense emotion. Surely the monogamous system was thoroughly entrenched in the Christian mores. Moreover, sexuality was viewed askance and sex indulgence was to be confined, in theory at least, to procreative purposes only. And yet here a combination of religious zeal and appeal to the deep instinct of sex made it possible to put the plurality scheme into effect within a few years. If any generalization is to be drawn from this, it is that there must be strong motivations before one can hope to bring about radical changes in human institutions and in the accompanying personal conduct.

Something should be said about the organization of this book. The first three chapters which serve as a prologue give three different views of Mormon polygamy. The first presents that of the antagonistic Gentiles who regarded plural marriage as a social cancer of the most dangerous variety. Second, there is the view of the faithful Mormons who regarded the system as divinely ordered and hence completely proper. The third chapter aims to give a factual description of polygamy as it operated in day-by-day living. Against the background of this prologue, there follow eleven chapters devoted largely to a psychological analysis of the way in which the spouses got along, how the children made out, and how the routine life of a plural family went on. There follow five chapters dealing chiefly with the public controversy that broke out over Mormon polygamy. For more than four decades it was one of the chief topics of public discussion in the United States. The book closes with a chapter—the epilogue—on the wider implications of plural marriage in modern society.

KIMBALL YOUNG

EVANSTON, ILLINOIS

# CONTENTS

# ISN'T ONE WIFE ENOUGH?

*. . . It is both the right and the imperative duty of Congress to prohibit in the territories those twin relics of barbarism —polygamy and slavery.*—From Platform of the Republican Party, adopted in Philadelphia, June 17, 1856.

# 1 THE MORMON CHAMBER OF HORRORS: THE GENTILE LOOKS AT POLYGAMY

THE MORMON CHURCH had barely been organized in 1830 when rumor had it that Joseph Smith was, by Christian standards, thoroughly immoral. This was the beginning of a long legend regarding the sexuality of the Latter-day Saints. Opposition to the Mormons, especially regarding polygamy, began as early as the Kirtland period and became even more intense during the Nauvoo episode. After the Civil War when the first relic of barbarism had been liquidated, at least officially, the attacks on the Mormons were intensified. Moral reformers, like hounds in pursuit of the fox, now had a new scent to follow. In the half-century from 1870 to 1920, Mormonism and polygamy rivaled with prostitution and prohibition as the main interest of American reformers. Polygamy was a menace to everything which puritanic Americans held sacred. Plural wifehood was an attack upon monogamy, the home and fireside, upon children, and—above all—upon the rising status of women. It was, therefore, the moral duty of all good Christians to help uproot this evil.

That the Mormon movement had become closely identified with polygamy in the minds of the educated as well as of the masses is neatly shown by C. Sheridan Jones who as late as 1920, in the introduction to a book, *The Truth About the Mormons,* remarked, "Mormonism spells polygamy, and polygamy means the enslavement of women." And recently a businessman who had had a college education asked me in all

1

seriousness: "Are they still practicing Mormonism in Utah?"
Obviously he meant polygamy.

The present chapter will give a brief picture of how the
Gentile—as the Mormons call the non-Mormon—viewed the
plural marriage system. Aside from early stories of Smith's
personal infidelities, spiritual wifism was bruited about as a
cover for the moral laxity of the Mormons, first in Kirtland,
Ohio, and later in Nauvoo, Illinois. Moreover, as the Mormons became a potential threat in the neat political balance
between the Whigs and the Democrats in the pre-Civil War
period, polygamy served as a convenient symbol to arouse
opposition.

In 1844 one Joseph Jackson published a violent attack on
"the depths of Mormon villainy" and a few years later, 1849,
appeared an anonymous book purporting to be "a full exposure of the iniquities of the pretended prophet, Joe Smith,"
which boldly stated: ". . . Immorality is the cornerstone of
the Mormon faith. The freedom of their conduct, however,
even exceeded the bounds which the warmest imagination
might ascribe to it, and exhibited the spiritual wife system in
a light altogether too glaring for exposure to the public eye."
Having thus whetted the emotional appetite of the reader,
the book goes on to give some of the exciting details of life
among the Mormons.

Writing before the Civil War, Metta V. Fuller, in her book,
*Mormon Wives*, wrote:

> Repulsive as slavery appears to us, we can but deem polygamy
> a thing more loathsome and poisonous to social and political pu-
> rity. Half-civilized states have ceased its practice as dangerous to
> happiness, and as outraging every instinct of the better nature
> within every breast; and as ages rolled away they left the institu-
> tion behind as one of the relics of barbarism which marked the
> half-developed state of man as a social being.

Truly Mormonism, a term most people thought synonymous
with plural wifism, was a topic of intense interest during
the latter half of the 19th century. To folks reared under the
strict monogamy of Christianity, the idea that a man might

with impunity and with open approval of his fellows share his bed with more than one wife was at the same time both shocking and yet more than intriguing. People in the larger cities, of course, had long winked at prostitution. Moreover, the bordello was defend̄ed by the upper *bourgeoisie* as a necessary evil, designed to protect innocent women. Moreover, in many small towns and rural districts premarital relations were not punished at all if the couple later married. But, on the whole, the Christian taboos on premarital and extramarital relations prevailed, and departures from such standards were considered both sinful and unlawful.

Many individuals wrote and lectured on the evils of Mormonism, especially polygamy. They got their materials, or said they did, from a wide variety of sources:

First, there were the stories of unhappy, abused, and disgruntled wives—both the plural ones as well as first wives. There were plenty of difficulties in polygamy and it was easy for the Gentiles to get some of these women to talk.

Second, there were the apostates, that is, those who had left the Mormon Church for one reason or another. Apostates from any faith are ever ready to reveal their experiences in an organization which they have abandoned. In fact, apostates are the religious equivalent of political traitors. And while the testimony of traitors is not usually regarded as completely valid, they frequently provide excellent intelligence for the militants on the opposite side of the fence. Moreover, when a nation feels strongly upset over the disappearance of one of its trusted persons to the other camp, it usually counterattacks him by accusing him of all kinds of dishonesties and immoralities. So it was with the struggle between the Gentiles and the Mormons. The Mormons regarded their apostates as evil persons and the Gentiles welcomed them into their arms so long as they could tell a good story—a story on which the Gentiles, in turn, could plan a campaign.

Then, too, many of those who wrote on Mormonism reported more or less formal interviews with various members of the Church. Finally, visitors to the Mormon communities made personal observations on the street, in the meeting houses, in the homes, and elsewhere. Facts gleaned in this way were used to supplement what they learned from conversation and formal interviews.

What the Gentiles heard and saw were abetted by a rich imagination and a strong desire to tell a good story. Some had sincere intentions to expose what they regarded as a great moral evil. Others, like the journalists and fiction writers, were out to tell a yarn which would sell. In any case, the Gentiles and Mormons alike amply illustrated a sound principle in perception. As G. T. W. Patrick, the philosopher, once said, "We see things not as they are but as we are." That is to say, the wish is father to the thought.

The tone and content of the serious religious-moral attack are illustrated in a report to the Cincinnati Methodist Conference in October, 1884, presented by its Committee on Mormon Polygamy. Among other things the report states:

> Mormonism is not a religion. It is a crime, therefore it cannot be entitled to protection and tolerance under the laws and Constitution of the United States as a matter of conscience. It is not a religious superstition but a system of masked sensuality, and hence subversive of every principle of morality, and abhorrent to every feeling of virtue . . . It is a preconcerted infernal scheme, partly mercenary, partly political, and chiefly licentious. It was originated in the deepest depravity, and is shared by three motives—money, power, and lust . . .
>
> It is already so rooted in the soil, the politics, the family life, and the religious fanaticism of that part of the country [Utah], that nothing but prompt and extreme measures will eradicate the evil. And unless the government shall immediately take decisive steps to exterminate the abomination, it will soon acquire such dimensions and potency as to render it impossible to remove the evil by legislation, or any civil measures. Indeed, it is the belief of some well informed men now that this dreadful ulcer can only be removed by a resort to arms . . .

The bulk of the persons who took up the moral cudgels against plural marriage were recruited from the ministry. The list of ministers who devoted hours, days, and years in attacking polygamy would have made a respectable Who's Who of the preachers of the day. The great and popular Reverend DeWitt Talmage of Brooklyn was one of the leaders. Shortly after the death of Brigham Young in 1877, Talmage strongly advocated that that was the time to give Mormonism its *coup de grâce,* if necessary, "at the point of the bayonet."

Yet these were not the only earnest people who were seriously concerned with this moral and religious problem. Having with her *Uncle Tom's Cabin* helped to dispose of slavery —the first relic of barbarism—Harriet Beecher Stowe, said in the preface to *An English Woman in Utah: The Story of a Life's Experience in Mormonism,* by Fanny Stenhouse: "May we not then hope that the hour is come to loose the bonds of cruel slavery whose chains have cut into the very hearts of thousands of our sisters—a slavery which debases and degrades womanhood, motherhood, and the family?" And Frances E. Willard, though giving most of her attention to problems of liquor abatement, took time out to write an introduction to a book by Jennie Anderson Froiseth, entitled, *The Women of Mormonism: Or the Story of Polygamy as Told by the Victims Themselves.* Among other things she said:

"Turkey is in our midst. Modern Mohammedanism has its Mecca at Salt Lake, where Prophet Heber C. Kimball speaks of his wives as 'cows.' Surely it is time that the Christian women of this nation arouse themselves to *organized action* against this son of all curses which can curse the sex not physically strong . . ."

A third type of material and method of presentation with which we are concerned are the alleged exposés of polygamy from inside the ranks. Without doubt the best known of these was written by Brigham's ex-wife, Ann Eliza Young. In 1868, at the age of 66 years, the Prophet married Ann Eliza Webb, then 24 years old. Seven years later she sued Brigham for divorce. While the courts threw out this case, since it could not admit that one could divorce a woman who was not legally married, Ann Eliza wrote a book entitled, *Wife Number 19.* It had wide circulation. Moreover she spent years lecturing on the evils of Mormonism and polygamy.

One of the most lurid accounts is that of William Jarman, an apostate polygamist. A side light on Jarman from the Mormon point of view, is provided in the journal of John Lewis for October 9, 1886, at the time Elder Lewis was attending the semiannual conference of the Church in Salt Lake City. He writes:

. . . Had quite a talk with Mrs. Hall who was once the wife of William Jarman who did so much to raise the feeling of the people in England against the Saints. She said that she was the polygamous wife of Jarman; the other wife was living at present in the 11th Ward of Salt Lake. She said he had many times locked her in a room and at the point of a knife or pistol extracted promises from her. He was as mean a man as could be . . . for although she had four children living by him, she could not say a good word of him and his book was a mass of lies from beginning to end with very few exceptions.

A good deal of the serious literature contra polygamy may be described as a combination of description and analysis. Such a book is Mrs. Froiseth's, already noted. So, too, was Mrs. C. V. Waite's, *The Mormon Prophet and His Harem; or, an Authentic History of Brigham Young, His Numerous Wives and Children* (1866). There is frequently an exposure of the evils of the system with various personal documents to support the argument. We shall note some of these later on.

In the fourth place, the line between fact and fantasy is often difficult to draw. There is a rather considerable body of fiction dealing with Mormons and especially with polygamy. In building the stereotype or image in people's minds about the Mormons and their practices, fiction is probably more effective than the more serious accounts of the moral reformers.

The fiction on polygamy ranges all the way from *A Study in Scarlet,* in which the redoubtable Sherlock Holmes is put on the trail of certain deceitful and treacherous Mormon missionaries, to the real tear jerkers such as Alfreda Eva Bell's, *Boadicea; The Mormon Wife, Life-Scenes in Utah* (1855.)

*Boadicea* is one of those yarns which combines the fictional approach with a good deal of moralizing. The central story is that of Hubert and his beautiful wife Boadicea, and her introduction to Utah, Mormonism, and especially to plural marriage. Early in the volume Boadicea tells of meeting Cephysia Edmonds. Mrs. Edmonds "informed me that she was one of Elder Manor's wives . . . glancing at Hubert in a manner that left no doubt in my mind as to her being his mistress." A little later Boadicea goes on to say, "Greatly to my astonishment, the brunet [Cephysia] informed me that she was commissioned to ask me if I felt willing to become the spiritual wife of Elder Aaron Manor, her husband, who, she informed me, had only ten wives already, and wished to add myself to his already 'small and respectable family . . .' " The story continues with the brunet telling Boadicea of the exchange of husbands and wives under the spiritual wife system. The account describes the whole system of plural marriage and brings out that, "No woman can enter Heaven on her own merits—that is, *without a man to take her there!!!*"

The lurid story continues to relate how the husband tried to convince the wife of his duty to take Cephysia as his plural wife, of how Boadicea, on hearing this, "felt as if turned to stone." The heartbroken Boadicea found that the new wife was attractive enough physically. A mean and passionate woman, she was also apparently an opium user as well as given to intoxicating liquor. Yet she was a zealous Mormon, especially in her strong adherence to plural marriage.

There follow many exciting details of the difficulties of Boadicea. She learns of the murder of a Mormon who has left the Church, and she barely escapes poisoning at the hand of the jealous second wife. After more adventures, interlarded with moralisms on the way the system "destroys the purity of the immortal soul," Boadicea finally manages to escape Utah with a party of friends. She concludes her tragic story in these words:

"Such events as I here laid bare before the reader, are *daily* occurrences among the Mormons. No better idea of pandemonium can be conceived; it is a veritable hell upon God's fair and beautiful earth. The blood of the murdered, the crushed hearts of the despairing call out for vengeance!"

There is still another body of anti-polygamy literature, that of wit and humor. This matter includes stories, poems, and cartoons. Two of America's best-known wits, Artemus Ward and Mark Twain, will serve as examples.

Ward's first pieces on the Mormons appeared before he had visited Salt Lake City and interviewed Brigham Young. Some time after his visit he wrote up his idea of a complex Mormon menage in these words:

I had a man pointed out to me who married an entire family. He had originally intended to marry Jane, but Jane did not want to leave her widowed mother. The other three sisters were not in the matrimonial market for the same reason; so this gallant man married the whole crowd, including the girls' grandmother, who had lost all her teeth, and had to be fed with a spoon. The family were in indigent circumstances, and they could not but congratulate themselves on securing a wealthy husband. It seemed to affect the grandmother deeply, for the first words she said on reaching her new home were, "Now, thank God! I shall have my gruel reg'lar!"

In another sketch Ward describes an imaginary Leap Year among the Mormons. He says that 17 young widows, wives of a deceased Mormon, offered him their hearts and hands. The account closes as follows:

They said—"Doth not like us?"
I said—"I doth—I doth!"
I also said—"I hope your intentions are honorable—as I am a lone child—my parents being far—far away."
They then said—"Wilt not marry us?"
I said—"Oh—no—it cannot was."
Again they asked me to marry them—and again I declined.
Then they cried—"Oh—cruel man! This is too much— Oh! too much!"
I told them that it was on account of the muchness that I declined.

The humor of Mark Twain was of a different character. It often carried underneath a certain pathos and deep appreciation of a given situation. In *Roughing It* he relates his first contact with Brigham Young in a somewhat allegorical fashion, describing how Brigham Young had once given an interview to a guest who in turn had given Brigham's children whistles. They raised such a rumpus with these that Brigham had the man pursued with an idea of punishing him . . . " 'But they never caught him. I am not cruel, sir. I am not vindictive except when sorely outraged; but if I had caught him, sir, so help me Joseph Smith, I would have locked him into the nursery 'til the brats whistled him to death.' "

In another part of this volume, Twain gives something of his more serious impression of the situation regarding polygamy. Stating that he felt it was a great wrong, he says:

. . . With the gushing self-sufficiency of youth I was feverish to plunge headlong and achieve a great reform here until I saw the Mormon women. Then I was touched. My heart was wiser than my head. It warmed me toward these poor, ungainly, and pathetically "homely" creatures, and as I turned to hide the generous moisture in my eyes, I said, "No—the man that marries one of them has done an act of Christian charity which entitled him to the kindly applause of mankind, not their harsh censor—and the man that marries sixty of them has done a deed of open-handed generosity so sublime that the nation should stand uncovered in his presence and worship in silence."

Clemens always maintained a rather tolerant attitude toward the Mormons. Later, when Kate Field, one of the more virulent crusaders, tried to get him to support her cause, he replied, among other things: "Considering our complaisant cant about this country of ours being a home of liberty of conscience, it seems to me that the attitude of our Congress and people toward the Mormon Church is a matter for limitless laughter and derision."

Other wits of the day turned their attention to polygamy in the form of verse. Out of a large collection of anti-Mormon verse, I give a tidbit from *Saint Abe and His Seven Wives, A Tale of Salt Lake City,* by Robert W. Buchanan, published in 1872. It is designed to show how a new wife, "Sister Anne," is regarded by the previous six. As might be expected the introduction of the new wife to the other wives was met by a combination of indifference or hostility:

Already she [the new wife] saddens and sinks and sighs,
Watched by the jealous dragonish eyes.
Even Amelia, sleepy and wan,
Sharpens her orbs as she looks at Anne;
While Sister Tabby, when she can spare
Her gaze from the Saint in his easy-chair,
Fixes her with a gorgon glare.

And a much more recent one in lighter vein, which was set to music, is this:

## I'D LIKE TO BE A MORMON

*Words by Horace Liveright*      *Music by W. L. Gwynne*

It must be nice to have six wives to tuck you in your bed,
Six bits of femininity to hold your aching head,
Six rosy mouths to kiss each night when home from work you come,
And likewise six to feed when your affairs are on the bum.
Twelve dainty hands to darn your socks, and go through all your
     clothes,
Twelve hands to find old letters from your Lizzies, Mags and Flos,
And when Christmas comes around, why bless your lucky stars,
Six wives to buy you made-up ties and no-tobaac cigars.

### Chorus

Oh, I'd like to be a Mormon, wouldn't you?
In Congress then I'd represent my state,
I'd lead a dozen lives and have a lot of wives,
Each one asking is my hat on straight.
Oh! I'd like to be a Mormon, wouldn't you?
I wouldn't mind the W.C.T.U.
I'd move to Salt Lake's shores with my Flos and Annie Moores.
Oh! I'd like to be a Mormon, wouldn't you?

The ammunition used by the Gentiles against Mormonism and polygamy was of various shapes, sizes, and effectiveness on the targets. The major targets against which they let go their salvos were Mormon priestcraft and its theory of salvation which gave a very low position to women. The second was its exaggeration and abuse of the sexual impulse. In the early history of Mormonism its critics were quick to seize upon the spiritual wife doctrine as an object of attack. If you believed that mating was done in heaven and that you might look forward to a predestined spouse in the spirit world hereafter, why should mortal man wait until he had crossed the bar before taking his spiritual wife to bed?

Yet, the attacks upon polygamy must be seen against the larger fact of the Latter-day Saints' ecclesiastical system and theology, especially as these were viewed by the non-Mormons. The Mormon Church is a close-knit system with a highly organized priesthood set up to regulate practically everything in the member's life. There is a fine gradation of power as one goes down the echelons from the Prophet, Seer and Revelator at the top, to the lowliest Deacon in the Ward who passes out communion on Sundays.

According to Mormon theology only a man could hold the priesthood; a woman could get her full salvation only by securing a Mormon husband under the Church's holy rites of matrimony. This principle, of course, applied equally to plural wives. The Gentiles quickly saw in this evidence of the low status of women under Mormondom and used it in their attacks.

Probably nothing upset the pious Christians and moral reformers of the United States and Europe more than what they considered to be the degradation and humiliation of Mormon women. The more ardent reformers among them, of course, saw the whole idea of the emancipation of women, for which they had fought so hard, threatened by this new development. Others saw the degradation in terms of the lust and sexual interest of Mormon men.

While J. H. Beadle, an ardent opponent, in his book, *Life in Utah; Or the Mysteries and Crimes of Mormons* (1870), says that: "The degradation of women . . . is the second great evil of polygamy," the first being jealousy and disharmony. Mrs. Froiseth remarks: "The cornerstone of polygamy is the degradation of woman, and it can flourish only where she is regarded and treated as a slave."

The inferior position of women is neatly brought out in Maria Ward's *Female Life Among the Mormons* (1855). The

courtship scene between Brigham Young and one Mrs. Bradish, whose hand he had asked in marriage, runs as follows:

Mrs. Bradish smiled a meaning smile. "I fear," she said, "that
my entrance into your household might not be relished by its
present inmates."
"And what of that?" he replied. "You should be the first and
greatest among them."
"No, that privilege belongs of right to the first wife."
"The husband has the liberty of conferring it on anyone he
pleases."
"The husband may assume that right, but I conceive that such
an assumption of prerogative is unjust."
"The husband is the head of the wife; her temporal and eternal
salvation depends on him."

Brigham left his would-be wife with no doubts about who
was boss not only in his own family but in the Mormon system
itself. It might be said that Mrs. Bradish declined Brigham's
hand.

According to Mrs. Froiseth some of the female defenders
of the system were "perfectly insane on the subject." On one
occasion a certain plural wife listened to a first wife's tale of
woe:

"Oh, I can not bear it," wailed the poor grief-stricken wife. "We
have been so happy together. I shall die if he takes another. I
cannot live and have another woman come between us."
"Die, then," responded the female apostle of polygamy. "There
are hundreds of better women than you lying up there in that
graveyard, who have died for the same cause!"

In another chapter, "Tools of the Priesthood," Mrs.
Froiseth says that to further the seduction of virgins, the Female Relief Society was organized at the command of the
church leaders and its principal function was to carry out the
"plans of a licentious and tyrannical priesthood."

The young girls are brought to these meetings every week and
the principles of polygamy thoroughly and systematically incul-
cated. With such a belief impressed upon the plastic hearts and
minds of children, what is the natural result? When they are four-

teen or sixteen years of age, and are told that they must be sealed to Brother So-and-So, and that thus their eternal happiness and glory will be assured, they go to the Endowment House and become the plural wives of the brothers selected, almost without hesitation.

Furthermore women tended to be viewed as mere property —another evidence of degradation. Such a view toward women, of course, showed that there was no place for tender sentiment or romantic love. Maria Ward relates a story of the interchange between two Mormon men, Brothers Melton and Weldy, to demonstrate this contention.

Brother Weldy, on the lookout for additional wives, came to Melton to see about marrying one of his daughters. Weldy was a well-to-do man and Melton drove a sharp bargain. In praising the good points of his daughters, Melton said, "You see, Brother Weldy, my girls are no common piece of woman flesh . . ." He went on to point out that they were trim and neat, handy with housework, and fairly obedient. ". . . The expense of their upbringing has been very great, Brother Weldy, consequently their husband must give me something commensurate. Beautiful girls like them should command rich husbands."

Weldy admitted he was well off but Melton reminded him that he was also getting along in years and that there were a good many younger men around who were quite attractive to the girls. Therefore, he wondered, if something might not be made in the way of a dower gift if he would agree to let him have one of his daughters.

"Why, yes," said Weldy, drawing his words, "I might give something rather handsome, I suppose, say, that gray mare; I'll give you her . . ."

"Say both horses, and it's a bargain. They're just such a span as I've been wanting to get."

"Couldn't, positively couldn't, unless you let me have both the girls; what do you say to that, eh?"

"Both my daughters! Really, I don't know. Would it be lawful for a man to marry two sisters?"

"Certainly, the patriarch Jacob did, you know."

"You would be welcome to the girls, both of them, provided you are willing to give me a suitable remuneration, but either one is worth both your mares, considering their age and beauty . . . I want them to marry a rich man, but I can't give them away; that wouldn't look well—wouldn't look as if I had any regard for them."

"You mustn't be too hard on a fellow, now; but I am willing to do right about it. Say both the girls, and I'll throw in that Durham cow."

"That's more like it; but it strikes me that if you were to see the girls, you'd still be more liberal. Let me go and call them."

The old-man and young-girl theme, as an expression of lust, was common enough in the Gentile literature. Austin Ward in *The Husband in Utah* (1857) describes a trip into the country with a group of Mormons. He writes:

Several married men were in the company. One, with whom I was slightly acquainted, and knew was the husband of six wives, was flirting and ogling most unmercifully with a delicate maiden of twelve years, who seemed decidedly pleased with his attentions, practicing all the arts and allurements of the most accomplished coquette. A more disgusting sight I never witnessed. Stranger still, the girl's mother was along, highly elated with the scene, and seeming to do all in her power to increase their intimacy.

The sex and lust theme was played upon almost ad infinitum and, viewed in cold, historical perspective, *ad nauseam*. Pious Christians of the day could hardly deny the facts of sex but they had various ideas about its place and various methods of controlling it. In Christian theology sex is recognized as necessary for procreation but the traditional view held that there should be no fun connected with it.

While admitting that the place of sex in the procreation of the species, Beadle, a violent opponent, contends that love has higher and nobler purposes of "companionship, society, love of congenial associates." It does not stop there, it "is, in part, divine . . . a nature in common with the angels." According to him the Mormons had little or no appreciation of these high virtues. Or, if they did, the introduction of plural marriage soon destroyed such sentiments. In discussing the extension of the system in Utah, Beadle says that in the early 1850's "Old men traded for young girls, and the new order was hailed as the great crowning glory and privilege of believers." And after the "Reformation" or revivalism of 1857, the new

. . . practice seemed for a while to reach a furious climax of unnatural and degrading obscenity. The duty and importance of polygamy was presented every Sunday; hundreds of girls of only twelve or thirteen years were forced or persuaded into its practice; and in numerous instances even younger girls were "sealed" to old reprobates upon the written agreement on the part of the latter to wait until the girls were more mature to act the part of wives . . .

To Beadle, it is only too plain "that the system results in the added destruction of domestic love and harmony. The Mormons themselves hesitatingly acknowledged, that 'the thing called love among the Gentiles' cannot exist under their system; but claim that they have instead, a purer feeling of respect, support and friendship." He goes on to remark, ". . . For a man to love six women, equally well, is manifestly impossible; but it is possible for him to be equally indifferent to all."

Beadle quotes Brigham Young as remarking in a sermon, " 'The women are everyday complaining of what they have to suffer in plurality. If it's any harder on them than it is on the men, God help them. Many of them seem to think that a man in plurality has nothing to do but listen to their troubles, and run at their beck and call . . .' "

Mrs. Froiseth frequently notes that her subjects, distraught and disgruntled plural wives, soon discovered that romantic love had no place in the scheme. Under the theory of romantic love, of course, jealousy is regarded as a signal of difficulties ahead and is a motive for doing something about keeping one's spouse. One plural wife quoted by Froiseth remarks that under polygamy a wife "is taught that to love her husband as her heart prompts her to do, and to feel that natural jealousy that comes from seeing her husband marry another woman, is wicked, and springs from her innate depravity; that she must crush out and annihilate all such feelings, and submit to whatever her husband and the Mormon Church dictate . . ."

Deception was said to be widely practiced. Writer after

writer cites, either in the name of actual fact or in fictional form, instances of the husband bringing home a plural wife without his first wife knowing anything about it. There are also cases where the second wife is first aware after her marriage that there is a first wife already on hand. In a chapter providing examples of deception, Mrs. Froiseth tells the story of how a Mormon missionary to England converted a young girl to Mormonism and further converted her to becoming his wife. They lived together for a time in Britain when the first wife, in search of health, and with the husband's consent, appeared on the scene. The first wife goes on to describe her distress when she had to live for two years in England as the sister of this Elder, while he cavorted all over the British Isles and the Continent with his new and second wife posing as his first. The account closes with these words: "But notwithstanding all the neglect she experienced, and the cruel treatment she endured, though she had lost both love for and faith in her husband, yet her devotion and loyalty to her religion never wavered one particle."

This is not all. Not only was there a general degradation of both men and women, not only was love replaced by lust, not only did men marry girls who were young enough to be their granddaughters, but the Gentiles had plenty of stories to tell of what they called "incest." In fact, this theme is repeated many times in some of the more lurid accounts.

Every student of social history knows that there are many meanings given to incest. Just how kinship by blood is reckoned and how taboos are placed upon the mating of close kin vary enormously. In a society where descent is traced in the father's line, taboos may prevent intermarriage of anybody in the paternal line even remotely removed. Where descent follows the mother's line, taboos may reach to very distant relatives in the maternal line. In the latter close intermarriage may be permitted in the father's line, just as where paternal descent counts, near relatives in the mother's line may and do marry. We live under a system of bilateral descent, counting it from both the mother and the father. With us the laws and social rules regarding consanguinity are applicable equally to both lines of descent.

In Christian history there has been a good deal of variation in theory and practice regarding the marriage of blood relatives. Certainly in the upper and aristocratic classes, on the theory of keeping the stock pure and the power in the family hands, marriages of close kin were not only tolerated but often encouraged. Biologically, of course, there is no reason why inbreeding should lead to degeneration of the stock. In fact, the purebreds among our domestic animals are the product of prearranged inbreeding. But the human animal has never been able to view himself in quite the same way that he does his horses, cattle, and dogs. Rather he has from time to time taken rather strong views on what constituted crossing the kinship line. In keeping with the Christian views, the Gentiles were horrified to find all kinds of amazing cases of Mormon men marrying two or more women who were sisters, or of men marrying a daughter and her widowed mother.

Regarding the situation among the Mormons, Beadle remarks, "To marry a mother and one or more of her daughters is even thought meritorious; and the Mormon authorities often advise a man to marry sisters, as they usually agreed better than others." Beadle then goes on to cite a number of cases. One man married three sisters. Two of Brigham's favorite wives were sisters, the Decker girls. In fact, in Utah, "The marriage of near relatives is so common that to remark on it would itself be considered remarkable." And William Hepworth Dixon, in reporting his visit to Utah in his *New America* (1867), says, "In one household in Utah may be seen the spectacle of three women, who stand toward each other in the relationship of child, mother and granddame, living in one man's harem as his wives!"

Dixon was not completely satisfied even with the admission of this kind of thing among the ordinary Mormons and once asked Brigham Young if he saw any objection from the Church's point of view of marriage of brother and sister. This was a little too much for the Prophet who said that, speaking

for himself, he would never approve such a thing. Nevertheless Fred Bennett, who for a long time was a deputy United
States marshal in Idaho, in his *A Detective's Experience
Among the Mormons* (1887), tells the story of an old Mormon
who married his own daughter. He does not say that he saw
this case for himself but reports that he had it from Mormon
friends of his.          •

This old fiend, desiring to go into polygamy, determined to take
his own daughter in as his second wife. She was taken into Salt
Lake City and was there regularly sealed to her father in the
Endowment House, her name having been changed for the purpose of the marriage. I do not mean to say that the church authorities were aware of all the circumstances in this case, but I do mean
to say that the system that renders such a terrible thing possible,
is an outrage on civilization, and that its lawmakers and lawgivers
are criminally negligent, and [Mormons] should be at all times
closely watched and brought to strict account for their misdeeds.
The old man who figured in this disgusting affair has since gone to
a Higher Tribunal but he was in good fellowship with the Mormon Church at the time of his death.

Many other tales are told of weird intermarriages. These
alleged incestuous matings probably served to induce hostility,
fear, and determination to uproot this system as much as any
single item in the long repertoire of alleged Mormon crimes
and vices.

The exploitation of plural wives through labor is also frequently noted. Austin Ward is describing his trip through
the Mormon countryside, "Still farther on, a woman was plow-
ing, with a very stubborn mule, that gave her an infinite deal
of trouble, to the great amusement of the loungers; and many
others were feeding the hogs and cattle, working in their small
gardens, or performing similar labors—the men loafing
around, as unconcerned spectators."

Under the law and custom of the mid-19th century, a man
had basic control of all the property of the family. It was not
at all uncommon for men under monogamy to desert their
women and leave them to the mercies of the poorhouse or
other charity. Occasionally cases did appear in the records of

the Mormons where a man tried to keep his first wife under control by threatening to cut her off without any money. When writers on Mormonism discovered such an instance, they blew it up into quite a story. Austin Ward writes:

> I encountered, one morning, in my walk a poor woman, middle-aged, faded, through hardship and exposure. She complained that her husband had deserted her and her children; and her house was cold, open, and exceedingly uncomfortable; that she had neither food, fuel, nor necessary clothing, though her lord resided with the younger and fairer wife, in a sumptuous mansion, there taking all the pleasures and luxuries of life.

The Gentile storytellers likewise made something of the sharp distinction between the large mass of Saints who lived in poverty and the elite and rich at the top. Fanny Stenhouse reports regarding her first initiation into Salt Lake with her husband, "We found among all but the leading families the greatest poverty and privation."

Critics of Mormonism regarded the degradation of women from two angles. With respect to the elite of the Church who could afford many wives, they described the whole system as essentially that of a harem where the wives lived in luxury and at the men's sexual bidding. At the other extreme, the plural wives were regarded not only as sexual tools but as a labor asset as well. Allegedly, they were exploited and many of them came to an early death as a result of the combination of heavy childbearing and undue physical labor. In terms of their dual class structure, the critic caught the Mormons on both horns of the dilemma.

Another favorite theme had to do with the relationship of the Mormon missionary system to polygamy. Mormon missionaries were pictured as swarming over the United States and Europe, but especially the latter, persuading young and innocent girls to join up in the name of the Lord and salvation, with fancy promises of rewards here and hereafter. These women, so the stories ran, inevitably found themselves the victims of the lecherous Elders who sooner or later seduced them into polygamy. There are many stories of distraught parents trying to rescue their daughters from such missionaries.

Mrs. Froiseth, who rings the changes on this as on almost all other themes, tells the story of a Latter-day Saint who left two wives in Salt Lake when he went on a British mission. "It seems he had obtained permission from Brigham Young to marry while he was abroad, but at the same time he was instructed to represent himself as a single man, so as not to become liable for bigamy under English law, in case he should find a new affinity." The Elder was decent enough to inform his two wives in Utah of the event but took good care to conceal the fact of prior marriages from his new wife in Europe.

Missionaries, like their superiors, the general church authorities, when confronted with such deceptions were ready with rationalizations. They argued that deceit was necessary to protect themselves, that polygamy was well accepted in Old Testament days, and that the Lord would forgive one for taking a plural wife in the name of the higher law. The ends justified the means. Clearly this is a type reaction of any strong ingroup against an out-group which is always viewed as a real threat. It is never a dishonor to deceive an enemy when at war. And the Mormons *were* at war with the Gentile world.

Once a plural household was established, trouble was bound to ensue. In short, another and prominent theme of the Gentiles was that plural marriage promoted marital conflict. In a work entitled *The Fate of Madame LaTour*, Mrs. A. G. Paddock, whose husband had once been a federal official in Utah, describes a monogamous family whose love, peace, and harmony were disturbed by the bringing in of a new wife.

Meanwhile, in the home that only a few months ago was so peaceful and happy, an evil spirit sat enthroned. The first wife, after a season of apathetic despair, woke to a full sense not only of her misery, but of her wrong; and bitter jealousy for the girl who stood between her and her husband, and hatred of the tyrant who placed her there, seemed to change her whole nature.

She would not feel so, she might get over it all in time, and bury the memory of the happy past—so she told herself—if every alternate week did not bring Philip back to the house; if she did not see his face and hear his voice day after day, knowing all the time that the tenderness which he tried to show toward her would be lavished on another woman next week; but the kisses which her outraged love refused would be given to that dark-eyed girl, whom she hated with a vindictiveness that frightened her when she stopped to reason about her feelings.

Several examples of the disruption of the home with the introduction of a new wife are told by Maria Ward. In the story of the Slocomb family she goes into detail of violent quarrels; the sadistic behavior of the sons of the first wife toward the second; the latter's killing of one of these boys in a fit of anger; her going insane as a result of guilt and remorse; and the final denouement in a double murder of her two youngest children, and her own suicide. The story ends thus:

The three had been found weltering in a pool of blood over the grave of William, she grasping in her cold hand the gory knife. Her gleaming eyes and incoherent words had been the subject of general remark.

Mr. Slocomb continues to live with Elizabeth, and has added two more wives to his domestic establishment.

Next to the mother, children have a high priority in American affections. To tell of the hardships and heartaches of the offspring of plural marriage was a "natural" for the Gentile zealots. We catch a little glimpse of the difficulties, as the critics saw it, in the Slocomb family. Yet the troubles did not consist merely in the quarreling among the various brothers and sisters or between them and the other wives. There was also a deeper matter involved in the basic conception of the influence of heredity upon the children.

The then current notions of heredity were not in line with those of today. During the time of which we are writing there was a widespread, if not universal, belief in "prenatal influence." This view held that if a woman being pregnant indulged in any kind of unusual activity or even unhappy thoughts, there might possibly be some carry-over of this to her offspring. For example, if a woman wanted her child to be a musician, she gave much attention to thinking about the matter or took up such practice as vocal lessons or playing the piano. Or stories were told of a woman who overindulged in eating watermelons only to find her beautiful baby was marred by a scar across the cheek in the form of a slice of watermelon with the seeds protruding.

In addition to this kind of nonsense there was a strong belief in the inheritance of acquired characteristics. The Lamarckian doctrine was well accepted by medical and biological students as well as by laymen. As a matter of fact, prenatal influence and the doctrine of acquired characteristics are closely intertwined, at least in the popular mind. Add to this the whole matter of the belief about the effects of incest and one has the basis for terrifying reactions to the plural marriage system.

Of the cross section of books which we have used to sample the attitudes of the Gentiles toward polygamy, no one has made more of this whole topic than Mrs. Froiseth who writes:

It is a notorious fact that ninety percent of these unholy alliances are contracted when the former wives are in that condition which most craves a husband's tender care and sympathy. It is not an uncommon occurrence for a wife to be near the hour of trial when a husband is off on a honeymoon with another woman. The inevitable mourning for the loss of her husband, the longing for his society, and the hatred of the other wife, exercise the most deleterious influences on the moral faculties of the children.

It sometimes happens that a wife under these circumstances will resort to the use of stimulants or potent drugs in order to drown her sorrows, and for the time being render her oblivious to her grief, or the triumphs of her rival. Taste and predelictions are thus imbibed and acquired by children, which often result in their early ruin . . .

The author then goes on to cite specific illustrations. One of the first is that young girls brought up in the notion that a man may be married to a number of women and have free access to them easily confuse this with prostitution. She cites "A certain noted woman in Salt Lake City" who had refused "admission to hundreds of young Mormon girls who would lead voluntary lives of shame."

She notes that the Mormon Church authorities frequently defended polygamy on the grounds that it took care of the sexual propensities of men and was thus a means of eliminating prostitution. She pooh-poohs this idea and cites a number of Mormon cases of premarital intercourse, which she regards as prostitution, as well as some outright instances of the same. She mentions a case of a bishop's son with three wives,

two of whom he married within a few weeks of each other, and both under compulsory circumstances. It was proved beyond the shadow of a doubt that the brutal instincts of this young Mormon came through his parents, and that every child of theirs has been almost on a par with this one—showing how truly Mormon polygamy makes beasts of nearly all who become entangled in its folds.

Mrs. Froiseth is not satisfied with some relatively mild examples. She goes on to cite an instance of a son who became a murderer and attributes this to the fact that his mother had homicidal thoughts. "A tree is known by its fruits." After a brutal murder, the son was lynched by an infuriated mob. The story continues that when various friends came to console the parents, including a "person high in authority in the Church," the mother told how happy she had been before polygamy

made our home like the abode of Satan. For months before the birth of that boy, I felt as if I wanted to kill his father's second wife, the woman who had destroyed our home and robbed me of my husband's love. Murder, and nothing but murder, was in my heart all the time. I never looked at her but I wanted to kill her. There were times when I would willingly have yielded up my own life, if I could have had the satisfaction of seeing her dead first, and by my hand. That poor, unfortunate boy has only paid the penalty of his father's sin and his mother's sorrow.

In a slightly different vein Beadle takes up the cudgels against the effects of polygamy by citing the high infant death rate in Utah. "A Mormon graveyard is the most melancholy sight on earth." He seems to believe that not only is polygamy responsible for high infant mortality but that there is plenty of evidence of physical deterioration in the form of weak eyes, various forms of crippling, and so on. He remarks that "The Asiatic institution was never meant to flourish on American soil, and has resulted here in a 'slaughter of the innocent' which is saddening to contemplate." And again, "The effects of their social bias are seen in a strange dullness of moral perception, a general ignorance and apparently inherited tendency to vice."

While this is not the place to take up the defense of the facts in this matter, it is well known by demographers that infant mortality during this period and especially under pioneer and frontier conditions was high everywhere. Beadle gives absolutely no facts regarding the differential death rate as between polygamist and monogamist families. The author would be willing to wager that there were no significant differences at all.

It was not only the young children who suffered. When we come to the adolescent and youth group, we find equally deleterious conditions. Another popular superstition of the time was that masturbation on the part of the young was likely to lead to moral and physical degeneration. It was further assumed, at least in the case of the writers involved, that such practice was the result of heredity. Beadle says, "I am convinced there is no part of America where youthful vice, of the peculiarly destructive and degrading kind, prevails so extensively as in Salt Lake City. And this is but a natural result; for polygamy is tenfold more unnatural to such a climate and race than in southern Asia or Africa."

How, following Gentile accounts, the Mormons kept their people under control has already been amply demonstrated in what has gone before. Here we can only add one or two items. The whole theory of the low status of women was itself a means, according to the Gentiles, of keeping them in hand. Other methods are noted by Mrs. Froiseth as, "the keeping of the people in ignorance and in poverty."

Beadle mentions still another, namely the use of slander.

He remarks that if a woman was seen associating with Gentile men at all, it was concluded "at once that she can have no pure motive in doing so, and among their own people they possess the power to ruin a woman's character entirely." In account after account the use of malicious gossip and slander as a technique of keeping the Saints in line is amply illustrated.

As might be expected in such a tight-knit society, officials in the church hierarchy were always on the alert for those members who might be inclined to depart from the way of the Lord. In particular, those who criticized the plural marriage system or refused to take part in it were frequently given severe reprimands. Sometimes these were in public and sometimes in private. According to some of the Gentile accounts matters went even beyond this, to include physical punishment and even death.

In a section entitled, "Mormon Barbarities," Maria Ward tells of one plural wife who told an immigrant in the hearing of a Mormon elder, "that polygamy was a system of abominations, and . . . repeated a few of her troubles and sufferings . . ." A night or two later when she went outside of her house she was seized, carried a mile into the woods, gagged, "stripped nude, tied to a tree and scourged until the blood ran from her wounds to the ground." She was left there all night and when her tormentors did return her to her husband's residence they just dropped her on the doorstep. The woman never recovered from this shock and died a year later. "Her husband's other wife refused to nurse and care for her."

Finally, it was said that outright murder of dissident persons, both male and female, was not uncommon. There is a whole legend of the operation of the Danites or the Destroying Angels.

The speakers and writers who gave such lurid pictures of the polygamous system doubtless thought that they were doing something directly to change the Mormon views of the matter; but in effect what they were doing was appealing to Gentile fantasy. The parallel with the use of atrocity stories in wartime propaganda comes to mind. Again and again it has been pointed out that the purpose of atrocity stories is not to stop the enemy from being cruel but to get the folks at home fighting mad and thus to build up their morale. The writings against the Mormons were designed in much this same manner and hope. Then, too, there was the close interplay of sex and Puritanism during this Victorian period where there was a strong repression of any overt sexuality. Moreover, it was a time when the double standard of morality was tacitly accepted. Men might be permitted certain indiscretions through prostitution but they were always held by the firm leash of romantic love and attachment to their wives and legitimate children. There was always hope that after sowing his wild oats, a man would come back to the home and hearth with humility in his heart from that time on.

There are a number of basic elements in the appeals which these stories had. Some operated at a more or less conscious level and some certainly at an unconscious one. First of all there was the sheer curiosity about this strange system. As we have already indicated, people quickly began to identify Mormonism with polygamy. How could such a system operate within the framework of a so-called civilized society? Men wanted to know about it and so did women. For the women there was a curious mixture of horror and fascination; they acted horrified and yet they were intrigued by what they heard and saw.

The analogy to women's interest in condemned murderers is evident. They certainly do not approve of taking another person's life; yet there is something sinisterly attractive in a man who would do such a thing. By the same token they were curious about both the men and women living under the system of plurality. And their fantasies were certainly titillated by what they read or heard on the lecture platform.

Then, too, projective mechanisms were at work. There were really two factors here. First, there was the projection of their own desires into this situation. Men were doubtless envious of the opportunities for sexual variationism afforded by having a number of wives with whom they could go to bed. In the same way the women, though they could not imagine having more than one man, could certainly indulge in a fantasy of sex under polygamy. At least the theory got around that the Mormon men were sexually highly potent. Second, there was evidence of the projection of their own guilt. On the part of women this would consist of feeling guilty for even having thoughts and curiosity about sex. In the case of men it would take either that form or might go so far as to be a projection of their own guilt regarding their overt sexual behavior which ran counter to the Christian mores.

On the basis of such projection, then, we have the foundation, as elsewhere, of strong feelings of rejection, repudiation, desire for punishment, and reformation of the wrongdoers. This is the psychology of the "do gooders" everywhere. Whatever the psychologist may say about its mechanisms, it has been one of the potent moral forces in the world. It doubtless played its part in the elimination of polygamy at the hands of the federal government and the Gentile moralists. The very process of repudiation and rejection, crying out for extreme punishment itself is part of the whole projective procedure with regard to their own sexual interest and guilt. It was simply a matter of thrusting it out on other people and building a basis for a social movement which would eliminate the wrongs. It probably played a part with the Mormons themselves. As we shall show over and over again, despite the rationalization of the principle of celestial marriage and plurality of wives, the good Saints could not completely eliminate their strong Christian and monogamous moral ideas.

There is, of course, another aspect of this matter. On the one hand, there are the moral ideals which are expressed at the conscious level and the moral reality of many of the individuals who were indulging in this campaign. The Mormons were quick to realize this and, partly as a defense of their own behavior, they made a great deal of the sinfulness and wickedness of the world outside.

Of course, the Gentiles did not stop with lecturing and writing pamphlets and books against the Mormons. Churches be-

gan sending missionaries to Utah to convert the Mormons
back to true Christianity. Schools were established in Utah
to rescue the young from the clutches of the Mormons. Ref-
uges for abandoned plural wives were set up though seldom
occupied. And a considerable number of anti-Mormon and
anti-polygamy organizations were founded. One of the best
known of these was the Woman's National Anti-Polygamy Society. More about its campaign and that of other organizations
will be indicated in later chapters.

*The Mormons are a peculiar people about marriage; we believe in marrying, not only for time, but for all eternity.*—Orson Pratt, in a sermon, 1854.

*As for its [polygamy] being degrading, it has proven to be the very opposite. It was exalting in its tendency and calculated to raise mankind from the degraded condition into which they had fallen under the practice of a corrupt and hypocritical system of enforced monogamy.*—Helen Mar Kimball Whitney, in Why We Practice Plural Marriage, 1884.

# 2 WOMEN AND CELESTIAL MARRIAGE IN ALL ITS GLORY: THE OFFICIAL MORMON VIEW

To UNDERSTAND the place of polygamy in Mormon history, we must realize that it was but a part of a grandiose scheme of salvation initiated by Joseph Smith and much elaborated by Brigham Young. These leaders—both living on the frontier—had been caught up in the American dream of perpetual social progress. All around them men believed in, and carried out, the successful and personally rewarding exploitation of natural resources. In their day these resources seemed endless. This Cinderella world excited the imagination of many. In fact, Joseph Smith, Brigham Young, and their colleagues were but a part of a larger mass of individuals who believed that—contrary to all lessons of history and psychology—man could finally "get something for nothing." Progress came to mean a continual and continuous expansion of mankind and his works. The Mormon leaders conjured up what they called "the doctrine of eternal progression."

Mormon theology taught that the Christian Trinity had only to do with this world. In addition to God the Father, his

son Jesus Christ, and the Holy Ghost, there were whole con-
geries of gods. The head god, Eloheim, had spawned millions
of worlds and spirits and permitted the latter bodies for occupancy of these worlds. Moreover, a host of like worlds
would in due course be created. These would provide habitation for still other spirits and bodies, presided over by
beings formerly men who had advanced to divine status. According to Mormon theology God himself had once been a
man and had advanced to the godlike state by this same means.
A favorite quotation of the Saints is: "As man is, God once
was; as God is, man may become."

Thus, if a good Latter-day Saint were faithful and married
a wife or wives under the "celestial marriage system" for time
and eternity, he might advance to be a god over his own
world with its inhabitants from his own family. On an uncertain frontier this idea of eternal progression of man from
mere dust to godhead had a tremendous appeal for rich and
poor alike.

To these believers, then, the more children they had the
better. Following the ancient prescription to "replenish the
earth," they foresaw an endless stream of generations expanding at a tremendous rate. They knew little or nothing of
Malthus but they sensed the cumulative factor in human re-
production. There would be no population problem in heaven
such as demographers worry about today.

There were and are a number of important theological
foundations of this doctrine of eternal progression. The basic
one is found in the theory of what Orson Pratt called the
Three Estates. First there is the pre-existence of man. This
phase of development was marked by the spiritual procreation
by God of myriads of spirits. This is the Maeterlinck bluebird
theme. But such spirits were anxious to move on to the next
stage, that of earthly possession of physical bodies. They could
not fulfill their destiny without taking on the flesh as human
beings. There was a certain population pressure in their state
of pre-existence to get down to earth as soon as possible.

Yet God in his infinite wisdom was both a good biologist
and psychologist. These heavenly spirits showed individual

differences in capacity. Some were predestined to be better than others, intellectually, emotionally, and especially, spiritually. In the words of Orson Pratt: "Among them are many spirits that are more noble, more intelligent than others, that were called the great and mighty ones, reserved until the dispensation of the fullness of time, to come forth upon the face of the earth, through a noble parentage that shall train their young and tender minds to the truths of eternity . . ."

Apparently there were large numbers of such superior spirits who had awaited "the day when all things would come to pass," that is, be fulfilled according to prophecy. It was therefore necessary to God's plan to make provision for this vast horde of the more promising spirits.

How could it be done? The most obvious way was to provide a method for these heavenly hosts to get down to earth and begin their next steps toward their ultimate salvation. The final estate would come after the second resurrection when the dead spirits would again be clothed in spiritual bodies—a combination of the spirit with a specially processed body that would survive forever.

According to Mormon doctrine a man may be married in three different ways: (a) The ordinary Christian or secular marriage is for *time* only, the bonds of matrimony being severed at the death of either spouse; and any Mormon who did not get married under the proper authorities and "sealed" in the proper manner, would be in this class. (b) The second form of marriage, and one which most Mormons followed, was that of being sealed for *time and eternity* by those who held the divine priesthood. This power had existed in ancient Hebraic times as well as during Christ's lifetime but later lost to be restored now by Joseph Smith. Such marriages bound a man and his wife not only until death did them part but forever and forever! (c) Then, finally, a person might be married for *eternity* only. This was a special provision for those who had spouses that had predeceased them without being properly sealed in the Church. For example, a widower who was a convert could have a dead wife married to him for eternity. They would be reunited in heaven.

This scheme likewise provided a man with an almost un-
limited number of wives in the hereafter. Many spinsters
were married to Mormons for the hereafter but not on earth.
Moreover, single women who had died without being married might be, and often were, sealed for eternity to some
good Saint.

The plan had other advantages. If a man married for time
and eternity should predecease his wife, the latter could in
turn be married for time only to some other man. Some of the
wives of Brigham Young and of Heber C. Kimball had been
sealed to Joseph Smith for time and eternity prior to Smith's
death. So far as we know these women had no issue from
Smith. Many of them later bore children by Young or Kimball
as the case might be. But according to Mormon theology, these
children would not belong to their earthly fathers, but would
belong to Smith in the hereafter.

This theory used to cause a good deal of amusement among
the grandchildren of the Young family. I recall teasing some
of my cousins by telling them that in the hereafter they
would not be Youngs but rather Smiths. This was an incisive
bit of sarcasm because many of the Youngs thought the Smiths
rather a peculiar sort compared to members of their own
family.

In the hereafter, however, there would be two classes of
citizens. First were those who had lived under the celestial
marriage plan and had been married for time and eternity.
These might go on to become gods of their own universes later.
The second group were those who had been wed for time
only, that is, in the manner of the ordinary Christian or secular marriage. This group also included unmarried people.
These second-class citizens would have no place in the marriage scheme in the hereafter but would serve a secondary
role as angels to minister to the individuals who had had the
superior blessing of the sealing on earth for time and/or
eternity.

The second stage then, that on earth, became a tremen-
dously important feature in the Mormon scheme of salvation. The ordinary monogamous marriage, at best, would

provide a place on earth for not more than from fifteen to twenty spirits. But if a man had plural wives, he could provide earthly bodies for more spirits. This became the rationale, in part, for plural marriage.

Clearly in such a scheme women would have an important place. Yet Mormon theology put man definitely in the driver's seat. Joseph Smith and his story of the true gospel and priesthood made sure that the male of the species was the center of God's plan. Only man could hold the divine priesthood. And only the priesthood could carry the proper messages from God to man. How then could God reconcile this masculine dominance with the need for a great many spirits anxious to be born? This was easy: Make every woman's salvation dependent upon her husband in the priesthood. In short, a woman's salvation here and hereafter was completely dependent upon her being married to a man who held the divine keys of admission to heaven. Moreover, since the spirits were pressing to be born, what could be simpler than to provide for them by making it possible for great numbers of them to take their place on earth through the system of plural wives.

There was ample evidence that God had put such a plan in motion at an earlier day. In the history of the Hebrews, Abraham took Hagar as a second wife. Isaac and Jacob had plural wives; and David had more spouses than he could count. Since the Mormons believed that they were taking part in the drama of the end of the world and that the plurality system was to play a part in this denouement, the Saints had no great difficulty in accepting the doctrine.

What was the nature of the divine revelation which Smith gave out as the defense of polygamy? The first was the requirement that all faithful Saints enter into marriage for time and eternity if they expected to get special benefits both here and in heaven. The second provision was that contained in a revelation given to Joseph Smith in Nauvoo, Illinois, July 12, 1843, entitled, "Celestial marriage; a revelation on the patriarchal order of matrimony, or plurality of wives." Certain dissident groups among the Mormons hold that this revelation was really the work of Brigham Young and that Smith had nothing to do with plural marriage. At this point we are simply giving the official view of those Mormons who held to polygamy. As is generally known, nearly ten years elapsed between 1843 and the open publication of the revelation after Brigham and his followers had arrived in Utah. Truly the alleged revelation was like most of Joseph Smith's other revelations—a long and windy document. The internal evidence shows, despite arguments to the contrary, that it must have been produced by Smith, for few others in his day wrote so verbosely and so confusedly!

The document opens with a statement by God that since Joseph Smith had inquired of Him regarding the possible justification of polygamy on the part of Abraham, Isaac, Jacob, Moses, David, Solomon, and other ancients, He would be glad to answer "as touching this matter." In fact, this was an opportune time for the Lord to give a new commandment to Smith: "For behold! I reveal unto you a new and everlasting covenant; and if ye abide not by that covenant, then are ye damned; for no one can reject this covenant, and be permitted to enter into my glory . . ."

The Lord first informed Joseph that unless a marriage bond was made under his jurisdiction it was not binding beyond the grave, but that if a man made a "covenant" with his bride for time and eternity under the Lord's power of sealing, then it would be binding after death as well as before. This is the basic instruction regarding being married for time and eternity.

The revelation goes on to describe the particular advantages which will come to those who follow the system of celestial and plural marriage, including the progression to godhead and the organization of a man's own universe which will make possible "a fullness and a continuation of the seeds for ever and ever."

The ancient system of polygamy practiced by Abraham and his descendants is used to support the argument for a plurality of wives. There is mention not only of plural wives but of concubines who bore Abraham children. However, God made

no provision under the new dispensation for a system of concubines. As we shall see, the Gentile world frequently viewed
the plural wives in just this light.

Then comes, in Section 16, a rationale by God, for the difference between plurality of wives and adultery. There is
strong admonition against adultery, but it is made clear to
Joseph Smith that marriage of plural wives under the covenant and by the proper authorities is not a case of adultery.

Section 24, however, contains the heart of the matter. The
full flavor of the revelation is contained in these words:

And again, as pertaining to the law of the priesthood: If any
man espouse a virgin, and desires to espouse another, and the first
give her consent; and if he espouse the second, and they are virgins,
and have avowed to no other man, then is he justified; he cannot
commit adultery, for they are given unto him; for he cannot
commit adultery with that that belongeth unto him, and to
no one else . . .

The revelation closes with the strong admonition and command on the part of women to abide by this new order. Those
who do not will be transgressors against the Lord's wishes.

As indicated by these quotations and as a fuller examination
of the complete document will show, there are scarcely any
specific directions in said revelation. Aside from one section
scolding Emma Smith for not forgiving Joseph his indiscretions, the matter is left to vague principles. Here was a whole
new system of matrimony and family organization for which
the Mormons had absolutely no preparation or information.
As we shall see in the chapters that follow, all sorts of devices
were developed to try to make this system work successfully.
A faithful member accepted this doctrine, however, and did
the best he could if he decided to try it out in practice.

At first the revelation was kept secret and given only to the
closest advisers of Joseph Smith. But as the system got under
way and as it became far more publicly practiced after the
Saints had migrated to Utah, the doctrine became more and
more thoroughly accepted.

There is an extensive literature giving the official explanations and defense of the plurality system. As typical of this material, we shall draw chiefly on two important Mormon sources. The first is that of Orson Pratt; the second, of Helen Mar Kimball Whitney.

Orson Pratt gave the first public and more or less complete official justification of celestial plural marriage. On August 29, 1852, the day the revelation on polygamy was publicly announced, Brigham asked Orson to prepare an explanation and defense of the same.

Orson Pratt had in mind both Mormon and non-Mormon readers, and his defense is broadly twofold: One is that polygamy was commanded by God; it is a sacred order to be fulfilled by the righteous followers. The other argument is a secular one; that is, it deals with the defense in terms of customs of polygamy in much of the world, alleged demographic effects, and various social benefits such as doing away with prostitution. The document itself is an elaborate and long-winded discussion in the then current argumentative style. Pratt frequently erected straw men of alleged Gentile arguments in order to demolish them.

Our discussion of Pratt's material will cover chiefly four major points: (a) It is the grand design of God! (b) Historical evidence supports the plurality of wives. (c) Polygamy has distinctive advantages and superiority over monogamy. (d) And, finally, it is to be carried out in certain ways.

It will be recalled that God's program for eternal progression involved "Three Estates." The first was the spirit stage; the second that of the earth where the spirits will take on bodies; and the third the renovated hereafter of clean spirits with resurrected bodies.

To facilitate the bringing of spirits to earth, the Lord established the plurality system of wives. Pratt argued that it was "embraced and practiced under divine sanction by the most righteous men who ever lived on earth: Holy Prophets and patriarchs . . ." And that "until we can find some law of God abolishing and prohibiting plurality of wives, we are compelled to believe it a divine institution . . ."

According to Pratt polygamy had a special place in the Mormon three-way marriage scheme. For example, if a man's wife died before he could be sealed to her for time and eternity, this ritual could be performed after her death by proxy; and what would be more sensible than for this "stand-in" to be the widower's second wife, taken after the death of the first? In other words, he would marry the second for time and eternity and then in a special ceremony this wife would serve as proxy for the first in order to insure his marriage to the latter in the hereafter. By the same token, a widow not married for time and eternity could marry her new husband for time only and then use him as a proxy to make sure that she had her first man in heaven.

It is noted, moreover, that those individuals who are not married under the sacred covenant by the authority of the priesthood, will not be permitted to continue their marriages in heaven. Their obligations as mere angels will be to serve the celestially wed husbands and wives in the Great Beyond. However, there is a way out for these people since the gospel plan provides for what is called "work for the dead." By proxy of living Saints such individuals may be baptized into the Kingdom of God and the holy ordinances of divine matrimony may be performed for them.

In explaining and defending plurality of wives for this world and the next, Pratt, representing the official point of view of the Mormon Church, went on to elaborate the whole matter with reference to the Principle as applied to God. If plurality of wives was good for man, it was good for God as well.

Regarding the procreation of spirits in the pre-existence estate, Pratt writes: "If none but gods will be permitted to multiply immortal children, it follows that each god must have one or more wives." But this was not enough. God the Father was also literally the father in the flesh of Jesus Christ.

It was the personage of the father who begat Jesus and it was for this reason Jesus is called "the only begotten of the father"; that is, the only one in this world whose fleshly body was begotten by the father. There were millions of sons and daughters whom he begat before the foundation of this world, but they were spirits, and not bodies of flesh and bones; whereas, both the spirit and body of Jesus were begotten by the father—the spirit having been begotten in heaven many ages before the tabernacle was begotten upon the earth.

The fleshly body of Jesus required a mother as well as a father. Therefore, the father and mother of Jesus, according to the flesh, must have been associated together in the capacity of husband and wife; hence the Virgin Mary must have been, for the time being, the lawful wife of God the Father: we use the term lawful wife, because it would be blasphemous in the highest degree to say that he overshadowed her or begat the Savior unlawfully . . . He had a lawful right to overshadow the Virgin Mary in the capacity of a husband, and begat a son, although she was espoused to another; for the law which he gave to govern men and women was not intended to govern himself, or to prescribe rules for his own conduct. It was also lawful in him, after having thus dealt with Mary, to give her to Joseph her espoused husband. Whether God the Father gave Mary to Joseph for time only or for time and eternity, we are not informed. Inasmuch as God was the first husband to her, it may be that he only gave her to be the wife of Joseph while in this mortal state, and that he intended after the resurrection to take her as his wife in eternity.

As God the Father begat the fleshly body of Jesus, so he, before the world began, begat his spirit. As the body required an earthly mother, so the spirit required a heavenly mother. As God associated in the capacity of a husband with the earthly mother, so likewise he associated in the same capacity with the heavenly one —earthly things being in the likeness of heavenly things; and that which is temporal being in the likeness of that which is eternal; or, in other words, the laws of generation upon the earth are after the order of the laws of generation in heaven. But if we have a heavenly mother as well as a heavenly father, is it not right that we should worship the mother of our spirits as well as the father? No; for the father of our spirit is the head of his household, and his wives and children are required to yield the most perfect obedience to their great head. It is lawful for the children to worship the king of heaven, but not the "queen of heaven . . ."

The Gentile World, especially its more religious and pious contingent, viewed such doctrines as unspeakable blasphemies. Here was evidence enough of the crude materialism and sexuality of the Mormons. Yet the faithful Saints held a quite different view. They firmly believed that God procreated the spirits and that he was literally the father of Jesus Christ by Mary. They took no stock in the generally accepted Christian view as to the role of the Holy Ghost *in re* the paternity of Jesus. However, they little realized that in giving the Virgin Mary over to Joseph, God was sanctioning what was, in effect, a form of polyandry since this meant that she had two husbands.

The whole notion of a mother in heaven is well recognized in Mormon theology but as a divine female she has never risen to the position of adoration as has the Virgin Mary in Roman Catholic dogma. Yet recognition of the importance of the female principle in the grand design of heaven is well brought out in the popular Mormon hymn entitled, "O My Father," written by Eliza R. Snow, who asks and answers her own question:

> In the heav'ns are parents single?
> No; the tho't makes reason stare!
> Truth is reason, truth eternal
> Tells me I've a mother there.

Mormon theologians did not let the matter rest there. Not only did God the Father and the other gods provide the pattern of plural marriage which the Saints might well emulate on earth, but Jesus Christ himself had a plurality of wives on this earth. This was in the divine scheme of things as foreshadowed by Isaiah who speaks of "the everlasting Father." Of Jesus, Pratt says: "It is necessary that he should have had one or more wives by whom he could multiply his seed, not for any limited period of time, but for ever and ever: thus he truly would be a father everlastingly, according to the name which was to be given him."

As to the earthly marriage of Jesus to one or more women, Pratt admits that the Gospels give no direct information on the matter, but goes on to say:

One thing is certain, there were several holy women that greatly loved Jesus—such as Mary, and Martha her sister, and Mary

Magdalene; and Jesus greatly loved them, and associated with them much; and when he arose from the dead, instead of first showing himself to his chosen witnesses, the Apostles, he appeared first to these women, or at least to one of them, namely, Mary Magdalene. Now, it would be very natural for a husband in the resurrection to appear first to his own dear wives, and afterwards show himself to his other friends.

In his defense of this point, the apologist becomes involved in a whole series of semantic and logical difficulties when he attempts to interpret literally various long-accepted figurative passages of the Bible having to do with Jesus as a bridegroom, and the discussion regarding the bride as "the lamb's wife" and other such matters. He also parades the popular Mormon notion that the miracle at Cana was on the occasion of Jesus' own marriage. While such arguments would carry little weight with faithful Christians, they gave the Mormon who was familiar with the Bible—and most of them were—ample proof of the sanctity of the plural system.

Pratt anticipated the shocked piety of the Christians of his time in closing the section in which he discusses the plurality of wives of both God the Father as well as of Jesus. Thus in a sarcastic tone:

There are many in this generation so pious that they would consider themselves greatly disgraced to be obliged to associate with a man having a plurality of wives; would it not be well for such to desire a place separate from the Kingdom of God, that they may not be contaminated with the society of these old polygamists? And then it would be so shocking to the modesty of the very pious ladies of Christendom to see Abraham and his wives, Jacob and his wives, Jesus and his honorable wives, all eating occasionally at the same table, and visiting one another, and conversing about their numerous children, and their kingdoms. O, ye delicate ladies of Christendom, how can you endure such a scene as this? . . .

The Mormons contended that the gospel of Jesus fulfilled but could not displace the ancient program of Hebrew life. He did not abolish polygamy; he actually sanctioned it. Certainly, argues Pratt, thousands of Hebrew converts to Jesus

Christ must have had plural wives. These they could not divorce since the early Church forbade such measures, hence the doctrine and practice of plural marriage must have been approved.

Curiously enough the historical support of polygamy from the Bible is not found in the *Book of Mormon,* the second of the sacred books of the Mormons. In the latter, polygamy is identified with adultery and both are strongly interdicted. The Gentiles, in criticizing Mormon polygamy, quickly seized upon many passages in the *Book of Mormon* which expressly forbade such practices. Yet Pratt was willing and able to use the *Book of Mormon* as a defense of polygamy by rationalizing its opposition in a shrewd way. He argues that unless God commands otherwise, monogamy is the proper form of marriage, and goes on to say that during the period when the Nephites inherited the Western continent polygamy was not necessary. In like manner, during the early history of the Mormon Church itself the Lord did not authorize the plural marriage system. It was only thirteen years after the first organization of the Latter-day Church that this new practice was revealed.

Pratt strongly challenged the Gentiles to exclude polygamy from the Scriptures. Moreover, in a spirit of ridicule, he invites the Gentiles to send their missionaries to Utah to convert the Mormons from the errors of their way, challenging them to bring their Bibles with them and prove by quoting the Scriptures that the Mormons are wrong.

Come, then, you missionary societies whose bosoms yearn over the dark and benighted heathen in foreign climes, awake to the awful conditions of the poor and outcast Latter-day Saints in your own land; send forth your master spirits . . .

Convince us that a plurality of wives is contrary to the gospel; let your light shine upon . . . Utah . . . peradventure . . . that she may be able to see some of the beauties of civilized society. The inhabitants of that dark and benighted land are so far sunk in the depths of barbarism, that they will not suffer a public prostitute to live in that territory: an adulterer or seducer is not considered fit to live in that barbarous land. These ornaments of civilized and Christian nations do not yet adorn the cities and towns of Utah . . .

While both the Hebrews and early Christians accepted polygamy, according to Mormon doctrine, it is further contended that in the second century after Christ there occurred what is termed "The Great Apostasy." Divine authority and priesthood were removed from the earth and for seventeen centuries the so-called Christian Church operated without proper divine sanction. The Roman Catholic Church had come to power and corrupted the original gospel as it had been given by Jesus and his Apostles. Among other things, contrary to God's will, the plurality of wives was abolished and in its place an unorthodox system of celibacy introduced. For centuries "the purposes of the Almighty in peopling the earth with its full measures of inhabitants" were thwarted.

It remained for Joseph Smith, "in the fullness of time," to restore the divine priesthood with authority, and as a part of this whole final program, to re-establish the ancient patriarchal order of marriage.

Another support for the system of plurality of wives was found in certain of its social benefits. The Mormons always drew a sharp distinction between their divinely ordained polygamy and adultery. This was a strong and recurrent claim of the Mormons, a point which the Gentiles refused to see. The latter usually considered adultery and polygamy as identical. In his original sermon in 1852, Pratt remarked: "Whoredom, adultery, and fornication have cursed the nations of the earth for many generations, and are increasing fearfully upon the community; but they must be entirely done away with from those who call themselves the people of God . . ." As to how prostitution can be avoided, he remarks, "It is to be prevented in the way the Lord devised in ancient times; that is, by giving to his faithful servants a plurality of wives, by which a numerous and faithful posterity can be raised up, and taught in the principles of righteousness and truth . . ."

The defender was quick to point out the superior virtue of the Saints in contrast to the Gentiles who criticized them so severely for plural marriage.

. . . Under the strict and rigid laws of virtue which prevail and are carried into general practice, wives are not in constant fear of inconstancy of their husbands; parents are not fearful of their children being seduced and their characters being destroyed . . .

They [the Gentiles] cry out, as though they were frightened out of their senses, because a territory practices a legal and lawful matrimony after a pattern set before them in the Scriptures; but they can swallow down comparatively easily, without scarcely uttering a groan, the polluted, wretched, most filthy stinks of iniquity which prevail to an alarming extent in all large towns, cities, and seaports, among the Gentile nations . . .

The thesis that polygamy was much superior to monogamy and was a defense against prostitution, is indicated in a resolution passed by a public assembly of Mormon women in January, 1870, at the time when the Cullom Bill was before Congress:

Resolved: That we acknowledge the institutions of the Church of Jesus Christ of Latter-day Saints as the only reliable safeguard of female virtue and innocence; and that the only sure protection against the fearful sin of prostitution and its attendant evils, now prevalent abroad, and, as such, we are and shall be united with our brethren in sustaining them against each and every encroachment.

While both male and female are necessary to fulfill God's plan this does not mean an equality of authority nor that a woman was entitled to more than one husband at a time. With respect to polyandry—an idea occasionally raised by the more curious Mormons—Pratt says: "No: such a principle was never sanctioned by scripture. The object of marriage is to multiply the species, according to the command of God." Polyandry, he implies would prevent a woman's having her quota of children and thus "frustrate the grand design" to bring spirits to earth. But just why a multiple paternity would stop any woman from having children he does not say. Perhaps the real answer is found by the editor of the *Utah Magazine*, October 2, 1869, who rationalizes alleged sex differences in the terms:

Man is endowed with polygamic qualities and woman with monogamic ones. This is no question of equality in intelligence or excellence, it turns on uncreated qualities of a man's being that enables him to be perfectly one with more than one woman. Woman is not so endowed. She can love many men in a degree, but she can be truly one with one only.

Contrary to a lot of Gentile nonsense, as the Mormons viewed it, the latter defended the principle of plurality as benefiting the women. Pratt contends:

Instead of a plurality of wives being a cause of sorrow to females, it is one of the greatest blessings of the last dispensation: it gives them the great privilege of being united to a righteous man, and of rearing a family according to the order of heaven. Instead of being compelled to remain single, or marry a wicked man who will ruin her and her offspring, she can enter a family where peace and salvation reign; . . . where the head of the family stands forth as a patriarch, a prince, and a savior to his whole household; where blessings unspeakable and eternal are sealed upon them and their generations after them; where glory is eternal and her joy is full. Rejoice, then, ye daughters of Zion, that ye live in this glorious era!

Long before Bernard Shaw made his famous quip about polygamy in *The Revolutionist's Handbook*, Pratt said, "What faithful, virtuous woman would not prefer to stand as the sixth or seventh wife of a good and faithful man, rather than to have no husband at all throughout the endless ages of eternity?"

Aside from such possible pursuit by unwed women, how was a man to go about getting a plural wife? Pratt outlines what were regarded as the approved steps:

First, he must consult the head of the Church who will seek a revelation about the matter. If a plural marriage is thus approved, the next step is to secure the consent of the parents. This in hand, he may then woo the prospective bride, but again not until he has the consent of the first wife.

Respecting the marriage ceremony itself, there shall be witnesses and the proper authority to unite them in marriage.

The President of the Church is that person, although he may delegate the power to others. Whoever this is

. . . calls upon the bridegroom and his wife, and the bride to arise, which they do, fronting the President. The wife stands on the left hand of her husband, while the bride stands on her left. The President then puts this question to the wife:

"Are you willing to give this woman to your husband to be his lawful and wedded wife, for time and for all eternity? If you are, you will manifest it by placing her right hand within the right hand of your husband." The right hands of the bridegroom and bride, being thus joined, the wife takes her husband by the left arm, as in the attitude of walking . . .

The President or his delegate then proceeds to ask the man and then the bride regarding their willingness to enter into the wedded state for time and eternity and also a number of questions regarding their obedience to the laws, rights, and ordinances pertaining to matrimony. If both of them answer in the affirmative, the President or his substitute then says:

"In the name of the Lord Jesus Christ, and by the authority of the Holy Priesthood, I pronounce you legally and lawfully husband and wife for time and for all eternity; and I seal upon you the blessings of the holy resurrection with power to come forth on the morning of the first resurrection, clothed in glory, immortality, and the eternal life; I seal upon you the blessings of thrones, and dominions, and principalities, and powers, and exaltations, together with the blessings of Abraham, Isaac, and Jacob; and say unto you, be fruitful, and multiply, and replenish the earth, that you may have joy and rejoicing in your posterity in the day of the Lord Jesus . . ."

The basic conflict between the Mormons and the non-Mormons over polygamy arose from the contention of the former that matters of religious belief, extending even to marriage, were not the concern of the state but were protected by inalienable rights of religious conscience and practice. Early in Pratt's defense of celestial marriage, it is contended that: "The constitution and laws of the United States, being founded upon the principles of freedom, do not inter-

fere with marriage relations, but leave the nation free to believe in and practice the doctrine of a plurality of wives, or to
confine themselves to the one wife system, just as they choose."
Pratt quotes the first amendment of the Constitution which
expressly forbids Congress to make any law "respecting an establishment of religion, or prohibiting the free exercise
thereof."

Pratt was wise enough to recognize that if the law of a given
state or country forbade a person from indulging in plural
marriage, the individual should obey said law. But he advised
people in such circumstances to "depart from under the jurisdiction of these illiberal state laws and go to Utah where religious liberty is tolerated, and where every people and sect
have the right to worship as they please, and marry as many
wives as they please, and be accountable to God and not to
man."

A second secular argument in favor of polygamy is the one
with which Pratt introduces his long discourse on celestial
marriage:

Plurality of wives is a doctrine very popular among most of mankind at the present day. It is practiced by the most powerful nations of Asia and Africa, and by numerous nations inhabiting the
islands of the sea, and by the aboriginal nations of the great Western Hemisphere. The one wife system is confined principally to a
few small nations inhabiting Europe, and to those who are of
European origin inhabiting America. It is estimated . . . that
about four-fifths of the population of the whole globe believe and
practice, according to their respective laws, the doctrine of a plurality of wives. If the popularity of a doctrine is in proportion to
the numbers who believe in it, then it follows that the plurality
system is four times more popular among the inhabitants of the
earth than the one wife system.

In June, 1879, in a discussion with Colonel Hollister, a
federal agent in Utah, John Taylor, once remarked in this
same vein: "While Great Britain is a monarchial government,
she can tolerate 180 million polygamists in India and throw
around them the protecting aegis of the law, while the United
States, a republican and professedly free government, is en-

acting laws prosecuting and proscribing so small a number as 150 in her territory."

Pratt also makes a strong point that polygamy is not contrary to the customs of Europe. In another article, he notes that Martin Luther and others approved of the plural marriage of Phillip, the Landgrave of Hesse, in the sixteenth century. Although the Catholics did, this was clear evidence that Protestants, at least, did not oppose polygamy.

In the eighth installment on celestial marriage in *The Seer*, Pratt devotes himself to those Gentiles who argue that polygamy produced poverty and was injurious to the economic welfare of society. Employing his straw-man tactics, he points out that though there are some cases of poverty, "in most of the cases, the plurality system would have a contrary tendency; instead of diminishing the wealth of a family, it would increase it." He then goes on to point out that the labor force made possible by additional wives and children would be a real asset in any household economy.

While God's basic principles on which polygamy rested were "fixed and immovable," so far as the day-to-day operation of the plural household was concerned there were no "rules to compel" the husband and father

. . . to act invariably in a certain way: this should be left for circumstances and the wisdom he has, to indicate and control; both wives and children should be perfectly satisfied to have the head of the family be in reality the head, and so as seemeth to him good . . . It is not for them to dictate to the head, but to pray for and administer to the head, that peradventure, through their kindness and meekness, and willing obedience, the head may be influenced to do right . . .

One basic principle, however, is that of love.

Love should be the predominant ruling principle in all family governments . . . Love, like all other gifts of God, can be cultivated and increased, or it can be neglected and diminished: it is subject to the control of the other faculties of the mind; it is not a principle such as is often described in novels, which act irresistably, forcing all other powers of the mind into subjection . . .

Yet, there was little place in this plurality system for what the Gentile world regarded as romantic love. There was, however, a kind of pure love which was to be supplemented by sexual conjugal love.

A man should love all the wives God may give him with a perfect love: it is impossible for him to love them too well, providing that his love is regulated and controlled in all things according to the law of righteousness. Can a man love more than one wife with all his heart? Yes, he can love each one God gives him with all his heart; and if he have a hundred, he can love them all with the same intensity that he could love one . . .

In common with the usual Mormon argument, Pratt also contends that a man can love more than one wife in the same manner in which he loves more than one child. This theme is repeated again and again in various Mormon justifications of plural marriage.

Pratt meets the argument that plurality destroys the rights of women in these words:

But what rights of women does it take away? If several women, voluntarily and from their own choice, with the consent of their relatives, wish to unite their destinies with one man, what rights have been taken away? What injuries have been sustained, either by themselves or by society in general? We answer, none at all. On the other hand, the rights of women are destroyed and taken from them in prohibiting them by law to have the man of their choice; they are compelled, by legislative enactments, to relinquish all hopes of marrying a man upon whom their affections are placed and are obliged, if they marry at all, to go contrary to every feeling of their nature—to be united with one for whom they have no love . . . Give women their right; let them marry the man of their choice . . .

It is said that plurality destroys the rights of the first wife, and, therefore, should not be tolerated by law . . .

Pratt meets this latter issue by saying that if a man contracts with his first wife prior to their marriage not to take another, he should be obliged to stick to this agreement, but he implies that to do so would be foolish. The usual procedure is to begin by securing the consent of the first wife. If she refuses to give approval, however, then the general authorities might give a worthy man their consent despite her objections. As we shall see, this provision for an appeal often served to force silence on the part of the first wife.

Closely related to this matter of the rights of women was the question of how to deal with jealousy. The apologia cavalierly disposes of the question in this way:

> If several women mutually agree to be the wives of the same man, and he treats them with impartiality, we see no cause existing for jealousy. Loss of confidence in a husband by his infidelity might give rise to jealousy but not when each wife knows that the other wives are as much entitled to the attention of the husband as she herself; she knows that such attentions are not criminal, therefore she does not lose confidence in him; though she may consider him partial, in some respects, yet she has constantly to know that his attentions toward them are strictly virtuous. Confidence being retained, the elements of happiness are retained . . .

The matter of jealousy is further disposed of by an analogue to children's jealousies. Pratt pooh-poohs the idea that jealousies of children mean anything; they pass away quickly and the harmony of the children is easily restored. So it should be the same with the relations of the wives to each other.

The whole official defense of polygamy is summarized thus by Pratt:

> The peculiar custom of plurality, practiced by some in Utah, in no way interferes with the rights of anyone: it is in no way immoral; it in no way injures the parties themselves, or anyone else; it is in no way unscriptural; it is in no way conflicting with the Constitution; it is in no way violating any of the laws of Utah, or any other laws to which the citizens of that territory are amenable. Therefore, there is no reason whatever for calling it a crime, or for passing legislative enactments against it.

Once having set up a household what were some of the duties and obligations of the members to each other? Clearly the husband is basically responsible. The wife is not to follow her own judgment but that of her husband.

The husband is the head of the family, and it is his duty to govern his wife or wives, and the children, according to the laws of righteousness; and it is the duty of his wife to be subject unto him in all things, even as the church is subject unto Christ . . . Each wife should seek counsel from her husband, and obey the same with all meekness and patience in all things.

Within this general framework the husband was supposed to care for all his families equally, including the touchy topic of the inheritance of property. To the Mormons there was no question about the legitimacy of the children of plural wives. "The children of each wife are considered perfectly legitimate and entitled to the proportionate shares of his property, in the same manner as if they were children of one wife."

As to household arrangements, "There is no particular rule, as regards the residence of the different branches of the family." Such matters come under the judgment of the husband and father and variations would occur depending upon the circumstances. Respecting children, Pratt stressed the fact that the purpose of marriage was not "mere multiplication of human beings" but their being reared in the proper doctrine.

In the two final articles dealing with celestial marriage, Pratt developed 27 rules for the making of successful families, living in peace, love, and union. Some of the rules apply only to, or chiefly, the men; others only to the wives; some to both parents; and some to parents and children. For example, the first 11 deal entirely with the problem of husband and father. He is advised first of all to seek the kingdom of God and its righteousness before he undertakes marriage. Secondly, he is to seek the wisdom of God in the choice of his wives. He is to give strength to his wives recognizing that they are "the weaker vessels" and that he as the stronger "must nourish, cherish, and protect" them.

There is some specific advice not to betray the confidence of one wife to another, nor speak of one wife's faults to another. The husband is told to avoid showing anger or a fretful disposition, and to deal impartially in all circumstances. "Call your wives and children together frequently and instruct them in their duties toward God, and towards yourself, and towards one another."

Then follows advice to the wives. No woman should enter polygamy unless she, "has fully resolved to submit herself wholly to his [husband's] counsel, and to let him govern as the head." Also, a wife should "never seek to prejudice the mind of her husband against any of his other wives, for the purpose of exalting herself in his estimation . . ." She should try to be the peacemaker in her family and speak no evil of her husband to any of the rest of the family. She should be willing to aid the other wives in times of trouble and illness. Each mother should "correct her own children, and see that they do not dispute and quarrel with each other, nor with any others; let her not correct the children of the others without liberty to do so, lest they give offence."

Both parents should have a hand in the training of the children according to their capacities and to teach them not only good sound Mormon doctrine but respect and love of the father and proper conduct generally.

Rule 23 says: "Suffer not children of different mothers to be haughty and abusive to each other; for they are own brothers and sisters the same as the children of patriarch Jacob; and one has no claim above another, only as his conduct merits it . . ." This gives the rationale in Mormondom for the fact that half brothers and sisters considered themselves full brothers and sisters.

And the final rule:

Let husbands, wives, sons, and daughters, continually realize that their relationships do not end with this short life, but will continue in eternity without end. Every qualification and disposition, therefore, which will render them happy here should be nourished, cherished, enlarged, and perfected, that their union may be indissoluble, and their happiness secured both for this world and for that which is to come.

The official Church had a number of female spokesmen for the success and glory of plural marriage. One of these was

Eliza R. Snow, the Mormon poetess, once wife of Joseph Smith, later—for time only—of Brigham Young. The Gentiles long viewed her as an official apologist for the plural system. In one of her articles defending polygamy, she said: "The action of the government can neither change nor annihilate a fundamental truth . . . This nation, in preventing the practice of plural marriage, shoulders a responsibility heavier than any other nation has ever assumed—with one exception, that of the ancient Jews."

Another widely cited and officially approved defender of plural marriage was Helen Mar Kimball Whitney, already referred to. She was a daughter of Heber C. Kimball and the first wife of Horace K. Whitney, one of the Twelve Apostles. Her pamphlet "Why We Practice Plural Marriage" (1884) was long regarded as one of the most substantial defenses of the system from the point of view of a wife and mother.

One of her basic themes is the sacrifice called for by living under polygamy: "To live one's religion," as it was euphemistically called, "meant sacrifice." That is, one had to put up with a good deal in this world in order to reap greater rewards in the hereafter. Pretending to be writing to a "nice" Gentile friend of hers, Mrs. Whitney remarks, "I did not try to conceal the fact of its having been a trial, but confessed that it had been one of the severest in my life; but that it had also proven one of the greatest blessings. I could truly say that it had done the most towards making me a saint and a free woman, in every sense of the word . . ."

Mrs. Whitney was "afraid of no man, but I feared to rebel against the Almighty," therefore she accepted the Principle. She found that it purified and exalted love, and cites a number of successful plural families which she knew.

She is fully aware, too, that the system was not easy for the men. ". . . those who think that men have no trials in the plural order of marriage, are greatly deceived. The wives have far greater liberty than the husband, and they have the power to make him happy or very unhappy . . ." On the rewards of bearing children:

Our children are considered stars in a mother's crown, and the more there are, if righteous, the more glory they will add to her and their father's eternal kingdom, for their parents on earth, if they continue righteous, will eventually become as Gods to reign in glory. Nothing but this, and a desire to please our Father in heaven, could tempt the majority of Mormon men or women either, to take upon themselves the burdens and responsibilities of plural marriage.

On the practical side she has some interesting things to say about the relations of the wives to each other:

My husband was advised by my father to take another wife. He studied my feelings and took one who he had cause to believe loved me and my children, and would cause me the least trouble. She lived with me in the same house till she had three children, and had it not been for this, and the care of my own little ones, we should never have separated. It was more agreeable for her to remain, as we had lived kindly together. Mr. Whitney built her a large comfortable house within a few feet of mine, and has deeded to each of us our homes. Our children have always lived more peacefully than many who have one mother. I am called "Aunt" by them and their mother is called the same by my children . . .

Like all good Mormons, Mrs. Whitney has plenty to say about the purity of the Saints and the sinfulness of the world. In allegedly writing to a Gentile who had inquired about whether he should live with a woman he loved when he could not divorce his wife, she writes,

To live with more than one woman, except you are sealed by one holding the Priesthood and authority from the Great Master, is nothing less than adultery . . . There is but one door open for us all, and through no other can we enter the Kingdom of Heaven. Repentance and baptism are the first steps. When you have obeyed those commandments, the Lord will fulfill His promise . . .

She goes on to advise this man to come to Zion and join the Church.

She has a good deal to say against prostitution and birth control and defends polygamy as a holy way to avoid such evils.

She takes a dig at DeWitt Talmage, the Brooklyn divine, who was so bitterly opposed to Mormonism and who contended in season and out that polygamy was essentially prostitution. She suggests that he clean up his own backyard, especially as regards "divorce and foeticide" before attacking the Mormons.

Neither are the Mormon women so dumb nor so enslaved as not to have considerable power. "We know the power we hold to declare polygamy illegal. If there was any necessity . . . we could assuredly . . . call upon the United States Army stationed here to protect us."

Regarding the Gentile plans to free "the poor downtrodden women from their polygamous yoke," she asked why do not these people do something for the women and wives in the industries of this country and Europe who are, in effect, but economic slaves. She contended that the Poland bill to disfranchise the Mormons was really but an attempt to break up the Latter-day Saints organization altogether.

Mrs. Whitney had some very sharp things to say about Senator Edmunds who introduced the bills into Congress which later put an end to polygamy.

Many senators told him [Mr. Edmunds] when he had his measure under way that it wouldn't have the slightest effect upon polygamy. He knew it better than any one of them. He didn't intend it to have any effect on polygamy. He aims it at the head of the Democratic Party. It answered his purpose in that respect perfectly. It gave the party of God and morality—the party of all the virtues, another chance to get up a howl about other people's vices. If it suppressed polygamy the chance would have been gone. . . . It was "something" that would furnish "good fighting" for a generation or so and offer a lasting foil for the superfluous moral indignation of the chaste and virtuous Republican masses . . . to remain still as a perpetual and handy, red "rag" to arouse Republican virtue to an annual frenzy of moral indignation and enthusiasm.

Yet Mrs. Whitney was not discouraged. New ideas or any "plan of improvement" is bound at first to meet some opposition. But she fully believed that in less than 50 years, plural marriage would have general acceptance. At the close of her document she puts in a general appeal to the faithful regarding polygamy:

> . . . How will it be with these political traitors and hireling priests . . . who are trying hard to destroy the power which holds this people together, who brand our wives as prostitutes, children as bastards, while at the same time they themselves are supporters of harlots, murderers of innocents, and framers of laws and secret societies to destroy those who are striving to remove ignorance and superstition . . . ?

Moreover, she is certain that most Mormon women will endorse what she has said. They are not "man-worshippers" but persons with their own mission, and if they prove to be good wives and mothers they will "have easier access to the throne of grace," and any suffering here will but "add greater laurels" to their crowns "in the world to come."

To the faithful Mormon, Joseph Smith had a sacred commission to restore the gospel. As a part of this gospel not only was the priesthood re-established, but the divine institution of plurality of wives was once more made available to the faithful. However, as we shall see, a good many Saints had trouble adjusting themselves to the plural marriage system, because of their strong puritan conscience and sense of guilt; but to the faithful it was the Word of God and there was nothing else to be done but to carry on.

*A narrative of facts stranger than fiction.*
—Metta V. Fuller *in* Mormon Wives
1856.

# 3  POLYGAMY IN FACT: "GOOD, BAD, AND INDIFFERENT"

AGAINST THE BACKGROUND of the strongly contrasting and even conflicting views just given, let us present a more realistic picture of plural family life. The student of human conduct wants to know just how polygamy operated on a day-to-day basis. We shall try to give an objective picture of just this. The present chapter will consist chiefly of a series of stories of selected polygamous families. On the basis of the author's own observations from living in polygamous households, observing them as neighbors, interviewing people who lived the system, and from the reading of a rather large number of family records, it is possible to set up a kind of norm, or ideal type, of a successful plural family. Such type-case should give a basis from which one could show differences in degrees of success in the particular families under study.

The author made an attempt, in fact, to rate the degree of success or failure of those plural families where his data were sufficiently full to warrant such a try. Of a total of 175 family records of varying merit and completeness, there were 110 sufficiently full to permit a rating. Five categories were set up as follows: (1) highly successful, marked by unusual harmony; (2) reasonably successful; (3) moderately successful with some conflict but on the whole fair adjustment; (4) considerable conflict and marital difficulty; and (5) severe conflict, including, in some instances, separation and/or divorce.

On the basis of these ratings, nearly 53 per cent, or more than half of our cases fall in the "highly successful" or "reasonably successful" classification, one-fourth of them fall in the middle or "moderate" position, and slightly less than one-quarter (23 per cent) were rated as "considerable conflict"

56

and "severe conflict." While it must be realized that I have no idea as to how representative my sample of family stories is, and while the judgments are my own, and, like other such ratings, subjective, nonetheless the figures do give some notion as to how these plural families look to a man who has been observing and studying them for practically a lifetime.

A rating was also made of the economic success of the families. Among our records we found 118 which had sufficient detail to permit an estimate of financial status. The criteria, for those of that historical period, so far as we could determine were: (1) high economic position, approximately our present category of "wealthy"; (2) reasonably high economic position, certainly above average; (3) medium or average economic status; (4) below medium economic condition; and (5) definitely on the borderline of poverty, or "poor."

Combining these ratings, we find that nearly one-half fall in the "high" or "above average" ranks, one-third in the "medium" or "average" grade, and one-sixth in the "below average" and borderline poverty group. Judging from these ratings, these data would tend to confirm the view that there was a positive correlation of the practice of plural marriage and higher economic status.

We shall begin by telling the story of a number of families which were rated as highly successful from the Mormon standpoint. In these harmony was clearly evident. We will then take up one or two cases that are obviously unsuccessful, in which conflict and even breakup of the family was the order of the day. Then there are certain moderate or middle-ground instances which were indifferently successful. We shall look at a few of those. Finally, there are some special types of problems presented, particularly those where the second wife was really in a definite secondary position to the first wife and her family; then again there were some families where the sharp age differential between the first and second wives made for a considerable amount of trouble. It must be borne in mind that these stories are presented to give the reader, at this juncture, a cross section of the kinds of material with which we will be dealing in more detail elsewhere in this book.

In the year 1851, Brother Hans Olson and his newly acquired wife, Emma, found themselves with 10 or 12 other
people to be the first converts to Mormonism in Sweden. As
good Latter-day Saints, they had a strong urge to leave for
the United States where they could join the main body of their
fellow-members in Zion. In the fall of 1852 they left for Utah,
traveling by way of New Orleans and up the Mississippi to
Keokuk. They spent the winter awaiting an opportunity to
get to Utah by ox-train. They arrived in Salt Lake City in
the summer of 1853. On the plains en route to Utah their first
son was born.

For his time, Olson was a rather well-educated man. He was
a skilled millwright, and there was great need for putting such
people to work. In keeping with the practice of the day, he
was sent to Ogden to build and operate a flour mill. He stayed
in Ogden until 1857 when he moved to Logan on orders of
the Church and set up two mills in that community.

While there is much evidence that polygamy had been practiced since at least the early 1840's, it was not officially announced until the very year that Olson arrived in Utah. In
common with other ardent Saints, he quickly espoused the
Principle, and in the space of eight or 10 years he had acquired
three additional wives. His first plural wife, Josephine, had
already been married for time and eternity to her first husband, who had died a few years before, leaving her with one
child. Under the rules of the Church, then, Olson could marry
her for time only, since she would belong to her first husband
in heaven.

Since all good Saints of that day wanted to increase the
amount of celestial glory which would accrue to them, Olson
soon acquired two other wives. He married wife number
three, Marie, in the late 1850's, and the fourth and final wife,
Annie, in 1860 or 1861. He was thus set up with four wives
on earth and three to take to heaven with him. All together
these four women bore him 32 children. But under the rules
of the Church, he would be able to claim 24 only in the hereafter. Those of his second wife would belong to her first husband when she got on the other side—a form of compensation,

no doubt, for Josephine's first husband for having died before he had a chance to sire a satisfactory number of children of his own.

Soon after Olson arrived in Logan he undertook to build himself a substantial house. He excavated and constructed a basement, but was unable to finish the house during the first year. He put a dirt roof over the basement and for the next year or so the family lived there. When he married his second wife, she was settled in a granary across the street. As soon as the large house was completed, he brought Josephine into the place as he did the other two plural wives who followed her shortly thereafter.

During the first 10 years in Logan the entire family lived in this one adobe house. Each wife had her own large room where she lived with her children. At first the family conducted a common kitchen and common dining room; later each wife did her own cooking in her own room and fed her own family. The largest room was occupied by the first wife; it was called "upstairs" by the children, although the house had only one story. Laundry was done in the basement where there was a fireplace. The children slept on the floor or in trundle beds.

Later, as Olson acquired more property, he built each wife a separate home on a large block nearby. Still later, he bought a farm in Hyde Park and moved one of the families there.

The wives he treated fairly and they got on well together. They never carried any of their troubles to Olson. They settled any difficulties they might have among themselves promptly and peacefully. To quote one informant: "You couldn't get a quarrel out of Aunt Emma. She was a good-humored woman and never had a cross word for anybody." The other wives held Emma in great respect for, although first wife, she made no effort to dominate the other wives.

As was common in pioneer families—monogamous or polygamous—the wives bore their children in rather rapid succession. There was little or no medical attention available and the women had their babies wherever it was most convenient. For example, the second wife had her first child in the granary

where she was living during the first year she was in Logan.
When a baby was born in the big house all the children were
hustled into other quarters during the childbirth.

While the day-by-day training of the young children was left
pretty largely to the mothers, as the children grew older they
came under more direct discipline by the father. Though he
had a strong authoritarian view of how children should be-
have, on the whole Olson got along with the children very
well and they with him. On occasion he did resort to physical
punishment when a child did not do as he expected; but at
other times he was most pleasant. There were always big times
in the household at Christmas and other festive days. While
the children were under the direct supervision of their own
mothers, the "aunts," as the other wives are called, did occasionally take a hand in the routine control of the children
of other wives. The children all had high respect for their
aunts and their own mothers would back up the latter in any
case where they had to be disciplined by one of them.

Training the boys in sound work habits began early. All
were given certain tasks and they soon learned to cooperate
in whatever they were doing. The same was true of the girls.

Since there were no adequate schools in Logan in those days,
during the winter months all the children of appropriate age
got up at four o'clock in the morning and had two hours of
schooling under the direction of their father. They sat around
a long table and Olson would go from child to child teaching
reading, spelling, writing, and other work. Later one or two
of the children attended school in Logan.

In 1875, or thereabouts, the fourth wife died leaving an infant son who was brought up by the first wife. At about that
time Olson secured some land near a neighboring town and
settled the second wife there.

From then on Olson made his headquarters more and more
with the first wife. He kept his clothes at her home and visited
the other wives less regularly than he had hitherto. Yet Olson
continued an old practice which had begun at the very outset
of his polygamous ménage. Supplies were bought as needed
and the wives were always treated as fairly as possible in re-

gard to all purchases. If one got a new chair, they each got a new chair. If one got a new dress, they each got a new dress.

While Olson operated completely on the theory of patriarchal domination of his family, he was always fair in his treatment of his wives and children. He organized their lives and they fitted neatly into the prearranged pattern. Moreover, the wives got along well among themselves. It might be pointed out in this connection that all the wives were Swedish. This meant that with their husband they all had somewhat the same European background. While the record does not show that this was of any great importance, I think it is a fair inference to hold that it was.

It is well to point out that this particular plural family was completed in the early days of Utah. Olson married all of his wives in the decade 1850–1860. The women were approximately of the same age and the children grew up together in about the same age groupings. Unlike some families which we shall examine later, there was no basis for conflict as sometimes happened when, after 20 or 25 years of monogamous life, a man suddenly decided to take a young and dashing bride for a second wife.

The family solidarity continued right down through Olson's life and afterwards. On his death he left a will and the family got together shortly after the funeral and within two hours the entire estate had been divided up amicably among all concerned. Each wife had had her own home deeded to her prior to his death as well as some additional property. There were no difficulties whatsoever in this family and to this day they are regarded as a closely knit group.

One final comment. This family story shows the fact that the psychological elements must not be overlooked in a consideration of these polygamous households. While it is true that the economic condition of this family became increasingly better, it is also true that there was mutual adaptability among the members under the patriarchal aegis of the father. All of the people concerned, that is, the husband and the four wives, had been brought up in a strictly Christian monogamous culture. All were converts to Mormonism with a firm faith in the Principle. All entered polygamy at a time when it was just beginning to be publicly recognized. Yet they adapted themselves to it very well. While separate households were usually regarded as more satisfactory, and while economic status was an important factor in the success or failure of plural families, in this particular family they began without much in the way of worldly goods and they began by living in a rather cramped and crowded condition in the same house. Nevertheless from the outset their family life was harmonious.

Another case in which the family was successful was that of John Vance. Vance represents one of the leading families of Utah having risen to a rather prominent place in church activities. He and his first wife, Lucy Stone, were English converts. John's affection for Lucy was said to be "love at first sight." They were married in 1856, left England in 1860, and arrived in Salt Lake the same year. Lucy was pregnant during the time of the trek from the Missouri River to Utah and her baby was born on the plains. The infant lived only a short time and was buried by the side of the road.

With the immigrant company was another girl, Ellen Johnson, a friend of Lucy's. Ellen had been driven out of her home by her parents for joining the Mormon Church. In London she had gone into domestic service where she had earned enough money to pay her way to Utah. She was a member of Vance's company and acted as companion to Lucy. Ellen lived with the Vances as helper and companion for Lucy for some years. In 1861 she married John. Later both families moved to a new community where they lived in one house until John married Susan Porter in 1868.

One informant, a son, who tried to present the family as the ideal type under polygamy, remarked about his father's choice of wives:

Father selected his wives with consideration of their natural function in mind—bringing forth children. He believed in the Principle implicitly, and considered all the aspects of the woman before he married her. There was nothing of romance like boys and girls have nowadays. His wives were selected with attention to heredity, education, and absence of defects. They later came to love and respect him, and were very glad to carry out their biological purpose.

Father consulted his first wife before he married his second and gained her consent. Before he married his third wife he counselled with both his first and second wives. Their consent was given willingly, probably because they themselves believed thoroughly in the Principle.

In the early days of their marriage all the wives shared the same log house. The relations among them were entirely peaceful. John had barely got a new house started for his wives when he was called to help settle another part of the country. He went to "Dixie" in southern Utah and started all over again. Here, at first, the two wives lived in the same house but in separate apartments, but with a connecting door between the two. The two women were great friends and frequently cooperated in their household duties. When Vance married his third wife, Susan, he built her a house about a block away. She seems to have been a little left out of the comradeship between Lucy and Ellen, although our informant contended that Susan never gave any appearance of feeling neglected. She visited with the other women quite often and the children were all mixed up in one large family. Later John built separate houses for the first two wives.

As to economic activities Vance first had a large farm and later a large ranch. As a matter of fact he never personally worked either one of these properties. He got into business and later became Collector of Internal Revenue. In addition to this his church activities grew apace and in his later years he had but little to do with his economic affairs. In the meantime his family had grown up and his boys took over for him. As one son puts it:

The farm and ranch were run by the boys. Always the oldest boy was the manager. When he got married and moved away, the next oldest took his place. I ran the outfit, hired and fired farm hands, did all the business of the farm and ranch when I was sixteen years old. While father never worked on the place, he always knew every detail of what was going on, coming around every two weeks or so and going over everything. He made it a special point to keep us busy. I remember once when he found me down on the main street of the town. Father asked me what I was doing away from the farm and I made some rather weak excuse, whereupon father said that if it turned out that there wasn't enough for his boys to do on the farm he would lend them to Brother Jones, a neighbor, who would keep them busy.

As to financial control, Vance held the purse strings of the family and a wife or child simply went to him and stated what was needed and usually got it.

Regarding the rotation of time among the wives, I quote another informant: "Father divided his time among his wives by spending a night with each one. He never missed this routine. But always before he went to bed he visited all his families, kissed all his wives and children goodnight, and then went to where he was spending the night. Father was an extremely affectionate man. Even when I was forty years old when he met me after not seeing me for several days, we kissed each other."

Vance treated his wives very fairly. They, in turn, reciprocated by great admiration and real fondness for him. When asked about whether there was any jealousy or difficulty among the wives, one son vehemently remarked that there was "absolutely none, the wives loved each other and father, and lived the Principle in this ideal form." While this illustrates the point that most prominent families would not admit any deviation from the ideal norm, it is apparent that this family got along exceptionally well. Certainly the children had no serious differences either during the father's life or afterwards.

While the wives were friendly to each other, nonetheless the first wife was always regarded as the person to whom the other wives turned for advice. The women always nursed each other through childbirths and illnesses. Ellen, the second wife, was an invalid during the last 20 years of her life.

Discipline was largely by the method of persuasion. Yet Vance was definitely the dominant figure even when he was not present in fact. When a child had done something of which the father did not approve, he would say, "Now wouldn't you like to do this instead?" with emphasis on the alternate course rather than the undesirable one. If the child refused, then the father would say, "I would just rather you didn't do that." And that was the end of the matter. Rarely was there any corporal punishment. The wives always supported the father in his wishes as to the children. He was away a great deal of the time and in terms of the general situation these women, like others, had the day-by-day care of the children and responsibility for their discipline and training. However, in case of any serious question about going some place if one of the children asked their mother, she almost invariably turned and said, "Ask your father." As the children grew older there was a certain amount of expectancy as to their companions, as to when they would get home from parties, and as to which party they would attend. As one of the daughters once said, if she didn't get home early as her father expected, she always had a certain guilt feeling in the matter.

John's control over his children is nicely illustrated in his attitudes toward their courtships. While he never forbade them to go with a particular person, he would take pains to point out the poor qualities of a particular individual. He cautioned the girls against new boys in the community saying that they ought to know a good deal about a man before they went out with him. A daughter tells this story:

I was writing to a young man in Beaver once. He was a fairly new boy in town, but I was writing to him. Father came in and asked me who I was writing to. I told him and he said that he thought I ought to know more about him before I put anything down on paper and send it to him. He said that he had heard some pretty detrimental reports about him, and how did I know that he was the only one that would handle my letter. I didn't write the letter and later I heard some very bad things about the young man, about how he was showing girls' letters around, and so on. I was awfully glad for father's advice.

The solidarity of this family is further illustrated in the division of the property on the father's death. Vance's first two wives predeceased him and these women had both accumulated a considerable amount of personal property which was

distributed to their own children. John left a will which stipu-
lated that the estate be held in trust for the use of his third
wife as long as she lived and that she should have whatever
she needed for living in comfort. This was to be paid out of
the interest of the estate and if it was not sufficient, then the
principle should be used. The will provided that after her
death the residue of the estate was to be distributed among
the children. There was no difficulty in the division of the
property, the wife was handsomely provided for, and upon her
death it was discovered that she had actually saved some money
out of her stipend which, in turn, was put into the general estate.

In the 1880's when the federal authorities began vigorously
to enforce the Edmunds Act, Vance, like many others, was
driven underground. After remaining on the Underground
for some time he was finally arrested and stood trial for unlawful cohabitation. However, he was acquitted.

As with the Olsons, the Vance family attained a high degree of solidarity. It was not a matter of separate households
alone or of economic status, but the fact that they really believed in the basic principle of polygamy and had every intention to carry it out. In addition, in this family we have a nice
illustration of the obligations which are laid upon the members of the community who belong to the social elite among
the Mormons. While Olson held certain local offices in the
Church, he was not regarded as a member of the upper class
of the Mormon Church. Vance, on the other hand, attained a
place in this class although in contrast to such families as the
Youngs, Smiths, Kimballs, Taylors, and others, he belonged
in the lower echelon of the upper class.

The disorganization of the polygamous family arose from a
number of varying circumstances. It sometimes happened
that the first wife picked up her baggage and left when or soon
after her husband took a second wife. Again there are families
in which the plural wife attempted to adjust and only after
a trial run did she give up. Obviously when the first wife left
after a man had married the second, he might be regarded,

in effect, as living in monogamy again. Of course, many of these men went on to marry subsequent wives. Some details and implications of such separations will be discussed in Chapter 11. Much more common, however, were those polygamous families which did not formally break up, but continued to exist under the conditions of considerable conflict. This was particularly true in the relations of the wives toward each other. Some aspects of this will be discussed in Chapter 9.

As we saw in Chapter 1, the popular anti-Mormon literature on plural marriages is filled with weird stories regarding the hardships of living under polygamy. There were, no doubt, many cases of real human tragedy. It so happens, however, that of the family records which I have collected and of which there is sufficient accuracy and detail, not mere hearsay, only a few would be regarded as really serious cases of disorganization. It must be recalled further that it would be difficult at this late date to get the full details on some of the families that were harassed by conflict when the system was in full swing. Nevertheless my materials do show that all was not well with the operation of the Principle and we shall now illustrate some family situations that were marked by severe difficulties.

Let us begin with the story of Andrew Pope as narrated to us by his second wife. Pope and his first wife were English converts. Like most of their fellow converts they soon set out for Zion to join the main body of the Saints and arrived in Utah in the early 1880's. As was common with converts already married, the Popes repaired to the Endowment House where they were sealed for time and eternity. Mrs. Pope, however, was lukewarm toward the gospel. In fact, she was so indifferent that she did not make any serious effort to bring up her three or four children in the way of the Church. As to polygamy, she always said that she would leave Pope if he ever entered into the plural system.

In 1887 Pope did take a plural wife, Elizabeth Shepherd. Elizabeth was the daughter of the second wife of a prosperous farmer near Ogden. At the time of her marriage she was about

18 years of age and 15 years the junior of the first wife. Of her marriage Elizabeth says:

I always believed in the principle of polygamy that it was a true and great one and I had been raised in it, so I didn't have any hesitation about it. But now when I look back on it, I sometimes wonder why I married into polygamy. My husband, Brother Pope, was a religious man but his first wife didn't want him to go to church very much and she would not allow the children to be raised Mormons. He, however, believed thoroughly in the principle of polygamy and he went to the church authorities about it. They told him he must not let a woman keep him from doing that which he thought was right. His wife told him, however, that if he ever married into polygamy she would leave him. Before they were married I had heard that she had made this statement but I didn't believe she would do it. But she did, and took the children with her. [The record does not report a divorce.] Brother Pope and I felt badly about it and we both tried hard to get her to join us again but she would not.

In effect, therefore, at the outset this was essentially, so far as Elizabeth was concerned, a monogamous family.

Pope courted his plural wife just before the Manifesto,* when the federal prosecutions were severe. In anticipation of trouble, Pope and Elizabeth were married in Mexico; shortly thereafter he moved his business to the Mormon colony there.

Pope was an energetic and hard-working individual. He had been a contractor and brick maker during his first residence in Utah. Later he went into the flour milling business in Mexico. Shortly after arriving in Mexico Pope also bought a store and took in a partner, a man named Wilson, who was regarded as a real asset because he spoke Spanish. The partner, however, later swindled Pope out of his property and returned to the States. During this early period in Mexico, Elizabeth had a hired girl named Alice, the wife of Wilson. She had two children by him. When Wilson absconded with the assets of the partnership, Alice went with him. Later she came back to the colonies when she discovered that her husband was, in her words, "no good."

* See pp. 376–378 for fuller discussion of the Manifesto.

A few years after Alice returned, having left her husband without a formal divorce, she married Pope. Of Alice the second Mrs. Pope said:

I felt something like Daddy's [meaning her husband] first wife when he married me. I did not think it was necessary for Brother Pope to marry Alice. Yet I believed in the Principle and I would not stand in his way. I guess there never were two people more unlike than Aunt Alice and myself. Alice and I never had to live in the same house and we never could. She was a good woman, however, but I just couldn't live with her. Brother Pope took her to the mill, located some distance from the town.

My children were growing up and I wanted them to go to school at the Academy in Juarez and I wouldn't leave. A man doesn't come first when there are children, I tell you. I used to take Alice's two children by her first marriage, and keep them in school and later she sent the other children. Whenever Brother Pope sent us money we were glad to get it, but we got along by ourselves when we had to. My father died while I was in Mexico and I had some money from his estate. Neighbors used to say to me, "Why don't you go out to the mill and take your rightful place," but I never wanted to do that. Daddy had married and the other wife's children were younger. Mine were growing up and could help me and we could get along. And Daddy didn't get along so well with the children. He was English and very strict and hard and believed in whipping and I couldn't stand for that. He whipped Alice's children, I know, and once he tried to whip my boy but I got in front of him. No, I knew that I could never stand for him to do that to my children. My children all stand together and love and respect me, but I didn't whip them.

All during these years there were strained relations between the two wives. Pope, whose business in Mexico was failing, took the second wife and family back to Utah. The first wife and her children followed: "but we paid our own way," she remarked. Her boys and girls got jobs to support her. Even an effort to pay a friendly call on Andrew and Alice led to great anxiety on Alice's part that Elizabeth and Pope might be reconciled. Later both families returned to Mexico, only to be driven out by the Villa revolution. The revolutionists burned Pope's mill and confiscated most of his other property.

Both families settled in El Paso, Texas, and shortly thereafter Alice died. And in the words of the first wife, long neglected: "There wasn't anything for me to do but to bring my husband here and take care of him."

A daughter of Elizabeth—herself married in polygamy—attributes much of the difficulty in the family to differences in the age of her father and Alice, and to the further fact that the latter having lost her first husband felt a deep need to hold fast to her new one, though in principle she was supposed to share him with another.

This family story neatly illustrates a number of important elements which will become more clear as we proceed. In the first place, complete faith in the Principle was a *sine qua non* for even its partial success. Mrs. Pope number one did not believe in the Principle and acted upon her belief by deserting when her husband took a plural wife. And, although the second wife was a child of a plural family, she had grave difficulty managing her emotions when her husband took still another wife. Externally the relations between the two families ran along reasonably well. But faced with a jealous and difficult person such as Alice, Elizabeth retreated from her husband and centered her affections upon her children. Although she continued to maintain that the Principle was the correct one, in her later years she had definite reservations in the matter and expressed some regrets at having entered the system. Psychologically she was giving verbal expression to the fact that she had for years suppressed her deeper affections and emotions. The final denouement in this case is interesting: In the latter years Elizabeth, who had separated from her husband, was obliged to take care of him in his declining years after Alice had died.

A case of a monogamous family that was marked by some domestic troubles to be followed by a plural marriage that, in effect, ended the first marriage is found in the case of William Root. Root and his first wife were converted in England in 1851 but did not migrate to Utah till the early 1860's. Root accumulated a reasonable amount of property and 30 years after his first marriage in 1873 took a second wife, a spinster of 30 years. Prior to this time, however, the relations of Root and his first wife were strained, to say the least. After the second marriage, Root and his first wife did not live together although he helped support her family. Wife number one had 10 children and was an able manager. There were no overt signs of conflict here, just a separation without divorce.

Today such a situation might easily lead to legal separation of the husband and first wife and marriage to the second. But such a procedure would have been highly censured by the Mormons of the day. As it was, he was but following the Principle when he married into polygamy and though his first wife did not like it and had nothing to do with him thereafter, no serious damage was done otherwise. This was, in effect, a case of two separate monogamous families tied together as a polygamous ménage by virtue of the lack of a formal divorce in the first instance.

Sometimes family troubles in polygamy which were focused on the first wife's objections, were dissipated when she left. This was true of the Oscar Dahlman family. The first wife was a troublemaker for years and finally divorced Dahlman. Although he had some sense of guilt about this, he was relieved— as were other members of his plural household. After her departure, in fact, this family might be considered a reasonably successful plural ménage.

It was not always the first wife who found difficulty in adapting herself to the plurality of wives. There are a number of families in which the second wife took her departure; sometimes even a third or subsequent wives. The David Osborn story is illustrative.

The breakup of the David Osborn plurality has a somewhat pathetic note. At the age of 21 years Osborn fell much in love and married his first wife, a girl of 16 years. Yet, to quote from an interview with David: "I talked to my girl about polygamy before I married her. All my life I had wanted to live in polygamy because I wanted a big family. That was why I believed in polygamy, it was to have a big family. I loved children, I was crazy about them, and I wanted to have two wives." His prospective bride did not like the idea at first, since she had heard a good deal about the trouble in polygamous families from her grandfather's situation.

Some eight or 10 years later, however, the first wife gave her consent to a second marriage and David secured a Recommend from President John Taylor, the usual and expected practice in securing a plural wife. Shortly thereafter he married his second spouse. This was during the height of the federal prosecution against plural marriages and a few years later the Osborns moved to the newly established Mormon haven in Mexico. David's comments on the sacrifices and difficulties attendant on practicing the Principle and on what led to the breakdown of his family life are revealing:

. . . But I want to tell you it is a hard thing for a wife to live in polygamy. She has to give up part of her husband's love and time and attention to another woman and it's a great trial for her . . . I want to tell you that my first wife has great blessings stored up in heaven for the way she lived in polygamy. She was patient and kind in everything. Down in Mexico, when I had separate houses for them, she would say to me, "What are you doing here? Your place is in the other home." But my second wife wasn't that way. She tried to win me away entirely, to get all of me and everything I had, but I wouldn't let her, I tell you I'd rather have died than do that . . .

. . . She was stubborn, my second wife was . . . and she wanted everything her own way. She couldn't ever give in. Down in Mexico I took her back for a visit to her father's place in the States and when I came for her, she said she couldn't come just then, but that she would meet me at the train. Well, never for one moment did she intend to meet me at the train. She wanted her freedom and independence. She couldn't accept a man to be the head of his own household. After that she never accepted home again. I tell you I felt terrible about letting her go. It's not easy to give up a wife and a child like that. [She had had seven children but all but one were stillborn.]

I wanted her back but she wanted to go her own way. She was a midwife and she was a good one. She made lots of money and wanted to be independent . . .

There was no divorce. The second wife simply severed all connections with Osborn and went her own way. Twice David tried for a reconciliation but failed.

According to our rating about one-quarter of our plural families had medium success in plural marriage. The Joseph Adamson family represents such moderate degree of adjustment. It is a good example of firm adherence to the Principle and difficulties in following it in practice.

Joseph Adamson was a son of the first wife of Judge Henry Adamson, a man well educated for his time. The father joined the Church in 1850 and soon after settled in Salt Lake City. Not long after this, his first wife died, but he soon acquired a number of plural spouses in keeping with Mormon custom. He moved to Ogden where he served on the bench. He was also a power in the Church.

Joseph was raised by one of the plural wives and he always regarded her as his real mother. He was a sensitive boy and there is some evidence that he was somewhat rebellious toward his father, an authoritarian character with a strong sense of justice and right. How Joseph's negative reaction to his father was transferred to other carriers of authority and power is illustrated in an experience which he had with the Church at the age of 20 and shortly after he had married for the first time.

Joseph had been working for the Church on what we would today regard as a public works project. When he was paid off, he felt that the Church owed him $40.00 more than he had been given in wages. He complained bitterly and loudly about his alleged mistreatment. The church authorities urged forbearance on him but he remained obstreperous. Finally this became so serious that he was disfellowshiped, though not excommunicated.

This was a severe blow to his ego and for some years he was cynical and disillusioned. Later, however, he was reinstated to full membership and was sent by his father to a new section of the country to head up the colonization there.

It is interesting to note that when Joseph was returned to full fellowship in the Church, his attitude changed completely

from that of insurgent to a docile follower who believed
everything that the authorities said and obeyed their orders
implicitly. We shall see more of this attitude later.

In the new community Joseph Adamson took a prominent
part in the selection of property for the colonists and the
management of the general operations there. Later he became
a Bishop and took an active part in all church affairs.

In the middle 1880's when the federal prosecutions for polygamy were becoming more intense the church officials, in
their counterattack, began urging the Saints to follow the
Principle more completely and in more wholehearted fashion
than ever before. As a good Mormon, Adamson felt it his duty
to obey this counsel.

A son of the first wife describes the consultation about taking a new wife in these words:

We lived in a three-room house. In such a house I couldn't help
overhearing my mother and father talking in their room at night.
I remember that for some time discussions went on about father's
going into polygamy. He usually said to mother that the authorities were insisting that he go into polygamy, threatening to release him from his bishopric if he didn't take another wife. Mother
would say finally that if this was really the case, she wouldn't stand
in his way. He could go ahead and take another wife if he had to.

I'm pretty sure mother was resentful of the whole thing; but in
such a situation a woman didn't dare stand in her husband's way,
because then she'd blame herself for whatever happened to him
ever afterwards, if she objected. In general a first wife realized
these things and didn't think of objecting. Yes, the first wife had
a severe emotional situation to cope with, especially my mother.
Father was none too well off, and he would have to support another family by marrying again. It was a severe trial.

Having secured Mary, the first wife's, consent to taking a
second wife, there is a story in the family that Mary helped
Adamson pick the proper person. There is another story in
the family, however, that Joseph asked a large number of
young girls to marry him with no success, but that finally
Louise Jensen did consent. She had been a student in a school
where Joseph had taught during the winter months. Her par-

ents approved of the match, especially when they learned that the first wife had agreed. At that time Joseph was 48 years old, the girl 17.

Louise had been brought up in an orthodox Mormon home and fully accepted the Principle. Her daughter says that her mother "felt as if something divine was happening to her, since she believed in the Principle of celestial marriage so completely. She felt much as Mary the mother of Jesus must have felt when she discovered she was to have a divine child."

Since the federal deputies were swarming over that section of the country in search of "cohabs," as they called polygamous men, she and Joseph quietly got out of town at night and went to a nearby Mormon temple where they were married. This was in 1888.

Though the first wife had given her consent, she was none too happy about the arrival of a young girl as a second bride. There were several children in the first family who were a good deal older than the second wife. In fact, the two oldest sons of Mary were violently opposed to their father's marriage and tried to stop their father but did not succeed.

Joseph built a second and better house not far from his first home, moved the first wife and her family into the new place, and put the new bride into the old house. He tried to be fair in his relationships with the two families and divided his time on a week-about basis.

Economically the family was never well off. Adamson gave so much of his time to church duties that he had little left for farming. However, the first wife was thrifty and hardworking and as her children grew up, they took over more and more responsibility in managing the farm. When the town was first established, Adamson had complete charge of the division of the available land and water rights. But in being just and in living up to the attitudes of complete honesty which were so characteristic of him, he took the poorest land for himself. This consisted of about 220 acres of fair land but without adequate water for irrigation.

Unlike the usual polygamous families the Adamsons never went in for home gardening. Neither did they take up home manufacture. What they got in the way of vegetables and clothes had to be purchased. Joseph tried to be fair about this and divided his purchases equally between his two wives. He was perpetually in debt and the two families really had a hard time of it.

The inter-family relations were none too cordial. For example, it is significant that in this ménage the wife and children of the second family never referred to the first wife, as Aunt. It will be recalled that the word "aunt" was almost universally used in the Mormon families to refer to the father's other wives. The first wife was always called "Mrs. Adamson."

On the other hand, the second wife's daughter remarks that one of the greatest problems which her mother had to face was the fact that never was she publicly recognized as "Mrs. Joseph Adamson." Because of the pressure of the federal authorities on the Mormons, Joseph had to appear as a monogamous man in his public life. When he went to church or to parties, he and his first wife went in the buggy; if the second wife went at all she walked.

It is clear that Mary never did fully accept the polygamous situation. She was rather jealous and envious of Louise. Louise was not only younger but she was a beautiful and attractive person. A son of the first wife remarks, "The difficulty between the two wives was probably more my mother's fault than it was Louise's. Mother was an independent woman and never made any especially friendly gestures toward Louise." The second wife was easygoing and friendly and would have gotten along all right with the first if the latter had been willing to yield a little. It was difficult for a woman 50 years of age to view with equanimity the arrival of a new wife of less than 20. Yet, for the most part the conflict between the two wives was kept under cover and only occasionally did the first wife break out into open expression of her strong feelings. Moreover, the children of the first wife rather strongly resented the second marriage. As a matter of fact, we have what in effect were really two separate families tied together by the husband and father alone. Louise lived a rather secluded life, taking little or no part in outside affairs.

The discipline of the children in this family was largely in the hands of Adamson himself. He was a great talker and was perpetually lecturing his children on morals and conduct. While for the most part his treatment of infractions was reasonably mild, on occasion he could be very severe and even indulge in physical punishment.

The first wife, when Joseph was not around, often tolerated behavior on the part of her children which he would not have condoned. For example, Adamson, as a Bishop, and in conformity with the standards of the official Church, was strongly opposed to card playing. When he was not around, however, Mary often let the older children play cards when they wished.

As a prominent man and as one who was admittedly polygamous as far as his official connections with the Church were concerned, Adamson was bound to be under indictment sooner or later. For a long time the officers tried to catch him. The second wife had moved to another community on the Underground but in time Joseph felt in conscience bound not to continue to evade the officers. Finally he gave himself up. He was found guilty of "unlawful cohabitation" and fined $200.00. He did not have the money but his friends rallied around and paid his fine.

The Adamsons are an instance of strong adherence to the basic principle of plurality of wives but who had considerable difficulty in carrying it out in practice. This was apparent not only in relationship to the economy of the household but also to the inter-personal relation of the wives and the children of the two families. The first wife was jealous of the second; she felt insecure in the matter of the economy of the household and had other difficulties. On her occasional outbursts toward Joseph, she was known to have said, "O.K. Go to your darling, then, if you wish."

The difficulties of a second family, especially of the children, are made clear by a daughter:

I remember how profound was my shock at hearing father say when I was about sixteen years of age that we children probably were not recognized at law. I thought over this matter a good deal because of my earlier bringing up in a polygamous situation.

The whole generation that were reared in polygamy underwent a profound shock in getting out into the world and finding out that some people did not think that our parents were legitimately married. We had to almost reorganize ourselves in changing from Utah where we were praised and looked up to the outside world where the attitude was entirely different.

From the standpoint of personality organization Adamson is interesting. A sensitive and somewhat emotional man, he had had a good deal of trouble in his early years adjusting to other people, especially those like his father who carried a strong authoritarian attitude. Later, as we know, his resistance to such attitudes were displaced on the church officials. Yet, after his episode of being disfellowshiped and on his return to the Church as a full member, he became more and more docile and obedient with regard to everything that the church officials demanded of him. On the other hand, he became increasingly authoritarian and rigid in his personal demands upon his family. This is a not uncommon instance of docility to the powers over one with the ambivalent severity to those whom one, in turn, controls.

A good illustration of Adamson's adherence to the Church is found in the remarks of a daughter of the second wife:

. . . When the Church repudiated plural marriage in 1890, father fell wholeheartedly in with the officials and deplored such marriages after the Manifesto. Our Bishop had four wives and was a fairly old man when he was called to go on a mission some years after the Manifesto. Before he went he took another wife, a young woman, and father was scathing in his remarks. He said that the Bishop just hadn't waked up to what he had done by marrying this girl illegally and without the authority of the priesthood. He said that when he did wake up to the terrible thing he had done, "he would go mad." And the Bishop did go mad and died.

As our records show and as general impressions confirm, there were many families not unlike this one. An outward arrangement was made but any internal harmony was hardly ever present.

We will now draw upon the impressions of polygamy given
us by a number of men who made observations of the Mormons
in the early days in Utah. These individuals were government
officials, like Captain J. W. Gunnison and Lester F. Ward, or
world travelers like Jules Remy, the great French traveler, and
Sir Richard Burton, best known for his translation of *The
Arabian Nights*. In fact, Burton is sometimes regarded as
somewhat too pro-Mormon for the Gentile world. His *City
of the Saints* has long been considered to be a fairly adequate
picture of the early days in Utah. He certainly was not shocked
by polygamy, having observed it in many other places in the
course of his extensive travels. None of these men were emotionally upset by what they heard and saw in polygamous
Utah. Moreover, most of them visited Utah before the moral-
religious campaign against the plural marriage system began.

Of the various observers Lester F. Ward, though opposed
to the practice, was reasonably perceptive regarding the system. In 1875, before Ward became well-known as a sociolo-
gist, and while he was still connected with the Smithsonian Institution as a paleobotanist, he made a number of trips to
Utah as a part of his fieldwork. During these trips he acted
as a correspondent for the *New York Tribune*. In one letter,
dated Gunnison, Utah, September 5, 1875, he describes the
Mormon communities and Mormon life and then takes up
the topic of polygamy.

Among other things he points out that the plural system
was limited in proportion to the total number of marriages,
and, furthermore, that it was confined largely to the upper
and wealthier class of Saints. He firmly maintained that polygamy worked a serious hardship on poor men. Moreover,
he contended that within the Mormon group the greatest opposition to the scheme came from the "intelligent middle
class."

As to the frequency of polygamy he writes:

From the acquaintance which I have formed here, from my observation of the people with whom I have come in contact, and
from careful inquiries in all quarters and fair and unbiased esti-
mates that I have solicited from candid and disinterested citizens

I derive the general conclusion that for the entire Mormon population the proportion of monogamous to polygamous men is about
as 6 to 1. In the town of Gunnison, where there were about 90
male heads of family only about 15 of these have more than one
wife. In Richfield, county seat of Sevier Co., where the church
officials reside, the ratio is somewhat less. In Glenwood, where I
have been longest, it is certainly considerably greater. And thus
it is throughout. So that the sacred institution is after all quite
limited in its control of the masses.

The greatest check upon the institution is the jealousy of the
women. They do not resist it so much by refusing to marry as by
refusing to live under the same roof with other wives. They demand separate establishments and ample support and the effect
is to limit polygamy. Cases do occur, it is true, with some of which
I am quite familiar, where two wives live together with a man,
but the idea is so generally distasteful to the present state of human
nature that, as we might anticipate, it is rarely possible to realize it.

Ward felt that plurality of wives led to the loss of deeper
sentiment and romance.

In Utah . . . all is cold calculation . . . That heroic attachment that welds one soul to another for life and defies the storms
of both the outer and the inner world . . . is swept down like a
gossamer by the poisonous breath of polygamy.

If asked what should be done with polygamy, I should answer,
as far as national interference is concerned, it should be left quite
alone. If my opinion of its probable destiny were solicited, I
should give it that the progress of intelligence, even as it is now
going on here, must at no very remote period, root it out of the
community. Although little practiced by the ignorant mass, it is
this great ignorant mass that renders its practice by others possible
and easy. Popular education, the panacea of all social as well as
political evils would be the only form of national interference that
any circumstances could justify.

As is well known, Ward was not interested in religion, but
he did have a strong moral sense. While he did not approve
of polygamy, he felt that education—his universal panacea
for all ills—would ultimately wipe out this disintegrating
force. It is interesting that he shows keen insight into some
of the most difficult problems associated with Mormon polyg-

amy such as the matter of handling the wives and the family, the disappearance of romantic love, and the economics of family life under the plural system.

There remains but a word to be said in concluding this chapter. Surely if we are to judge by our rating of marital success or failure, or by the sample family stories which we have given in some detail, or from the relatively objective observations of early and reasonably unbiased observers, we must realize that while polygamy was by no means an unmixed blessing, even where externally the plural families got on well together, by the same token it was neither the horrible system pictured by the anti-Mormon reformers nor the marital bed of roses alleged by the church officials of the Latter-day Saints. In the chapters which follow we shall have ample opportunity to document all the important phases of this family system, so novel for its time and place—19th-century puritanical America. Attention will be given to husband-wife relations, inter-wife contacts, the place of the children under the system and many other aspects of the day-by-day life of these families. Also attention will be given to polygamy as a symbol of a deep conflict—moral, economic, and political—between the Mormon adherents of the system and the much larger body of anti-Mormons, both within and outside of Utah.

# 4 ORIGIN AND DEVELOPMENT OF MORMON POLYGAMY: OFFICIAL AND OTHERWISE

THE ORIGINS and development of polygamy must be seen against the background of the rise of Mormonism itself. The major features of this larger story are relatively well known, yet many facts are lacking which, if known, would be helpful to the historian and social scientist. Within a few years after the formal organization of the Church, the whole story of the founding and development of the Mormon movement becomes a mixture of fact and fancy. With regard to the plural marriage system the mystery of its origin is peculiarly tantalizing. Certainly the precise steps in its emergence are almost impossible to trace, as this chapter will make clear.

The audacity of an ignorant and half-educated adolescent, Joseph Smith, in announcing that he was chosen of God to restore the lost gospel and to initiate the last dispensation of time, struck many people as either stupid or ludicrous. And yet the very boldness of his claims intrigued others and Smith soon had followers. Nor did all of these come from the untutored masses. In his day people were looking for some belief which would be a rock of refuge on an uncertain frontier. The time was full of many sectarian claims of the "true gospel" and if Joseph Smith had not appeared, perhaps some other prophet would have.

For one, I have never been fully convinced that at the outset Joseph Smith intended to found a new church. There is some historical and psychological evidence that he was a parapath, that is, one who cannot always tell fact from fantasy. As a youth, he was a great spinner of tall yarns. It is more than likely that with the telling and retelling of these stories, he came to believe them to be true. Moreover, when he found others accepting them as facts, he was all the more inclined to believe them himself. As parapathic behavior is common enough among the formulators of religions the world over, of magic makers, and the proposers of all sorts of social utopias, we should not be surprised, then, that Smith, as a product of his time, was caught up in this kind of psychological climate.

Smith reported a variety of visions and revelations as occurring to him in the late 1820's. So, too, he produced the *Book of Mormon,* allegedly taken from "golden plates" buried by one Moroni at the end of a long history of the early inhabitants of the Western Hemisphere. These people are said to have fled from Jerusalem under an edict of God and to have settled in the Western Hemisphere. The story goes on to say that some of them departed from the true faith and were cursed by God with a dark skin. From these latter come the American Indians, known in the *Book of Mormon* as the Lamanites. Their white brethren, the Nephites, carried on for many centuries until they, because of their own wickedness and their military inefficiency, were wiped out by the Lamanites. The last of the Nephites, a "last of the Mohicans" in reverse, wrote up their whole history on golden plates in "reformed" Egyptian hieroglyphics and buried the same in what came to be known as the Hill Cumorah. Many centuries later, Smith, under divine guidance, found this book, and translated it with the help of the Urim and Thummin. These he alleged to be a pair of spectacles which would enable him to read the ancient documents. In his ignorance Smith did not know that the Urim and Thummin were a kind of lot or dice cast by ancient priests in discovering the divine will. On April 6, 1830, Smith formally incorporated a church which became officially known as the Church of Jesus Christ of the Latter-day Saints. Missionaries were sent out, people were converted, and the movement began.

Whether he believed it or not, Smith soon found large numbers of people accepting his message. In the early 1830's he received many revelations from God regarding the organization of the Church. Rules were set down, and the Mormon movement grew in numbers and in complexity of structure.

To get a somewhat fuller understanding of the operation of the Church, a brief excursion into the nature of the priesthood and its relation to the social controls will be in order.

The essential matter in the "restoration of the gospel" by Joseph Smith was the giving to him by God of the proper priestly authority. There are two basic priesthoods which compose the ecclesiastical hierarchy of the Mormon Church: The first of these is that of Melchizedek, named for an ancient Hebrew king and priest; the lesser or second priesthood is the Aaronic, named for Aaron, the brother of Moses. In addition to the priesthood there are certain authorities who are concerned with the temporal welfare of the Saints; there are also what are known as "auxiliary" organizations.

The Melchizedek priesthood is charged with the fundamental functions of spiritual salvation. There are three gradations in this priesthood: The first is that of the Elder who is supposed to spend a good deal of his time in preaching the gospel both at home and abroad. The second estate is that of the Seventy; he, too, is charged with preaching the gospel and with certain additional functions in the way of supervisory work in the Church. The third and highest grade is that of the High Priest; he holds the fundamental keys to the divine power and all the important positions in Mormondom are held by men in this category.

The secondary or Aaronic priesthood is likewise divided into three estates, the lowest being the Deacon, the second, the Teacher, and the third, the Priest. They act to perpetuate the gospel and to keep the faithful in line but have certain special functions. For example, the Deacons aid in the passing of the Lord's Supper at the sacramental services. The Teachers go about the Wards exhorting the Saints to be faithful and to perform their sacred duties. The Priests are charged with the function of blessing the communion and participating in other activities having to do with local affairs. However, no member of the Aaronic priesthood can baptize a new member into the Church, or perform such functions as christening, or perform a marriage ceremony. These offices must be performed by some member of the Melchizedek priesthood.

The temporal organization of the Church follows a geographical pattern. At the bottom is the Ward, or parish as it would be called in other denominations. This is definitely a spatial unit. The Ward is headed up by a Bishop and two counselors. The Bishops and their counselors have charge of the meetings of the Ward, supervise the various activities of the Aaronic priesthood, and perform other temporal as well as spiritual functions. In addition there is a Prayer Circle made up of members of the Melchizedek priesthood in the Ward; and, on occasion, there may be invoked a Bishop's Court to settle various disputes among the members.

The next unit is the Stake, made up of a number of Wards. It is headed by a President and two counselors. The government of the Stake is in the hands of the Stake High Council. This is made up of High Priests chosen to perform certain legislative and judicial functions.

At the top of the Mormon Church stand the President and the Twelve Apostles. The President is known officially as "The Prophet, Seer, and Revelator." He has two counselors. The President has the divine power of God and all others in the Church are subservient to his authority. Beneath the First Presidency and the Twelve Apostles are the Seven Presidents of Seventy who supervise the various quorums of Seventies and, in general, have an important hand in the missionary work of the Church. In addition to these so-called "general authorities" is the Presiding Bishop and his two counselors. They have more or less oversight and control of such temporal affairs as the collection of tithing, management of church property, and investments. There is a Church Patriarch who supervises the Ward Patriarchs. These men give "patriarchal blessings"—a kind of private prayer for individual members telling them in vague clichés their place in the divine plan of salvation.

The oldest of the auxiliary organizations is the Female Relief Society founded March 17, 1842, in Nauvoo. Sunday schools were begun in December, 1849. Later, two youth organizations, the Young Men's Mutual Improvement Association and the Young Ladies' Mutual Improvement Association, were established. These two have some control over the recreational as well as educational activities of the adolescent members of the Church. They function at the Ward level but, as is true in the Sunday School, there are stake and general church supervisory officers. In addition to these there are the Primary and Religion class groups. Originally these were two separate organizations but have now been merged into one. They aim at giving religious instruction to children of elementary school age.

In addition to these there is another auxiliary organization of sorts which might be mentioned. I refer to the practice which has grown up in Mormon communities of having Seminaries, as they are called, attached to the various high schools and colleges wherever the Mormons count in any numbers. These Seminaries are under the general authorities of the Church and are supposed to give the people of high school and college age religious instruction. They are similar to the Christian and Jewish organizations affiliated with American colleges and universities.

In its early days, the Church had complete dominance of all phases of education from elementary level on through to the college or university. Today, aside from one university, it confines its educational efforts to its auxiliary organizations. On the whole, its religious instruction and training are highly effective.

The Church had hardly begun when persecution set in. People in central New York who had known the Smiths well doubted the whole story of the golden plates, and Joseph and his cohorts were subject to a good deal of abuse by those who thought it a lot of nonsense. Under divine guidance, Smith moved on with his followers to Kirtland, Ohio. Here he built the first temple and initiated the first of the sacred rituals of the Church. It is well to understand that the Mormon Church is really a form of secret society. The basic rituals are taken from those of the Masonic order, of which Smith and the three subsequent presidents of the Church were all high-ranking members.

While in Kirtland, Smith began having revelations about founding a new Jerusalem on the Missouri frontier. He sent missionaries there and they returned with glowing reports of the availability of ample land and other resources. Affairs in Kirtland were in a bad way, what with financial difficulties, apostasy, and some rumors of plural marriage. Smith, in anticipation of increased trouble, sent a vanguard of the Church to Jackson County, Missouri, designated by Smith to be the Zion of the New Order. Smith and the main body of the Saints followed some time later. But the Mormons had hardly begun to settle in their new locality when trouble ensued. Smith had committed himself against slavery and after a bitter time of it, the Saints were forced out of Jackson County. They settled next in Davis and Clay counties with their center at Far West. Again the story is repeated and they were finally driven out of Missouri to find refuge in West Central Illinois in what came to be known as the City of Nauvoo.

The Nauvoo period is interesting from various angles. First of all Smith obtained a most remarkable charter from the state legislature. Nauvoo was in effect a state within a state. It had its own court system, its own military establishment, and the mayor was practically its political dictator. The Saints went to work and the place grew in importance, both economically and politically. However, trouble with the non-Mormon elements arose. The beginnings of polygamy, which we shall discuss fully later in this chapter, began to be a symbol of sharp differences even within the Church. Apostasy was frequent. Nevertheless Nauvoo grew in size, especially with the influx of Mormon converts from other parts of this country and from Europe.

Following the killing of Smith and his brother in Carthage jail, the main body of the Mormons were under the guidance of Brigham Young. After a short time in Iowa, they moved on to the Great Basin. At first, they thought they were free from the United States and set up their own government, known as the State of Deseret. However, the Mexican War having been settled in the meantime, they found themselves still a part of the United States. Brigham Young was appointed the first

territorial governor of Utah. During these early years, however, the distinction between the ecclesiastical and the civil
government was slight indeed. The Church established its own
organization everywhere and the civil government was really
dominated by the ecclesiastical order. We shall have something to say about this in later chapters. Let us now turn to
examine the beginnings of Mormon polygamy.

The end of the 18th and the beginning of the 19th centuries
saw a tremendous upsurge of religious interest and enthusiasm
in this country. There were really two great centers of revivalism, one in the Kentucky and Tennessee area, the other in
parts of New England and New York. While the revivalism in
the latter area never reached quite the mob and mass expression that occurred in the Cumberland Valley, nevertheless
there was a real outburst of religious fervor among the people
of New England and New York.

Among other, to us, bizarre doctrines which emerged was
one known as "spiritual wifehood." The essential features of
this belief is that men and women are mated in heaven as
spirits. It is a concept of "natural mates," to quote William
Hepworth Dixon. But since there was no method by which
the mating before birth could be communicated to those on
earth, men and women were free to find their spiritual mates
here. When the individual, by some inspiration, divine or
otherwise, was able to detect his spiritual mate, he was supposed to be free to join with the said mate. This new conjunc-
tion of the sexes was sometimes of a purely platonic nature. In
other cases it was an easy step from spiritual mating to living
together in more mundane relations.

The doctrine of spiritual wives had periodic currency in
Europe, but the emergence of a similar doctrine in the United
States seems to have been associated with the whole perfec-
tionist movement with which the names of John Humphrey
Noyes, Matthias the Prophet, and others are associated. One
of these groups, known as The Perfect Church, had a strong
organization in New York and another in New Haven. There
were many women as well as men leaders in these movements

and they soon developed the idea and practice of spiritual mating. In some instances this was of an idealized sort, intended to test the individual's capacity to overcome the flesh. In others, there was a much more open admission of the sexual factor. This was true in the case of Noyes and his Oneida community where there was no giving or taking in marriage. Noyes had the idea that marriage itself was sinful and contrary to good Christianity because of its essential possessiveness. The Platonic aspect of spiritual mating is nicely illustrated in the Shakers who permitted no procreative activities at all.

The doctrine of spiritual wifism was part of the "strenuous evangelism" that swept over New England and central New York in Smith's day. While it is quite unlikely that Smith ever heard of the European movements, he could hardly have avoided picking up ideas about the doctrine nearer home. There is one legend that Matthias the Prophet did visit Smith at Nauvoo but whether Smith got any ideas from him on the matter at that time is unknown. Spiritual wifism was in the air and, as with other items in Mormonism, Smith was quick to absorb current and even bizarre ideas.

Maria Ward in her novelized account of the early days of the Church, maintains that plural marriage was accepted and practiced even before Smith and his followers left New York State. Certainly there is considerable evidence that Smith toyed with the idea very early and at least he gave his close associates, such as Brigham Young, to understand that he had had a revelation on the matter of plurality of wives even before the founding of the Church.

Jonathan Baker in his journal, July 26, 1872, writes:

At night went to the fourteenth Ward meeting. Brother Brigham . . . [said] that while Joseph and Oliver were translating the *Book of Mormon* they had a revelation that the order of patriarchal marriage and the sealing was right. Oliver said unto Joseph, "Brother Joseph why don't we go into the order of polygamy, and practice it as the ancients did? We know it is true, then why delay?" Joseph's reply was: "I know that we know that it is true and from God but the time has not yet come." This did not seem to suit Oliver who expressed a determination to go into the order of plural marriage anyhow although he was ignorant of the order and pattern and the results. Joseph said, "Oliver if you go into this thing it is not with my faith or consent." Disregarding the counsel of Joseph, Oliver took to wife Miss Anne Lyman, cousin to George A. Smith. From that time he went into darkness and lost the spirit. Anne Lyman is still alive, a witness to these things . . .

Whatever the source of this story which Brigham told his audience, it shows clearly that the Mormons realized that plural marriage, at least as an idea, was early in the Church. Another indication of its early appearance comes from Orson Pratt, who in a pamphlet, declared that the "Principle" was first made known to Joseph Smith in 1831. Pratt claims, however, that Smith did not enter into the practice of this until a good ten years later. W. W. Phelps, another early Mormon leader, once remarked that Smith told him that polygamy would be a practice of the Church. This was during the Kirtland period while Joseph was translating the *Book of Abraham*.

Certainly there were rumors and counter-rumors during this time which had to do with the secret plural marriages and adultery. One Philastus Hurlbut was excommunicated from the Church on the grounds of adultery and he began a strong attack upon Smith. Among Hurlbut's charges was the practice of polygamy. (See Chapter 15.)

There is ample evidence that Smith, like other founders of religion, was concerned with matters of sex. For one thing he and Emma, his wife, did not get along and there was much rumor that Joseph was not adverse to paying attention to other women. It was also said that he was given to drinking and gambling.

One is reminded of the statement attributed to Brigham Young regarding Smith which Young made shortly after he was converted. "If he [Smith] acts like a devil, he has brought forth a doctrine that will save us, if we abide by it. He may get drunk every day of his life, sleep with his neighbor's wife every night, run horses and gamble . . . but the doctrine he has produced will save you and me and the whole world."

Whatever may have been the personal origin of Mormon polygamy, Fawn McKay Brodie in *No Man Knows My History* (1945), a biography of Smith has stated the matter aptly in these words: "But Joseph was no careless libertine who could be content with clandestine mistresses. There was too much of the Puritan in him, and he could not rest until he had redefined the nature of sin and erected a stupendous theological edifice to support his new theories on marriage."

Among the various stories is one that linked Nancy Marinda Johnson's name with Joseph Smith as early as 1832. Three years later it was rumored that he had seduced Miss Alger, an orphan girl of 17 years whom Emma had taken into the family. Emma was so enraged that she forced her to leave the house although the girl was pregnant. Mrs. Brodie lists her as the first plural wife of the Prophet.

In September, 1842, in an affidavit Fannie Brewer said she resided in Kirtland in 1837 and that "There was much excitement against the prophet, on another account, likewise,—an unlawful intercourse between himself and a young orphan girl residing in his family, and under his protection!!! Mr. Martin Harris told me that the prophet was most notorious for lying and licentiousness!!"

During these years the doctrine was kept secret and the official Church denied any such practice. In a public statement in the *Millennial Star*, Smith said that the Mormons did not believe in "a community of wives," and that such a thing was "an abomination in the sight of the Lord." Yet at the very time Smith was giving attention to the whole idea of plural marriage.

Many of his women followers adulated Smith. Nancy Rigdon, daughter of Joseph's chief lieutenant, had testified in his favor at the Richmond trial and he was more and more of a mind to follow up her friendliness. In fact there had been gossip at Kirtland that Sidney Rigdon had a quarrel with Smith because the latter wanted to take Nancy as a plural wife. Then, too, during his period in jail in Richmond, Missouri, Lucinda Huntington Buell, whose husband had apostasized, visited Joseph in February and tried to do so again in March but was refused permission by the jailer the second time. Subsequently Smith wrote her a letter saying that he had a great plan afoot that he would soon unfold to his most faithful followers. During part of his sojourn in Missouri Smith stayed at the home of Lucinda Morgan Harris who many years later admitted to having been the Prophet's mistress at the time. Later Smith married both Mrs. Buell and Mrs. Harris as plural wives.

By 1839 or 1840 Smith had worked out a theory or "Principle" regarding the plurality of wives. Parley P. Pratt states in his autobiography that about 1840, in Philadelphia, the Prophet told him about an idea "of eternal family organization and the eternal union of the sexes in those inexpressible endearing relationships in which none but the highly intellectual, the refined and pure in heart know how to apprise . . ." Also, George A. Smith frequently remarked that Smith had taught him the principle of polygamy in 1839. All this was done in secrecy and the official revelation is not supposed to have been given until July 12, 1843. Smith was building up a background for the open approval of polygamy, at least by the leaders of the Church. In 1842 one Udney Hay Jacob published a pamphlet defending polygamy, first, in terms of Old Testament history, and, second, as one way of solving marital troubles. Jacob also made clear that God regarded women as definitely inferior to men and that they had no rights to more than one husband. Although Smith's own press had printed this pamphlet, the Prophet publicly denounced it. Yet it was probably a feeler of public sentiment, and many of its arguments were those used later by the officials of the Church in defense of plurality.

There is still other evidence that plurality of wives was being talked about as well as practiced. Benjamin Johnson's journal reports that prior to 1842 a Mormon named Granger in Rochester, New York, announced a divine revelation setting forth the doctrine of polygamy. Apparently he derived this from the theory of spiritual wifism. Writing of this matter somewhat later, Johnson says: "Men and women of previous respectability were now in free love disgracefully and insanely mixed up . . ." He regarded this as "a trick of the Devil to forestall with disgrace and bring contempt upon a sacred and holy law that the Lord was about to reveal."

That Johnson had some foreknowledge of what was to come is told in his journal. He says that in April, 1843 Joseph Smith explained to him the principle of plural marriage and asked him to intercede in his efforts to secure his sister, Almera Johnson, as a plural wife. To this Benjamin reacted: "Brother Joseph, this is all new to me. It may all be true. You know, but I do not. To my education, it is all wrong, but I am going, with the help of the Lord, to do just what you say. But I promise you that if you do this tō degrade my sister, I will kill you."

Subsequently Benjamin, "filled with the Holy Ghost," converted his sister to this plan and she was sealed to the Prophet. The journal continues: "Soon after that the Prophet was at my house again, where he occupied my sister Almera's room and bed, and then he asked for my younger sister, Esther." But Esther was promised to Benjamin's brother-in-law, so the Prophet dropped the matter. The latter, however, went on to tell Johnson more details of the whole system of celestial marriage, and in fact insisted on repeating the marriage ceremony of Melissa and Benjamin "by the law of the Lord" so as to make it divinely legal. The Prophet then promoted the marriage of Johnson and an orphan girl, Mary Ann Hale, who had been brought up by Benjamin's mother. Joseph promised Johnson that if he would marry the girl "you will all be blessed." The journal remarks: "This seemed like hurrying up my blessings pretty fast, but the spirit of it came upon me and from that hour I thought of her as my wife that the Lord had given me."

There is ample evidence that Smith married more and more plural wives in the years previous to the announcement of the revelation itself. Brodie lists 26 women as being married to Smith between 1840 and the summer of 1843. Her tabulation reports that he married an additional 18 women between the time the revelation is supposed to have been given him and his death.

It will be recalled that the revelation provides that the first wife should give her consent to the husband before he takes a plural wife. Smith probably had his Emma in mind when he concocted this idea. At any rate, by the spring of 1843 Joseph seems to have finally convinced Emma of the inevitability of the new system, although Jonathan Baker's journal points out her "spite and vindictiveness" in the matter. She reluctantly admitted the Principle but said she would like to choose the wives of the Prophet. The Smiths had four young girls living with them at the time under their guardianship: Eliza and Emily Partridge and Sarah and Marie Lawrence. These girls were orphans and had been taken in by Emma and Joseph. Emily and Eliza Partridge were married to Smith on May 11, 1843, with Emma's consent. Unknown to Emma these girls had already been married to Smith some two months previously. A little later Smith married the two Lawrence sisters. While Emma knew about these marriages, she probably never knew just how many spiritual mates the Prophet really had.

The early days of the Mormons were never quiet. Yet the Kirtland and Missouri troubles were mild compared to those in Nauvoo. A man who played an important role in Nauvoo, first as friend and then as enemy of Smith, was Dr. John Cook Bennett. At the age of 35, in the summer of 1840, he was baptized into the Church. He was a dapper young man of dark complexion and a facile tongue. His medical background is obscure but at the time he was secretary of the medical society of Illinois and Quartermaster General of the state militia. Smith was greatly attracted to him. For a time they were inseparable and Bennett replaced many of the older leaders who had been so close to Smith in former years. At one point Bennett was referred to as the assistant to the Prophet or to the President of the Church. In addition to helping train the Nauvoo Legion, the military arm of the Mormons, Bennett seems to have been intrigued by the doctrine of spiritual wives.

For nearly two years Bennett and Smith acted in close cooperation. Then came a break marked by an elaborate exposure of Smith and Mormonism by Bennett and by counter-charges that Bennett had been seducing innocent women on the promise of marriage.

It is said that the immediate cause of the break between the two men had come about because of conflicting solicitations for the hand of Nancy Rigdon. The legend of the courtship of Nancy Rigdon has been repeated many times in various anti-Mormon books. It seems that Smith had long harbored the wish to marry this attractive girl. The story, as Bennett later made public, is about as follows:

A rendezvous was arranged with Nancy by Smith at the home of Mrs. Orson Hyde. But Bennett had given Nancy some prior information about the Prophet's intentions and she did not take kindly to his proposition. Rather she threatened to scream the whole thing to the entire town and said that unless he let her go home she would kick up a fuss.

The next day Smith dictated a letter to her which, in part, said:

Happiness is the object and design of our existence; it will be the end thereof, if we pursue the path that leads to it; and this path is virtue, uprightness, and faithfulness, holiness, and keeping all the commandments of God, but we cannot keep all the commandments without first knowing them . . .

Whatever God requires is right, no matter what it is, although we may not see the reason thereof until long after the events transpire . . .

Nancy showed the letter to her father and told him of Joseph's advances. Whether Rigdon had been aware that polygamy was being practiced secretly in Nauvoo is unknown. He sent immediately for Smith and although at first Joseph denied everything, when Rigdon produced the letter, he broke down and admitted the truth. He made a lame excuse that he was merely trying to test Nancy's virtue. Despite efforts at secrecy, the story got around that Nancy had refused the Prophet's hand in marriage. But this was only one of several stories of attempts to put spiritual wifehood into earthly practice.

Another widespread story concerned a convert from England, Martha Brotherton, and Brigham Young. The chief source of the story is found in an affidavit, sworn to on July 13, 1842, in St. Louis. Martha alleged that she had been trapped into a secret meeting with Brigham Young. In a room over a store in Nauvoo, Brigham asked her to be one of his plural wives. She was indignant at this proposal but asked for time to consider it. As she continued to demur, Brigham asked her if she would be willing to talk to Joseph about the matter. He locked her in the room when he went for Smith. Shortly the two returned and the following conversation is alleged to have taken place:

". . . Well, Martha," said Joseph. "It is lawful and right before God—I know it is. Look here, Sister, don't you believe in me?" I did not answer. "Well, Martha," said Joseph, "just go ahead and do as Brigham wants you to—he is the best man in the world except me." "Oh," said Brigham, "then you are as good! . . ." And, further, Joseph went on to say that "If there is any sin in it, I will answer for it before God; and I have the keys of the kingdom, and whatever I bind on earth is bound in heaven, and whatever I loose on earth is loosed in heaven—and if you will accept of Brigham, you will be blessed—God shall bless you, and my blessing shall rest upon you, and if you will be led by him you will do well; for I know Brigham will take care of you, and if he don't do his duty to you, come to me and I will make him—and if you do not like it in a month or two, come to me and I will make you free again; and if he turns you off, I will take you on."

There follow further details on trying to persuade her to accept Brigham and at the end they made great efforts to get her to commit herself to complete secrecy. She finally got away and promised to think the matter over. The next day, on Sunday, at the close of services, Young asked her again if she was ready with an answer. She demurred once more and went off with her sister. Shortly thereafter she left Nauvoo for St. Louis where the whole story was subscribed and sworn to before a justice of the peace.

This story leaked out and at the April conference of 1842 mention was made by Hyrum Smith that some nasty rumors were afloat that a Sister had been shut up in a room for several days while some of the leaders were trying to persuade her to believe in the plural wife system. Such stories, he said, were the work of their enemies. At this same conference, Joseph, using a familiar technique, delivered a strong sermon against all adulterers and those who indulged in various kinds of sexual crime. "If God should speak from heaven, he would command you not to steal, not to commit adultery, not to covet nor to deceive, but be faithful over a few things."

While Smith never referred directly to the Brotherton episode, both Heber C. Kimball and Brigham Young called her story a base falsehood. Moreover, Martha's two sisters and brother-in-law, who had remained true to the Church, produced a document that made out that she was not only a liar but also immoral. It is interesting to note that Elizabeth Brotherton, who signed one of the statements against Martha, became the plural wife of Parley P. Pratt on July 24, 1843, just 12 days after Smith had his revelation regarding polygamy.

There were other scandals. Smith is said to have taken the wife of Orson Hyde, an apostate, as a plural wife; and while Orson Pratt was absent on a mission, Joseph made overtures to his wife, Sarah. Bennett reports Smith as having said to her, "Sister Pratt, the Lord has given you to me as one of my spiritual wives. I have the blessings of Jacob granted me, as God granted holy men of old and as I have long looked upon you with favor, and in earnest desire of connubial bliss, I hope you will not repulse or deny me."

Mrs. Pratt refused him and Smith is supposed to have threatened to ruin her reputation. This little episode, whether true or not, became the basis of more gossip. Mrs. Pratt years later denied that there was anything to this. On the other hand, the anti-Mormons made much of it. It is a fact that there were serious difficulties between Orson Pratt and Smith after the latter had returned from his mission to England, but whether over Smith's solicitations to Pratt's wife is not known.

Whatever troubles may have arisen among some of the leaders regarding matters of wife-swapping and the taking of virgins for plural wives, officially the Church continued publicly to deny the practice. Members who were not *au courant* with the top echelons were summarily dealt with if they preached the new dispensation. For example, the official *Times and Seasons* for February 1, 1844, reports the excommunication of Elder Hiram Brown for "preaching polygamy . . . in the county of Lapeer, state of Michigan."

During this period another difficulty arose respecting women converts who had left their husbands to join the Saints. Taking such a woman as a wife, plural or not, posed certain problems. Apparently in many instances the women did not bother about a divorce. On the frontier and far removed from their former homes, and under the sanction of those with divine authority, there seemed no need to obtain legal separation. One such was the first plural wife of William Smith, a brother of Joseph, married in April, 1843. She was Mary Ann Sheffield who on conversion to Mormonism had left her husband in England.

There appears to be ample evidence that the plurality system was well established among a good many of the leading Mormons prior to the date of the official revelation. It has been claimed that John C. Bennett suggested a revelation to Smith in order to cover up his tracks. It is also alleged that during the late spring and early summer of 1843, realizing the growing criticism and threats of open revolt, Smith decided to announce the Lord's sanction of plural marriage.

The story of the revelation regarding polygamy—Smith's final and in some ways most devastating message from God— is told by William Clayton, the Prophet's confidential secretary. It was to him that the revelation was dictated. In an affidavit under the date of February 16, 1874, Clayton tells of its background. As secretary he was aware of the public and private business of Smith. He knew about the tithing records, the donations, the land and other business. Also, he was well acquainted with Emma Smith. Moreover, Clayton was appointed Temple Recorder and kept all the records of the endowments and marriages therein performed.

In February, 1843, Clayton and Smith, at the latter's request, took a long walk during which the Prophet said that he was aware that Clayton was fond of a certain woman convert in England. He asked Clayton why he did not send for her. Clayton said he had no authority to send for her. Moreover, he did not have the money to pay her expenses. To this Smith replied that he would give him authority and provide the means if he wished it. The affidavit goes on to say:

This was the first time that Prophet Joseph talked to me on the subject of plural marriage. He informed me that the doctrine and principle was right in the sight of our Heavenly Father, and that it was a doctrine which pertained to celestial order and glory. After giving me lengthy instructions and information concerning the doctrine of celestial or plural marriage, he concluded his remarks with the words, "It is your privilege to have all the wives you want."

From then on their conversations about this new system were more frequent. If Smith would talk to his secretary in this way, he was certain to talk to many of the leading authorities in the Church. There is evidence from Clayton that Smith and others of the leaders took plural wives. Hyrum is certainly one who took more than one wife and it was he who suggested finally to Joseph:

"If you will write the revelation on celestial marriage, I will take and read it to Emma, and I believe I can convince her of its truth, and you will hereafter have peace." Joseph smiled and remarked, "You do not know Emma as well as I do." Hyrum remarked, "The doctrine is so plain, I can convince any reasonable man or woman of its truth, purity and heavenly origin," or words to that effect. Joseph then said, "Well, I will write the revelation and we will see." He then requested me to get paper and prepare to write. Hyrum very urgently requested Joseph to write the revelation by means of the Urim and Thummin but Joseph in reply said he did not need to, for he knew the revelation perfectly from beginning to end.

Joseph and Hyrum then sat down and Joseph commenced to dictate the revelation on celestial marriage, and I wrote it, sentence by sentence as he dictated. After the whole was written, Joseph asked me to read it through slowly and carefully, which I did, and he pronounced it correct. He then remarked that there was much more that he could write on the same subject, but what was written was sufficient for the present.

Clayton goes on to remark that he and Joseph waited for Hyrum to try out the revelation on Emma. Hyrum returned to report that Emma was bitter and full of resentment and hostility about the whole thing.

During the same day the revelation was read to several of the Church authorities. Later still Bishop Newell K. Whitney asked Joseph if he had any objection to his making a copy of the revelation. Next day it was carefully copied by Joseph C. Kingsbury.

A few days following, Smith told his intimates that under Emma's teasing and pressure, he had finally consented to destroy the document; but he said he did not worry about it because he knew it by heart. Moreover, there was the copy which Kingsbury had made. Clayton further says that the copy was carefully preserved by Bishop Whitney. Few people knew about it, however, until in 1846 it became more generally known at least among the chief authorities. This was at Winter Quarters, Iowa, following the exodus from Nauvoo.

Clayton concludes with these paragraphs:

After the revelation on celestial marriage was written Joseph continued his instructions, privately, on the doctrine, to myself and others, and during the last year of his life we were scarcely ever together, alone, but he was talking on the subject and explaining that doctrine and principles connected with it. He appeared to enjoy great liberty and freedom in his teachings, and also to find great relief in having a few to whom he could unbosom his feelings on that great and glorious subject.

From him I learned that the doctrine of plural and celestial marriage is the most holy and important doctrine ever revealed to man on the earth, and that without obedience to that principle no person can ever attain to the fullness of exaltation and celestial glory.

Although the revelation was not generally made public for some time and not actually printed for circulation till nearly 10 years had passed, there was a growing rift among the leaders of the Church over the doctrine and its practice. William Law and his brother Wilson had long been faithful members and trusted lieutenants of Smith. They were strongly opposed to polygamy and with others actually set about reforming the Church.

The whole thing came to a head in April, 1844 when several prominent members of the Church were excommunicated on charges of "un-Christianlike conduct" and without any trial. Among these was Robert D. Foster, William and Wilson Law, and Jane Law. A few weeks later another dissenter, F. M. Higbee, had Smith arrested on charges of slander. The warrant was issued by the clerk of the circuit court of Carthage, but Smith secured a writ of habeas corpus and was tried before the municipal court of Nauvoo. He was discharged as one might expect. A little later, in the month of May, Higbee, Austin Cowles, and other critics were cut off from the Church on charges of apostasy.

After their excommunication Law and his friends set up a newspaper called the *Nauvoo Expositor*. The air was full of slander and counterslander and the Prophet faced a real schism. The first and only issue of the *Nauvoo Expositor* on June 7, 1844, consisted chiefly of a serious editorial which outlined in some detail, but mentioned no names, some of the difficulties in the Church, including polygamy and the danger of uniting church and state. The newspaper had the effect of putting Smith on trial before his whole people. He quickly retaliated by having the paper declared a public nuisance and under court orders the entire plant was destroyed.

The Bennett and the *Expositor* episodes are both illustrations of the strong attacks against polygamy and will be discussed in detail in Chapter 15. They are mentioned at this juncture to show that there is evidence that plural marriage was already well established while Smith was still alive.

In concluding this chapter, we need but say that the practice and the dogma in defense of polygamy were themselves a gradual growth in Smith's mind and among the Mormons. Whatever be the truth of the accusations that Smith was an adulterer from the start, we must recognize that in time the doctrine of celestial marriage and the accompanying one of plurality of wives emerged from the whole background of Mormon theology and social organization. The plurality idea was likewise applied to the whole doctrine of the godhead as we have seen. Smith was elaborate in his fantasies and the notion of eons of time and endless numbers of worlds and universes in which human beings would in time emerge as gods provided at least some rationalization for the return to the patriarchal order of marriage.

On the other hand, and on a more practical level, it may well be that the doctrine was first announced as a rationalization for Smith's own infidelities. Yet the doctrine of spiritual wives was in the religious atmosphere of the time.

The Josephites' claim that polygamy was the product of Brigham Young and his followers after the death of Joseph Smith has never been substantiated. There is some argument on their side but the weight of the evidence today seems to be quite to the contrary. In any case though there was much talk about polygamy in Nauvoo and among both Mormons and non-Mormons before Smith's death. The whole system did not get into full swing until the Mormons were isolated in the valleys of Utah a few years later. It was then, in 1852, that formal public announcement was made.

*And God said unto them, be fruitful, and
multiply, and replenish the earth.*—Genesis 2:28.

*This is the reason why the doctrine of
plurality of wives was revealed, that
the noble spirits waiting for tabernacles
might be brought forth.*—Brigham
Young.

# 5 REASONS AND EXCUSES: THE QUANTUM THEORY OF SALVATION

FROM THE official point of view men and women entered
polygamy to fulfill the Lord's commandment to "multiply
and replenish the earth" by providing physical bodies for the
infinite swarm of procreated spirits waiting in heaven for a
chance to be born on earth. As James Powell, an ardent follower of the Principle, wrote in his diary for October 2, 1871:
"Celestial marriage is one of the most sacred and essential
principles of the gospel, for without it neither we nor our fore-
fathers can claim our wives, nor our wives claim us, and enter
upon our exaltation in the eternal worlds."

This was the official reason. Yet, so far as the individual is
concerned, motivations are always difficult to untangle. The
reasons for most human conduct lie buried in the unconscious
bases of drives, attitudes, and values. The Mormons' acceptance of the principle of plurality of wives was linked with their
deep convictions that Joseph Smith was a "true prophet of the
Most High" who had restored to mankind the only true doctrines of salvation and the only priesthood which could bring
this salvation about. Under the concept of "continuous revelation" they felt bound to obey new commandments God chose
to give to his Prophet. The strength of such a belief is evident
in the autobiography of Kurt Sturm written shortly before
his death for members of his family. Sturm, who had two
wives and 18 children, wrote to his family:

I wish to impress this fact upon the minds of my children that to discredit the principle of plural marriage is the same as discrediting any other principle of the Mormon doctrine as they all come from the same source. Joseph Smith, the Prophet, was commanded to establish the same in the Church. I testify to you that I know my father entered into the Principle in full faith of receiving a generous reward from our Heavenly Father for his honest efforts to live it properly. The same can be said of my father-in-law, George L. James, and I testify to you myself after twenty-eight years' experience in trying to live it that I know the Principle is divine. Although it is at the present time unlawful both from the Church view as well as from the standpoint of the state, I know it was established by God. Those who have lived it faithfully and well will receive a very enviable reward in the world to come . . .

In line with this general reasoning Mormon polygamists almost universally defended their actions in terms of the Principle. As the biographer of one pioneer put it: "Father had abiding faith in the authority of the priesthood and regarded the law as divine." And as the system became more widely accepted and practiced, the rationalizations under the Principle became easier. Mormon children, in monogamous and plural families alike, were openly taught the sacredness of the plan. One pious believer, with two wives, put it thus: "I believed in polygamy because it had always been taught me and we lived it at home. I always wanted to marry in polygamy, and I'm glad that I did."

Yet there was never 100 per cent acceptance of the Principle. But during the four decades when polygamy was openly practiced among the Saints those who had their doubts about its divinity and practicality had to remain silent or leave the Church. Some reflections on this topic will be offered in later chapters.

The present chapter will deal chiefly with personal and more specific motives, especially as they related to class status, desire for children, desire for multiple wives, and various other needs. Yet all of these must be seen against the broad and general acceptance of the sacredness of the Principle.

While polygamy was open—within the general regulations —to all members of the Church, we saw in Chapter 3 that it tended to be confined to those men who held higher ecclesiastical office or who had made a success of their financial enterprises. In Mormondom these two measures of personal prestige were, and are today, positively and highly correlated. We have some instances where men married in polygamy after they had begun to make money and sometimes these men never held any important church office. We have a few examples of men in serious poverty trying polygamy. But far and away most of our families reflect middle or high status among the Latter-day Saints. For our purposes we may say that median status is reflected in one's being a Bishop or counselor to a Bishop, and/or a member of the High Council of a Stake. High status obtains for those who are stake Presidents, Patriarchs, and especially among the general authorities of the Church. These latter include the Presiding Bishopric, head Patriarch, the Seven Presidents of Seventies, the Apostles, and highest of all, membership in the First Presidency of the entire Church.

In pioneer Utah it was often more a matter of ambition and enterprise, both in gaining wealth and in getting ahead in the Church, than the precise fulfillment of the spiritual norm that determined a man's going into plural marriage. However, aside from a handful of top leaders, few Mormons in the 40-year period when polygamy flourished, accumulated any marked wealth as measured by present-day standards. Yet against the level of living of the time, plural families were generally recruited from among men of substance and of better-than-average church standing.

Facts regarding official church positions held by polygamist husbands are difficult to come by. Unfortunately our own records are scanty in this regard. However, an estimate of polygamous Mormon men listed in the *Latter-Day Saint Biographical Encyclopedia* showed that a high proportion of those reporting plural families held offices of bishopric or higher order.

When members of polygamous families talk or write about the reasons for entering the system, they almost invariably justify their own family history in terms of the divinity of the Principle. Yet in many instances further probing brought out the fact that individuals had other and more personal motives for setting up plural families. People often act in certain ways in terms of what their fellows expect as well as from more personal interests. So far as the Mormons go, it should not be forgotten that plurality of wives was a permissive, not a mandatory, feature of their lives. It was an additional aspect of the larger scheme of celestial marriage. True, to practice the Principle gave one added status, here and in the hereafter; but one was not, strictly speaking, compelled to practice polygamy.

The general Mormon atmosphere, however, encouraged entrance into plural marriage. The doctrine was advocated from the pulpit by Mormon leaders, and more specific stimulation took the form of counseling a given man to take more wives. Thus of the 33 instances in our records where mention is made of the reasons for entering the system, only three stated definitely that there had been no official stimulation, general or specific. Thirty noted that they had been advised to enter the plural marriage system. Of these 30, 21 said it was of a general sort, and nine that it consisted of specific instruction of some official: Bishop, Stake President, Apostle, or even the President of the Church himself.

General official stimulation through preaching was common from the time plural marriage was publicly announced in 1852 until it was officially abolished by the Manifesto of 1890. There were, however, two periods within these four decades, marked by special encouragement to practice polygamy. The first was during the so-called "Reformation" in 1856–57 when a revivalist spirit swept through the Church and there was a widespread movement for rebaptism of members for the remission of their sins, for them to take their covenants in the Endowment House, and to take additional wives. For example, of this period which coincided with the dispatch of the United States army forces to Utah under General Albert Sidney Johnston, one Mormon's biography says:

. . . President Young advised the men folks to marry the available young women so they would have a home and protector if the soldiers were quartered in our midst. One ardent follower, on the basis of such advice, married a young girl of fifteen named Rachel Scott who had no people of her own in the city. Another addition was made to the house, and all were provided for since the farm yielded plenty for the family.

The second intensive preaching of the doctrine of polygamy came during the early 1880's at the very time when the federal government was making its most effective drive to wipe out the system. The leaders not only advised generally that men take plural wives but more and more took the position that those Elders of Zion who held important posts should enter into the patriarchal order of marriage. Jonathan Baker reports that Apostle George Q. Cannon on January 20, 1884, at St. George said that he did "not feel like holding up his hand to sustain anyone as a presiding officer who had not entered into the patriarchal order of marriage . . ."

And Jerome Sweet writes of this period:

I came to Mexico so that I would be able to marry Alice Lee, a widow with four children. My first wife had always been anxious that I marry in polygamy and for a long time I did not consider it. It was taught to me always that it was the correct Principle and we were urged to do it. I went to a special priesthood meeting where Joseph F. Smith [later President of the Church] was the speaker and he said that men holding positions in the priesthood should either marry in polygamy or they should step down and let someone who would marry have the position.

Others report much the same thing. "Polygamy was being preached from the stand in all the churches." Or again, "They [the church authorities] were all preaching to the men to marry the girls, and I guess it was very useful. You look around you nowadays and see plenty of unmarried young girls and old maids, but not in those days." And another, "Our Bishops practically forced us into it. We were counseled all the time to go into polygamy." One man recalled a Stake conference in Southern Utah where the brethren were bluntly told to marry in polygamy or "resign their church offices."

Reactions to such pressure varied. Some members refused to heed the counsel. One Bishop's counselor in Hyde Park, where a strong pro-polygamy campaign was underway, talked the matter over with his wife and in the end declined to follow the directions of his superiors. While he was not officially disciplined for his refusal, many people in the community disapproved of his failure to follow the church leaders. But about this same time, one of his neighbors, also in a ward position, was not so hesitant and soon took himself another spouse. In fact, for the most part, the Saints obeyed orders.

A first wife's reaction to official advice is illustrated in the journal of Elizabeth Street:

In the fall . . . Job [her husband] concluded to take another wife as it was counseled. I was quite willing. We all went to Conference and on the ninth of November, Sister Stella Hoskins was sealed to him. I was there. Eliza R. Snow asked me if I was willing. I said "yes." Then she asked me if I thought I could live in that Principle. I answered that I was quite willing to try, that my mother and sister lived in it and I thought I could do as much, and besides I wanted my husband to go into the Principle before I was too old, that I thought it was right. She said my reward would be great because I was willing and that I would never get old.

Some husbands, however, refused such requests, although it is not likely that taking a wife under such circumstances would gravely endanger previous family solidarity. Dennis Gallagher's wife so completely believed in the Principle, and felt so strongly that her own glory would be lessened by her husband's flat refusal to follow her urgent pleas to take another wife, that she divorced him after two years. Shortly thereafter she married as a plural wife a man well along in years.

As to more specific and direct advice, a number of informants relate that Brigham Young himself told them to take a plural wife. The third wife of Adam Winthrop tells that though her husband had two wives, when he was called to colonize in Dixie, Brigham Young advised him to marry again. "You ought to take a third wife so you will have a family circle." This idea of a "circle" was popular for a time on the theory that since the godhead was a trinity, by analogy a man should have three wives. Winthrop demurred but the account continues:

"Brother Brigham, I don't want to get married and I don't feel that I should. It's only been a year since I married Lillian [the second wife] and I don't feel that I can possibly support another family. And I don't know what it will be like in the new country."

"That's just why you need another wife," Brigham Young said. "You will need your family there. And it's a commandment that has been put upon us and we must obey. I know it will be hard but you marry and the way will be opened before you . . ."

When Brigham said a thing, we did it, just like he was an angel from heaven. After we had given up everything for our faith, it wasn't hard to accept another commandment.

Mrs. Winthrop number three goes on to relate that when Adam asked her to marry him, she at first declined on the grounds of being too young (she was only 16 years old at the time) and of wishing to get her parents' consent. The latter had not yet arrived in Utah. Somewhat discouraged, Winthrop returned to tell Brigham Young, who remarked:

"Adam, you bring the young lady here in the morning and I'll talk to her."

Of course, I went. I wouldn't have thought of anything else. When we got there, Brigham had a mischievous twinkle in his eye and said, "So: You don't want to marry Adam?" I said, "No, I don't want to marry anybody." Then he asked me if there was anybody else I cared for and I told him I didn't know anybody else. Then he talked to me and told me about it being a commandment and how we would be blessed if we followed it and lived up to it and if we didn't we would be condemned. He said that if I did it, I would be blessed and happy and never regret it. He said it would be all right with my parents and that it was the thing to do.

He convinced me and we were married in October and went to St. George in November.

Not every Saint, however, fell so directly under the influence of their great leader, yet there are numerous cases which mention Bishops, Stake Presidents, and Apostles who gave direct advice to men and women to enter into the plural system.

Aside from official encouragement, either general or specific, there was persistent unofficial stimulation. Much of this fell within the larger framework of complete belief in the Principle. The social climate of the time fostered obedience to the system. While most of my own documents rationalize adherence to the Principle either in general terms of conviction and/or in terms of more or less official stimulation, some give a more personal and mystic interpretation. For example, in a sketch of his life, John Manning writes:

> On the 14th of October, 1850, myself, wife, sisters . . . and brother . . . were baptized into the church . . .
> At Keg Creek I first became acquainted with Laura Farnsworth Smith, who is the widow of Hyrum Smith, the Patriarch. In the winter of 1851 the Lord sent a messenger to me; he came in a circle of light . . . This messenger told me many beautiful things, told me to take this Laura Farnsworth, with my wife, Susan Riggs and go to Utah and have them both sealed to me by the Prophet Brigham, and I should be greatly blessed. I was then living more than 1000 miles from Salt Lake City, and this messenger showed me the city and the Temple that would be partly reared. I saw the cornerstone of this Temple laid. I saw myself pass through and receive my endowments, and had a new name given me. Saw the Prophet sealing the woman to me, and many other beautiful things . . .
> . . . We arrived in Salt Lake City, August 22, 1852 . . . We received our endowments and sealings . . . [My] wife Susan was sealed to me for time and all eternity . . . and Laura Farnsworth for time and to Hyrum Smith for eternity . . .

Some years later, and when he had become a successful settler in southern Utah, he had another vision about plural marriage:

> . . . I started for Salt Lake on business. And while on the journey the Lord showed four women to me and also the place where to find them, although I had never seen them in the flesh before

me. I told President Young of these things and he said, bring them on and he would seal them to me, for I was a man he wanted to see go ahead. When I got to the city I went where these people lived and knew them without speaking to them. Their names were Elaine Snow and Caroline Brown . . .

While there was some discrepancy between the number promised in the vision and the actuality, he courted these two women and married them in short order.

Specific stimulation to enter the system might come from the wives, from parents and other relatives, and from neighbors and friends. While women living under monogamy may find it difficult to imagine permitting a man to marry a sister, under the general acceptance of the system, and in view of the inter-personal and economic circumstances of the time, it is not surprising.

Of our family records, 19 per cent of them report that the men married sisters. It cannot be claimed that this percentage is typical of all Mormon polygamous families, but it is a reasonable inference that a considerable fraction of Mormon plural families had at least some plural wives who were sisters. Of these 30 cases all but one marriage were to full sisters; in this one it was to a half-sister. In one family a man married four sisters; in another he took twins as numbers one and two and a half-sister as wife number three. In still another a man married two sisters and their widowed mother! Of the 29 families of full-sister marriages, one-half of them made up wives one and two respectively, one-quarter were numbers two and three. The balance were scattered among the higher brackets of numbers of wives.

The role of a sister in promoting a match is illustrated in the Albert Procter family. Procter met his first wife Gertrude Adams when, as fellow-Mormons, they were en route to Utah from England. She was traveling with her brother. Shortly after arriving in Salt Lake City Procter married Gertrude and they moved to the Bear Lake country. About two years later the rest of the Adams family arrived, among them a sister, Daisy. Subsequently when Albert began talking of entering polygamy, Gertrude suggested her sister. Daisy was popular and had "plenty of suitors." She was attracted to one young man but as he was violently opposed to the very idea of plural marriage, she dismissed him as not being a good Mormon. Some time later she married Brother Procter as his second wife.

Parental concern for a daughter was sometimes a factor in stimulating plural marriages. The Charles Cook story indicates such interest in their unmarried daughter's future and a plan to provide her with a good husband—all within the family, as it were.

Constance, a sister of Cook's first wife, was being courted by a young man known to have tuberculosis. The father of Constance—he was the Bishop—and her mother, anticipated that any such match would be a poor risk. So one day they called upon their son-in-law "whom they loved very much" and the Bishop put this proposition to him: "Charles, do you know what Mother and I have been thinking? We've been thinking that maybe you'd want to marry Constance."

Charles protested that this was far from his mind but promised to consult his wife, Josephine. The latter said that if he wanted to go into the Principle, Constance would be her own choice over any other girl. So Charles made the deal and "Josephine placed Constance's hand in Charles' at the sealing."

The informants in this case—the man himself and his first wife—insisted that it was not the father's counsel as Bishop which persuaded Charles but the father's concern for his daughter's future. Assuming this to be so, we have a neat example of a culturally approved pattern upon which is projected a more personal motivation.

Many Mormon women took a thoroughly practical view of their situation.

A wife might take a hand in stimulating another marriage because she believed that sooner or later her husband would take such a step anyway. Many wives felt that the issue should be met as soon as possible. Delay might mean that the husband later might marry a much younger woman and that the first wife by such a step would lose her position of control.

One husband reported: "My wife says to me 'If you're going to get married, I want you to do it while I am still young. I don't want you to wait until I'm old and good for nothing and then bring in a young wife.' "

The first wife of Ebenezer Whyte had begun to lose her dominance in family affairs to the second wife and urged her man to marry her younger sister, recently arrived from Denmark, as a third. She thought in this way that she would have two votes to her rival's one when it came to handling her husband and in deciding many problems of the family. As it turned out the younger sister, a quiet person who refused to enter into the family disputes, finally became Whyte's favorite wife. At the time of the marriage, however, she was not particularly impressed with Whyte and married him "because she had nothing else to do."

In societies where there is a high premium on childbearing, sterility is viewed as a disgrace. So it was among the Mormons for whom childbearing, associated with celestial marriage, is the *sine qua non* of the obligation and the glory which parents anticipate both in this world and in the next. A strong belief in the Principle often served as a motive for a wife to urge polygamy on her husband after she realized that she could not have children of her own.

A number of plural households were established because the first wife, being sterile, asked her husband to bring in another. Daisy Barclay tells of her courtship with one of her teachers. Barclay and his first wife came to visit Daisy in her parental home. Daisy had refused to go walking with Brother Barclay unless the wife went along, defending her stand on the ground that Sister Barclay was her guest and to go out without her would be an offense against good manners. The next day, while taking Daisy for a buggy ride, the wife brought up the subject of plural marriage and observed that apparently Daisy was indifferent to her husband's attention. To this Daisy replied that ". . . Without your approval, our interest in each other will go no farther." The wife then remarked that although she had been brought up in a rather unhappy polygamous family and felt a certain aversion to the whole system, she had been married five years without having any children. "I can't deprive Brother Barclay of a family," she concluded, "and of all the girls I know, you are my choice."

Nephi King's first wife likewise deeply regretted having no children and was "eager to have her husband marry again." In fact, he took several plural wives. Years later the first wife proudly lined up a considerable number of King's children by his other wives and said to a visiting apostle, Erastus Snow: "See, this is what polygamy has done for my husband. Without it he would have been childless." In this family, the second wife who bore King nine sons, gave over her second boy to be raised by the first wife "as her very own."

A first wife who was sterile selected for her man's second a girl of 20 years who had been a seamstress in her home. The latter related: "The first wife courted me more than her husband, and she was the one to first ask me if I would be willing to be a polygamist's wife." The second wife proudly bore her husband seven children, the first two of whom were taken by the first wife to raise.

In another case a second marriage, motivated in part by the evidence of the first wife's sterility, had a somewhat "miraculous" consequence. Edward Quinn, whose first wife had borne him no children, was called on a mission to South Carolina. While there he converted the Williams family and urged them to move to Utah. He had fallen in love with the eldest daughter, but she said that she was not interested in polygamy. However, she said she was sure that her younger sister, Minerva, was. Quinn then turned to the latter and they were married. According to the informant in this case—a son of the first wife—the motivation was twofold: (a) a certain sense of obligation to the Williamses, and (b) uncertainty that his first wife would bear him any children. It was clearly a marriage of convenience. Interestingly enough *after* the plural marriage the first wife bore him four healthy children. The second wife had the same number.

The economic motives in Mormon polygamy have often been noted. Some have rationalized the whole scheme as an effort to have a larger labor force in a frontier community.

This is far too simple, but officially it was easy to link up the idea of a high birth rate which provided more physical bodies for heavenly spirits and the material advantage of having many hands for purposes of work.

As we shall see when we discuss the economy of plural households, both wives and children usually proved important economic assets. However, when we examine the more personal records at our disposal, we find only occasional and indirect mention of economic motivation. If it was present —as it doubtless was in many cases—it was disguised behind the ideal of celestial marriage and the divine requirement to provide bodies for the waiting spirits in heaven. In some cases we find that the first wife suggested a domestic servant as another spouse with an eye—more or less camouflaged—to her continued economic service to the family.

A second wife, who came to Utah with her mother from Switzerland, went into domestic service at the Isaac Lamberts. She says, "I nearly raised the Lambert family before I married Isaac, working for the first wife and doing everything in the house. I scrubbed this kitchen floor until it is worn out right now." At that she was only 17 years old when she became wife number two.

Propinquity and congeniality both played a part. Such an obvious source of another wife would not escape a man's attention. Source and stimulation to polygamy obviously went hand in hand.

Then, too, plural marriage might have another implication, as illustrated in the second wife of Wallace Bain, a prominent leader. She was at first a domestic in the household and her subsequent marriage to Bain definitely raised her social status. Despite the fact that already in Utah class lines were beginning to separate the top leaders of the Church from the great bulk of members of lower economic status, such marriages as this—either monogamous or plural—for the girl reflected advancement in social position.

In a society where polygamy has a high social reward and where the number of young women available was somewhat limited there was bound to be competition between single men and married men for wives. At times such rivalry related to differences in economic and official status, as we shall see in describing courtship under the plural system.

Another perennial question—and, compared with the economic aspect, more exciting—asked about polygamy concerns the place of romantic love and direct sexual interest in Mormon courtship, marriage, and family life. To the Gentile lust was firmly believed to be the original and continuing reason for the whole system. Actually there was far less direct sexual interest in Mormon polygamy than might be imagined. The Mormons were thoroughly puritanic about such matters; to them the whole scheme of plural wifehood was a divine principle, not a mundane one to be idly followed. It must never be forgotten that this new family scheme was a revolutionary departure from traditional Christian monogamy into which had been introduced certain notions of romantic love. Thus in Colonial, and even more so in frontier America, a system of romantic freedom of mating had emerged in contrast to the practices of Britain from which we got most of our customs of marriage, control of children, dower rights, property inheritance, and other elements of our family system. In particular the importance of class status and the rights of parents to choose their children's partners had been rather thoroughly abandoned in our democratic West.

The Mormons, definitely a frontier society, accepted these more liberal ideas and practices. At the outset their marriage system was monogamous and followed these newer features of free choice in mating. It was into this system that plural wifehood was introduced.

Does it follow that romantic love disappeared among the Mormons? Or was it only to be found in the case of first wives? Did the taking of additional spouses mean that these were but religiously sanctioned *mariages de convenance?* What place did sexual interest play in polygamy?

While it is difficult to get answers to such questions, either from personal documents or from interviews with plural spouses or the children of such marriages, nevertheless there is some evidence on the topics.

The surviving first wife of a polygamist practically broke up an interview with the husband by scoffing at the whole idea that plurality of wives was divinely instituted. She contended that it was a device to satisfy man's passions and that of all the polygamous families she had known, only one or two had been successful. Another informant, a daughter of a prominent Mormon who had five wives and many children, bluntly said: "I don't think those polygamists knew what romantic love means." Certainly any number of informants bear witness to the fact that taking a plural wife or wives was looked on as a matter of duty, or as one man put it, "as a business proposition."

Yet the reading of the rich materials from personal documents and interviews with polygamous families leaves one with the impression that there was a good deal of tender feeling, high moral principle, and personal sacrifice—the hallmarks of romantic love. However, from the official point of view it was realized that romantic love might cause a considerable amount of difficulty. Surely the rivalry and jealousy which emerged in many multiple households, to be examined in another chapter, give some evidence of an underlying romanticism. The comment of the third wife of Earl Vernon is interesting:

I always thought of it [plural marriage] as a natural thing. Father was a polygamist and all his families lived together and we got along very well. I don't think I thought anything about the Principle . . . when I married. I fell in love with my husband and married him, just as a girl would today, only it was in polygamy. He was twenty years older than I was, but he never seemed old. I think I loved him even when I was a little girl.

But in this instance, as in many others, such romantic love did not necessarily make for satisfactory inter-family adjustment. The first and second wives in this family were twin sisters and, moreover, half-sisters to the third wife. Both these women resented the introduction of the third wife into their ménage.

The point is, however, that romantic love of a rough

pioneer variety was doubtless evident in many plural marriages, but under the puritanic taboos free expression of this was held back in many instances; or, in the interest of a workable harmony, expression of such affection was inhibited. We shall have ample occasion later to look more closely at the relation of love to the success or failure of plural family life.

On the other hand, we cannot gloss over the fact that there were instances where more direct sexual interests, not dressed up in romantic love, played a part in a man's plural courtship and marriage. Some reference to such cases will be noted in the next chapter on courtship.

In addition to the above factors which stimulated plural marriages, there were some which developed out of a variety of fortuitous circumstances. In one case a man took a plural wife as a retreat and solace from marriage to his first, who had taken to periodic drinking much to the annoyance and disgrace of the entire family. In another instance a man met a girl whom he later married when he relinquished his steamship ticket to her so that she could go to Utah. In another family a man took as a plural wife a woman who for years had nursed his invalid first wife. One man unintentionally found himself in the situation where he married two girls on the same day. One of these he did "not know so well and he thought she had been wished off on him by her father." On his wedding trip he complained to the favorite wife that he "wished he hadn't brought Julia along!"

When we examine the wide range of motives which appear in our records of polygamous families, we note that there is nearly always the basic faith in the principle of plurality of wives. While individuals must have varied in the intensity of their belief in this matter, on the whole the system had become deeply imbedded in Mormon culture. It was thought to have divine sanction and to promise rewards here and in the hereafter. It was practiced chiefly by the leaders on whom the mass of members looked with respect, awe, and a sense of complete obedience. In time it became a symbol of the very difference from the Gentile world which did much to set the Mormons apart, and to their minds was proof that they were a "unique" and "chosen" people. Against the background of this cultural expectancy and acceptance all sorts of secondary or derived motives emerged. But since the deeper motives of our conduct are hidden below the surface of our daily habits, it is not to be expected that writers of personal documents or informants in interviews would be able to expose their deeper desires in these matters. At best, we have to draw our inferences from rather limited data.

# 6 COURTSHIP AND MARRIAGE

THE OFFICIAL REGULATIONS of the patriarchal order of marriage gave no practical directions regarding courtship. Moreover, Mormondom remained a monogamous society in which polygamy was permissive, never obligatory. The would-be polygamist seeking a new bride fell back upon the traditions and customs of monogamy for guidance. These might follow a romantic pattern of courtship. Romantic ideals also at times appeared in polygamy. Yet in Mormon society, as elsewhere, women were often sought after with an eye to potential childbearing, household competence, or economic advancement, rather than in terms of rosy romanticism.

The present chapter will take up the matter of consent of wife number one, the sources of plural wives, some of the tactics in polygamous courtship, and the competition between single men and polygamous men for brides. We shall also discuss the marriage, wedding festivities, and the honeymoon. The chapter will close with comments on the attitudes and practices as regards later legal marriage to plural wives if and when the first wife predeceased the husband and his other spouses.

Once a worthy Mormon husband had made up his mind to seek a plural wife, what was the next step? Officially no man was supposed to take another wife without the full and free consent of the first. Some critics maintain that this theory was more honored in the breach than otherwise; but judging from our records there was usually explicit, or at least implicit, consent.

In some instances the first wife earnestly urged her husband to take another wife. In one family the second wife, when asked about the first wife's consent, replied: "The first wife

120

sanctioned it! She was more anxious about it than he was."
The husband was 45 years old at the time, the prospective
bride 17.

There is ample evidence that to say "Yes" to one's husband's
taking another wife was a severe emotional strain to the first.
Talking it over with one's spouse in terms of the glories of the
Principle might assuage the conscious fears and potential
jealousies, but at the deeper unconscious levels it meant a
hard personal sacrifice. In some families there was an agreement at the time of the initial marriage that sooner or later a
second, or maybe a third or fourth wife might be introduced.
Brother Frank Alexander told of such an arrangement with
his first wife but said that when she asked how long this might
be, he "injudiciously" and somewhat jocularly said, "about
10 years." The first wife apparently went along on that expectation and raised some objections when he was wed for the second time within five years after his first marriage.

A great many Mormon women necessarily took for granted
the whole prospect of polygamy in their own families. Since
really there was not much that a good Sister could do and
since any worthy Elder could persuade his Bishop in the matter, many doubtless took the hardhearted realistic view of a
first wife who bluntly told her man: "Well, you may as well
marry 'em as to want 'em!"

Elder John Emmet relates that on his return from a European mission, all six of his closest ex-missionary friends entered the patriarchal order. The entire community was
heartily in favor of the practice and he gradually began to
accept the idea. After prolonged discussion of the topic with
his wife she reluctantly agreed. She was a daughter of a second wife and was not opposed to the Principle, but she feared
the impending loss of the close ties to her spouse.

There was another problem about consent that arose to
haunt those who wanted third, fourth, or more wives. Was it
necessary to secure the consent of all the prior spouses before
taking another? It is my impression that many plural marriages to third, fourth, or more wives were in no way dependent on the consent of other plural spouses. For example, the

third wife of Oscar Dahlman stated definitely that "the first knew about" his proposal to marry her and gave her consent, but that the second had not been consulted. She "guessed second wives hadn't much to say in such arrangements, anyhow."

Yet in a number of cases, chiefly in the families of the elite, it was the norm to consult all the wives about any further ventures in matrimony. Joseph F. Smith, who had six wives, always got the consent of all the others: but in such prominent families it is doubtful if a wife would dare not follow the wishes of her lord and master. Social position demanded conformity in such matters.

There were, however, many instances where the husband, securing a Bishop's approval, married again without any consultation with the first wife. Jonathan Baker, who had been married for over 16 years, came home one day and quietly told his wife he wanted "his temple clothes" made ready. A daughter goes on to say, "Ma thought he was just going to do some [church] work. She asked him what he intended to do and he said he was going to marry Eliza Bowen. It was a blow to Ma and naturally she resented it and never got over it."

On occasion, taking a second wife may have been motivated by marital conflict. One elder who had had trouble with his wife, on his return from a mission began courting a daughter of a rather prominent family in Dixie. The girl consented to be his plural wife and without their consulting her father or the first wife, went to Salt Lake City to be sealed in the Endowment House. On their return home the newlyweds called on the bride's father. The father had that very day first discovered the situation and had been upbraided by the first wife on the matter, who asked, "Why did you allow your daughter to marry my husband without making things right with me?" He was much upset by the matter and when his daughter asked for his blessing on the event, he turned on her with these words: "You have come to me too late for a blessing. Carey did wrong in marrying another wife without first making things right with his other family . . . It is too sacred an obligation to be outraged in such a manner . . . My daughter, you have made your bed and you must lie in it!" The couple left shortly afterward, the new wife "sad and downcast." In fact, this event led to her ostracism from her family and she never saw her father again, nor would her near relatives in the community where they settled have anything to do with her.

Doubtless in many situations the first wife's refusal ended any plans a man might have to take a second wife, but this fact would hardly show up in our records. The author, however, knows of a number of families where despite pressure and general preaching, on consultation with his wife a man decided against such a step.

Sometimes the decision was not without emotion. One elder in Paragoonah wanted a second wife, but he feared to ask the consent of his first. Finally, he told her he had had a revelation to marry a certain girl and that in the face of such divine instructions, she must give her consent. The next morning she announced that in the night she, too, had received a revelation "to shoot any woman who became his plural wife." Being the more drastic, her revelation ended the matter once and for all.

When asked why he never took another wife when so many of his friends did, Brother Richard Gordon of St. George nodded toward his wife and said, "She wouldn't let me." This brought on a strong emotional outburst from the wife. "I told him," Sister Gordon said, "that if he ever took another wife, when he brought her in the front door I would go out the back. And when I told his mother what I said she told me, 'If I had only a quilt, you would be welcome to half of it when you left him.'"

Where did the Mormons recruit their plural wives? A widespread Gentile belief was that most of them were zealous but deluded young women whom Mormon missionaries dragged to Utah. On the basis of this theory, many anti-Mormon writers assumed that women greatly outnumbered men in the early days of Utah. More objective persons are not impressed with this contention. Knowing that in most pioneer communities, men of marriageable ages are greatly in excess of women of like ages, they wish to know how plurality of wives worked out in terms of the usual frontier distribution of the sexes. If such pioneer condition held for Utah, then a great many men must have done without marriage.

Did polygamy in fact produce a large crop of bachelors? Actually the censuses of the territory for 1850 through 1890— the period in question—show that the expected disparity of the sexes did not exist. While there was a slight preponderance of males, it was not striking. Clearly such an approximate equality of the sexes of marriageable ages would mean that under polygamy some men would have to remain unwed. This is doubtless what happened, but it is not possible to obtain from the censuses anything like an accurate picture of the frequency of plural marriages. For example, my examination of certain census tabulation sheets from Washington County, Utah—the Dixie country, so-called—gives clear evidence that plural wives, known as such from other records, frequently were reported as single. The fear of exposure to the federal police was so great that the Saints did not trust the census enumerators.

While the Gentiles have always delighted in stories of lecherous Mormon men enticing young women converts to Utah with an eye to plural matrimony, there is little to substantiate such legends. For the most part, the church leaders preferred and encouraged the family type of migrant to the lone person since for purposes of colonization families suited their program better than did single individuals.

This is not to deny that a great many single women were converted. They were, and most of them sooner or later showed up in Zion, many of them to become the plural wives of the faithful. In fact, it was not uncommon for a man to select a plural mate from among recent arrivals of converts in Salt Lake City. A second wife, speaking of this period, says: ". . . Utah in those days was full of girls and women who had come from the European countries and from the Eastern states [as converts]. Brigham Young used to say to the men: 'Marry these girls and give them a home and provide for and protect them. Let them be wives and mothers.' So all men who could looked upon it as a duty."

The counsel obviously applied to both single and married men and doubtless afforded support for the system of looking over a new crop of women converts on their arrival. This was a kind of open matrimonial market and men, on hearing of the coming of attractive girls, would seek them out with an eye to courtship and possible marriage.

The chief source of possible new wives was within a man's own community. The Mormon village form of settlement is unique in American rural history and it served not only as a center for economic, religious, and political life, but it provided a means for people to get to know each other easily and naturally. Newcomers soon became acquainted with those who had arrived earlier. There was a high degree of congeniality among the Mormons, as one would expect in any society with strong in-group sentiments.

Somewhat more formal but nonetheless effective contacts of older married men with unmarried girls would be provided through the medium of Ward teaching and home missionary work. Under this program selected Elders made periodic visits to the homes of Mormon families. Here hymns were sung, prayers offered, and instructions and discussions engaged in with a view to strengthening the faith of the members. It was an excellent and not-neglected opportunity for married men to become better acquainted with the available young women of the community.

Judging from our records, a good many plural marriages took place among individuals who themselves had come from polygamous homes. This practice must have become cumulative. While only the top elite practiced plural wifehood in Nauvoo, the system spread rapidly in the first decade in their new home in Utah. And as we approach the official abandonment of the system in 1890, we find more and more evidence of husband and wives alike coming from polygamous homes.

Thus, in the Benjamin Wolfe ménage the two wives were sisters who came from a plural family and another sister of theirs married their husband's brother as a plural wife. Benjamin's father had three wives, he being a son of one of the plural ones. In the Alexander Todd family—one most prominent in their community—the husband and all but one of his six wives came from polygamous households. The father of the second wife of Joseph Wright had three wives and she said, "Nothing in my father's household made me dislike polygamy. I always believed . . . it was a true Principle, and through it and it alone could we obtain the greatest blessings and live as fully as we should."

We saw in Chapter 5 that occasionally a man would find a plural wife right in his own home. We have a number of records which report the marriage of a man to a girl who had been a domestic in the home or a companion to his wife or otherwise connected with the family. Moreover, some of the immigrant girls who had been domestics before they were plural wives might more easily continue to recognize the first wife as the head of the household afterwards. In some instances they did, in others they did not. This was especially likely to be so if the plural wife of recent immigration was much younger than the first.

A common practice was to take another wife from the same family from which the first had come. Of those records of ours which are fairly complete, nearly one-fifth report that the men married sisters. Of the 30 families, with adequate details, in which sisters or half-sisters were spouses of the same man, three-fifths of them may be rated as very successful or moderately successful; seven families were definitely not successful; of the others there is too little data on inter-family adjustment to warrant making a judgment as to success or failure.

Another legend among anti-Mormon writings is that older married men on occasion traded off their young and attractive daughters to other polygamists, who in turn accorded them the privilege of their own daughters as plural wives. The extent of such conduct is difficult to discover. A daughter of a plural wife contended to me that a number of such cases were well known in the town where she grew up. However, on questioning she could not cite specific details. There is little doubt that under the pressure of sermons to take plural spouses and motivated by masculine interest, many older men looked with favor upon the younger unmarried daughters of their friends. It is to be expected that in some instances, an occasional swap would be openly or tacitly arranged between the suitor of the girl and her father according to the terms of which the latter was given a like privilege to seek the hand of one of the former's grown daughters.

Widows were a limited source of plural wives. The hazards of the frontier were such that it was not infrequent for a woman, still of childbearing age, to lose a husband through illness, occupational accident, or by violence at the hands of hostile Indians or desperadoes. There was only one serious hitch in this scheme, however. If the widow was properly married in the first instance—that is, sealed for time and eternity —the second marriage could, by the rules of the Church, be for time only. This meant that the man could claim neither this particular spouse nor his children born to her as a part of his glory in the hereafter. Certainly Brigham Young, Heber C. Kimball, and other leaders took over for time only the wives of the slain Prophet Joseph Smith and of his brother, Hyrum. On the basis of their own practice, the authorities of the Church frequently urged the brethren to look to the widows of the community in seeking another wife; but judging from some of our records, many of the brethren demurred. If the glory hereafter was to be reckoned in the number of wives and in the number of children one had on earth, it seemed to many a bit unreasonable to go through the difficulties in the here and now only to have another man move in for the glory in the world to come. Nevertheless, the practice did go on.

We also have a few examples of a man seeking a daughter or daughters in wedlock, agreeing to take a widowed mother into the bargain. In his journal John D. Lee says that he had 19 wives and one woman—mother of another of his wives— whom he married for "her soul's sake." However, he goes on to say he never counted her as one of his spouses.

Occasionally a man would marry his dead brother's wife, but certainly the levirate was never officially required. The

Mormon arrangements for the next world doubtless blocked the development of this particular marriage custom.

Finally, there were occasional marriages to divorcees, or to women who had deserted their spouses but who were accepted in the community as free to marry again. The former were chiefly those who had been granted divorces by the Church for a plural marriage that failed. While the Mormons take much the view that the Roman Catholics do regarding divorce, during polygamy their leaders had to grant divorces to some in those situations where the conflict was so serious as to cause a breakdown of the whole polygamous arrangement. This matter will be discussed at length in Chapter 11. The other source was chiefly from those women who, on joining the Church, walked out on their husbands when the latter refused to accept the gospel.

The *cause célèbre* was that of Apostle Parley P. Pratt who took as his twelfth and final wife Mrs. Elenore J. McComb McLean, the estranged wife of Hector McLean. Mrs. McLean had been converted to Mormonism in California over the violent opposition of her husband. It was in San Francisco that she met Parley and one of his plural wives. She became much attached to them. Later, after her husband had secretly sent her three children to her father in New Orleans and she had failed to recover them, she settled in Utah. Again she resided with the Pratts. Her story aroused great sympathy not only among the members of the Pratt family but among all those who knew it. Some months after settling in Salt Lake City, she and Pratt were sealed, again without arousing any community reaction.

The next year (1857) she made another attempt to get her children, but when her father refused she kidnaped them. According to prearrangement, she and Parley were to meet in Arkansas and from there they were to go on to Florence, Nebraska, to join a company of Saints bound for Utah. Hector McLean, who had been informed of Elenore's actions and who discovered hers and Parley's movements, intercepted them and had them both arrested. When brought before a judge, however, the charge, a flimsy one of having stolen Hector's clothes for Mrs. McLean's children, was held insufficient and Pratt was released. However, before he could get away, McLean and his friends overtook him. He was stabbed and shot to death by McLean. The Gentiles hailed this a just vengeance for a Mormon wife-stealer. The Saints viewed Parley as a martyr.

Like so many other features of plural family life, the courtship practices tended to follow the customs and traditions of monogamy. New ways of courting a prospective bride, however, did arise as situations varied from those in a strictly monogamous society.

Since the undertaking of courtship is normally the prerogative of the male, we will discuss first the conduct of the Mormon man in search of an additional wife. Unlike the conditions under monogamy, married men in Mormondom were free to court any likely candidates among the fair and the young. As a four-time married man put it, "It was common enough for married men to spark around among the girls." However, as the federal prosecution in the 1880's became more and more effective, the whole plural marriage system was driven under cover and both courtship and marriage in polygamy became more hazardous and hence more secretive. In fact, the situation had so changed by the late 1880's that the fourth wife of Hyrum Stratton, married in 1887, has this to say: "Married men didn't do any courting of their plural wives. Why, we would have thought it dishonorable for a mature married man to go sparking around like a young man. They just came and asked us, and if we wanted them, we agreed."

Under the combination of continuous preaching of plurality of wives and the development of additional patriarchal prerogatives, some men went to work in earnest. Brother George Mackay was one of the more eager type. All his life, so a daughter of his sixth wife reports, he kept his eye open for prospective wives. He had seven. He usually got the consent of all his other wives before he took a new one, however. His chief technique was to get up large sleighride parties of young girls. Afterwards he would take the girl or girls home for supper, for his wives to observe. Obviously Mackay, being well-to-do, had certain advantages over single men of little means. In general, however, George's courtships were short and matter of fact. The girls always professed to be much surprised at his proposals.

Like Mackay, Elder Hyrum Stratton went through life with an eye out for a prospective mate. He wed his first wife when she was 16; before she was 19 he had taken another. And although number one consented she was most unhappy about it. As Stratton got older he seemed to become even more interested in marrying. His eldest daughter said that "Father was always acting silly around young girls" often to the embarrassment of his wives and children.

In the mid-1870's, with two wives and growing families at hand, he began making serious gestures to a young girl who was employed by the first wife. Two daughters of the latter discovered his plan to take the maid to Logan to be married in the temple there. The girls got hold of the maid and filled her full of yarns about the horrors of polygamy, saying that if she became a plural wife it would be no bed of roses but rather "she would have to spend the rest of her days scrubbing floors" and doing jobs such as milking and gardening. While this story ended that particular courtship, the father went right on to other pastures. When he began courting Elizabeth, who later became the third wife, the eldest daughter of the first wife reported to the latter that father "was acting silly again" this time over Elizabeth. To this news the mother calmly replied: "Don't look around too much" and that her "father would do just as he pleased." The daughter further remarked that her mother was fully aware of her husband's "sparking around" but "never said anything. I guess she had a broken heart; but it was suppressed."

Just as the first Mrs. Stratton disliked the coming of the second, so the latter complained bitterly to the first wife when number three appeared, asking her if she did not resent it. At this, wife number one reminded number two that she had been through all this when Stratton married the second time.

Curiously enough, the third wife in turn felt much abused when at the age of 58 he wed a fourth time, a girl 40 years his junior. Here was a curious "hierarchy of heartbreaks" as the field interviewer put it. Yet, despite this, the inter-family relations were quite satisfactory. For one thing, Stratton was well-to-do.

Another man whose taste for polygamy was "highly cultivated" was a certain Bishop Price of Paris, Idaho. He eventually had four wives, one of them taken after the Manifesto. That the Bishop had a way with women is shown in a little ditty, long popular in his community:

> Old Bishop Price is very nice,
> As nice as you'd be wishing;
> But girls, look out for Price's bait
> When he goes 'round a-fishing.

These stories aside—if we may judge by the bulk of our records—the usual approach to the prospective new bride was rather restrained. The general advice given by John Taylor, later President of the Latter-day Saints, that the courtship should be short and direct was pretty generally followed.

While most polygamous courtships were rather short if not sweet in the romantic sense, occasionally a courtship might last for some years, as the following case shows. The second wife of Benjamin Wolfe, who was born in a polygamous family, tells the story of how she fell deeply in love with her brother-in-law. She had been a domestic and from time to time when not employed had resided with the sister and her husband. While she went out with other men, she admitted that Brother Wolfe "was the only man for me."

I was in love with him for years before we were married, and we courted each other for years. Nowadays I guess the girl would try to take the man away from his wife, but not in polygamy. My sister agreed that I could have a share in her man but that I could not take him away from her. And so we lived in polygamy, and I am proud of it. He was the best man that ever lived, and good-looking, too.

In contrast, the second wife of Joseph Wright, likewise from a plural family, had more difficulty in adapting herself to the prospective new situation:

I found it hard to go into polygamy. My husband courted me for five years—and courtships weren't usually so long in those days. Oh, I went out with other boys and men and considered some of them. I often told Dad [meaning her husband] that the only reason I married him was because he pestered me so much.

During the courtship the first wife came to see the girl and told her that she wanted her to be her husband's second wife, but she remarked:

[I] could not make up my mind to marry him. Even when I promised, I was doubtful . . . It was just before the Manifesto was issued that I finally promised him. People all over Utah were upset and harried and there was beginning to be a different feeling about polygamy. I believed in it utterly but I wondered if I should be strong enough to live it. There were a number of fine men who wanted to marry me and I couldn't decide.

The girl consulted her mother who also expressed some doubt about the matter until she had a dream which instructed her that it was quite correct for her daughter to marry into polygamy. The daughter continues, "After that, she was convinced that it was the best thing to do. I did it and I have never regretted it."

Often enough the courtship was not so well accepted by the first wife. Making advances to a domestic, for example, right under the nose of the first wife might and often did produce strong negative attitudes. In the Roger Knight family the first wife was none too pleased when her husband, under the impress of preaching, began paying attention to the hired girl in the home. Moreover, the manner in which he carried on did not improve the first wife's readiness to accept another into the family. Wife number one was pregnant at the time and he would bring the girl into their home nights and make love to her while his wife looked on. "I felt so ungainly and awkward at the time that it was more than I could endure to see the attractive young girl sitting on my husband's lap, being kissed and fondled by him." She hated the girl before she came into the home as a wife and the years did not much improve her first reactions.

Sheer hedonism is clear in the story of Andrew Terry. While not regarded as strong in the faith, he had given money to the Perpetual Emigrating Fund—a fund used by the Church to aid needy converts to migrate to Utah. Some time later, an immigrant girl who had been assisted by this Fund came to live with the Terrys to pay back her passage money in work. They were living in a two-room adobe house at the time. The husband was rather lazy and the wife had to work hard to make both ends meet. She was pregnant at the time her husband began courting the girl. Sister Terry did not approve of the prospective match:

I'd watch her and after the work was done, she would run away down to the cherry trees. They were in bloom then, and he'd meet her there and they'd carry on.

He'd take her to parties and high-foot it around, while I'd have to stay home till the work was done, then take the kids and go to the party by myself to watch him doing it.

She did not object to polygamy, but was convinced that her husband "had no business marrying another wife when he couldn't support one."

Occasionally a zealous and courageous Saint would try courting two women at the same time. I have but three such examples and details in two of them are lacking. The third was one of a widower with five orphaned children who were being cared for by a housekeeper. Apparently he had his one eye on the housekeeper who was a widow and the other on a popular girl of 20 years. The latter has provided the facts.

The girl had plenty of chances to get married, but said she "didn't really care about marriage." Then one day Richard Norton, a widower, appeared at their home and proposed marriage. The girl's father liked him—her mother was dead—but still she could not make up her mind. She had three other suitors at the time and was confused as to what to do. "I picked up a flower," she relates, "calling off their names as I plucked the petals and the last one was Brother Norton."

But her problem was not so simply solved. Having agreed to marry Norton, he then took her to her father and in the latter's presence told her that he had a widow keeping house for him and wanted to know if the girl who had just consented to be his bride would have any objections to his marrying the widow also. She concludes her story in these words: "I hadn't wanted to live in polygamy but I believed in it and thought it was the right thing for me to do. I didn't mind his doing it. I suppose I'm not of a jealous disposition and I wasn't in love with him, so I never had a second's jealousy. I was married first and was the legal wife."

James Hunter's entire family knew of his plural courtship and even took part in it. The eldest daughter of the first wife said that when her father and mother began casting about for a second wife, they often took the children with them as they visited about among the townspeople whom they knew. She recalls one time at a neighbor's home when a young lady was singing and she "wondered if father was going to marry that one." As it happened he wed another and the daughter did not find it out until her new Aunt had her first baby.

Many wives were not very generous, even though they gave their consent. One of Douglas Moody's plural wives, Betsy, tells the story that one day her husband brought a girl he was courting to have dinner in her home. Betsy thought Douglas had enough wives and was quite upset at the idea of his taking another. After the dinner was cleared away, some of Betsy's children began to cry and make a lot of other disturbances. At this, their father said, "Betsy, take these children out so we can have some peace." It seems he wanted the parlor for further pursuit of his courtship. The wife, instead of hushing the children and taking them out of the room, said, "Children, howl all you want to!"

The opposition to plural marriage was sometimes mixed with doubts on the part of the prospective new bride. The first and second wives of Brother Theodore Gregg were sisters, but unlike a good many such families, the first wife rather strongly opposed her husband marrying the sister. The girl's parents, who were recent converts, shared this view.

The sister had been fully converted to Mormonism and believed all that was taught her. She says that the Mormon hymns "filled me full of fire," and she was anxious to live her religion. The courtship itself was secretive throughout. The wife had no idea that her husband was seeing the sister. "We did most of our courting," said the second wife, "in the corral, milking cows." During these periods and while they went together gathering berries and wood, the husband talked religion to the sister-in-law and asked if she would like to marry in polygamy and, if so, he would like to have the first chance. Later he made a definite proposal to her but she pled for time.

At a later date, Gregg and his first wife returned to the community where the sister was living with her family. Gregg again proposed to her and gave her a two-week period in which to decide. To this she replied that she would marry him if "it was all right with my sister." The sister had a great deal of difficulty in making up her mind, but finally said to her husband regarding the sister, "Don't you bring her back before you marry her, if she *is* coming back." And to her sister in turn she remarked, "I know this is the true Church and this Principle is just as true as any of them. I don't see how you can go into it, being that you are my sister; but if you are going back with us, I don't want you to go as a young woman, I want you to go as a married woman."

The sister then discussed the matter with her father and mother. On hearing the news, the father said, "I would rather bury you. But I won't put a straw in your way. I have always told my children that they should choose what they want as long as they live a good life. If you are going to marry into polygamy just let me know a few days before you go to St. George."

The girl still had many doubts and the prospective husband was beginning to get impatient. He said that he would like to have her consult the Bishop and his Counselors. At this meeting the church authorities told the doubting sister in no uncertain terms that she should follow through on the proposition. With quoting the scripture and a variety of testimony she was finally convinced. She says, "I wanted to do it;

it was my duty. I would have to do it." A few weeks later they were married but the sister did not, as is usual, accompany them to the temple. The second wife concludes, "It nearly broke her heart. That is what made it so hard for me."

So far we have dealt chiefly with the roles of the husband and the first wife in the selection of the prospective bride. Not infrequently, however, the latter also had some reactions which further complicated the courtship. While the securing of the first wife's consent was the general practice, occasionally a prospective plural wife was not satisfied with any vague indications of approval.

The second wife of George Yates came to Utah from England with her father. She had been baptized by Yates some years previously when he was in Britain on a mission. She pointed out that it was not uncommon "for some of the brethren to come to Salt Lake to meet some of the young women who might be their wives." Evidently some such impulse led Yates to travel all the way from Beaver to Salt Lake to visit Alice. In her own words:

Brother Yates wanted me to be his plural wife, but I was not sure about it because I did not have a "knowledge" of it. [That is, she was not fully convinced of the Principle.] Furthermore, I was not sure of it because I did not know whether his first wife, Martha, had a "knowledge" of polygamy. I asked him to find this out for me.

Some months went by and the next spring when he and his wife were in Salt Lake City for a semiannual conference of the Church, both of them went to her home to call upon her and he again pressed his suit.

I asked his wife if she had a "knowledge." She said "No," but she was "sure I was the one for Brother Yates." I was not satisfied with this. Later, after she had returned to her home I wrote a letter asking again. She wrote back saying that Brother Yates and I should get married and then when we were she hoped to get a "knowledge." She again said that she felt that "I was the one for him."

Alice was still unconvinced but Yates "kept after [her] to marry him." She again declined. Then he hit on the idea of having her visit his home in southern Utah, which she did. After remaining there for a few months, she returned to Salt Lake and shortly thereafter they were married in the Endowment House.

Young Mormon women were not unaware of some of the pitfalls as well as the advantages of entering polygamy. Not only was the glory of a plural family to be balanced against being an only but truly legal wife, but these girls knew, as the second wife of Frank Alexander reports, that "there were some unscrupulous men who used polygamy" as a handy device to get a new wife, and sometimes abandoned their plural families when they got tired of them. The so-called "winter Mormons" were the most serious offenders. After the Civil War ex-soldiers en route to California would occasionally settle in a Mormon community, become converted to the Church and then marry a Mormon girl or maybe more than one. Later most of these men—but not all—deserted their families and moved on.

There were some Mormon women who showed a good deal of aggression in courtship. Fully converted to the Principle, and badly wanting a man, some of the Sisters undertook not only romantic devices to snare a husband, but in some cases were much more direct. The eldest child of Richard Field said that her father, who was a popular Bishop in the community, was much sought after by women who asked him to marry them. "And they were fine intelligent girls, too, but a man has just as much right to refuse as a girl has." A third wife tells this story: "Brother Winthrop had a fourth wife. She was my brother's daughter, Emily. I won't say anything about her, she was a good woman. But she wanted to marry Brother Winthrop and she did the proposing. In those days when a woman wanted to marry a man, the man felt it was his duty to marry her. Brother Winthrop married her but he didn't want to."

The reverse of the widely circulated stories which describe how evil Mormon missionaries pursue innocent British girls with a view to seducing them into polygamy, is the case of Carrie Smith who became the third wife of Albert Procter.

When Albert was 35 he was sent on a mission to England. He already had two wives who were sisters, and a family of 10 children, six of them by his first wife, four by the second. While in England he met Carrie, an attractive convert of 17, who definitely "set her cap" for him and followed him "over a lot of territory" trying to persuade him to marry her. Her pursuit could not be kept from her fellow Saints and from Procter's many relatives with whom he visited. Moreover, word got back to the wives at home. His father especially took violent exception to the courtship of his son and Carrie and once referred to her as "that filthy wench."

Evidently Procter was not unimpressed by the girl and she emigrated to Utah at the same time as he returned from his mission. He took her to Salt Lake to stay until he could prepare a house for her. As soon as an old log house of his could be replastered and repaired by his sons, he was ready for her. His two wives let him have the cash to return to Salt Lake to be married.

All in all, the tribulations and pleasures of polygamous courtship were in most instances more evident than they are in monogamy. Romantic love was difficult to demonstrate in a world where it had become identified with monogamy. Despite the acceptance of a married man's full right to seek another wife, the hangover of ideals and attitudes of monogamy must have made many men feel not only a little silly but also a certain sense of guilt at courting when they already had a wife and children. True, full faith in the Principle provided a cover for the sense of guilt and shame, yet they probably operated unconsciously.

At the opening of this chapter we noted that the distribution of men and women in the population of early Utah, unlike the usual situation in pioneer regions, was about equal in numbers. This meant that there were not enough women on hand to provide extra wives for many of the Saints unless other men went unwed. As a matter of fact, despite the common acceptance of the principle of plurality of wives, there was always an implicit if not an open competition for the available women. While many young men were taken up with colonizing, going on missions, and otherwise helping to build up Zion, thus delaying their entrance into marriage, they were at the same time under official pressure to marry and make a home in which they could raise up their children to God. Such men were bound to come into competition with those already married but who were seeking to increase their status by going into polygamy.

We have already seen that women occasionally had a chance to marry single men but chose to enter polygamy instead. As a matter of fact we have a number of instances where distinctive rivalry between married men and single men was a factor in the courtship. When polygamy was in flower in Utah the chances of marriage was no problem to women. A girl was considered to be an old maid after she was 25 years of age, but even so she might have her opportunity. The men thought it a moral duty to see that every woman was married. When they had two or three wives it did not matter much if they took a spinster or a blind girl or an unattractive one as an additional wife.

In the relation of single to married men in courtship a kind of code developed. Unless a married man was fairly young and seriously in love with a young girl, he would try to learn if she had an unmarried suitor or was in love with another man. If a girl had no suitors then she was considered "open game" by the married men. Another important factor was whether the girl with whom one had a courtship really believed in the principle of polygamy. If she did—and every religious woman was supposed to—then she received his proposal.

Under the pressure of the system of celestial marriage single men were often very active in their courting. They realized that they were in competition with married men and frequently brought pressure to bear on their prospective spouses. On the other hand, attractive married men who also had considerable property often had the "inside track" in courtship. As a result of this economic advantage young single men frequently resented the competition with the older men in their seeking the younger girls of a given locality. This was poach-

ing in its worst sense. They did not mind if a man who already had a wife, or wives, took an older woman or a widow,
but they were hostile to the idea of his taking a young girl
even if she was not all that romantic idealism would wish.

Finally, a woman's great glory in those days was her ability
to bear many children. One who could not was bound to end
up in a lesser social sphere both here and in the hereafter.
Nearly all of the older polygamous women mentioned the "old
maid" with utter contempt. One said to me, "My husband
married Edith Swenson but, then, she was an *old maid*."

Again there were as many variations in the competitive pattern as there were differentials in the motivations which led
a girl to accept a married man in preference to a single one.
The third Sister Dahlman reported that she was surprised
when Oscar proposed to her. "I never thought of anything
like that until he proposed to me. Mother and I talked it
over afterward and we knew Brother Dahlman was a good man
in the community and so I accepted him." She was 17 years
of age, he was 46. When asked whether a girl in her day would
prefer a polygamist, well established, over a young man who
was just starting out, she replied:

A girl would do just as I did. I had offers from single ones,
but none of them suited me, and when Brother Dahlman came
along he was about what I wanted and I took him. A girl would
judge the man and if he suited her she would take him in those
days and not pay much attention to polygamy . . . No, I don't
think the wife of a polygamist will get any higher glory in the
Celestial Kingdom than a single wife will get. We knew the Principle was right, however.

An amusing story is told of one old polygamist. Well-
advanced in years, he decided to take another plural wife, so
he bluntly asked a young girl of 16, who as promptly told the
old man that under no conditions would she marry in polygamy. "So he huffed off," as the story goes, "and asked another,
who said she would marry him." From the afternoon's operations he started back home, "all warmed up with his victory."
As he was passing the home of the girl who had refused him,

she came out to the picket fence and told him she had talked the matter over with her mother, and that she had decided she would marry him after all. Shortly thereafter the happy man took both his young brides to the altar.

It should not be imagined that the polygamists always won out in their competition for the young women of the community. Although many a young girl took a practical view of the possible advantages in marrying a well-established Saint, especially if he was a pleasant and good-looking man as well, romantic or other interests sometimes served to block the proposals of married men.

The official requirements were that a prospective polygamous husband have (a) the consent of the first wife, (b) the consent of the Bishop with his Recommend, properly approved by the Stake President, and (c) that the ceremony of sealing be performed in a temple or in the Endowment House by a member of the Melchizedek priesthood. On the basis of these bare essentials, however, a number of more or less widely accepted practices arose. Sociologically the whole system of Mormon polygamy demonstrates how institutions emerge out of theories once these are put into practice. To draw an example from courtship and marriage: From the idea and usual practice that the first wife must consent to a husband's taking a second arose the belief that all the prior wives should also agree to taking still more wives. While this idea was not carried out generally, it was done in many families and the practice was doubtless found to be a sensible one. Future harmony among the wives might be more satisfactory by virtue of such action taken in advance.

Another practice was that the first wife should accompany her husband and the prospective plural wife to the temple for the sealing. This became much more widely accepted, both in theory and practice, than did the custom of getting the consent of all the wives before taking on an additional one.

As to the sealing itself, the procedure for plural wives was the same as for first marriages. By ordinary Christian standards there was no glamour in this ceremony. The participants are clothed in their official underwear, a full length union-suit over which is worn a loose white cotton or linen robe.

The bride and groom kneel before a simple altar. There are no crucifix, candles, or other paraphernalia of the usual Christian sort. The couple clasp hands over the altar and the ecclesiastic in charge than directs the marriage vows.

Both attitude and circumstances determined whether the first wife would accompany the husband and his prospective bride to the sealing. Travel was hard, distances were long, and it was often necessary for someone to remain to care for the household and children. In some families—especially where the first wife's consent was not given at all or reluctantly given—there was no motivation to go along.

Since, as we shall see later, status differences were bound to arise in some families in terms of who was first and who was second wife, Brother Herbert Sumner had his own way of avoiding that difficulty. To quote from his journal:

I got married in 1876 to Myrtle and Edith in the Endowment House on the same day. But I never told anyone who was the first wife. They that was there knew, of course. People have tried to make me tell which was the first wife, but I took 'em both at the same time. They was willing or else I wouldn't have married them . . .

Joseph Carey wanted to marry a certain widow, but she only consented if he would agree to also marry her two daughters when they grew up. They were then in their early teens. A few years after he wed the widow, she accompanied him to the temple where he married his two stepdaughters on the same day.

The frequency and openness with which the first wife accompanied her husband and his fiancée to a temple or the Endowment House was affected by the increasing attempts of the federal deputies to stop plural marriages. To take along the first wife made movement through the streets more obvious to passers-by, and furthermore, if a wife witnessed a plural marriage of her husband, she might some day in the courts be questioned under oath on the matter. It was the part of wisdom, then, for the first wife to know nothing about the plural marriage. Moreover, this fact encouraged some men to marry secretly without the consent of the first wife.

At the time Maxwell Kirby had become engaged to his prospective third wife the federal officers were active. As a result the couple had to be secretive about their courtship. The girl's family knew that she intended to marry and while they were not entirely in favor of it, they did not block the step. When the day came that they were to be married, the bride merely told her mother that she was going to the temple. Kirby was being watched and he had a hard time getting away from the office. He walked around several blocks and finally showed up at the temple. Sister Kirby number three goes on to remark, "We were married and I came home alone and spent the night alone. 'In three years,' my husband told me, 'we will celebrate this event.'"

Marriage under such conditions must have been at best rather troublesome. Under the conditions of secrecy the Mormons developed a whole set of new institutions including the "Underground." We shall have something to say about this whole system in Chapter 18.

Due to a variety of circumstances some deviations in the system of sealing emerged. The normal procedure, of course, was for all the wives to be married for time and eternity. Due to frontier hardships of travel, it was not always possible for men to take their first spouses to the Endowment House in Salt Lake City or to the St. George Temple, the two places where sealing of this kind could be done in those days. Hence it was not uncommon for a justice of the peace or a Bishop (often these two offices were held by the same man) or some higher ecclesiastic to marry the man and his wife for the time only in a civil ceremony. As a rule, a couple would at the earliest opportunity be sealed properly for time and eternity in a sacred edifice. There are several instances where the first wife and husband who had had only a civil marriage, were sealed on the same day that the husband also wed a plural wife.

Under special circumstances men and women were sealed with an eye to the hereafter only. Howard Keith was sealed to a woman shortly before her death. She was never a member of the household; he never lived with her. The other wives and their children never considered this woman as a wife at all. The story of Mathilda Cook is interesting in this connection. She was keeping company with a young man to whom her father had violent objections. The young man became seriously ill and was not expected to live. He let it be known through his friends and neighbors that he had no ill-feelings for anyone but Charles Cook who had taken such a dislike for him. Charles went to see him and was reconciled. As the young man was about to die, the father now interceded with his daughter who agreed to be sealed to the dying man for time and eternity.

Subsequently Mathilda had six offers to marry, but all the men gave up their suit when informed that she could only marry for time only, since she was already wed for time and eternity to another. Later she became the plural wife of a man who did not mind the fact that she would not be his in the hereafter.

Sometimes people arranged for marriages for eternity to take place after their death. Joseph Carey, Jr., tells in his diary that he went to the temple and gave the name of an old friend of his to the president of the temple saying, "She wished to be sealed to Elder Joseph Carey, Jr., as a wife for time and all eternity." The president of the temple copied this message and filed it away. His son Joseph M. Carey likewise remarks on the fact that his father and uncle both told him that Aunt Alice Conklin wished to be sealed to Joseph Carey, Jr., when her husband Samuel Conklin was dead. The son goes on to say that all understood and agreed to this arrangement. The wife of Conklin in turn proposed that he have sealed to him Miss Marie White of Michigan after Conklin was dead. Evidently it was thought that arrangements of this kind might be made here to be worked out in heaven. This kind of mating for the hereafter may have been relatively common although my own records do not show many examples of such.

From his journals it seems that the son, Joseph M. Carey, attempted to follow his father's footsteps in this matter. He relates that when he was living in Dixie as a young man he became engaged to one Hazel Green. While he was away at school in 1871 she broke the engagement and later married a man named Johnson. To quote the journal:

After a silence of fifty-six years she wrote me again, in October 1927, from New Castle, Utah, asking to be sealed to me at death. After discussing and explaining this matter to my wife, Elnora, and the president of the temple, I answered Hazel in the affirmative. So now I consider that we are engaged a second time, but only to be effective after death comes to one or both of us and I now, December 30, 1929, declare it to be my wish that after my death Hazel Green Johnson be sealed to me Joseph M. Carey.

Five years later his diary carried an entry that Mrs. Johnson had died in Iron County, Utah. After hearing this news Carey approached the president of the Salt Lake Temple and explained the prior arrangement. Carey was informed, however, that the sealing "must not be done without the approval of a majority of the children." Carey then went to work and wrote each of the seven children about the matter but failed to get their approval. Moreover, the chief recorder of the Salt Lake Temple subsequently told Carey that three of Hazel's children had been there and testified that their mother before her death had expressed her desire to be sealed to her husband, D. H. Johnson, the father of all her children, although she and her husband had been married by civil law only.

Carey concludes sadly: "So, this is final; and I *cannot* keep my promise to have her sealed to me after death. I must of necessity abandon all further activities relating to this matter, but I am not responsible for the break; I certainly wish that joy and happiness may come to her through all eternity."

The common practice, and one free from restraint, was to marry plural wives from among unmarried women who had died. We have a number of illustrations of this in our records but just how widespread this practice is or has been in Mormonism can only be determined by an examination of confidential records of the Church itself. Rita Stanley in her biography of Parley P. Pratt, entitled, *The Archer of Paradise* (1937), says that Brigham Young had hundreds of women sealed to him for eternity only, though she adduces no proof. One of the informants for this study said that her uncle had "some hundreds of wives sealed to him for eternity only." Again there is no documentary evidence on this matter. I do know, however, that it was a common practice to secure additional plural wives by being sealed to deceased unmarried women. It must be remembered that theologically speaking plurality of wives is still a principle of Mormonism and this at least is one way of providing for future happiness and glory.

Social festivities following a plural wedding varied with the economic status of the man, with the reactions of the first and/or other wives to the newcomer, and with the general community situation such as regards the need for secrecy, so often the case in the 1880's.

Jennie, the sixth wife of George Mackay, was 19 years old at the time of her marriage. After the sealing in the Endowment House she was brought to Provo where Mackay had one huge household for all his families. The other wives had prepared a wedding feast for the bride and groom and they ate together while the other five wives served the dinner. Jennie said that she could "have sunk through the floor" as she thought of eating her first meal under the watchful eyes of her husband's five other wives. The latter were naturally interested to know the kind of woman their husband was adding to the household.

Certain aspects of the community reaction to plural marriages are revealed in the use of the charivari. One informant said that in his community a man always got a much noisier and more ribald charivari when he brought home his second spouse than on the first occasion. Catcalls such as "Why did he want to marry another woman when he couldn't keep up with the first one?" disturbed the newlyweds. It was common, too, that the groom must treat the boys who put on the charivari to food and perhaps beer or wine. Just how the first wife, or the plural one, took such public demonstrations is not made clear, but doubtless many of them found it none too pleasant an occasion.

As federal pressure against polygamy increased, it became more and more hazardous for any festivities to be held in celebration of a plural marriage. As the practice was driven more and more underground, plural wives often went home to their parents and continued to go about in their former role as single women.

Daisy Barclay was married to John Barclay, as his second wife, in Logan. They took the first train available to return to Salt Lake City. But Barclay thought it wise to drop his new bride off at her own home in Brigham City while he continued on to his first wife in Salt Lake City. Daisy writes of her return:

The family had finished the evening meal. As I sat down to a glass of bread and milk the thought came to me. "Well, this is my wedding supper." In those few minutes I recalled the elaborate banquets I had helped to prepare and the many lovely brides among my friends. I even began to compare their wedding gowns. I was conscious of the obscurity of my own first evening after marriage.

"What a contrast," I said to myself. "No one will ever congratulate *me!*"

Another second wife tells a similar story. After a long and hard trip by team she was left in a small cabin on the outskirts of an unknown community. "At the house there was no one to welcome me. He just told me to go into the little room and sleep and he would stay in the wagon. And that was my wedding night! I was frightened to death and lay there praying for God to take care of me."

In like measure, the wedding night was often an uncomfortable experience for the first wife. When James Hunter took his second wife, the first who had accompanied the couple to the Endowment House for the ceremony could not sleep and walked the floor all night as she thought of her husband lying in the arms of his new bride. The first wife of John Emmet who had, as we saw, reluctantly given her consent to his plural marriage, went through much the same heartache. So as not to show her feelings she "used to go down to the granary and cry." Finally John discovered her and "tried to comfort" her and "make things easier." Years later Emmet admitted to his first wife that he had handled the situation foolishly and apologized, saying "I didn't realize what an awful thing I had done to you."

A person brought up in a polygamous household and in a town in which there were a great many plural households told this story: "There is one real tragedy in polygamy that I can remember. One evening a man brought home a second wife. It was in the winter and the first wife was very upset. That night she climbed onto the roof and froze to death."

In those families where the first wife opposed the plural marriage the wedding night must have proved a particularly severe trial. Sometimes conflict broke out almost from the start. One man took a second wife despite the opposition of his first spouse. He provided a new house and furnishings for the prospective bride before taking her to Salt Lake City to be married. On the return trip, by team, they stopped with friends who had helped promote the match. Late that night they continued on to their new home, but they found the place locked. On breaking in, they discovered that all the furniture, bedding, kitchenware, and other household goods had been removed. They had to go back to their friends who took them in for the balance of the night. As the husband suspected, this was not meant for a joke but had been carried out by the first wife as a form of revenge on the newlyweds.

In closing this chapter, a comment must be made on the legal status of plural wives. Actually, of course, no plural marriage was legitimate in the eyes of the law. The Mormons were well aware of this, especially insofar as it had to do with the division of property. Therefore it became rather common practice for a man to marry his second wife if his first wife divorced or predeceased him. So far as I know, the general authorities took no formal stand on this matter. In the eyes of the official Church and of the faithful members, one wife was as "legal" and "proper" as another. Yet the Mormons could not in a few decades shake off their attitudes, ideas, and habits built up around monogamy. We shall see how strong this was when we discuss such topics as division of property, post-Manifesto reactions, and others.

Some of these legal marriages, when they took place years after the Manifesto and when both the families and the communities had lost any zest for polygamy, upset family members considerably. The two wives of Benjamin Wolfe were sisters, and after the first wife died, Benjamin married the second in order to protect her rights in his property. On learning of the legal marriage the children and grandchildren of the first wife were quite disturbed. It came as a complete surprise to them as it did to the community. Many of them felt that they had to bear the brunt of unpleasant public gossip which followed this event. However, some of this reaction was probably motivated by fear of loss of rights to the father's property on the part of some members of the first family.

It is clear that in these matters, as in so many other aspects of Mormon polygamy, there were few standardized practices. Under the terms of the "Revelation" on plural marriage, the institution got underway. But as to consent of the first wife, courtship practices, the role of the first wife with regard to the marriage ceremony, the wedding festivities, the wedding night and the honeymoon, there was a great deal of variation. The system did not last long enough for deep-seated official and customary practices to emerge. Mormon polygamy still remained after nearly 50 years an appendage to Mormon monogamy.

> *If he take him another wife, her food, her raiment, and her duty of marriage, shall he not diminish.*—Exodus 21:10.

> *A man should have three wives: two to beg and one to sew sacks.*—Mormon folklore.

# 7 THE ECONOMICS OF THE PLURAL HOUSEHOLD

ONCE A man had taken a plural wife the problem of adjusting the new family unit to the prior monogamous one became paramount. The nature and success of such rearrangements were qualified by the economic adequacy of the husband, by the actual and potential housing facilities, by the attitude of the first wife and family, and especially by the emotional and social relations which developed between the wives and families. The present chapter deals with the economics of plural families. The subtler and more difficult tasks of inter-personal relations of the wives and families will be presented later. Yet to understand the household economics of either the monogamous or polygamous family in Mormondom, we must first describe the larger community organization as it developed in the Great Basin under pioneer conditions.

Most frontier agriculture in Western United States took the form of individual farmsteads scattered over a given region. Villages and towns which arose to serve as marketing centers were located at traffic crossroads or at county seats where the economic and political functions developed together. But the typical rural pattern was that of households located on each farm and separated by varying distances from each other. In a time of difficult travel this made for personal and family isolation.

Mormon community organization differed sharply from this. Almost from the outset the Mormons settled in towns or cities formally laid out in rectangular pattern. Their agricultural operations were carried on in the surrounding farmlands, but family residence was located in the town or city, not on the remote farm itself. This pattern, as a planned feature of their life, began in the Missouri and Illinois phases and was carried into the Great Basin when they migrated thence in the late 1840's and thereafter. The procedure in founding Salt Lake City became the pattern to be followed elsewhere. A few days after the first company of 143 persons entered the valley of the Salt Lake, Brigham Young and his Apostles laid out the city. Wilford Woodruff, later President of the Church, reports:

. . . It was also moved and carried that the city be laid out into lots of ten rods by twenty each, exclusive of the streets, and into blocks of eight lots, being ten acres to the block, and one and a quarter in each lot.

It was further moved and carried that each street be laid out eight rods wide, and that there be a sidewalk on each side, twenty feet wide, and that each house be built in the center of the lot twenty feet from the front, that there might be uniformity throughout the city.

While the size of the blocks and the width of the streets in other communities varied somewhat, the general ground plan of each community followed that of Salt Lake City. The land lying outside the city or town limits was also subdivided, usually into 10- or 20-acre farm plots. At the founding of any community it was a common practice for both city property and farms to be chosen by lot or assigned by someone in charge of the distribution.

Such community planning was adapted to the cooperative irrigation systems on which Mormon agriculture depended. Moreover, it suited the districting of church members into Wards or fixed areas like a parish. Also the location of families in a compact village, town, or city made possible more effective protection against hostile Indians than would be the case if the settlers lived on scattered farms. Finally, such a community layout made for closer inter-personal and inter-familial contacts. Neighborhoods arose within the community and church and civic meetings and entertainments could be more frequent and better attended than if the inhabitants were widely dispersed on separate farms.

From the outset the Church controlled community development. Planned colonization was begun in the very year of initial settlement of Utah, that is, in 1847. The Church usually assumed some responsibility for providing capital for equipment and sufficient foodstuffs to launch each new community. But individuals and families were supposed to furnish the bulk of their own material goods: teams, wagons, tools, plows, and other necessary equipment as well as their own household goods.

The selection of persons to colonize, however, was not haphazard. There was official realization of the need for quotas of individuals with particular skills and knowledge under assigned leaders. Hence a definite allotment was made as to farmers, masons, carpenters, millers, hat-makers, weavers, shoemakers, and others essential to any well-organized economic community.

The initial Mormon settlements were near Salt Lake City— north to the Weber River and south into Utah Valley. In time they spread, usually along the valley lines and parallel to the Wasatch Mountains, till they reached to the Gila River in Arizona and to the Snake River valley and beyond in Idaho. In the years 1847–57, 100 such communities were established; in the next decade an additional 135; and between 1868 and 1877, another 127. Thus in 30 years over 360 villages and towns were settled. For the most part these communities remain today the chief Mormon centers.

One fundamental aim of Brigham Young and his fellow-leaders was to make the Mormons economically self-sufficient and thus independent of the rest of the country. Their previous experience in trying to live in the midst of non-Mormons had left them doubtful that any satisfactory *modus vivendi* could be worked out. They and their followers were bitter toward the Gentile world because of repeated conflicts. The Mormons sought a remote area in order to escape any contact or contamination with Babylon, as they dubbed the hostile world outside.

The fates, however, decided otherwise. Hardly had Salt Lake and nearby settlements been founded than the discovery of gold in California—an event in which certain Mormons had participated—set loose a mad rush of migrants to the Golden West. Brigham Young forbade the Saints to follow the lure of gold, but the Mormons took advantage of certain economic opportunities related to the Gold Rush. Whatever surpluses of food, draught animals, and vehicles they had they sold at big profits to California-bound fortune seekers.

This temporary economic windfall, however, symbolized something else. The Mormons could not long remain completely separated from the rest of the United States. They lived astride the main transcontinental highways from the Middle West to the Pacific coast. Later when the telegraph and the railroads were built the isolation was further dissipated. As one prominent Mormon pioneer said regarding the implications of the new transcontinental railroad connections of 1869: "Our days of isolation were now forever past and with our steam and electrical communications we could stand face-to-face with all the good and evil that modern civilization represents."

It was within this more or less church-controlled village and rural organization that the Mormon family had its life. The family was the basic economic unit in fulfilling the aim of self-sufficiency. The head of the family ventures, of course, was the husband and father. Women folk, both married and single, took a submissive role under this masculine dominance. The patriarchal pattern served well the demands of strenuous pioneer-frontier conditions. Finally, the system was intimately a part of the Latter-day Saint theology, priesthood hierarchy, and its socio-religious community organization.

Moreover, polygamy had to be fitted into this scheme of life and society. After all, the plural family was really but an appendage to the basic patriarchal monogamous family. In matters such as the location of the families—whether under the same roof all together, or in separate households, in the same community or in different localities—there were no definite rules. Neither was there any official advice as to distribution of income or on details of day-by-day control of the domestic economy.

A variety of circumstances influenced the location of the new plural family. If the husband was not financially well-fixed, the usual practice was to place the families under one roof. Later, as economic conditions improved, the wives might be given separate homes. Well-to-do men often provided separate households from the outset; yet, in some instances where wealth was not a consideration, all the families occupied the same dwelling. Sometimes there was a mixed arrangement: one or more wives lived in their own separate dwellings, the balance under one roof. In fact, this was the pattern in the large ménage of Brigham Young after the Lion and Beehive Houses were built. Most of his families lived in these large establishments, where each wife had an apartment for herself and her children and the family shared a common dining room. Nevertheless, separate houses were provided for some of the wives who did not readily adapt themselves to this communal program. But the households of Brigham Young were a special case. While his wives had considerable responsibility for the care of their own children and for certain features of the household economy, his wealth and position enabled him to provide domestic servants for much of the household drudgery. The large families of Young, Kimball, and a few others, in fact, are probably the foundation for the widespread Gentile myth that Mormon polygamy was organized along the lines of extensive harems. Nevertheless, in 99 per cent of the Mormon plural families there were no such numbers of wives or children nor the economic means to set up and run such elaborate establishments.

In short, it should not be thought that the spatial arrangements were determined by economic considerations only. Other factors entered into particular family situations: the presence or absence of inter-wife conflict or the removal of families to a new locality, as happened when men with plural families were selected to colonize a new section of the country. Then, too, as federal prosecution of polygamists was intensified in the 1880's, prior arrangements were often disturbed by the husband or plural wife going on the Underground to avoid arrest.

The operation of a single or joint household itself varied with respect to details. Sometimes the meals were prepared together for all families who used a common kitchen and dining room although each wife would have her own room or apartment for herself and her children. In one of our families while each wife had her own apartment, as the children grew older the families began to put the boys in one room to sleep and the girls in another—mixed up without regard to which mother they belonged to.

The housework was done by the wives and their daughters. Ordinarily each wife took on a certain line of duty. For example, in one family a third wife who had no children, although she took care of some of the others, managed the kitchen and the culinary operations. The other wives, in addition to the care of their large families, carded and spun wool for cloth. They also helped with the housework and did the sewing. A picture of mealtime from a son is rather intriguing:

The meals were taken by all members of the family at one table. On the one side was the father and his three wives, with all the girls ranked according to age. On the other side sat all the boys also arranged according to age. The children were mixed without reference to their mothers "because they were advised to run their families like that." That is, the children were all regarded as full brothers and sisters and were so treated.

In another family the first wife was the business head and general manager and since she had no children, she made periodic trips to Salt Lake City to take produce from the farm on Mill Creek to trade for other commodities. The other wives were given other assignments; some did the weaving, others did the housework, and so on.

On the whole, plural families made better adjustments when they lived in separate dwellings with a corresponding independence in most day-by-day routines; yet in some families there was evident harmony under the single dwelling plan. One man remarked of the later difficulties between his two wives, "It was when I got them separate homes that the trouble began." That is, envy and struggle for status began to influence their relations. Let us look at some illustrations of such spatial arrangements.

In some instances the residence was arranged as a duplex, all under the same roof, but each family having a full complement of kitchen, dining, and sleeping facilities. George Yates thus describes the house plan which his father-in-law made at the time the latter took a second wife:

Father planned how he wanted his house built. It was to be arranged for two families, in the shape of an "H." Two rooms on the north, one 16 x 19, and the other 16 x 15 and two rooms on the south of the same dimensions and a room 16 feet square in between. The front was to extend back 6 feet allowing for a porch 6 feet deep, and 16 feet wide. On the back of this middle room were to be two kitchens each 8 x 10. The two back rooms were to be partitioned, making two bedrooms. The work was to start at once and I was to oversee it.

Sometimes there were combinations of joint and separate households. One man [Heber Thomas] arranged his households in this fashion. Two wives lived in the same house and the third in another a few yards in the rear. The single dwelling was really a duplex because each family had its own apartment, kitchen and all. The three kitchens, however, opened on a small yard about 10 yards square. This provided an opportunity for the wives to see each other many times during the day. There was one cellar for the three families but the food was stored separately. Each wife had her own barrels and bins for supplies. While there was occasional borrowing of such things as bread, these items were always paid back. Each wife had her own cows and made her own butter and cheese; likewise each had her own flock of chickens. There was a large orchard with apple, peach, and plum trees, and gooseberry bushes. When the orchard began to bear, the father counted off the trees according to the number of children in the respective families. He was particular in dividing up the fruit and food and he thought this a method by which all would be fairly treated.

Where there were separate houses for each wife, the spatial arrangements varied considerably. Most frequently the families lived in the same village, town, or city. Occasionally some arrangement between a farm for one or more wives and other houses in town for still other wives was worked out. Where the families lived in the same community, the houses were frequently on adjoining lots and certainly for the most part they were in the same neighborhood.

While circumstances sometimes dictated the locating of plural households in different villages or towns, this practice became a deliberate one after the federal prosecutions of the 1880's led to increased secrecy, caution, and outright deceit to mislead the officers. Amasa Lang moved his second wife and her brood to Hyde Park, some 60 miles away, where for nearly eight years they lived under the name of Logan. He built a house in Hyde Park and visited his plural family whenever circumstances permitted. He was at this time Bishop of the second Ward in Ogden.

A percentage analysis of the occupations of the father of our polygamous families provides a background for a discussion of income and expenditures. We tabulated the male heads of family into five more or less standard occupational groupings: (1) Professional, including here high Mormon officials, that is, beyond the bishopric level; (2) Proprietary, including bankers, farm or ranch owner-operator, manufacturing, merchandising, and freighting; (3) Clerical and white-collar workers; (4) Skilled craftsmen; and (5) Semiskilled and unskilled.

The tabulations were made for the chief occupation, as nearly as this could be determined from the records. The figures show that in slightly more than two-thirds of our families, farming or ranching was the major source of income. Adding the other proprietary fields to this we find that this category accounts for four-fifths of those families on which we have

adequate data. In contrast, few of our cases fall into the professional category—six high Mormon officials and one college
professor. There was one in the clerical class and three each
in the other two categories.

As to money earnings of our group, our data are sketchy and
inadequate. As a matter of fact, money wages were not too
common. Income was often paid in kind. Moreover, the Mormons developed the use of script as a medium of exchange, especially with regard to their official building programs, such as
the temples, and as a means of disposing to consumers any
produce paid into the Church as tithing or other contributions. Then, too, production for home use would be difficult to evaluate. In brief, it would be useless to attempt to
estimate real wages or, for that matter, to attempt to find a
monetary index to the level of living standards which would
be comparable to contemporary figures. Rather than attempt
this, we use a rating of economic success as judged against the
total experience in pioneer Mormondom. These data are
given in Chapter 3. On the basis of occupation and our rating
of economic status, we shall discuss the range of wealth among
our plural families. Examples will be given for the chief occupational classes.

The professions were scantily represented either in the
general population of early Utah or in our own records. In
view of status and income, the elite of the Church fulfill the
usual criteria of a profession. The early leaders of the Latter-
day Saints—to a man recruited from modest economic circumstances—in time began to assume a superior professional attitude regarding their positions in the Church and the civic
hierarchy. While the Church still maintains the system of lay
ministry, as early as 1877 the "general authorities"—President, Apostles, Seven Presidents of Seventies, and some others
—were given fixed salaries because they had to give their
major time and effort to ecclesiastical duties. Even so, for a
long time, most of those holding such positions continued to
engage in other enterprises in order to add to their incomes.

In the early days, Brigham Young and some of his close
lieutenants soon became interested in large-scale operations of

freighting, developing lines of communication, such as the pony express, and later the telegraph lines. With the coming of the railroads Young, John Sharp, and others made a good deal of money from construction contracts. Their wealth increased considerably and their household arrangements were quite atypical in comparison with the run-of-the-mill Mormons, whether polygamist or not. However, the story of John Taylor resembles that of most of the leaders of the Church and will serve to illustrate a common pattern among the elite.

In his earlier years Taylor had been a wood turner and cooper. At the age of 28 years he was converted to Mormonism and in little more than a year became one of the Apostles. This meant that he had increasingly to give his time and energy to official duties. Nonetheless, he had to provide for his families. While on various missions he was supported by the Church, but at home, in addition to his church work, he engaged in the publishing business and in teaching. After the migration to Utah, he also went in for farming, construction work, and other business ventures.

With regard to the proprietary group, farming and ranching made up over half of the occupations among our plural families. This proportion is probably true not only for the polygamous families generally, but for the entire Mormon population of this period as well. An example of a highly successful entrepreneur is that of Henry Zeller.

Henry Zeller, born in Europe in 1825, was a watchmaker by trade. He had migrated to Australia as a young man and set up what soon became a successful jewelry business there. He became interested in Mormonism and left Australia for London where he joined the Church. Imbued with the spirit of religious communism—the order of Enoch was just then being preached by the Mormons—he offered to turn all his worldly goods over to the Church, but he was told that a tithe would be sufficient.

He migrated to Utah in 1865 with a large stock of jewelry and enough slate shingles to make a substantial roof for his jewelry store which he set up on Main Street in Salt Lake City. He resided in the two floors above the store. Some time after his arrival he married. Seventeen years later, and by that time a prosperous businessman, he married again, and shortly after that a third time—to a sister of his second wife.

In the mid-1890's he sold his jewelry business, retired to Provo where he built some fine homes for his wives, and in his latter years dealt in stocks and bonds. He was a faithful Mormon, but despite his wealth and civic prominence he never held any important office in the church hierarchy.

Like Zeller, who was a skilled craftsman, many others with special trades did not long remain mere wage-earners, but set up in business for themselves. Herbert Winslow, a stone-cutter by trade shortly set up his own business and became successful. He also bought a farm to supplement his income.

So too, Mathew Hale, a skilled blacksmith, shortly after his arrival in Salt Lake City, was sent to an outlying settlement that needed such services. He set up his shop there and in a few years had become an entrepreneur with several journeymen and apprentices in his employ. A few years after settling in this community, he married a plural wife and 12 years later he took a third, the widow of one of his friends. In addition to managing a blacksmithing enterprise, Hale had a small farm which helped support his families. While he never accumulated any extensive property, he left his families with good houses, the blacksmith shop, and the farm.

Of course, not all skilled craftsmen became entrepreneurs but among our records there are very few polygamists who could be classified, strictly speaking, as skilled or unskilled workmen. In fact, there is evidence, already noted in Chapter 3, that plural marriage tended to be confined to enterprising and relatively successful men either from an economic standpoint or as members of the elite of the Church, or both. While polygamy made severe economic demands, it also, of course, provided additional economic assets as the children grew up and were put to work. However, demands of the leaders for men to aid in colonizing new sections or to go on missions sometimes put a damper on their accumulation of property. In other instances mobility of residence did not prove a handicap.

Some economic and other effects of frequent mobility of residence linked with recurrent calls for service by the Church as colonizers, are nicely illustrated in the life story of Henry Spaulding, one of the most prominent contributors to the settlement of Utah's Dixie.

Spaulding was born in Scotland in 1819 and was brought to Canada by his parents as a young child. At the age of 26 and already married, he joined the Mormon Church. He and his father had an excellent farm which they sold at a sacrifice and set out to join the Saints at Winter Quarters on the Missouri. Spaulding was among the first groups to reach the great Salt Lake Valley in 1847. Although some early economic adventures were unsuccessful, he soon had a thriving sawmill on Mill Creek and began to develop a number of farms. Within five years he writes as follows in his journal: "About this time I was getting in comfortable circumstances. I had a good mill, a good farm, a good pasture well fenced, two span of horses, two yoke of oxen, and twelve head of milch cows, and a good comfortable house, and out of debt. In all I was worth in property about ten thousand dollars."

A few years later, he reports:

I have plenty of house room and had all my family under one roof and ate at one table and had plenty to eat. (He had three wives by that time.) There were sixteen in the family old enough to eat with knife and fork at the table beside the number of little ones. This was the happiest time of my life, for all was peace and good feelings, and no one need tell me that there cannot be peace and enjoyment in a family where there is plurality of wives in one house, where I had tried it with three wives, and all their children under one roof.

Yet this was not to last. Spaulding went on a mission which set him back financially. Moreover, he suffered further severe losses on his return. At the age of 40 he began once more to rebuild his property, and in a few years was well fixed; but he was called to Dixie by Brigham Young to help colonize that area of Utah. Again he disposed of his property at a considerable loss and took some of his family South to begin the settlement there. Subsequently he took all of his families to southern Utah.

Spaulding's journal is filled with accounts of the recurrent difficulties in developing irrigation in that arid, sandy region. As he acutely put it: "It was hard to get the water and the land to connect." In fact one of the most heartbreaking aspects of colonization in the Dixie country was the perpetual problem of building dams and ditches, only to have them washed out during torrential rains or go dry for long periods when the water in the streams disappeared.

The decade from 1864 on was extremely difficult. He was active during the construction of the St. George Temple and for several years devoted full time to getting out the lumber used in this building. His families resided at various places. As the children grew up, each family had more and more to shift for itself. The families were moved about so often that it became almost second nature for them. The third wife used to tell her children a yarn about their frequent moving: "Every time the chickens heard a wagon start moving, they would run out in the road of their own accord, lie on their backs with their feet straight in the air, waiting to have their legs tied."

The third wife, in fact, finally got to the point where she could no longer take it and left Spaulding. He gave her one-fourth of his property and she and her children were on their own from that time on. There was no divorce though Spaulding offered to give her one.

Yet through his own efforts and with the help of his families Spaulding finally accumulated a great deal of property. He writes in his journal:

From my early manhood I have been a hard worker, and inasmuch as I was called into that country with my four families, I was required to devote most of my time to public service without pay, so that it was quite difficult to accumulate much means after supporting my wives and children. It was a hard country in which to make a living. I raised twenty-seven children and made an effort to provide for them as best I could. I have never felt [a desire] to complain over my lot. I am thankful to the Lord for his manifold blessings to me and mine.

In contrast, however, to the Henry Spaulding story, we have that of Douglas Moody who became increasingly well-to-do though he was also highly mobile during certain periods of his life.

Moody was born in England in 1821. In 1843, a year after his marriage, he and his wife were converted to Mormonism and migrated to Nauvoo. Moody was a hard-working and energetic man and though he had expended all his savings on his trip to America, he went to work at once to recoup his finances. He helped get the Saints out of Illinois in 1845, later served with the Mormon battalion in the Mexican War, and ended up his service in California.

In 1850 he returned to England where he married a second wife and brought her to Salt Lake within a year or two. By this time he had sufficient capital to buy good teams, wagons and other equipment, 100 head of cattle including several blooded Durhams, and the first threshing machine in Utah. He built himself a fine house in Salt Lake and in the fall of 1852 he took still another wife. Later that year he moved his families to the Jordan and began rather large ranching operations there. Within a year he bought another farm and engaged in other enterprises and moved back to Salt Lake. There he set up a butcher shop and went into other enterprises. He married again in 1854 and by this time had acquired a large number of city lots in Salt Lake which in 1855 he sold to Brigham Young who advised him to go to Tooele to settle. The year after that he took still another wife and shortly thereafter was called by the Church to settle in Carson Valley, Nevada; but this colonization project was not very successful and Moody was recalled about a year later.

The year 1859 found him engaged in a profitable trading business between Utah and Montana, in addition to managing farms and a retail store. He bought more farm land and continued to expand his operations. In 1862 he was made

Bishop of Farmington which led him to buy more city lots and construct additional dwellings for his growing family. As his sons were growing up by that time he put them in charge of a large fruit farm. In this same year he married his sixth wife. The year following he purchased one of the first reapers to be used in Utah and also planted, so his diary says, the first alfalfa in the territory.

In 1864 his third wife died of cancer but within four months he had taken still another wife. His business was expanding in all directions but he was not satisfied; he got into politics and served several terms in the territorial legislature.

In the late 1860's he first began to experiment with dry farming, a type of agriculture which met with much disapproval from those who had become convinced that only irrigated farming would pay in that arid region. Prosperity continued and his family grew. When he was nearly 50 years of age he took his eighth wife. By that time he had become a director of the Utah Central Railroad and had begun to operate a sawmill.

All during these years he continued to make money, but in 1880 he was forced to go on the Underground much against his pride. Finally, he accepted a call to settle in Arizona where it was thought the federal pressure on the polygamists would be less severe. He became president of the St. Joseph Stake in 1883. In Arizona he acquired farms, grist mills, and entered other businesses. In the late 1880's he was one among several who explored the possibilities of setting up a refuge for the Saints in Mexico.

While he had always looked forward to returning to Farmington to retire, he did not go there until he was 77 years of age, and he died a few months after his arrival in his old home.

Although only 15 per cent of our families were rated under Class 4—moderately unsuccessful—a reading of their records shows that rather than helping, polygamy seems to have hindered a good many families. Conditions were difficult at best in settling a semiarid region and for some the economic demands were rather overwhelming. From the story of Jerome Sweet it is apparent that one wife and family were about all he could manage. He made a try or two at farming in San Pete before he finally found a more satisfactory place at Pond Town near Payson. Throughout his life Sweet supplemented his meager income by playing the violin for community dances. He also tried his hand with a sawmill in one of the nearby canyons. Later, when his finances permitted, he served on a mission. Being a zealous Saint and believing with his wife in the divinity of plural marriage, he migrated in 1900 to Mexico so as to take another wife.

Two years later he took a third spouse. Life in the Mormon Mexican colonies was difficult at best and Sweet had a hard time of it. Altogether his three wives bore him 25 children. When he, with the other Saints, were forced out of the state of Chihuahua by the Revolution, he lost what property he had acquired. From that time on he had increasing difficulties and his families had to shift for themselves. An informant who knew the situation well put the whole matter briefly thus: "Without polygamy, Brother Sweet would have been, no doubt, in comfortable circumstances today. He is a man who knows nothing but hard work and faith in the Church—truly a gentleman of the old school."

Following our rating referred to above, only three families out of 118 on which we have data on the economic situation, fall in Class 5—very unsuccessful. Brief note may be made of these.

Jacob Voss with two wives suffered "continual poverty" through his lifetime. He was described by an informant as a "rolling stone"; he resided in nine or ten widely separated sections of the Mormon country in the years between 1850 and 1890. He tried his hand at various jobs, including sheep raising, freighting, and farming. At none was he much of a success. In fact, the support of the families fell heavily on the wives. His first wife was an expert weaver and her earnings were almost always more than his. He must have recognized this, for one of his children by his second wife, after complaining of the father's ineptitude, said, "He bought a nice loom for Aunt Eliza though." The second wife in time built up a small business selling eggs, butter, and cheese. Whatever the two women were able to make they always generously shared with each other. Voss always tried to be impartial in the support of his two households but he was a poor manager and was known by his family and friends as rather shiftless, irresponsible, and at times even erratic.

Occasionally a polygamist was characterized, as was Andrew Terry, as "a lazy, no account man." He worked only as he felt like it and smoked and drank at times—in short, he was not a good Mormon.

Whether the total population of polygamists would show the same proportions of families in our economic categories is unknown; but if the records on which this book are based are at all typical—and I believe that they are fairly so—the data tend to confirm the assumption that on the whole plural marriages were confined to men of better-than-average economic status.

While the major occupation of the father as chief breadwinner usually made up the largest fraction of income, his supplementary jobs added to the total budget as did the contributory earnings of the wives and the older children. While about two-thirds of our records show that the chief resource was agriculture, nearly every family among the professionals, proprietary, and the skilled or unskilled workmen had plots of farmland and/or gardens and orchards from which they added to their living. The more prosperous farm families were practically economically self-sufficient. They sold their surplus for cash or tithing script with which to purchase goods and services they could not themselves furnish.

As for the wives, the chief income came either from gardens, orchards, chickens, and milch cows, or from the use of special skills, such as weaving, dressmaking, tailoring, hatmaking, school teaching, clerical work, or telegraphy. From our records it seems that gardening was more a common means of supplementation than the application of special skills. As for the contribution of the children, it was usually in the form of additional labor force, though in a few instances sons worked for wages from which source the family got some funds. In a few families the management of farms or other enterprises fell entirely upon the women folk as in the example of Albert Jones cited below. In line with widespread custom the sale of any surplus from gardens, chickens, or milch cows which were under the wife's care, was considered her own. Sometimes, however, a husband's earnings were so meager that any profit from gardens, eggs, milk and the like had to be turned in to the family budget.

Obviously, however, operations differed in terms of whether the polygamous families were housed in a single abode or in separate homes. In the former gardens, chickens, and cows might be managed cooperatively by the wives, or there might be a work division of some sort.

The family operation of the Andrew Anderson family was different. There were four or five wives all domiciled in a large house on a farm devoted to dairying and a nursery. The garden was managed cooperatively and provided things for the whole household. Potatoes, cabbages, beets, parsnips, and celery were common crops. The wives made butter and cheese, and candles from tallow taken whenever a "beef critter" was slaughtered. A daughter said, "We made molasses from beets, but it was a dark ugly color. Molasses made from parsnips was best; it was light and sweet and was an especial treat (*sic*)."

The demand for tailors, seamstresses, milliners, and related occupations was such that any women who had skills with needle and thread could always earn extra money. And where the birth rate was as high as it was in pioneer regions, midwives were in demand. Also after the coming of the telegraph there was considerable demand for women who acquired skill in telegraphy.

Sometimes a wife was given capital and full managerial responsibility to operate various enterprises. A striking illustration is that of the Albert Jones ménage. Jones and his wife were converts who arrived in Utah in 1864. During his first decade there he married two other women. Almost from the outset he was a successful farmer, trader, and freighter. At first he had a common storehouse and doled out supplies to his families as they needed them. When he had accumulated considerable property, he hit on the novel plan of giving each

wife certain capital—land, houses, or money—and then have
them set up their own enterprises. His first wife was established in a hotel venture which did very well. The second
wife, whose six children were all girls, was given a large farm
and she had some difficulty in managing it at times. The third
wife he left in town in her own house and she depended on the
earnings of her sons for her support.

Jones drew upon his sons for his labor supply but all the
boys were paid good wages. From time to time he might supply his wives with additional capital or occasionally give some
little direct help financially for current expenses. But, in general, he left to each wife and household the details of management while he devoted himself to his freighting, trading,
running a stage coach line, a threshing business, and other
ventures. The effect was to put each wife and family on their
mettle and a genuine competition developed among the three
families.

The money economy, as we know it, in which income is derived from money paid as wages, rent, interest, or dividends
had relatively little place in the Mormon system of self-
sufficiency. Aside from a few instances of accumulation of
considerable capital, most of our families operated with small
funds in the form of cash and tithing script. Hence, when we
examine the facts as to family expenditures, rather than
sources of income, we find a variety of practices as to manner
of spending and controlling incomes. In general the patriarchal prerogatives obtained, though with considerable variation due to number and dispersion of the plural households
and level of financial resources. It is clear, too, that the
methods of controlling and dispensing income were often
linked up with inter-wife and inter-family rivalry or cooperation. The psychological aspects of these topics will be
treated later.

Most husbands apparently tried to follow the counsel to
be fair and equal in the treatment of their various families.
A few of our records report the husband's trying to maintain
this in practice by buying identical items for each wife:

furnishings, and clothes, foodstuffs, and so forth. Joseph F. Smith, who prided himself on his complete fairness, followed this practice. As one of his daughters reports:

> Father bought alike for his wives and his children. If he gave one a black dress, he gave them [each] a black silk dress, and they were made alike. Mother and Aunt Julina, who were sisters, would fit the dresses on each other, and they would help each other sew. When father gave one a cameo, he gave all. They were great big ones and the only difference was that the names were on the back. He always put the names and dates on everything. We lived by dates in our family. Once I went to a funeral and I saw three of father's wives sitting there in their black silk dresses he bought and with their cameos, as big as a hand, and I thought I would go into hysterics.

Practices as to dispensing supplies or funds varied with the type of household arrangement and with economic condition, and in terms of the attitudes and values of the husband and his wives. Benjamin Wolfe was a big and successful farmer-owner. His second wife, sister to the first, reports:

> We always had cash money . . . We never went in for charge accounts; we paid cash for everything. Our husband never gave us an allowance . . . He wanted to be boss in money matters. But any time we wanted money we got it . . .
> Brother Wolfe bought good stuff, clothes, shoes, and so on. For years he kept the best horses in the community and when automobiles came in, he bought good cars . . .
> He tried to put everything in his homes to make the work lighter. But he never did anything for me that he didn't do for her [his other wife] . . .

Some men, while they did buy identical things for each wife, kept a tight rein on expenditures. Others left more to the decision of the wives. Some men, like Heber Thomas, tried to operate his households on the "United Order" basis and any money earned by any members was supposed to go into the common fund. Purchases were made with money or script largely in terms of the particular need. There was little purchasing outside because there was little cash.

Thomas' son, John, who had two wives, was apparently much more emotionally identified with his role as head of the household than was his father. His earnings were never very ample from his varied occupations such as merchant, rancher, elementary teacher, and others. His wives had to contribute a good deal to keep their families going. One of them was a good seamstress. But John would never listen to any suggestion of a system of allowances. The economic life centered in him and the wives had to ask for every item they needed. He tried to be fair in his treatment, but the second wife sometimes felt that the first wife's children were getting more than their share. Here economic hardship doubtless became a symbol of some mild conflict.

Regular allowances were provided in some families, though this was likely to occur where there was a good or better money income. Amasa Lang, who was a farmer and public official, gave his second family a regular allowance. This was partly due to the fact that the second wife was living under an assumed name in a different town so as to avoid coming to the knowledge of the federal officers. Henry Zeller, whose story as a successful jeweler has been told above, gave each of his wives a definite allowance: $50.00 each per month. In addition such staples as flour, sugar and coal were bought in bulk and given out as required. Spencer Neil, who had a successful blacksmith shop, maintained two absolutely independent households. Each wife was given a definite allowance each week on which she was supposed to manage. His income from blacksmithing was supplemented from a farm. Mathew Hale, another blacksmith, also used an allowance system. He, too, was a successful farmer.

The amounts of allowances varied with economic position; also they were not always completely equitable. The second wife of Isaac Lambert who had to live on the Underground for some years got only $10.00 a month. This was supplemented by her own efforts. The first wife was an invalid and Lambert who had but a modest salary for his work in the Logan Temple had a hard time of it.

The system of charge accounts, like that of allowances, meant a capacity to operate within a money economy. Daniel Lawrence, though none too successful financially, permitted his wives to have charge accounts at the Z.C.M.I.—a church-controlled cooperative merchandising enterprise. As Bishop he had charge of considerable tithes and the Church permitted him a small percentage for handling the funds and goods which came in as tithing. He had three wives, each operating an independent household, with gardens, chickens, cows, and the usual domestic assets. Groceries and clothes were the principal items which had to be purchased commercially. At one time he owned considerable land but gave much of it away to poverty-stricken converts in order to help them get a start. Many of the top officials in the Church, because of their salaries and their investments, were able to provide allowances and/or charge accounts for their wives.

It is difficult to generalize about such varied household economics as this chapter has revealed. Four elements in the situation may be noted in summary of basic factors to be taken into account.

First of all the Mormon family, whether monogamous or plural in character, followed the Mormon pioneer pattern of self-sufficiency. Then, secondly, our polygamous families revealed clearly a concentration of occupation and income in the higher socio-economic brackets as measured in terms of conditions in the Far West in the second half of the 19th century. In the third place, plural families provided a larger labor force and thus contributed to more rapid settlement and a faster accumulation of wealth. However, polygamists were not universally successful in their economic ventures. Fourth, the patriarchal pattern, so deeply imbedded in Mormonism, was adapted and extended in the plural family operations. Yet the spatial relations—separate houses and dispersion of families in different localities—as well as familial management problems made for certain feminine independence both in earning and spending.

Finally, the social and psychological implications of the

plural marriage system begin to emerge in discussing their economic arrangements. Earning and spending habits are related to attitudes and values, to struggles for status and control, and to jealousy and envy which often lie beneath the surface. We shall examine some of these features of polygamy in the next three chapters.

*When he went, I let him go. And, when he came back, I treated him decent and just like he hadn't been gone.*—Comment of a first wife regarding her husband's rotation system among his wives.

 8 THE RELATIONS OF THE
SPOUSES IN PLURAL FAMILIES

THE HABITS and ideas which developed around the plural family derived from monogamy. But, obviously, the customary relations of the spouses and the children were altered by the introduction of a second wife. Then, later on, if she had children of her own—as she usually did—there would be other changes in inter-personal relations. These usually involved, if not separate houses, at least separate living quarters for each wife and her children. Moreover, there would be new obligations of the husband and father as to support, discipline of children, and division of time with the wives. The changes sometimes induced frustrations on the part of the wives leading to envy, jealousy, and conflict. The husband, too, had his personal problems in trying to be fair, to keep harmony among his households, and to avoid potential pressures from the first wife, or from a possible favorite wife, or from combinations of wives who might through cooperation secure together that which they could not get singly. Many wives in polygamy found that "in union there is strength" just as some husbands found that one way to keep the upper hand was to "divide and conquer."

In the present chapter we shall first present the ideal norm of the roles which the family members were supposed to play and then, against the background of the expected relations, we shall discuss certain of the day-by-day contacts of the husband and his wives.

The husband's role as a partner in procreation and as the chief wage earner carried over directly from monogamy. However, there were no formal norms as to the amount of time a man should spend with a given wife nor was there, beyond the broad assumptions of equal treatment to all, any official code as to the division of income. In keeping with the Mormon theology, of course, the husband and father was lord and master in his household. This patriarchal function found expression not only in ordinary daily discipline and authority but in his role as spiritual head and guide for all members of his family. Upon him fell the major responsibility for the moral-religious training of his children though the wives were supposed not only to carry out his instructions in these matters, but to aid him generally in fulfilling the obligations of parenthood. Family instructions included prayer, Bible reading, explanations of the gospel, and insistence on strict adherence to the moral rules of the Church including the Word of Wisdom—a document which forbade the use of tea, coffee, tobacco and alcoholic beverages.

The Mormon wife's primary role was that of childbearer. Brigham Young, in a sermon in 1861, laid down the ideal and more or less official view on this matter in these words:

I am almost daily sealing young girls to men of age and experience. Love your duties, sisters. Are you sealed to a good man? Yes; to a man of God . . . Sisters, do you wish to make yourselves happy? Then what is your duty? It is for you to bear children, in the name of the Lord, that are full of faith and the power of God, —to receive, conceive, bear, and bring forth in the name of Israel's God, that you may have the honor of being the mothers of great and good men—of kings, princes, and potentates that shall live on the earth and govern and control the nations. Do you look forward to that? Or are you tormenting yourselves by thinking that your husbands do not love you? I would not care whether they loved a particle or not; but I would cry out, like one of old, in the joy of my heart, "I have got a man from the Lord!" "Hallelujah! I am a mother—I have borne an image of God!"

The wife had definite responsibilities in the rearing of her children. To quote Brigham again: "Let the mothers commence to teach their children while in their laps, there do you teach them to love the Lord, and keep his commandments . . ." And again, "The duty of the mother is to watch over her children and give them their early education, for impressions received in infancy are lasting . . ."

The role of the housewife followed the puritanical, pioneer vein. Wives were supposed to be thrifty, hard-working, "to keep their houses, furniture, and beds pure and clean," to be good cooks, and above all to be orderly, neat, and systematic. "Have a place for everything and everything in its place," was Brigham's advice.

The wife was also to be a helpmeet and companion to her husband. While they had but a secondary place in the Kingdom of God, nonetheless their role was important. The scriptural statement that "man is not without the woman, neither is the woman without the man in the Lord" was frequently quoted. As Brigham idealized it:

It is the calling of the wife and mother to know what to do with everything that is brought into the house, laboring to make her home desirable to her husband and children, making herself an Eve in the midst of a little paradise of her own creating, securing the husband's love and confidence, and tying her offspring to her, with a love that is stronger than death, for an everlasting inheritance.

The ideal apparently did not call for any striking evidences of romantic love. As we saw in Chapter 6, courtship was to be brief and to the point. Certainly there was no overt recognition of the place of sex as a means of personal pleasure; rather the puritanic view was commonly accepted that sex was to be used only for procreative ends. Brigham bluntly warned: "If the plurality of wives is to pander to the low passions of men and women, the sooner it is abolished the better." Yet the romantic spirit could not be gainsaid, even in polygamy, and we shall see some evidences of its effects in our later discussion; but so far as any ideal or official view on the matter, it was largely negative.

The role of children will be discussed in some detail in Chapter 12. At this point we note that there were some ideals or norms which applied equally to all children, whether born in polygamy or monogamy. First of all, children are considered the earthly bearers of eternal spirits, and as part of the divine plan. In this sense, Mormonism was a child-centered culture. As Heber C. Kimball once put it in a strong sermon against birth control: "Suffice it to say I have a good many wives and lots of young mustards that are growing . . . The Lord told me to get them. 'What for?' To raise up young Mormons, not to have women to commit whoredoms with, to gratify the lusts of the flesh, but to raise up children."

Under such a belief the more children a man had, the higher his status both in this world and in the world to come. Women held a similar belief. As we shall see in many plural families there was not infrequently considerable rivalry among the wives as to frequency of childbirth.

Finally, under the ideal norm children were considered definite economic assets. In fact, as the earlier strong faith in the Principle was dissipated and especially at present, when official Mormondom wishes to forget polygamy in keeping with its desire for respectability, a frequent justification for the system is that it helped populate and exploit a frontier.

Age differences between husband and wives and among the wives varied considerably in Mormon polygamy. It has been generally assumed that great discrepancy in ages made for difficulties in plural households. Trouble probably did not arise from the age differences between husbands and the newer wives but rather when there were striking discrepancies in the ages of the wives. Obviously age differences alone did not make for harmony or disharmony in plural families; they were but one contributing factor. The economic condition of the husband, the spatial arrangement of homes, the temperamental differences among wives, and any number of other elements were important.

In the case of the much-married Howard Keith, the taking of a new bride as wife number six caused some irritation among the other women. The new wife became known as a "tattle-tale" in her efforts to establish a place for herself but, on the whole, this family made a fair adjustment. Perhaps the

…ary saint bargaining for wives. From Maria Ward, *The Mormon Wife,* 1873.

…risis of life—entering into polygamy. From Fanny Stenhouse, *An English-…an in Utah,* 1880.

The old wife jealous of the new (at top of picture). The old wife washing the new wife's feet (at bottom of picture). From W. Jarman, *U.S.A. Uncle Sam's Abscess*, 1884.

*bove:* Polygamy in low life—the poor man's family. From Fanny Stenhouse,
*An Englishwoman in Utah,* 1880.

*ow:* Polygamy in high life—the Prophet's mansion. From Fanny Stenhouse,
*An Englishwoman in Utah,* 1880.

*Above:* Eleven P.M. in a Mormon household, retiring for the night. F[rom] W. Jarman, *U.S.A. Uncle Sam's Abscess,* 1884.

*Below:* The last (wife) shall be first, and the first, last. From W. Jarman, *U.[S.A.] Uncle Sam's Abscess,* 1884.

# U.S.A.

### UNCLE SAM'S ABSCESS,

OR

# HELL UPON EARTH

FOR

## U.S.

#### UNCLE SAM.

BY

## W. JARMAN, ESQ., K.G.L., T.C.K.,

*Knight of the Grand Legion of North America,*

WHO SUFFERED TWELVE YEARS IN

### THE MORMON HELL ON EARTH,

AS ONE OF THE

"VIRGINS WITHOUT GUILE,"

AND

#### A PRIEST AFTER THE ORDER OF MELCHIZEDEK:

WHERE

### POLYGAMY, INCEST, AND MURDER

ARE TAUGHT AND PRACTISED AS RELIGION UNDER THE

#### "ALL SEEING EYE,"

AND THE SIGN

### "HOLINESS UNTO THE LORD."

*Copyright secured in both Hemispheres.*

EXETER: ENGLAND, 1884.

PRINTED AT H. LEDUC'S STEAM PRINTING WORKS, EXETER, ENGLAND.

*U.S.A. Uncle Sam's Abscess* title page.

rs. Maxfield murdered before her husband and children for revealing endowent secrets. From W. Jarman, *U.S.A. Uncle Sam's Abscess,* 1884.

Arrest of the bashful, but muchly married, Brother Handy. From W. Jarma
*U.S.A. Uncle Sam's Abscess,* 1884.

## GOVERNOR BRIGHAM YOUNG AND HIS NEW TOY.

GOVERNOR BRIGHAM—I'm delighted with this new jack, sent by Brother Cannon [fro]m Washington. It jumps just as I want it to, and will amuse our "best society." I'll [kee]p well lubricated with Axtell grease. Indeed I never had a plaything it took so [much] grease to run my way.

From the *Salt Lake Tribune*, February 28, 1875.

FOOTNOTES TO AMERICAN HISTORY

An enterprising salesman interests Brigham Young in the first group-insura
policy. Reproduced by permission. Copyright, 1946, The New Yorker Magazi
Inc.

chief difficulty was economic since Keith never had much in the way of worldly goods and the various wives had to work hard to make a go of it.

Often the coming of a young bride as a plural wife made no trouble at all. Sometimes she was positively welcome. When he was 55 years of age, Daniel Lawrence took a plural wife of 18 years. The first wife had consented and the domestic arrangements worked out satisfactorily, each having her own home and being amply provided for.

The first wife of Isaac Lambert was bedridden for nearly 50 years though she bore him nine healthy children during this time. At 45 years Isaac took a second wife of only 17 years. She had been a domestic in the home. Though she was given a house of her own, she continued to help manage the first wife's household.

By present-day standards a bride of 17 or 18 years is considered rather unusual but under pioneer conditions there was nothing atypical about this. Occasionally, however, there were very striking divergences in age. One of the many wives of Judge A. H. Adamson, a prominent leader and father of Joseph, was only 14 years old at the time of her marriage. Also Apostle C. C. Rich took a bride of 14 years though he did not live with her until she was 18 years old. She played the role of one of his children after the marriage until her husband set her up in her own place when she came of age.

Next to the question as to how many wives a Mormon had, curious-minded, monogamous Christians were always inquisitive as to how a man divided up his days and especially his nights among them. In one of his sermons Brigham Young good-naturedly ridiculed the Gentiles for always secretly wishing to ask him: "How many wives have you, Mr. Young?" . . . or "I wonder whom he slept with last night." From his point of view this was not the kind of interest in Mormonism people should have.

. . . I would rather see them anxious to learn about the Gospel. Having wives is a secondary consideration; it is within the pale of duty, and consequently, it is all right. But to . . . save the chil-

dren of men, build up the kingdom of God, produce righteousness
in the midst of the people . . . to clear the world of wickedness
. . . and to usher in the reign of universal peace, is our business,
no matter how many wives a man has got . . .

Brigham's relative indifference to these matters did not
lessen the world's curiosity nor did it gainsay the fact that the
success or failure of plural marriages was particularly influenced by the division of time and attention among the wives.
Of the 50 family records, among our total, which give adequate information on the time division, in slightly more than
a quarter of the families the husband spent alternate days with
each wife, about the same proportion took them week-about,
and the same percentage were irregular, that is, had no fixed
schedule. The balance were scattered into two-day, three-day,
and fortnightly arrangements. A few fell into special groupings, such as, seasonal variations where the families were
widely scattered in the summertime but might be living in
the same village during the winter, or where a plural wife's
long absence on the Underground would require considerable
change in former regularities.

The use of the same dwelling for multiple families or the
location of separate houses adjacent to each other would make
for more frequent rotation than if the families were scattered
on widely separated farms or ranches. Illness in one family
might cause a schedule to be broken temporarily. A third wife
related of her husband: "Brother Vernon had no set time for
spending time with his wives. If he was needed, he was there.
Whenever there was sickness, he stayed at that home. Sometimes he had to be on the farm and sometimes in town." With
many men who had widely scattered business interests, it was
rather difficult to set up any regular rotation. As a daughter of
Hyrum Stratton put it, "Father just stayed where night overtook him. We learned to expect him when he showed up . . ."

So, too, psychological elements might enter in. Prolonged
coolness between a man and a particular wife might reduce
visiting. Or the dominance of the husband by a favorite wife
might induce irregularity of visits to the other women.

The division of time among the families gave rise to a variety of habits and rationalizations. Doubtless because of the cultural expectancies of monogamy, many husbands were anxious to give their wives as little occasion for envy, jealousy, recrimination, and sense of neglect as possible. Stephan Workman, who had three wives and who rotated at two-day intervals among them defended his time schedule by saying that he felt to go a whole week, "as some of the Brethren" did, was "too long a time to be absent from any one family." He believed that the families needed him more often than that.

Various daily habits grew up in an effort to be fair to all wives. Thus, George Reynolds, one of the leading officials of the Church, located his first two families in adjacent houses. Although he spent alternate weeks with each wife, he made it a daily practice to call on the other wife to "kiss her good morning as he was on his way to his office" and again, on his way home, in the evening, he would "stop in to kiss her good night." Later when he took a third wife, she was housed a mile and a half distant and such an arrangement was out of the question for her. Still later when he was under indictment by the federal courts, he and his plural wives went on the Underground which, of course, forced an abandonment of the former routine.

Other habits emerged. A daughter of Allen Tiffen recalled:

Father spent one week with each wife. When he got up in the morning, he made the fire, called the family and fed the cattle. Then he would go over to the other house, make their fires, call the family, and feed the livestock there. After that he would go back to the place where he was staying and have his breakfast. The wife where he stayed was supposed to wash and mend his clothes. But the first wife would often leave this for my mother to do.

Still other men used other devices to keep up the idea of complete equality of treatment. Frederick James, at the time he had three wives, housed each in a well-built attractive home of her own. He spent a week with each wife in turn and when he went out in public—to church, public dinners, dances, or other entertainment—he always took "the wife of that week" with him. The other wives were not permitted to sit next to

him if he appeared at church alone, or with the wife of the
week. They might sit nearby, however. When he took a pleasure drive in his large and roomy automobile, he took all the
wives along, but again the place of honor next to him in the
front seat was reserved for that wife with whom he was staying
at the time. If she were unable to go along, the place remained
vacant. When he bought presents for them, he always got three
but had them draw lots to see what they received. He permitted them to trade their gifts around later, if they wished;
he felt that his responsibility ended by this demonstration of
equalitarian treatment.

One rather common means of showing absolute equality
was to purchase similar or identical things for each wife and
especially to allot the same income or property to each. Illustrations of this were given in Chapter 7.

For the pious Christian the central cause of Mormon polygamy was the unrestrained lust of unredeemed men. A recurrent theme of the Gentile accounts was that of over-sexed
Elders seducing innocent young women into plural marriage.
From the official Mormon view these yarns were deliberate
lies concocted to mislead the world regarding one of God's
most sacred institutions. The truth seems to rest somewhere
between these extremes. In theory, the Mormons, like other
Christians, viewed sexual relations as a necessary evil for
purposes of procreation only. Polygamous unions were expected to resemble monogamy in this as in most other matters.

Yet the readjustment to the novel system of plurality must
have caused much conscious and unconscious conflict, not always fully assuaged by official approval and by individual conversion to the Principle. No doubt there was a great deal of
suppression of these inner conflicts the outlets of which appeared in various forms.

The fact that polygamy was so divergent from the long
Christian tradition is probably one reason why it was difficult
to get much intimate data on the topic of love, sexual attitudes,
and sexual habits. There was a strong resistance, in common
with their monogamous neighbors, to giving any information

about these matters. As a result our data are scanty and often of indirect sort.

From the limited sources, however, there is evidence that in many families there was deep and genuine love between a husband and his wives. In others there was equally frank admission that there was little or no affection.

With respect to the first group, a frequent question by persons reared under monogamy is: "How can a man love more than one wife?" One of Wilhelm Zeeman's daughters tells of her curiosity: "I used to ask father if it was possible for a man to love more than one woman. He always answered by asking me if a woman could love more than one child." This rationalization was not uncommon. While Zeeman had some difficulty with his first wife, largely due to temperamental incompatibility, his relations with his other three wives and the latter with each other were amiable. Two daughters of Mathew Hale, who had three wives, report their father to have been "very affectionate. When he wanted to 'love up' his wives, they had to stop whatever they were doing and be hugged and kissed." However, the father was careful never to show such affection for one wife in the presence of another. "He knew what the consequences might have been," they added. As his daughters grew up he used to hug and kiss them and hold them on his lap and ask them if their young men were kind to them.

A husband's responsiveness is much affected by a wife's attitudes and response. John Porter's first wife was rather matter-of-fact while number two was more expressive and it is clear that John's overt affection for the latter and her daughter were, in part, dependent on this fact. There are many other such instances. In fact, polygamy exposed somewhat analogous variations to those found in monogamy especially in contemporary cases where a divorced spouse, having been under considerable inhibition from a first partner, reveals in a subsequent marriage more expressiveness and congeniality.

In many families, of course, there was more restraint. One informant from the Kurt Sturm family—the husband was of German-Swiss background—says he did not recall much dem-

onstration of affection. His father "kissed his mother as husbands do," apparently in a perfunctory way. Even so, Sturm
was careful, as was Hale, not to show any affection for either
of his wives in public. So, too, there was a certain restraint
vis-à-vis the community. The likelihood of gossip that a man
favored one wife more than another might keep him from
showing affection in public.

In contrast are those families in which the plural wives
were greatly in love with their husbands but in anticipation
of romantic reciprocity were doomed to suffer considerable
disappointment. The second wife of J. W. Nystad tried to
identify herself with the first wife, as a device to make a go of
plural marriage. It was not too successful.

The first wife, Esther, gave her consent to her husband's
taking a second wife. She thought it a privilege and would not
deny him his glory. The prospective bride, Rose, told Nystad
that she knew of the deep love between him and Esther. Of
the beginning of her life as a plural wife she says, "I went to
live with them and because everything Esther did was perfect
in his eyes, I tried to do everything as she did. I tried to keep
house, to cook like her, to *be* Esther. It was the biggest mistake
I ever made. I should have been myself."

The husband tried in every way to be just to the new wife
and both women made a genuine effort to live harmoniously.
"Until the day of her death, Esther would not allow him to
favor her. She was all for me and so I was the same with her.
We were the shining example in the entire colonies of a happy
polygamous family." And while the husband tried to avoid
admitting it, he was well aware that he could not love his second wife as he did his first. Rose continues: [She] "did everything she could to make me happy. I think she told him ways
in which he slighted me, for when he did he came to beg my
pardon. As time went on such slights grew less, but he never
came to fully love me—to love me as he did her. I don't think
it possible for a man to love two women at once, not in ways
that are the same."

Gradually Rose came to realize that her efforts at identification were not successful and she insisted on Nystad building

her a house of her own. He wanted to keep the two women together and Esther backed him up. In the end Rose won out in this debate. When she was settled in a place of her own, she remarks, "I began to be myself and I was happier. I came, as he grew to love the children, to have a place in his heart . . . He did all a man could do to be good and just."

The courtship and marriage of the dashing Edmund Barclay and Daisy Yates whom he took as his second wife were related in Chapter 6. It will be recalled that because of the need for secrecy, Barclay somewhat unceremoniously dropped her at her parents' home while he returned to his first original spouse. After describing her meager meal alone—her family had dined hours before—she continues her story:

> Yet I was sure I had taken the right step and recall feeling confident that something really worth-while had been accomplished. Finally I broke the silence.
> "The experience wasn't half bad."
> "You haven't half begun yet," father replied.
> I realized the truthfulness of his remark two weeks later, when Mr. Barclay failed to keep his appointment to come to see me. I was so disappointed that it seemed to me that the very angels wept with me.

Barclay had various church duties as well as wide business interests and the romantic daydreams of Daisy were due for a shattering experience. Her story continues:

> I craved some assurance of his love after placing "my all" on the marriage altar. When he treated so lightly his appointment to come to see me two weeks after our marriage, is there any wonder that I was brokenhearted. A week later he came but my enthusiasm was gone . . . In time I learned to steel myself against disappointment of his failure to come. However, I learned to love my husband dearly, and I wondered later if anyone was a more ardent lover than myself.
> I was active, at this time, in church work. To everyone I was known as Miss Yates. Not even my closest friends had a suspicion that I was married. Mr. Barclay's visits were not often, as his attentions were now on another young lady, Margaret Dewey. Too, he was getting ready to leave for Europe to fill a mission as soon as the school year ended.

So, within six months of my wedding day, he had married again and was off to Europe. I had not seen the third wife, but I did wonder wherein I lacked that so soon he would take another wife. Then I remembered the doctrine of the trinity as taught by the Church—that if one wanted to attain the very pinnacle of glory in the next world there must be, at least three wives. I reminded myself that that may have been the reason my own father had married the third time, and so I was reconciled.

An instance of romantic love for a man who already had a wife, followed by a matter-of-fact remarriage, is that of Mary Jane Ruge. She married her uncle, John Zimmerman, although a neighbor, Jacob Ruge, had been courting her, too. Of her uncle-husband, she wrote: "None of the young men appealed to me so much as did my uncle . . . He was much older than I, was married to my father's sister, and had four children. But he was kind and joyous and everyone liked him . . . His wife, Aunt Lena, helped me make my wedding outfit . . . I was then nineteen years old."

Zimmerman took his prospective bride to Salt Lake, by team, to be married in the Endowment House. In 10 days they were back in Santa Clara. The day following, Zimmerman was killed by a runaway team in the presence of his two wives and the children of the first wife. Mary Jane continues her story:

. . . That was a sad finish to my honeymoon, and I went back home to live with my father and mother. In as much as they were getting old and times were hard, they thought it best that I should marry again. Soon Jacob Ruge came courting me. I told him I would be his wife, though my heart was not in the answer.

Just four months after my first trip to be married, I was journeying again to Salt Lake . . . But this trip seemed different. I cried when I left home, and cried often all the way up and back. Jacob was kind to me and did everything he could to comfort and please me. But somehow I could not get over caring for my first husband.

After three years of uncertainty and heartache, Mary Jane finally became reconciled to her situation and lived to raise a splendid and competent family. She once told one of her granddaughters that at no time did she love Jacob Ruge, yet she bore him seven children. She thought this was a "woman's duty."

A daughter of Alexander Todd says that though all six of his wives "profoundly respected" their husband, except for his first wife, he had no "particular" love. "I don't think those polygamists knew what romantic love means," was her final comment.

There are a good many examples among our records of men taking plural wives out of a sense of duty and, moreover, where the second family remained throughout more or less an appendage to the first and dominant one. On the other hand, there are contrasting families where the first wife was relatively indifferent to demonstrations of love and where a plural wife came to fulfill a man's needs for overt affection. Thus the first wife of Henry Roper, though she bore him 15 children, was an undemonstrative person. The second wife, who was brought into the family after 14 years of monogamy and who was a quiet and lonely young woman, provided Henry an emotional outlet he had not had before. The first wife retrospectively remarked:

> Guess I had enough love to do for him as he ought to be done by. I didn't care for all that hugging and kissing stuff. I used to do everything for him. I knitted socks, made his shirts, and got his shoes for him. What more did a man need?
> I learned in Relief Society to set my mind on the children and my home . . . I never let any feeling enter into it. You just can't be always thinking about what they are doing and watching for him all the time in polygamy. It wouldn't work.

The third wife of Maxwell Kirby was reminiscing about plural marriage:

> . . . It hasn't been an easy life, but I wouldn't wish to undo it, though I don't want my children to live in polygamy. Young people today couldn't live in polygamy. We were raised to regard it as sacred and to live in it for the good of all. We weren't familiar with the opposite sex then as they are now. Men and women were taught that lust must not enter into polygamous relations and our husbands regarded us highly.

In theory, the sexual habits of the Mormons, either in monogamy or polygamy, were supposed to be confined to purposes of procreation only. In actuality, however, these habits would be influenced by time schedules among the families, by frequency of pregnancies, by adherence to the strict code of procreative aim only, and by more hedonistic and personal interests.

Again there was no clear official view on the whole matter, though sometimes some rather frank talk was given the Saints by their leaders. Jonathan Baker reports in his journal about a Stake conference at which

President McAllister spoke of some men bringing on premature decay and an early death by the too frequent use of sexual intercourse, showed the folly of a man entailing disease and suffering on his posterity through not governing himself during the time his wife was bearing children or nursing them. He spoke of the saying, "He that looks upon a woman to lust after her, has already committed adultery in his heart." Showed that a man could look upon a woman that was comely and beautiful and admire her without sin and could desire her and if not engaged to another, with proper consent, could woo her and win her and in all holiness in the authority of the Holy Priesthood marry her. But if he looked on her with a desire in his heart to have unlawful connexion (sic) with her and would do so if he could get the chance, was guilty before the Lord of adultery, for he had planned and conceived the sin in his heart and only lacked the opportunity of carrying it out.

He dwelt upon the beauties of plural marriage as ordained of God for the purpose of raising up a pure seed unto God, and the sanctifying influence of his Holy ordinance of eternal marriage and that men should, like men of Zion, govern and restrain their passions and school their spirits and bring every passion and desire unto the will of God, and so promote longevity to himself and posterity.

He spoke of the baneful effects of the sin of masturbation . . . bringing in some instances of chronic and lifelong debility and insanity . . . He also dwelt on the propriety of gratifying women during pregnancy where it was right and consistent that they might not entail on their offspring unholy desires and appetites that would render them miserable and unhappy all their lives.

With slight variation, McAllister's views were representative of the time. Some of the brethren would have condemned intercourse at any time after a wife was known to be pregnant. Hans Olson once proudly told his Bishop that as soon as he discovered that one of his wives "was in a family way," he didn't "have any more to do with her until her child was born." This was a common taboo but we have no information as to how strictly it was obeyed. The usual advice was to be considerate of a wife's condition—counsel vague and general enough to permit wide latitude in practice. McAllister's remarks also show the common conceptions of the time about prenatal influence and the serious effects of masturbation.

Apparently a common practice—in both monogamy and polygamy—was to "let nature take its course." Usually if and when intercourse with a pregnant wife was too obviously unpleasant the man would defer to her wishes. That not all men were so considerate, however, is revealed in a complaint that came before the High Council in Jaurez Stake. The second wife of Russell Bradley, himself a member of the High Council, brought charges against him that in his marital relations "he was more the animal than man," that he would want to live with his wife a day or so before her child was born. It is said that the first wife also felt strongly about such abuses, but that she hushed the matter up and "did not want the second wife to talk about it." She talked, however, and the case was brought to trial, though the charges were not entered in the official record. Such instances were probably rare. Certainly most wives would take the view of the first wife and keep silent on such things. But the second wife had become bitter from her whole experience and in later years had nothing to do with her husband.

There are some legends about sexual jealousy which reveal some of the difficulties in marital relations. A first wife wanted her husband to marry in polygamy so as to get the glory but she did not want him to marry for any other reason. He wed two other women. During a period of long economic struggle all three wives slept in a wagon box—the first wife in an upper bunk, the other two below. When the first wife thought they needed a child, she permitted the husband to go down, but she made him return again and spend the rest of the night with her.

A daughter of Hyrum Stratton said she knew "one first wife who was all right about the second marriage until she could hear her husband's boots drop on the floor in the second wife's room. You know," she said, "it's those little things that must have hurt."

Sometimes a woman developed a considerable aversion to intercourse, as is shown in the story of the third wife of Ezra Austin. He paid her somewhat infrequent visits and gave her rather inadequate financial support. She had become indifferent to him and on one occasion when he came to her home unexpectedly, her younger sister was staying with her. The latter left to return to her own home as the Austins had but one bed. The third wife was much upset by this. She knew that Ezra would expect sexual favors and this could have been prevented if her sister had remained the night.

Sometimes the frigid and unwelcome attitude of a wife was perhaps due more to her own observations and reactions to sex in her earlier years than to anything which happened in polygamy. This was evidently so with Howard Wilson's third wife. She was a Bach in whose family much open conflict had centered around sexual jealousy. Out of this experience as she said, "I grew up with a horror of sex in marriage," and part of her own subsequent difficulty with Wilson may be traced to this.

There is little doubt that sexual interest played a part in the marriage of some older men to younger women. We recall that Hyrum Stratton, who had altogether four wives, always showed a lot of interest in the early phases of his marriages only later to turn his attentions to another prospective bride. Similar stories are told of Merlin York who seems to have fallen in love easily and frequently. He had four wives but never more than three at any one time. On one occasion he expressed in his journal his regret at having passed up a chance to court a young girl for fear of offending his first wife.

On the 7 July, 1857, Hannah [his first wife] gave birth to our first child, Annabelle. Lydia Hopkins acted as midwife. We hired a girl, Jane Spencer, daughter of a particular friend. We fell in love and both her parents desired me to take her for a wife. I was afraid to hurt Hannah and let the opportunity pass. From that time on for twenty years I mourned and repented and feared I would not get another chance.

Birth control has always been officially tabooed among the Mormons, and to this day the ecclesiastical hierarchy inveighs against it. This view, of course, is in line with the thesis that a couple should bring as many spirits into this world as possible. Brigham Young put the matter in these words: ". . . There are multitudes of pure and holy spirits waiting to take tabernacles, now what is your duty? It is the duty of every righteous man and woman to prepare tabernacles for all the spirits they can . . ." And a few years later he said:

To check the increase of our race has its advocates among the influential and powerful circles in our nation and in other nations. Infanticide is very prevalent in our nation. It is a crime that comes within the purview of the law, and is therefore not so boldly practiced as is the other equally great crime, which no doubt, to a great extent, prevents the necessity of infanticide. The unnatural style of living, the extensive use of narcotics, the attempts to destroy and dry up the fountains of life, are fast destroying the American element of the nation . . .

These views were accepted by most strong churchmen, Protestant and Catholic, at the time. Joseph Adamson's daughter relates that whenever her father would suspect that a neighbor was practicing birth control, he would say: "Don't you notice that he can't look you straight in the eye lately?"; and "His memory seems to be failing these last few months, doesn't it?" She adds: "Father, of course, never used any such techniques."

A common belief then, as now, was that a woman was not likely to become pregnant so long as she continued to nurse her baby. There is evidence that this was not unusual among Mormon families.

Large families, however, were definitely the rule and while

some women may have tried to keep from getting pregnant too soon after childbirth, any extensive period of time between births—say anything beyond a two-year span—was likely to lead to shaking of heads and considerable gossip. In fact, the general high moral value put upon having children led in many plural families to a friendly race among the wives to see who could have the most children. To surpass another wife in such matters enhanced one's prestige, rhetorically called "adding jewels to one's crown of glory in the hereafter." We shall discuss the race for babies in the next chapter.

Under pioneer life the conditions surrounding childbirth were difficult. Babies came often and there was a high infant mortality. This applied equally to monogamy and polygamy. From our present-day standpoint many of these people had a somewhat casual attitude toward the actualities. A family just took it for granted that it would be bound to lose, by death, a certain number of children and the loss was rationalized as "God's will."

The usual practice at child birth was to have a midwife, if one were available; and the wife was expected to go back to work about 10 days following the delivery. The second wife of Richard Yancey recalled: "My, it was terrible on women then. I never had a doctor in my life and most of the time no midwife with my children. It was just take whom I could get. And, hot, oh my! The summers were terrible, flies, no screens, dirt and no one to help. It's no wonder my children died." She had 13 children in all, five of whom died before they were three years of age. This was not at all unusual.

*Polygamy isn't a thing you go into once
and have it over; it's something that lasts
every day of your life and you have it always to contend with.*—A plural wife's
advice to a second wife, just wed.

# 9 PLURAL WIVES IN COMPETITION AND CONFLICT

STRUGGLE IS a law of life. Yet what we strive for varies with what we value most and with the amount of effort we are willing to use to get what we desire. Sometimes we fight it out with others. In other instances, especially if the reward may be shared, we may get others to help us in our struggles. In this chapter we will look at certain aspects of competition and conflict among the wives in Mormon plural families.

What is the psychology of human struggle? Struggle is an aspect of man's relations to his fellows everywhere. Sometimes it takes a rather mild form which we call competition. In other cases it is more violent and we call this conflict. The roots of struggle lie in the scarcity of rewards, material or otherwise. Sometimes these consist of economic wealth. At other times people strive for status or prestige. Both aims were held in high regard by the Mormons. Some aspects of the struggle for wealth were discussed in Chapter 7. Other features of the same struggle will be treated in Chapter 13 which deals with the inheritance of property. So far as the striving for property and status concerned plural families, there were few if any predetermined rules of the game among the Mormons. Their system did not last long enough to develop any standards.

Status or social prestige must be regarded as a scarce item in human society. Otherwise high social position would be meaningless. A person in high position is one who has a certain power that others do not have. Moreover, such power cannot at the same time be retained and yet shared with others.

So far as the Mormon husband or father was concerned under the patriarchal system, he was supposed to treat all members of his family justly and equally, both as to property and status. While some men tried to do so, there are many instances where they failed or did not even try. From the standpoint of the wives, sometimes such efforts to be equal in all matters stimulated rather than abated competition or conflict.

The efforts to obtain and to hold top position was a matter of grave concern in many plural families. Yet there were instances in which the plural wives definitely accepted a role and status inferior to those of the first wife. Top status, of course, is something that cannot be shared. Here we shall see how people struggled to secure it and how, once acquired, they fought to hold it.

Our records reveal four basic devices that a woman could use in striving to get status and to keep it. The first of these concerned household economy, including such things as the use of spending money, maintaining a good and profitable garden, and efficient conduct of the household. A second device was to secure external evidence of affection and attention from the husband. Under monogamy, of course, any outside threats to these demonstrations is normally met by jealousy. As we know, attempts to use this device under polygamy often had disastrous results. The third way was success in childbearing and child-rearing. Finally, there was the matter of the larger public regard for the wife in the community. Sometimes a woman used her place in the family as a means to support her position outside. In other instances she was able to affect her status in the family because of her activity in the community.

There were a variety of factors which would influence the inter-wife contacts and hence affect either competition or cooperation. First, there were those plural families set up many years after the firm establishment of a monogamous family. Only in a few instances—in our sample at least—did a man start off by marrying two or more wives on the same day. In the second place, polygamous households were often established soon after the first marriage. This meant that before a monogamous family could get its roots down, arrangements had to be made to accommodate more than one family. In the third place, difficulties frequently arose in a plural family if two wives had been established a long time and their relations had been reasonably good only to be disturbed by the husband introducing a third or more wives. This broke into an already accommodated routine and often made for trouble.

An example of an already established plural family being upset by the later appearance of a still further plural wife, is clear in the Stephan Workman story. Stephan, who had already been successful in business, at the age of 30 in 1889 married for the first time. The bride came from a prominent Mormon family and symbolized for Workman, the son of humble parentage, a definite upward step in status. The next year he took a second wife, Joan, who came from another prominent family known for their literary interests and abilities. This further enhanced his social position. While there were some mild difficulties between the two wives in the early period of the plural households in St. George, on the whole they became rather well adjusted to each other. Because of federal prosecution Workman moved to Mexico with both families. He prospered there and became one of the leaders in the refugee colony.

In 1900, at the age of 41, he married the attractive and dashing Rose Lee, 16 years old. She turned out to be a demanding person and caused a lot of trouble in an otherwise well-run plural establishment. Not only did the children of the first and second wives resent her but the community at large tended to disapprove of her attitudes.

Status likewise had its place in the conduct of the spouses at local entertainments, at church meetings, and other public gatherings. Sometimes, as with the George L. James family, the wife at whose home the husband stayed, was for that period given preference in dancing or in sitting with him in church.

Circumstances tended to determine the form of such activities. During the later phases of polygamy, when federal raids were common, men were more cautious about being seen in public with their plural wives. Such a situation, of course, tended to give the first and legal wife a definite advantage in control and prestige.

There were many little symbolisms of status. Hans Olson always spoke of his "week-about boarding with his wives," as if this were a somewhat temporary and secondary arrangement. He considered "home" to be his first wife's place. Forms of address sometimes revealed differences of status. While the most common practice was to designate another wife by the term "aunt," in some families a different appellation was given the first wife. Adam Winthrop has always called his first wife "Sister Winthrop" as did the other wives and their children. The plural wives were called "aunt." "Sister Winthrop" was definitely head wife, and on her death wife number two took over. Still later, when the second died, this status fell upon the third wife. In the Joseph Adamson family, the first wife was addressed as "Mrs. Adamson." This was a sharp departure from Mormon custom, however, since to this day the usual term is "Sister" not "Mrs." when addressing a married woman-member of the Church.

The factors which made for differentials in status and for assumption of dominance were thus both psychological and situational. First, there was the conscious and unconscious acceptance of the first wife as head wife because she was legally the only wife. These people with their strong Christian mores regarding monogamy could not so easily get rid of their fundamental values and habits. Linked to this continuance of the monogamous ideal was the lurking sense of guilt which many must have had even though they fully accepted the Principle. Then, too, there were differences in age, intelligence, and community status among the wives which, in turn, influenced a wife's position in the hierarchy of a given polygamous family.

The most striking deviations from the equalitarian theory are found in those instances where the plural wife was regarded as in a servant status, as a dependent, or even as a guest. We have already noted a number of examples of a servant becoming a plural wife and continuing thereafter in an inferior role.

Closely akin to the master-servant relation between wives is that which psychologically resembles a mother-daughter relationship. Our records reveal a few such cases.

Hyrum Stratton's third wife, whom he married when he was 50 years old, was a shy girl of 20 years. She was taken to the home of the first wife. A daughter of the latter said of her: "She was so young and quiet and timid that she was treated like one of the children. She had her own room, but during the day she joined in the housework exactly as one of the daughters . . ."

The family background of the wives sometimes served as a cue to the assumption of status superiority. Myra, the first wife of Henry Roper, took a dominant position toward the second wife, Elizabeth. She did not want Roper to enter polygamy and justified her opposition on the ground that her own family, the Grants, were socially much above that of the second wife. During the first two years of the plural arrangement Elizabeth lived in the same house with Myra. The two wives maintained a common kitchen and a common dining table but had their separate bedrooms. This program was changed by the first wife taking matters into her own hands. While Henry and Elizabeth were at a church conference in Salt Lake City, the first wife took all of Elizabeth's clothing, furniture, and other belongings out of the house and put them in another place three blocks away.

When the first wife was asked about this matter of moving the second wife elsewhere, she remarked:

I gave her a little heating stove, and took down the bedstead and sent all that with her clothes and bedding up to the other house. I never saw the house; I think it had one room. An old woman lived there and she died. I don't know what time they got back from the conference. I went to bed early. I guess they had to find the place and set up the bedstead before they could go to sleep. My husband never said a word about this, neither did Elizabeth.

The first wife kept close watch on her husband and his new wife. For example, Myra was in the habit of getting up early and doing her household chores promptly. If she found that Roper and the second wife were still lying abed, she would go over and throw rocks on the roof to awaken them and get them up.

On one occasion Roper gave Elizabeth a rather fine heating stove. This vexed Myra a great deal. All she had was an old-fashioned potbellied base burner. While the second wife was out of her house, Myra sent one of her boys over to dismantle and bring the new stove to her. Roper grumbled a good deal at this rather highhanded action but did nothing to rectify it. As the first wife put it, "He couldn't do anything because I had the stove set up and a fire in it before he knew anything about it."

Under monogamy a wife was supposed to be a good house-keeper, to handle well matters of sewing and laundering, and to manage a garden. The successful performance of these duties not only contributed to the household economy but was supposed to evidence good management which, in turn, would please the husband and father. While there was a good deal of cooperation in these matters among plural families, there was also much competition. Wives in plural households came to feel that if they were good housekeepers, kept profitable gardens and managed other home problems well, they would secure added attention from their husbands and thus acquire a certain amount of status. In the monogamous marriage system this is the kind of competition which goes on among neighbors. What we have in Mormon polygamy is simply the borrowing from the pattern of neighborhood rivalry applied to the polygamous family. If a woman could not meet the competition with another wife in any other way, in these matters she might be able to show up the first or other wife.

The Kurt Sturm family is a neat illustration of such competition which was met successfully by the first wife. Mabel, the second wife, had a definitely lower status. This inferiority was emphasized by the energy and effectiveness with which Clara, the first wife, handled her affairs. Thinking to follow suit and to get some of the privilege that came from good housekeeping Mabel tried to meet the competition on equal terms. A son of the second wife, remarked, "Mother has felt many times that she'd been better off physically if the pace had not been so hard. She didn't want to appear to be a shirker, so she really worked harder than she was able to work. Not that they were imposing on her though." The informant continues, "Father obviously could do nothing about the situation. Auntie was pretty much in charge, and mother wouldn't complain, so father perhaps hardly suspected that anything was wrong." As Mabel found herself facing defeat, she rationalized her failure in terms of differences in the physical capacity for work.

Moreover, Clara continued throughout to be the prominent wife insofar as the outside status was concerned. Mabel always resented the fact that she could never be seen in public with her husband. Her son puts the matter in approximately the following words, "If there was ever the question of father appearing in public with a wife, he showed up with his first wife; my mother always came later with her children. There seems to have been a specific understanding to this effect among the three of them, in order to effect a satisfactory adjustment in the marriage." The son recalled further that as a boy of twelve he could never understand why he always went with his mother while his Aunt Clara went with his father.

The Jacob Ruge family is a good example of a well-established monogamous household, followed by a plural ménage including three new wives. Yet throughout the entire time, the first wife never lost her top status. She felt socially much superior to the other wives, especially to wife number two, whom she regarded as of peasant stock. Jacob was born in Switzerland in 1838 and in 1860 was converted to Mormonism. Shortly thereafter he migrated to Utah. Ruge had some capital with which to begin life on the frontier. A month after his arrival in September 1861 Ruge was sent to the Dixie colony by Brigham Young. There Jacob prospered and accumulated a great deal of property.

Just before settling in the colony Jacob married his Swiss friend, Francine Richet. An informant reports:

> The first wife was a very proud and jealous woman. She considered herself superior to the town and thought she was doing her husband a great favor to live in Kanab. She had come from a well-to-do Swiss family. Her family did not like Utah and had gone on to California. She was not particularly religious and did

not approve of polygamy. She considered that the best was hers and that the other wives would have to take what she discarded. Jacob tried at all times to be just to his wives but wife number one remained the dominent character and he was inclined to give in to her.

The obvious evidence of top status was to live in the largest and finest house the economy permitted. Closely associated with this material symbol of headship was the practice of considering one particular home as the husband's headquarters. In the Porter family the headquarters of the father was definitely at the home of the first wife. The second wife occasionally tried to get him to build a barn at her house or set out an orchard or a garden, but he always refused saying he wanted everything at one place. Besides he did not want to use any more of the farm land for garden and orchard. The first wife had a good garden and the second had to go there to get produce. However, Porter treated his families with reasonable equality as to funds. He was well-to-do and there was no problem of economic hardship.

The complex of factors which entered into the dominance of a first wife is described by Daisy Yates Barclay in writing about her father's domestic organization. The two families lived on opposite sides of the same street. The center of control was in the first wife's home. Although Yates was well-to-do, his

idea of living polygamy was to give the first wife first consideration. Whenever we went in the carriage, it waited for us at the first home, and when we returned, it was unloaded there. It was assumed to be the proper thing for Aunt Harriet [the first wife] to be always in the front seat with father, and mother in the back. This was the case whether we went on the train to conference in Salt Lake or drove in the carriage. It was frequently a surprise for us to see how quickly Aunt Harriet got ready to accompany father on every occasion. "See, there she goes," my mother would remark as father would drive off with Aunt Harriet. "She never lets him go without her."

The first wife had charge of dispensing household supplies, a control which the husband fully approved, for "if mother began a complaint when my father was in our house, about the meager supply of provisions which were doled out by Aunt Harriet, he walked out. He was following President Young's idea of having distribution of supplies from the first home."

All the entertaining of leading Mormon officials was done at the first wife's place. The right or privilege of entertaining the visiting dignitaries of the Church was an important symbol of superior status. It was, and is, a common practice for the general authorities to pay periodic visits to the various localities, preaching and supervising the spiritual and material welfare of the Saints. For a wife to provide meals and lodging for an Apostle or other high official of the Church gave her a sense of social success and clear evidence of top prestige among the wives. It was usually the first wife who had this prerogative. Occasionally, as with George Mackay after his removal to Mexico, since his sixth wife had the largest house the visiting officials were entertained there. Otherwise, in this family, the first wife was considered definitely the head.

Such mundane matters as doing a husband's laundry, and mending, and keeping his Sunday clothes often became indicators of difference in status. While many men followed the practice of Abram March, who, on a week-about schedule, kept his clothes at both places and had his laundry and mending done "when and where needed," others made quite a point of having these things attended to at the headquarters home. A daughter of Joseph Adamson by his second wife remarked on the high significance of doing the laundry: "I have seen my mother in tears because father didn't bring his laundry for mother to do. She was so afraid she hadn't done it right last time."

In plural households, in particular, to gain the attention and affection of one's husband was the focal point of all competitive activities of the various wives. Yet it was the reward least easy to share with others. Certainly the expectation of the wives with regard to their role in marriage contemplated exclusive possession of the husband. At least this was the monogamous ideal on which they had been nurtured. If they could not carry this ideal fully over into polygamy how small a compromise on this exclusiveness was a person able to manage? Clearly a great many different devices were attempted. Sometimes there was a good deal of outright aggression and open hostility; in other situations the rivalry was more mild and suppressed. In some instances devices such as neurotic invalidism appeared.

There was no way of predicting how much aggression would be shown or what particular methods might be used in the given families. Such things as the wives' attitudes toward each other, their relative status in the family, and the particular situation at the time all have to be taken into account. Certainly the emotional tone of the whole interaction was important and it was on these matters that frequently the informants were the least willing to talk or else did not know.

The intellectual adherence to polygamy as a Principle, of course, was much easier than was the emotional acceptance of it in practice. This fact is most evident in the inter-wife relationships. A good example is the Winslow story.

Herbert Winslow had three wives. He married all of them within a period of four years. This family was highly organized and operated economically more or less as a unit.

Herbert was thoroughly converted to polygamy and during his courting frankly told his prospective wife, Mary, that he intended to practice the Principle. Not long after he set up his first household he began courting Norah and Rebecca. In fact, he brought both girls to his home and obtained the first wife's consent. Mary tells her story in these words:

After he had married the other women, every night he would come to see me, and every morning also, to see that I was all right. [This may have reflected a sense of guilt on the part of Winslow.] Well I felt pretty bad the first few months. He had been good to me though and I thought a bit and it helped me to feel better. He told me that he believed in the Principle and didn't want me to feel bad, so I tried not to feel bad about it.

Norah was a good girl, and she couldn't even look at him if she thought I wouldn't like it. But Rebecca, this one just gloried when she could get out alone with him. There's all the difference in the world between those two women.

Three of us lived in the same house for a year. I said I couldn't stand it, I was going to lose my mind. I couldn't stand to see him fondle over the others. Oh, he had to show them a little affection . . . No, he never slighted me, but I just couldn't stand it. I'm not the jealous kind, though.

By "jealous" Mary apparently meant a woman who caused difficulties. Later when separate households were set up, the three wives made a fairly reasonable adjustment although the third wife was regarded by the other two as inclined to be a little troublesome at times.

While Asa Kendall's first wife, Ellen, had at first encouraged his marriage to the attractive Catherine Baker, it later developed that Ellen was an exceedingly jealous woman. Although she thought she could live the Principle, she found that the strain was "too much for her." She had difficulty in competing with a much younger and more beautiful woman.

Some examples may be mentioned. Kendall used to take part in the local dramatics. On one occasion when he kissed a woman in the play, Ellen, who was in the audience, fainted dead away. On another occasion there was a funeral in Paris of a close relative of the second wife and the husband insisted on going with the second wife and left Ellen in Logan. She was highly resentful of this and decided to do something about it. She took a spell and announced that she was dying, and when the husband arrived home, Ellen had raised such a fuss that the neighbors had come in to see what the matter was.

One informant goes on to say, "One other time when she created such a disturbance and was being carried off to bed, father turned the bed down and said, 'Well, when I turned Catherine's bed down it always smelled like a laundry.' This implication that Ellen was not as good a housekeeper as the other wife set her off into another temper tantrum."

A daughter of the second wife, who was raised by the first one after her mother's death, remarked:

Ellen won't even let father put a gravestone at Catherine's grave. We children had put up cement curbing and once when father was in the cemetery after a funeral I got him to come over and see the grave. He wanted to wait and get Ellen to go with

him, but I knew right away she would not come. We tried to get
father to agree to put up a stone but he said that it was taken care
of in his will. He wouldn't dare to make Ellen more jealous by
putting a stone at Catherine's grave.

They wouldn't even let mother be buried where they were
going to be buried, in a six thousand dollar vault in Logan. Mother
is buried in Paris alone.

The difficulty in practicing the Principle, although people
strongly believed in it, is also clear in the John Emmet family,
where the motivation for plurality in this instance was a general community expectancy and more particularly the example set John by his ex-missionary friends. The second wife
soon became troublesome. The first wife, Eileen, is speaking:

Bertha was two years older than I was and she was determined to
have things. She told me once, not long after they were married,
that I had had John alone for five years and that she would have
the same number of years with him. I told her that she didn't
have an understanding of polygamy. I made up my mind that I
was going to do everything to be good and just. But Bertha hasn't
always tried to do her part.

One source of irritation on the part of the first wife was that
the second was always secretive about what she did. While
John tried to be fair to both wives, Bertha was forever trying
to get something for herself without letting the first wife know
about it. As a neighbor who knew these women well remarked:

The first wife was deeply in love with her husband and affection
would do marvels for her, while the second wife, while liking affection, wants more substantial demonstration.

The husband makes every effort not only to be fair and just
about material things but also he's very careful to keep the confidences which he gets from one wife or the other. He is fully aware
of the difficulty with Bertha, as illustrated when his first wife
occasionally gets upset and expresses the same fact to him. He's
very likely to say, "Don't you get upon your ear. I've got all I can
stand with Bertha, and I can't have you cross or complaining."

Sometimes the strong feelings lasted throughout a life time.
The attitude of the first wife of Roger Knight toward his sec-

ond one reveal intense emotional response. Some years after Jane—the first wife—and Roger had set up housekeeping, they hired a girl, Annie Strong, as a domestic.

Later Roger took Annie as a second wife although Jane had not approved this match. The years only served to make the arrangement increasingly more difficult for her although she bore Roger five additional children after he had taken a plural wife. Jane always maintained that she loved Roger deeply but any mention of the second wife turned her to pure gall. A friend of the family put it thus:

I think I have never seen more unadulterated hatred than she shows when speaking of this woman. She tells how she herself had refused to visit her husband on his death bed though her children told her that he had been calling for her all day and begged her to go to him. She boasts that "I haven't spoken to Annie for thirty years and don't expect to speak to her for thirty more if I live that long."

The attitude of the second wife and her family was not unfavorable. While the second wife did not particularly care to discuss polygamy, on some prodding she had this to say:

I was just eighteen when I got married and I didn't think much of anything about it.

My granddaughter said to me just the other day, "Grandma, I don't see how you could love a man that already had a wife." I told her she didn't know, that it was just as easy to love a man with a wife as without one. You see we accepted polygamy so much then. We'd heard it preached all our lives and we believed it was the true Principle. It was preached and preached and preached at us. When they weren't preaching that, they preached marriage.

In contrast to open signs of jealousy, rivalrous feelings were sometimes covered over. Earl Vernon's first two wives were twin sisters who were married to him at the same ceremony. A few years later he married Louisa Newton, a half-sister of the first wives. Of the adjustment, the third wife had this to say:

We got along pretty well, about as well as most families do in monogamy, I guess. We couldn't help being jealous, any of us, but

we learned to control it. When difficulties would come up, I'd
think, "Now what would I do if I were placed in that situation,"
and I could see that they had acted for the best. Sometimes the
treatment of the children would bother me, but I would always try
to put myself in the other one's place. One of my sisters was as
fair and just and good to me as anyone could be.

Apparently she did not feel quite so good about the other
half-sister. This story brings out nicely the fact that her point
of reference and her rationalization rest on her basic belief in
monogamy.

In discussing their interrelationships, Maud, the second
wife of Frank Alexander, remarked: "Oh, yes, there were
jealousies. Occasionally brought on by oversights and slight-
ings on the part of the husband. But this was the Lord testing
their strength in the Principle. If a girl felt jealousies or resentment rising within her, she must suppress them."

Philip Bach had the following to say about the situation in
his family in these words:

As soon as I got back from my mission I married my second wife.
No, my first wife did not like the idea at first. She was upset, but
she got used to it. If my second wife had been as good as my first
wife and as considerate, I would have had much more domestic
happiness than I had . . . My second wife was selfish and jealous
and wanted too much. I would take her aside and talk to her and
tell her how things must be, but she kept on being jealous and I
was sometimes disgusted with her. I got two houses because a man
is happier and the women happier in separate homes.

One device which apparently was not at all uncommon is
nicely described by Mrs. William Emmet, the second wife.
One of the problems in that family, though not serious, was
that the first wife was always "honeying around" her husband
seeking favors. We have a number of instances of attempts to
use a certain amount of sexual charm as a device to intrigue
the husband's attention. In some quarters such devices were
regarded as unfair; they smacked of romantic love which was
not in official favor.

There is a poser here: Plural families were supposed to
provide outlets for love just as were monogamous ones, and

yet when overt affection was used as a device to secure the attention of a husband, its expression was likely to get one in trouble. In other societies where plural marriages have long been established, there is seldom any such thing as romantic love. In such societies many of the difficulties of inter-personal jealousy probably do not arise, but in Mormon polygamy the attempts to carry over from monogamy the devices of overt affection and jealousy usually led to conflict.

On occasion a wife might throw a temper tantrum as a way to secure her own way. Benjamin Wolfe married two sisters, Gertrude and Christine. The second marriage, however, had followed 15 years after the first. Unlike some of our families where marrying sisters made for harmony, in this instance both women showed strong feelings of jealousy. The second wife was constantly distressed that she could not wrest the complete dominance from Gertrude. A daughter of the first wife tells this story:

Once a large group of relatives came up from Logan for the week-end to the farm where Christine lived. Among them were other sisters of Christine and Gertrude. Both wives were present, and on Sunday afternoon when everybody was ready to leave for home, father decided to go back to town with Gertrude to spend Sunday night. This, of course, meant that Christine would have to remain on the farm alone. This precipitated an explosion. The second wife made a terrific scene as we were about to depart. She could be heard screaming a long time after the party left. Father was about to turn back to stay with Christine when two of her own sisters intervened saying, "Don't you dare give in to her." This shamed him into going on into town with mother. They explained that their sister had always used such means to get her own way. During all this time mother sat very quietly and said nothing.

The use of invalidism as a power device by neurotics is well known, ranging all the way from the conversion symptoms to the outright malingering. The following account illustrates how this device was used in a plural family. Although Lucile, the first wife of Isaac Lambert, bore him nine healthy children, she was bedfast during the last 40 years of her life.

Lucile had her first baby on the plains and was carried in the baggage wagon. In crossing the Platte River at one point the wagon overturned, injuring her and the baby. The infant died soon after and was buried beside the road. This accident made a slight cripple out of Lucile and the next 40 years "[she] lay continuously on her right side . . ."

The husband was much concerned about her. She was afraid of electricity, she was afraid of fresh air and she played on her husband's sympathies. As one informant puts it, "Father gave mother a great deal of attention."

Although there may have been some physical basis for Lucile's condition, all the evidence points to the conclusion that her invalidism was motivated psychologically. She had a definite shock at the loss of her baby and she never made any effort to get up from her bed. The family life revolved around her. In fact, the second wife, who had entered the household as a servant, remained to marry the husband a few years later with Lucile's full consent. There are other examples of the use of prolonged illness as a method of getting attention, but none quite so extended in time as this one was.

We can write a footnote to the case of Lucile. When Lambert became very ill about a year before he died, Lucile did get out of bed. She told her children that she wanted to get up and help her husband. Apparently this was a dramatic occasion and Lucile got all the attention she could out of the incident. Having once got up she was able to get up again and for a time she was up and around the neighborhood and even went to see Clara, the second wife, several times. In about six months, however, when she was reaching to wind up a clock, she again "dislocated her spine" and went back to bed. She died soon after this.

If the Principle called for providing spirits in heaven with physical bodies on earth, it was only natural that a good deal of stress should be put upon childbearing. As a phase of the struggle for attention and status there was often a real race for babies. To have a large family was rhetorically called "Adding jewels to one's crown of glory in the hereafter."

The first wife of Henry Roper had this to say about the second wife:

Elizabeth was pretty vexed because her children came so slowly. It was two years after she was married before she had her first child, and five years between each of her other children . . . She had plenty of opportunity to have children, but she just didn't. No, she didn't do anything to keep from having them. She felt bad about not having more . . . She certainly had as much chance to have them as I had. My children came along about every two years. I had 15 fine children, eight boys and seven girls. Three of the girls died, but I raised all the boys.

In this family the competition was mild and not very conscious. It was much the same with the wives of John Thomas, the first of whom had 10 children, the second nine. The two women were half-sisters and, on the whole, got on well; they always helped each other at the time of childbirth, and apparently got on to a certain routine for a considerable number of the children came at about the same time—usually not more than two months apart.

In the John Porter family, in contrast, a real struggle for superiority began. When John married the second time, he told his new wife that he wanted to have 25 children. There is some evidence that he had the idea of emulating his sister who was a wife of John Vance and who at that time had already had eight children. She later had seven more. At any rate there began a kind of competitive childbearing by the two Porter wives. The second wife said: "Mary [the first wife] got nine months ahead of me once, but by the time our last few children were born, we were about together again."

Apparently Porter had intercourse whenever he wished and took the view that his wives should bear children as often as they could without injuring their health. A few months after Porter left for a mission, the two wives bore him a girl each: the first wife on the last day of January 1886, the second about five weeks later, on March 7th. The two wives always viewed these two girls as twins.

The Morgan family was much the same. The first wife had 10 children, the second, nine. A daughter of the second wife

explained: "Their children were born about the same time
and when the first wife had a child, I can remember my
brothers and sisters saying that 'Mother will be having one
soon.' "

As in any family, monogamous or plural, it was only natural that as the children grew up they should be closely identified with their mothers. Sometimes a first or a plural wife who
felt abused would appeal directly to her children for sympathy
by relating to them the hardships of marriage. Frequently
these problems were not apparent when the children were
younger but as they grew older they became aware of them.
For example, a son of the second wife in the Kurt Sturm
family has this to say:

All these difficulties became apparent when I was grown. The
parents never let their differences become obvious to the children.
I never knew until I was a mature man and talked with mother
that there were any differences between the wives and that there
was an agreement that she was not to accompany father in public.
Father seems to have had a little of the old world attitude towards
marriage which resulted in his presenting his first wife as his
official wife. Mother felt that it was her first cross to bear.

In many families the child must have experienced a combination of uncertainty about polygamy, including a diminu-
tion of loyalty to other members of the family, and a strong
identification with his own mother. After all, his status rose
or fell with hers and at times his hostility to his half-brothers
and half-sisters might be quite evident. On occasion the children actually promoted conflict in the interest of their mother.
This was apparently what happened in the Winslow family
where the older children of the first wife, feeling that they
were not always justly treated by the father, would cause quite
an uproar. As a matter of fact, this family, though welded together along economic lines under the firm hand of the father,
had a reputation of being a rather boisterous and quarrelsome
lot at times.

While the handling of children in the plural families,
especially in the early years, could draw on the patterns of be-

havior developed under monogamy, there certainly was no standard by which a man could know how to settle difficulties among his wives. In most cases the husband made a genuine effort to solve the problem. One instance is recorded where the husband insisted on one wife cooking a dinner for both wives and all sitting down together and trying to solve a problem that had arisen during the day.

Grant Ball told his wives that when they were in trouble with each other they should use a system of making sacred covenants with each other to avoid difficulties in the future. In addition, he suggested prayer as a device to make for harmony. Many men tried to avoid a head-on intrusion into the difficulties of their wives. Often they would rather withdraw or avoid the issue.

In closing we need only repeat that while there is plenty of evidence of difficulties in polygamous families, it should by no means be assumed that conflict was the inevitable aspect of plural family life. The real problem was that the difficulties could not be easily settled because the culture did not provide any standardized ways for handling these conflicts. For the most part, these people genuinely tried to live according to the Principle, but when they applied the rules of the game borrowed from monogamy, such as not controlling feelings of jealousy, they got into real trouble. Perhaps Brigham Young and others were wise when they pooh-poohed romantic love as a factor in polygamous situations. Certainly there is some evidence in a few of our records that where the wives did not seem to be particularly fond of their husbands in the romantic sense, they were able to make a better adjustment than were those who were romantically involved with their spouses. Yet the next chapter will show that there was a great deal of cooperation, not only among the wives but among the children as well.

*This co-operative movement is only a
stepping stone to what is called the Order
of Enoch, but which in reality is the Order
of Heaven.*—Brigham Young.

# 10 COOPERATION
## AMONG WIVES

EARLY IN their history the Mormon leaders became interested
in initiating some form of religious communism. Various
Utopian programs were in the air and Joseph Smith did not
long delay thinking up the Order of Enoch. This was a scheme
of property stewardship—the Bishops would hold the community property for the Saints. The production and distribution of wealth would be organized among cooperative lines.
Against the background of agitation and actual attempts at
founding the United Order—as it was later called—it might
be thought that cooperative attitudes and habits would be
found in Mormon families generally.

Two forces militated against the practical success of the
Order of Enoch. First, it was tried out in a society that was
deeply imbued with the spirit of competitive capitalism and
private enterprise. It was hard to make a scheme of economic
equality work when there was great pressure for every man
to make a stake for himself. The other factor which made
democratic cooperation difficult in practice was the growing
power of what became, especially under Brigham Young, the
closely knit, ecclesiastical system in Mormonism itself. The
doctrine of divine revelation, coupled as it was with authoritarian gradation of power, did not easily integrate with the
supposed egalitarianism of the United Order. Thus while
families were urged to pattern their own organization after
the Order of Enoch, cooperation usually ended at the kinship
limits of the family. While the family was often a solid economic unit, its cooperative enterprises were directed inward.
Beyond the boundaries of the family competition was the
practice.

The cooperative pattern was present and had some effect on the Mormon plural households. Though the individualistic, competitive attitude came to dominate the Mormons—in common with most Americans—a high degree of coordination and solidarity in Church and community alike showed that certain aspects of cooperation have been present all along.

In the previous chapter we saw that plural families often fell into strong inter-personal and inter-family opposition. But there is ample evidence that this was only one side of the story. In many families direct efforts were made to bring about cooperation, not only among the members of a given wife's family but between or among the families.

A number of interrelated factors determine whether a member of a family would pursue his goal by cooperation or by competition. These factors include (a) the assumed scarcity of the value sought; (b) whether once gained it could be shared; (c) the attitudes of the rivals toward each other, based on their previous experiences; (d) the behavior prescribed by the culture for that particular situation; (e) the sense of one's security or insecurity; and (f) the controlling influence of the father as the dominant leader of the family. The role of the husband and father has already been indicated. In particular, his powers to give or withhold rewards were important factors in the prestige and status of the wife and of her children.

In discussing the cooperative behavior of the wives, we shall follow somewhat the same approach as in the previous chapter. We shall pay attention to the motivation of such behavior, the values or rewards expected to be secured by cooperation, and something of the techniques employed. Here as elsewhere, the plural wife depended chiefly upon the pattern of monogamy to guide her in her relations to her husband. The wife in a monogamous family was supposed to carry on certain duties such as good housekeeping and proper care of the children, and provide the satisfaction of her husband's desires, both biological and economic, and act as his affectionate companion. In terms of her own expectancy and that of the community, her status resulted as she fulfilled this role successfully. If in a plural family a wife could satisfy these demands and still maintain her ego security and status, then cooperative relationships could be built up. But, as we saw in the previous chapter, threats from the other wives often resulted not in cooperation but in competition and/or conflict. While the general sanctions of plurality of wives made clear that cooperation ought to occur, such threats frequently resulted in quite other behavior. The reconciliation of the exclusive aspects of monogamous role taking, such as being a mate, bearing children, housekeeping, child care, and supplying the husband's various wants with expected nonexclusive elements in polygamy of sharing the husband, his property, and his children presented problems for which few had any answers.

The reconciliation of these divergent ends and means might take place outwardly and mechanically, yet with certain costs of compulsion from outside and certain heartaches from within. Our records bear ample evidence of the fact that wives might cooperate in some matters and yet fall into conflicting relations with regard to others, such as the husband's affections. As a matter of fact, this situation made for a certain split in the personality.

We have defined cooperation as the striving together of individuals for a goal or reward which may be and usually is shared. Certainly under the idealized principle of plurality, cooperation was possible. We noted in the John Vance story, for example, that it exemplified a community recognition of family life that approached the ideal. There were strains and stresses, but as among other prominent families, the strains were covered up so far as the outside world was concerned. The same thing was true of the Joseph F. Smith family. Our informants gave a much idealized picture of that family with the exception of one daughter who once referred to herself as deviant from the expected attitudes.

Most conscientious Saints made a real, deliberate attempt to live the Principle. This was true in the Calvin Williams family. He and his first wife were much in love and both were convinced that polygamy was a divine Principle. As the informants remark, their father did not marry again because he was in love with the second and third wives, but rather because he thought it was his duty. The first wife gave her consent and made up her mind she would live in the Principle. Moreover, both the second and third wives were depicted as being

. . . mature enough to know what they were doing. They were attractive young women and had plenty of beaux. In fact, they were both engaged to young men. Yet they decided they wanted to live in polygamy and they admired Father. He was a bright man and a kind man. They wanted him enough to marry him in polygamy. Father was a wise man. He chose well. All three of his wives had the same ideas. They wanted education and culture, and they wanted a peaceful home.

The informant did say that the second and third wives were somewhat more aggressive than the first wife, yet all three got along together. "They knew that they had to consider each other's rights. There is nothing in the world so good as polygamy to make people unselfish, once they have made up their minds that they will live it for the rest of their lives."

The informant further remarked that the father never made any show of affections to one wife in the presence of the other, nor was there any carrying of tales from one wife to the other. "They all wanted harmony and they were strong for loyalty and harmony in the home. They were all proud, proud of the fact that they could live together. Auntie [the first wife] believed that the family should be united and she did everything to make it possible."

While this is a somewhat idealized picture given many years after the events, it does show something of a real effort to make a success of the system. Surely such high expectations frequently helped to motivate people to live the Principle. On the other hand, as we have repeatedly remarked, temperamental differences among the wives made for problems of various kinds.

One of the important factors making for cooperation was that the status relationship among the wives be well structured and mutually agreed upon. Jealousy obviously exposes a lack of such consensus. In family after family where one wife— the first or other—was clearly recognized as dominant, we find excellent examples of cooperation. This was true of the Vance family where the first wife was always regarded as the head. So, too, it was true in the Winthrop family even though Helen, the third wife, later became the favored and dominant one.

At least in the earlier years of its plurality, the Keith families were reasonably cooperative. Soon after Keith married a second time, he built a better and more substantial place nearby for the first wife. The second wife continued to occupy the older one-room loghouse in which all had lived while the new house was being built. When Keith took a third wife, he moved her in with the second. These two women got along satisfactorily but neither forgot that the first wife had the highest status.

The third wife reports:

We had our first babies there and did all our work together. We worked shoulder-to-shoulder. We used to agree on what part of the work we would do. When we were doing the washing, sometimes she'd take the first tub and then I'd take the second tub and sometimes it was the other way around. We got along famously. [Later, this family had considerable difficulty with subsequent plural wives.]

In some of the larger plural families, two or more wives might be very close and work together in contrast to their relations to the other wives. The Strattons furnish an illustration. Stratton had four wives. The relationship between the first wife, who remained in many ways the dominant member, and the fourth was most intimate. For some time they lived together in the same house and shared their work. Even after they had separate homes, they were the closest of any of the wives to one another. On occasion these two wives would cooperate to get something from Stratton when they felt that to tackle him singly would lead to failure. One of

these women remarked: "He always said he had two to fight."
In spite of the 25-year difference between their ages, the fourth
wife, the informant in this case, said her attitude toward the
first wife was one of absolute equality. She never looked up to
her to make decisions yet their contacts were most friendly.

Procter's first two wives were sisters. They were the greatest
of friends and agreed on everything. Ten years later he married his third wife, Carrie. While the coming of the third wife
disrupted this family considerably, it apparently strength-
ened the comradeship of the first two wives. In fact, as years
went by, "They got so they didn't care what their husband
did." These two wives combined frequently against the third
wife.

Another illustration of an attempt to make polygamy work
in terms of a certain rational view of the process is that of
the Gilmore family. The second wife had this to say:

I married with an intense desire to make a go of it. I felt that
going in as I did, I should not assert myself over the other wives,
and that I should do the best I could to make a place for myself
in the household.

I felt that I was living the holy Principle and that I must conform my life to it. Polygamy makes people more tolerant, more
understanding, and more unselfish. It gives them more contact
with reality and a wider circle to love and do for . . . It's not an
easy way to live. We never fully conquer ourselves . . . It's not
jealousy so much, for I had made up my mind to that, but the constant pressure of adjusting yourself to another woman. Each
woman should be a queen in her own home, my mother always
said, and it is the natural way.

This is a good illustration of a recognition on the part of
a plural wife of some of the difficulties of trying to adapt polygamy to the monogamous theory of complete identification
with a one-wife role. The Joseph Carey, Jr., family was somewhat similar to this. Joseph courted two sisters. But the mother
would not consent to their marriage unless she herself were
also married to Joseph. To this he agreed. In fact, he married
the mother before he married the two daughters, thus making
the mother his legal wife. His first wife had died some time

before this. One of the sisters says, "We all lived together. We were very happy. We didn't have any trouble in polygamy. I had two girls and one boy and they all lived. My sister didn't have any, but she was just as fond of my children as if they had been her own, and they could scarcely tell the difference between them. She always liked to do the outdoor work and I would do the work inside."

We have already discussed the material on the economics of the plural households in Chapter 7. In this section we shall describe various cooperative patterns which developed in the plural households. Sometimes the mutual regard and co-operation emerged more or less spontaneously from initial friendly relations. Sometimes the cooperation and division of labor were deliberately planned and the operations laid out by some dominant member of the family. This latter might be the husband, but sometimes it was the head wife.

Oliver Owens had been married 11 years when he decided to take a plural wife. The second wife remarks, "When I married I was younger than the first wife and I tried to do the hardest part of the work, but we didn't have any division. We just worked till it was done. There wasn't ever very much money to divide, we shared alike. We both worked hard."

An example of a somewhat more organized household was that of the William Marsh families. The two wives lived in separate houses but on the same block. William's toolshed lay between the two houses. Each wife had her own corral and cows, her own chickens, but there was a common haystack. The two women worked together in good harmony. While there was occasionally some little strain in this family, on the whole the members cooperated very well. The second wife was a little more successful with her garden and chickens than was the first wife, and the latter was anxious to be equally good in all things. There was, in fact, a certain amount of friendly rivalry as well as cooperation.

In contrast to this somewhat spontaneous and natural evo-lution of cooperation and division of labor, let us look at a few instances where cooperative activities and division of

labor were highly organized and systematic. In her autobiography Belle Thompson has described how the arrangements worked out in their joint household. There were three
wives at that time. During the period of which she wrote there
was considerable official encouragement that family economy
—monogamous or plural—be organized along cooperative
lines as exemplified in the United Order. Mrs. Thompson
writes:

We had our work so systematized and so well ordered that we
could with ease do a great deal. One would for a period superin-
tend the cooking and kitchen work with the help of the girls, another would make beds and sweep, another combed and washed
all the children. At seven-thirty all would be ready to sit down to
breakfast. Wilma [the second wife] was always ready to go to her
sewing at eight or nine o'clock. She was also the best saleswoman
in the house. She generally did most of the buying, especially the
shoes. She was a good judge of leather. Auntie [the first wife] did
darning and repairing. I seldom patched anything; she did it all
for me. She never ironed the clothes; I did most of that. When
wash day came, all hands were employed except the one who was
then doing the cooking. On that day we liked the boiled pudding.
Noon saw our family wash on the line.

We usually bought cloth by the bolt and whoever needed most
was served first. In fact we had in our home an almost perfect
United Order. No one can tell the advantages of that system until
he has lived it. We enjoyed many privileges that single wifery
never knew. We did not often all go out together. One always
stayed home and took care of the children and the house. In that
way we generally came home with a correct idea of what was given
in the sermon.

Whenever one was indisposed she was not obliged to tie up her
head and keep serving about the house, but she could go to her
room and lie down knowing that her children and all her share
of the work would be attended to. No one was obliged to bend over
the washtub when she was in delicate health or condition. All
stepped into the breach and helped each other.

We acted as nurses for each other during confinement. We were
too poor to hire nurses. One suit or outfit for new babies and confinement did for us all, and when one piece wore out, it was supplied by another. For many years we lived thus, working together,

cooking over the same large stove with the same kettles, eating at the same long table without a word of unpleasantness or jar in our feelings portrayed. The children we bore while we lived together in that poor home loved each other more than those that came to us after the raid on polygamists came on and we were obliged to separate and flee in different directions.

Another illustration of a well-organized household was that of George Mackay. He had six wives. For 18 years they lived together in a large house especially built for them. Each wife had her own bedroom but there was a common kitchen and dining room. There was a living room which was used by the husband as his office. He also had his own bedroom. The duties of the wives were systematically organized by the husband. Some were assigned to the laundry or to cleaning the house; others to the sewing room, or the kitchen. Each one's task was a duty performed for all the family. The fourth wife, for example, "loved to cook" but didn't like sewing, so she used to trade jobs with one of the other wives who liked sewing. Each wife took care of her own bedroom.

Another excellent instance of a highly organized family with division of labor down to the last detail was that of the Herbert Winslow family. Winslow had three wives who bore him altogether 33 children. He had a successful tombstone business as well as a good farm. He took the old proverb "The devil finds work for idle hands to do" literally and kept his wives and children working under a systematic plan. Their labor helped him develop his farm and his tombstone enterprise and, later, a mill.

A daughter of the third wife described the organization of work in about these words:

The whole family worked as a unit. Father was systematic, and every child had definite chores to do. The tombstone plant was run to capacity by the wives and children up to Decoration Day, and then the whole family would move out to the farm and do the spring planting. When the children worked in the mill, they were paid wages which they could use just as they pleased.

The third wife added further details:

All the children—a whole army of them—worked on tomb-stones, doing everything. Some of the girls got to be good at letter-ing and ornamenting stone. They used to be allowed so much a let-ter. Some of them made as much as $12.00 per week in rush sea-sons. The wives also did lots of work in the mill.

When the children got to be so old, father gave the girls $1.00 and the boys $2.00 a week. They were supposed to take care of all their incidental purchases with it, and not to spend it foolishly on candy and other knickknacks. The boys got more because they went out courting and needed extra money for their girls.

And this from the first wife:

Years ago, when Brother Winslow first started up in his business, us women was the men in the shop. (*sic*) I was surely glad when we graduated from that. Then the children got bigger and they began to do the work like cutting, polishing, and lettering.

Every spring he'd take all the boys out to the farm to work. It was a beautiful farm. He made six large reservoirs himself and made a barren bench productive.

We all worked together in everything we did, most of the time. You wouldn't believe I'd cook 23 and 24 loaves of bread every day when peach harvesting time was on. Then everybody was working in the orchard and the packing shed. I tell you, it looked like an army coming up to meals from the orchard.

Yet, along with this regimentation of the productive forces of the family, each wife had her own cows and could use as she pleased the profits from any sale of milk, butter, or cheese. However, Winslow assumed ownership of the stock and sold the cows and calves whenever he wished and kept whatever he made from these transactions.

While in many families there was a race for babies, never-theless in the child-caring activities of plural families, there was a good deal of mutual aid. In a way this represents the other side of the competition for children. The second wife of Paul Lamb, who had married sisters, remarks:

We had our houses just across the street from each other and we went places together and did many things together . . . I nursed a great many of the other wife's children. She had trouble with her milk and I didn't, so when we had children together I would always help take care of them. When she was sick I went right into her house and stayed with her and many is the night I have gone to stay with her when she's been sick or when he was away.

The members of this family had a little trouble after the Manifesto when the question came up about the legal wife, but previous to that they were quite congenial.

The first wife of Walter Reeves said: "I had no discord in polygamy. We did not quarrel and we were harmonious in our relations. I loved Emma—the other wife—very much." Reeves had married Emma during the period of the Underground and therefore she had to keep out of sight a good deal of the time. When Amelia, the first, found out that Emma was going to have a baby, she made a complete layette for her and sent it to her hideout.

On cooperation, one of the daughters of Mathew Hale has this to say:

We girls often were sent to help with housework at the other house. Father would come in and say, "Georgia needs you today" and that was all there was to it. We went. Father sometimes varied his routine of where he spent his time. I can remember when Aunt Georgia's children were ill, Father must have been over there during the day because I heard him and mother talking about it. Later mother said, "Mathew, I'm sure Georgia needs you with those sick children, so suppose you go over there and stay tonight."

A good illustration of the existence of both competition and cooperation is found in the Dahlman story. A son of the second wife tells of the cooperation of the wives during times of sickness and childbirth. He clearly remembered going to the house of one of the other wives for soiled baby clothes which his mother washed and returned. Though midwives attended all the confinements, the other wives helped out as much as they could in times of childbirth. He noticed no particular reaction of any sort in the other wives at such times. "They just took childbirth as a part of life, and were neither proud nor sorry when another wife had a child." Yet in other things, this family showed considerable conflict.

One common way of fostering harmony and cooperation in a family was the holding of special festivals where all the family participated during holidays or birthdays or on other occasions. But again practices varied. In some families Christmas, New Year's, and other holidays were a conjoint affair involving all the families. On other occasions each family had its own celebration and the father rotated around from house to house or family to family during the festivities.

The first wife of Winslow said:

We wives and family were together in everything. We celebrated Christmas and his birthdays all together, mostly at my house because I had the most room. In those days we all had fun that we made ourselves; none of your factory-made amusements then like nowadays. We used to have big parties at my place.

We wives just got so we loved each other's company. I just got so I felt I couldn't work alone. We all took our turns and everything went on all right.

A daughter of the second wife of Stanley Winters has this to say:

Mother and Lillian, the first wife, got along just fine. I can't remember anything differently. Aunt Lillian liked children and she used to play with us and help us more than Mother did. We had right good times when we were children. Aunt Lillian would teach us dialogues and little plays and on holidays we would give programs. On Christmas we nearly broke our necks to see which one would get to the other house first. On holidays we always had our dinner together. One holiday Father gave us all a dime each and on our way uptown my half-brother swallowed his and we divided with him. I can remember seeing Father going up the aisle of a church with one wife on either side. He took them both to all public places. He said where one went the other would go too.

All in all, cooperation worked out reasonably well. In the first place, cooperation was preached in the pulpit and attempts were made to practice it. It is clear that certain goals or rewards could be shared, and in these matters there was no reason why wives could not learn to cooperate. On the other hand, there were some situations which did not make for mutual aid but rather for competition and even conflict. Where the wives felt that they could not share the husband's affections, property, or other goods or rewards, friction was likely to arise. I am impressed by the fact that among my records are a good many instances of successful cooperation where the women were sisters or developed a situation not unlike that of congenial sisters. We saw in the previous chapter, however, that there were a few instances of bitter rivalry between sisters. Evidently temperamental differences played a large part in determining the degree to which people were able to cooperate rather than to fall into conflict.

There are a number of examples also where the husbands, or the wives and husbands together, worked out a *modus operandi* of having what was, in effect, completely separate and rather independent households. This was true of President John Taylor and of Apostle Erastus Snow. These men and others really set up segregated establishments which had little interaction. The husband rotated among these establishments as patriarchal head, but the wives and families had relatively little to do with each other. This had the effect really of limiting a certain amount of either conflict or cooperation. It fostered, of course, the enhancement of the relationships of a mother to her particular children.

Then, too, there was the matter of the idealization of plural family. We indicated earlier that in the leading families of the Mormon Church there was a kind of expectancy that they would be able to make the system work. The Joseph F. Smith family is a good illustration of this. On the whole the families were cordial to each other. Each wife centered her attentions on her husband and his role and on their own particular families. They all worked hard and tried to assist in making the family a success. In this family, true, certain kinds of cliques developed between certain wives. For example, the fourth and sixth wives had developed a system of reciprocal gifts, which did not apply to the other members of the family. The sixth wife, in fact, was perhaps the least well integrated into the total family. She was married during the height of federal prosecutions, had to keep out of sight, and was never really as closely tied into the total establishment as were the earlier and older families.

Whether individuals will use devices of opposition or co-operation to get what they want, will depend in large measure upon their training at home and the larger cultural acceptance and expectancy regarding the use of one device or the other. In Western society there is a heavy stress on competition with regard to both material goods and social status. No matter how the Mormon leaders may have tried to prevent or block economic competition among the Saints, it was not an easy thing to do. For example, effort after effort was made to set up what were socialistic communities where there would be no private property, but all the goods were to be held in common. Yet, time after time these communities broke down because people could not accommodate themselves to the system. It was not a matter of instinct, it was a matter of strong habit and value which they had learned in a highly competitive capitalistic society. It is only natural, therefore, that even in matters of inter-personal relations, rivalry should be strong and ways of cooperating relatively weak or absent.

Likewise in this situation the problems of ego security and sense of pride loomed large. Two factors operate here: One is the capacity or willingness of the person to identify himself with others and to see things as they do; the other is the group expectancy of sympathetic as against conflictive behavior. High status rests upon sympathetic and supporting responses on the part of others.

The getting and holding of high status was clearly a central thought of the wives in many plural families. An individual who is in a superior position with respect to the group may believe that his position depends upon maintaining that group's *status quo*. Such a person will likely greet with hostility any newcomer or any attempted change in the group organization. Many plural wives viewed the coming of additional plural wives with anxiety just as did the first wife when she faced the coming of the second. On the other hand, a person might regard his status as so secure that a change in family organization with the coming of a new member would not constitute any threat. For example, if a man accepted the Principle so thoroughly and carried it out in practice so completely as to feel secure in the matter and with a high degree of status, he could not possibly regard any threat as coming from the addition of more wives. The same thing would apply to the wives. Nevertheless, as we have already seen and as we shall indicate still further, no matter how strong and safe a woman might feel about the Principle, she frequently had difficulty in adapting herself to the threat of losing status when she was in a plural household.

Then, too, there was the important factor of the husband's leadership. The husband might force cooperation or its outward semblance. Or if the approval of the head of the family was the thing being sought—and this was true in many polygamous families—the father could withdraw it from the more hostile members. Or he might maintain an equal distribution of consideration among all the members. Or, in turn he might direct the competitive and conflictive attitudes of the members into new channels.

In the oppositional and cooperative relations of people to each other additional factors come into play. Constitutional elements, such as strength of drive, physical attractiveness, and differences in social-emotional qualities, and in native intelligence all have a place. Also the sense of intimacy with others, or per contra, sense of avoidance and difference will affect, in turn, capacity for identification with group aims and group standards of success and status. It is not to be implied that these variations depend only on innate or constitutional qualities. They are probably a combination of such elements with learned reactions. For example, the lowly European peasant who was a convert to Mormonism might willingly and easily accept an inferior position in the community or in a plural household. In contrast, a member of the Church from middle-class backgrounds in the United States with all the emphasis on upward striving for higher status would not be inclined to accept gracefully a lowly position. There is no doubt that both men and women enmeshed in polygamy varied in their views and attitudes in these matters. Certainly many men went into polygamy because of the felt pressure to rise in the church hierarchy and hence in general status.

Finally, we must recognize the emotional components in competition and conflict in contrast with cooperation. A noticeable feature of opposition is the expenditure of energy in an aggressive way. The emotional accompaniment of such effort is that of strain and dislike or fear of the persons with whom one is in competition or conflict. In severe conflict the emotions frequently carry one far afield. We noted this in cases of severe neurotic anxieties and temper tantrums. In contrast, in cooperation the emotional accompaniments are rather of a milder, more friendly and sympathetic sort. The individual identifies himself with those with whom he is cooperating in a congenial way. Of course, people use identification in conflict but there the image of the other person is frequently one of a threatening and hostile rather than of a friendly individual.

*And my wives have got to do one of two things; either round up their shoulders to endure the afflictions of this world, and live their religion, or they may leave, for I will not have them about me. I will go into heaven alone, rather than have them scratching and fighting around me. I will set all at liberty. "What, the first wife, too?" Yes, I will liberate you all.*—Brigham Young in a sermon, September 21, 1856.

# 11 SOME COULDN'T TAKE IT: DESERTION AND DIVORCE

THE ORIGINAL CREED of the Latter-day Saints was as firm against divorce as that of the Roman Catholics. Long before plural marriage was publicly announced, Joseph Smith and other early leaders made clear the sacredness of the marriage bond and pointed out that it was not to be lightly broken. Yet under the pressure of serious family difficulties in plural households some device had to be worked out to sanction separation. This chapter will bring out the interesting and important fact that a marriage and family system such as polygamy, superimposed as it was upon Christian monogamy with all its values, was, at times, bound to induce such stress as to require some official form of divorce.

While there is much evidence that plural marriages were practiced before Joseph Smith's death, we must recall that the public admission of the Ancient Patriarchal Order of Matrimony or Plurality of Wives was not made until August 1852, when the Saints, then located beyond the Rocky Mountains, felt secure from outside interference. Equally interesting is the fact that within four years after this official announcement of this "great social innovation," as Edward W. Tullidge, Mormon biographer called it, Brigham Young made it clear that if the women of Mormondom did not like the new system,

226

they could leave their husbands and the Church. His remarks in a sermon on September 21, 1856, are plain enough:

> I wish my own women to understand that what I am going to say is for them as well as others, and I want those who are here to tell their sisters, yes, all the women of this community, and then write it back to the States, and do as you please with it. I am going to give you from this time to the 6th of October next, for reflection, that you may determine whether you wish to stay with your husbands or not, and then I am going to set every woman at liberty and say to them, now go your way, my women with the rest, go your way . . .
>
> Let every man thus treat his wives, keeping raiment enough to clothe his body; and say to your wives, "Take all that I have and be set at liberty; but if you stay with me you shall comply with the law of God, and that too without any murmuring and whining. You must fulfill the law of God in every respect, and round up your shoulders to walk to the mark without any grunting."

At the outset, however, the whole process of separation, divorce, and possible remarriage was a hit-and-miss affair. As happened in announcing the system of celestial marriage itself, the church officials had no blueprint for the faithful to follow in case their marriages—monogamous or plural—went on the rocks. Only gradually did some sort of orderly procedure emerge. Moreover, a certain looseness of action with regard to getting married or splitting up reflected the personal freedom of the frontier. If a couple could not make a go of marriage, one or the other might merely pick up and leave. At least in the earlier phases of Mormon pioneering such practices were not unknown.

While in time the Mormons developed some institutional ways of granting divorces, there were a great many informal separations. In some instances the separation was marked by little emotional feeling on anyone's part. This was true in the William Root family mentioned in Chapter 3. Somewhat similar is the account of John Yancey who married his first wife, Elizabeth Ann Smith, in 1833. Fifteen years later, shortly before he left for a mission to England, he took a second, Jessie

Williams, who accompanied him to England. He returned in January, 1850, and settled in Salt Lake City. A year later his first wife left him. This did not discourage Brother Yancey because by early 1858 he had taken a total of 10 wives. There are various legends about Yancey. One is that he cut the throat of one of his wives because she objected to polygamy. Another is that he did so because she was unfaithful to him.

In the Andrew Pope family the first wife was apparently never more than lukewarm about the gospel and although she was married in the Endowment House, she lost interest in the Church and refused to permit her children to be baptized. She told her husband many times that if he ever married in polygamy she would leave him, and she did. Neither of them bothered about a divorce. So it was with Rachel Haswell, a first wife who was not in favor of polygamy. When her husband took a second, she just packed up and left him and did not bother with a divorce. A few years later she remarried.

Milton Sutter's first wife, Hazel, put up with the second marriage for a year or so and then just drifted out of Sutter's life. Somewhat similar was the departure of the first wife of Ezra Austin. She settled in another community in a house built by her husband, but she never again had anything to do with him. There was no divorce.

How one man, Henry Spaulding, reacted to the departure of one of his plural wives, years after the marriage, is set forth in his journal:

My third wife, Rosemary, became dissatisfied and had been for some time, and wished to leave me. She would not give me the reason for so doing, only because she wanted to do it, because she could do better for herself than I could do for her, inasmuch as I had such a large family to support. She thought that if she had her share of my property she could handle it, with her ability, to more profit for herself than I could do for her. She could live better without me than with me. She used to curse poverty, and did not like to meet the times as they came along, as I had to do. She liked to live and be on the upper shelf. She was a smart woman and had many noble traits in her character. The breaking up of the family at that was a hard stroke on me. (sic) To part with the

children and a home was hard to endure. It was especially hard
to part with her. The property I cared nothing about.

I gave her one-fourth of what I had. [There were four wives.] She
receipted me for it as payment in full. I offered her a bill of divorce,
but . . . she would not take that. She declared she would not accept that, so she belongs to me yet. I wish my family to treat her
and her six children kindly for my sake.

While there were many separations without any formal
recognition by the Church, in time, more formal procedures
were developed. Obviously because plural marriages were not
legal, there could strictly speaking be no legal divorces of
such marriages through the territorial or state courts.

The official view on procedure for a church divorce was
well described by George Reynolds, a high Mormon official,
who was a witness at the hearings in 1903 before the Senate
Committee on Privileges and Elections in the matter of the
seating of Senator Reed Smoot from Utah:

*Mr. Tayler.* "As you have a certain method of joining in marriage,
do you also have one for severing the marriage relation?"
*Mr. Reynolds.* "Yes, sir; the Church grants divorce of those who
have been married for time and eternity. For the legal wives that
is not done until the courts have acted and separated the parties.
For plural wives—that is, marriages which are not recognized by
the law—they are granted divorces on application, without any
action of the courts, because the courts will take no action, as they
do not recognize the marriage."

Unfortunately our data regarding divorce, either judicial
or ecclesiastical, are rather scanty. It must not be forgotten
that the Saints did not approve divorce. For most of those who
had to go through with it, it was a guilt-laden experience. Nor
was it, from their standpoint, a "nice thing" to talk about
later. Neither the material from diaries, journals, or other
records made at the time, nor data from recalled facts—obtained through interviews or life stories written later—contain much if any detail as to the procedure used in obtaining
a formal separation.

In the second place, it must be recalled that practically all

forms of social control were dominated by the Mormon
Church. Each Ward, under the management of its Bishop, had
a court of initial jurisdiction. But these courts by no means
confined themselves to religious matters. In the early days
they were often used to settle disputes which we would view
as strictly secular. These included differences over land, water
rights, debts, and accusations of personal slander. Such moral
questions as sexual misconduct were handled almost completely by the Bishops' courts. At that time Mormons had little or no faith in regularly constituted courts. This attitude
was rationalized in terms of their earlier brushes with the law
in Ohio, Missouri, and Illinois.

Yet in most instances where a divorce concerned the first
and legal wife, the parties repaired to the regular territorial
or state courts for legal dissolution of their marriage. Thus,
Hannibal Lowman's first wife divorced him shortly after the
appearance of the second wife on the family scene. Number
one had been married and divorced before marrying Lowman.
Later she married again, only to get a divorce the third time.
It is interesting to note that this woman did not leave the
community but settled down there, and on not too unfriendly
terms with her former spouse.

Anna, the first wife of Oscar Dahlman, divorced him after
years of inter-family and inter-personal troubles. Oscar had
married his first wife, a widow with nine children, before he
left his native Norway to join the Saints in Utah. About 1872,
only a short time after arriving in Logan, he took another
wife. Then, 17 years later he married a third time. Externally
wives one and two seem to have gotten along reasonably well.
But over the years Anna had more and more sought emotional
release through drinking. About a year after Dahlman's third
matrimonial venture, Anna's children by her first marriage
induced her to get a divorce. It is alleged by other children
of the family that they had in mind a satisfactory financial settlement. She used "failure to provide" as the ground for
divorce and was given $300.00 in cash to build a house, and a
small alimony. Oscar, then a Bishop, and with some property,
made no defense. Anna died shortly after the divorce and ac-

tually had only received $100.00 of the amount allotted her by the court.

The third wife, in recounting the story, remarked, "I really believe Bishop Dahlman was perfectly willing to let her go. He didn't care much for her, and her drinking caused him a great deal of worry."

The complications of family life and recourse to divorce as a solution to difficulties is well illustrated in the story of Wilhelm Zeeman. All told, Wilhelm, a convert from Denmark, had five wives. His first, Maria, died about a year after the marriage in 1863. He remained a widower for several years. Then he married Rebecca, a widow for whom he was working. She was 20 years his senior and had had several children by a prior marriage. There is a family legend that "Rebecca talked him into marrying her" and that he did so "because he was sorry for her." In any case she bore him only one child. At that time officials of the Church were encouraging the brethren to enter the Principle and within three years of his marrying Rebecca, Wilhelm wed again. This new wife had one child that died in early infancy and a few months later she passed away. Two years later he married two women, Elizabeth and Sophia, close friends, who had but recently arrived from Denmark. This was in 1878. At about this time, Rebecca with whom he had had difficulties, left him. The last two wives got on famously, however. Both had large families and for several years the households were relatively serene. When the federal efforts to suppress polygamy became increasingly severe, Wilhelm was arrested, tried, and sent to the territorial penitentiary. Just before this, Rebecca who had become his legal wife divorced him. He was assessed $8.50 a month alimony.

Like many other Saints who had been in trouble with the law over polygamy, Zeeman wanted to avoid further complication, so when he was released, he lived with his Bishop. During this time, and by mutual agreement, Elizabeth and he obtained a church divorce. When this was done he married Sophia as his legal wife. While he never lived with Elizabeth afterwards, he maintained her household and continued to

divide his time between her place and Sophia's. This accommodation to a difficult situation was largely engineered by
Elizabeth who rationalized it by contending that Sophia was
younger and needed him more than she did. Sophia had five
additional children after the Manifesto.

During the post-Manifesto period divorces were sometimes
resorted to in an effort to bring about family harmony. This
was so even among some of the families who settled in Mexico
in order to escape federal prosecution. (See Chapter 19.)

A prolonged marital conflict which began before the Manifesto and was reopened years afterward is that of Joseph M.
Carey and his first wife. It is a somewhat pathetic story of
thwarted love, hurt pride, and guilt intermixed with legal
difficulties over both polygamy and divorce.

Joseph M. was born in Salt Lake City in 1851, a son of
Joseph Carey, Jr., and his first wife, Joan Miller. Joseph M.
had a good education for that day and at the age of 23 years
while teaching school in Coalville he courted and married
Hannah Hepzibah Marinda Almira Johnson for time and
eternity. As a friend remarked, "Any girl with a name like
that should have made him suspicious."

Late in 1877 Joseph M. joined with Lot Smith and others
at Sunset, Arizona, to establish the United Order there. He
combined teaching and farming as a means of livelihood. In
1879 he decided to take another wife but somewhat against
the wishes of his first.

In December, 1879, he began the long trek from Sunset to
St. George with his prospective new bride, Elnora Miller.
They were sealed for time and eternity in the temple. While
on this matrimonial errand, Almira and two small children
left Sunset for Utah. Almira stopped off at Kanab, Utah, and
for some time boarded with friends. On learning that his first
wife had left him, Carey made arrangements for a property
settlement and to establish her in Toquerville, though not
without some difficulties with the law arising from a writ of
attachment being served on him for failure to pay the board
bill for Almira and the children. To complicate matters all
around, Almira gave birth to a third baby shortly after arriv-

ing in Toquerville. Later that year, she returned to her parents' home in Coalville. In the meantime Carey had gone back to Sunset. A few years later the cooperative venture there failed and Carey settled in Woodruff, Arizona.

In September, 1883, Carey was married to Elnora's sister, Alice, in the St. George Temple. But further residence in Arizona was to be cut short.

Under the pressure of federal prosecution, late in 1884, Carey and his two plural spouses, along with other Mormon plural families, decamped for Mexico. They returned to the States in 1889 and he was not bothered again. In 1891 this entry appears in his journal:

. . . I have had some correspondence with my first wife, Almira, but we can not be reconciled. I have sent her some money; but am not able to do much. She feels so bitter that I have not made any attempt to see either her or my three children since they left Sunset 13 years ago. She still lives in Coalville with her relatives . . .

From time to time Carey tried further reconciliation once offering, as his journal states, "to meet her before President W. Woodruff . . . and abide by whatever *decision* he might render as to our troubles. This she scornfully refused but continued to threaten us with the law." Then, in mid-summer 1899, Almira and her oldest son appeared in Woodruff without any warning "in the same old unreasonable, hostile, and warlike mode." The journal continues:

She said she had "shed her garments, got rid of them long ago." That she was no Mormon, the Church officials were false and corrupt; that I had been whoring with these two women [meaning Elnora and Alice]; they were whores and their children bastards. She would feel like pitching them into the streets, that I and all I possessed belong to her and her children.

Efforts on Carey's part to effect a settlement and peaceful separation failed. Instead, early in January, 1900 Almira swore out a complaint in the district court regarding his "conduct, and asking the court to grant her a divorce and one-half of my property with costs, attorney's fees, etc."

In July of that same year, on the basis of Almira's statements, Carey was brought before the Grand Jury and indicted on charges of adultery and unlawful cohabitation with Elnora and Alice. He was released on bonds provided by friends. In February, 1901, while Almira's divorce action was pending, he appeared in court, pled guilty on the advice of his lawyer and was fined $100.00 and released. In the fall of that same year Almira got her divorce. She had asked for a large property settlement but in the end got nothing, although Carey paid the court costs and attorney's fee. The entry in his journal for March 11, 1902, contains this item:

She got her divorce and is now free; but instead of getting *all* my property she gets no property, so she, having scornfully refused an equal division of my property before any legal proceedings were instituted, making the unreasonable demand that I should pay her $4,500.00 in cash, she finds herself now without anything. She dug a pit for Elnora and Alice, but she finds herself now in that pit. She threatened to land them in the street but she is there herself . . . The Lord has delivered me from the evil designs in direct answer to my prayers.

While this comment has the tone of more than sweet revenge, Carey kept hoping through the subsequent years to get into more friendly relations with Almira and her children. He tried time and again to get a reconciliation. As late as December 31, 1927, not long before his death, appears this entry: "But Almira and her children, living at Burley, Idaho, still maintain a very cool and distant attitude toward me. . . . I hope they will all see differently some time, either in this life or in the next . . ."

We have included this rather long account because it gives the flavor of the views and attitudes of a man who had the strongest faith in the Principle, who was prominent in his own locality, and well regarded by the general authorities of the Church. That he was faithful to the Principle until his death is clear from the instances of being sealed for eternity to certain women friends who had predeceased him. Polygamy for the hereafter was not subject to any Manifesto.

We have no adequate information as to the number of church divorces, granted annually or in toto. These were supposed to be handled through the Bishops' courts; but apparently some separations were managed by the President of the Church directly.

The marital troubles of Belle Harris became the basis for a legend that had wide circulation among the Saints. Her family, which had been in the Church almost from its outset, was rather prominent. When Belle—a most attractive girl— was 16 years old she met the dashing Clarence Merrill, likewise of a prominent family. He was in his upper 20's and married already to Bathsheba Smith, daughter of Apostle George A. Smith, one of Brigham's chief lieutenants.

For Belle it was love at first sight. She remarked years later:

> When I met Clarence, he was like the romantic hero I had imagined. He was polite, refined, educated, and seemed to offer me all I wanted in a man. We had a romantic courtship . . . He did all those lovely things a girl longs for. He wrote me beautiful letters, sent me books with dainty handkerchiefs in them, and perfumes that I had never had. Oh, I loved him all right then, or thought I did, and I believed that polygamy was a divine Principle. We were married when I was eighteen, and though I didn't know anything then, it wasn't long before I began to learn.

One of the first lessons to follow this romantic affair was that Clarence could not support his first wife and her family let alone another. During the first year Belle lived in Fillmore with the first family. Bathsheba was friendly enough, but it was soon apparent that Clarence's economic deficiency was a constant threat to the fulfillment of all that Belle had daydreamed about. She continues her story: ". . . My trouble was simply that he couldn't make a living and I couldn't live that way. I had to have a man who could assure me of a living and education for my children or I had to do it myself . . ."

When Belle had her first baby she was determined to have a home of her own. She moved to Richfield "in a tiny place." Within a few months she was pregnant for a second time. ". . . I did some thinking. I decided that I must leave Mr. Merrill before I had any more children." She consulted with various church authorities and with her father and they all gave their consent. Her father handled the details of obtaining a church divorce.

While the matter of the divorce was underway, Merrill was indicted for polygamy before a grand jury in Fillmore and Belle was subpoenaed as a witness. She refused to testify, was sentenced to the territorial penitentiary for contempt of court, and became quite a heroine in Mormon folklore.

Nothing so highlighted this conflict, especially as it concerned judicial as contrasted to ecclesiastical actions regarding divorce, as the famous suit of Ann Eliza Young against Brigham Young. When Judge James B. McKean, sworn enemy of Mormonism and polygamy, granted her a divorce and awarded Eliza an annual alimony of $9,500.00 a year, both Mormons and non-Mormons everywhere were quick to catch the import of this judicial sanction of polygamy. An editorial in the New York *Post,* reprinted in the *Deseret News* for March 17, 1875, remarked:

By the law of Congress made especially for Utah, and the common law of the land, any other woman taken by him (a man) to his bed and board after his first legal marriage is not his wife. This is the very point that Judge McKean has heretofore considered it his special mission to establish.

By this decision the Judge receded from his own principles and may fairly be hailed by the Mormon Church as a convert to the doctrine of polygamy.

In less than a month after his decision McKean was removed from office, and Judge David B. Lowe took his place. In May Lowe ruled that there had been no legal marriage between Brigham and Ann Eliza and hence there could be neither divorce nor alimony.

Yet Ann Eliza and her sponsors did not give up. There followed for some years various decisions, some favoring her, some Brigham. For a time the latter was incarcerated in his own home under guard for refusal to pay alimony. Finally, on April 27, 1877, the whole case came to an end when Judge Michael Schaeffer ruled that Ann Eliza had never been legally married to Brigham Young and could not, therefore, obtain

a divorce. The alimony payments were remanded but Young
had to pay the court costs.

In a great many instances the reasons for divorce among
the early Mormons were probably much like those reported
among Americans today. Temperamental differences of the
spouses, problems of economic hardship, the breakdown of
earlier romanticized expectations, and a host of other factors
doubtless played their part. In addition to these, polygamy
put a strain on many who tried to live under its mandate. The
basic tenets of monogamy are so firm in our Western culture
that even the deep emotional conviction about the Principle
could not completely wipe out an unconscious sense of guilt
among many of those who tried it out in practice.

It may well be, however, that some of those reared as Latter-
day Saints and especially those who as children had been members of plural families could and did fully accept polygamy at
the emotional level, and if they in turn—as many did—took
plural wives, they might well be able to live in it without suffering an undue load of guilt. Of course it did not follow that
because one was brought up in a polygamous household one
necessarily approved of the system. In fact, several of our
family records show a good deal of resentment if not downright disbelief in the system. This is clearly evident in those
instances where the first wife deserted or secured a legal
divorce after her spouse took a plural wife.

On the other hand, many Mormon women swallowed their
pride and hurt feelings and stayed on despite deep emotional
wounds. Yet a man's taking another wife might serve as a
convenient excuse for a separation, the roots of which might
lie deep in temperamental or other differences between the
original pair. For example, in the Reuben Jacobs story, the
plural wife deserted him though she always contended it was
not due to his having taken another wife. She and her husband had been at odds for years. She remarked to her
daughter: "Understand this. It was not polygamy that made
me leave your father. It was just that I would not put up with
him any longer. Polygamy had nothing to do with it." The

divorce in the Dahlman family has much in common with this one.

Undoubtedly economic factors played a part in some desertions and divorces; but again, neither poverty nor disputes over the distribution of income or property were sufficient to bring about wholesale separations. The internal convictions, on the one hand, and the public pressure of fellow Mormons, on the other, usually served to keep the wives in line.

Among the Mormons, as with others, there was usually more than one "cause" for the breakup of a family. The Daisy Yates Barclay story, which we have already told, was one in which romantic polygamous marriage dissolved for a variety of reasons. Belle Harris had begun her marriage with Merrill full of romantic daydreams only to find them shattered on the rocks of economic deprivation. But there may well have been some temperamental problems in that match as well, as indicated in her strong ambition for her sons. She was not willing to play the role of a poverty-ridden wife. Certainly many of those wives who rationalized their leaving because of nonbelief in the Principle could not face plural family life because of threats to their role and status. Or they left because they saw expected income and property being taken from them and their children and divided among or given to others. Surely, if we had the more intimate personal data on these people, we would find a variety and multiplicity of elements that could be set down as the real "causes" for the dissolution of their marriages.

One part of the grand plan of the Patriarchal Order of plural marriage provided that a man could marry by proxy women who had predeceased him. These sealings, of course, would be for eternity only. Thousands of such matches for the hereafter have been consummated. If a Saint can properly marry a dead person so as to enjoy the benefits of the Principle in heaven, is there any logical reason why divorces may not be granted so as to separate a living spouse from one who had already passed to his reward? This is a difficult question and while neither church officials nor the ordinary run-of-the-mill

Mormon ever talked much about it, the whole topic came up for an airing during the Reed Smoot hearings already mentioned. The testimony of George Reynolds is interesting in this connection. He was being questioned regarding the Mormon system of marriage and divorce:

*Senator Foraker.* "Are these divorce proceedings confined to the living? You spoke of marriages after death."

*Mr. Reynolds.* "I have known very rarely of a woman seeking to be separated from her husband after he was dead, and the president of the Church hearing her statement had directed that the marriage be canceled on the records."

*Senator Foraker.* "Do you say you have heard of that frequently or infrequently?"

*Mr. Reynolds.* "No, sir; not frequently. Once in a long while."

*Mr. Tayler.* "Is it not also customary for those who have been married solely for eternity—that is to say, a living person married to a dead person—to have that marriage also dissolved?"

*Mr. Reynolds.* "I have no recollection of ever having heard of such a thing or having to do with anything of that kind. I presume it is possible."

*Mr. Tayler.* "It is possible?"

*Mr. Reynolds.* "It is possible; but it has not come in my experience, according to my present recollection."

*Mr. Tayler.* "How often have you known of a divorce being granted by the church to a man or woman whose husband or wife, as the case may be, had died?"

*Mr. Reynolds.* "I cannot answer that question."

*Mr. Tayler.* "Many times?"

*Mr. Reynolds.* "I should not call it many, a few I should say."

*Senator Foraker.* "You confined your statement, as I understood you, to cases where women had applied for divorces from husbands who were deceased?"

*Mr. Reynolds.* "Yes, sir."

*Senator Foraker.* "Have there been any cases where the husband has applied for a divorce from his wife who was deceased?"

*Mr. Reynolds.* "Never to my knowledge . . ."

*Senator Foraker.* "I should like to ask another question before we get away from the matter. It is about these divorces that are granted to women from their husbands who are deceased. Is that divorce, in the few cases you have referred to, granted on account of something that the man did in lifetime or something he is supposed to have done after death?"

*Mr. Reynolds.* "In lifetime. We do not know anything they do after death."

*Senator Foraker.* "The proceeding is taken against him without making him a party or giving him a chance to be heard?"

*Mr. Reynolds.* "That is exactly it, and that is why so few have been granted, because it is regarded as unjust to the person who could not appear. But when the wife produced evidence sufficient to cause it to be evident that he had done certain things, making him unworthy of being her husband, then the divorce has sometimes been granted."

*Senator Foraker.* "Is anyone appointed to defend the dead man in such cases?"

*Mr. Reynolds.* "No, sir."

*Senator Foraker.* "The proceeding is purely ex parte?"

*Mr. Reynolds.* "Purely."

*Mr. Tayler.* "The man who dies, the fortunate possessor of a half a dozen wives, has no assurance that he will find them at the end; that is to say, the church on earth has the power to dissolve after a man's death the bonds of matrimony that have tied him to several wives?"

*Mr. Reynolds.* "Yes, sir."

Although the Senators had their little fun with Mr. Reynolds, it should never be forgotten that the Mormons took all these matters very seriously. They hoped they would be successful in their plural marriages but if they were not, they also trusted in their church authorities to disentangle them from the troubles they had encountered in trying to make the Principle work. It was not always an easy burden for the faithful Saints to bear.

*It was easier to be a child than a wife of polygamy.*—A daughter in a plural family.

# 12
# POLYGAMY

## THE CHILDREN OF

THE TRAINING of children under polygamy was essentially the same as that under monogamy. Yet the inter-personal relations in plural households were complicated by the fact of parallel families under the same father. In the first place there were the child's contacts in his own immediate family consisting of his relations to his parents and his own brothers and sisters. Then there were the child's relations with the other wives who, as we know, were almost always called "aunts." There were also his contacts with his half-siblings, that is, the children of another wife but of the same father. Finally, these inter-family situations were qualified by the relations of the child's own mother with the other wives. All these factors brought about certain changes and complications in family practices which often contrasted sharply with those found under monogamy. To get a proper perspective about the situation in plural households, we shall begin by noting briefly the main features of the rearing of children in the Mormon pioneer family, whether plural or not.

Child rearing in the days of the frontier and at a time when puritanic practices and mores were the social norm was probably quite different from either the ideal or actuality in urban, middle-class families of today. Earlier strong patriarchal and authoritarian sanctions have given way to much more permissive attitudes.

We have already described the patriarchal tradition in the Mormon family and its relationship to the male-centered ecclesiastical system of the Church. Mention, too, has been made of the high value put upon childbearing. A husband and wife were remiss if they failed to fulfill their duty of "bringing as

241

many spirits" to the earth through the bearing of children as
was possible. Obviously this was a useful religious and moral
rationalization for a high birth rate of the kind common in
rural and pioneer communities.

Against the background of this patriarchal system the
family was expected to function not only in childbearing and
early care but in training the child "in the way of the Lord."
Among other values there was strong stress upon obedience to
authority, loyalty to the Church, conformity to the codes, and
individual effort to make good in the material things of this
world. From the official point of view of the Church the family
was supposed to provide all the fundamental traits of character which would later enable a person to conduct himself as a
good and proper Saint.

From the point of view of modern psychology the parental
training of the Mormon child ranged from that which was
relatively indulgent, friendly, and helpful to the other extreme of severe discipline and the rigid imposition of authority. This wide variation reflected not only the usual deviations in American families of that date, but differences
among the European families who came to Utah as converts
during the period when polygamy was in vogue. Pioneer life,
with its great hardships, made for considerable variations in
the forms of early indulgence or discipline. Moreover, the prolonged absence from home of a husband on many occasions
such as came about from spending time with other families,
going on a mission, or exploring new sites for colonies, threw
a great deal of responsibility upon the mother.

As to specific features of childbearing and early training,
there was first of all little medical care for expectant mothers
or for attendance at childbirth. There were practically no
physicians in the early Mormon communities. While there
were a number of common superstitions about childbearing
such as the doctrine of prenatal influence, there was likewise
a certain amount of sound tradition about personal hygiene
and care, especially as the time of delivery approached. While
there were midwives in the larger towns, it was not at all uncommon for a woman to bear her babies with only the as-

sistance of whatever relatives or neighbors might be at hand. There were plenty of instances where parturient mothers had no help at all.

Mothers were supposed to nurse their own babies except under special circumstances. In the matter of feeding schedules, there was no standard formula, but, in general, the nursing of the children was worked into the routine of the household duties. Sometimes there was a fixed feeding schedule; sometimes feeding times were quite permissive.

Weaning took place toward the end of the first year or certainly during the early part of the second year. It was usually attempted gradually, but again there was individual variation. Sometimes mothers shut off their nursing almost at once. In other instances the whole process was a much less severe experience for the infant.

In this connection there was a widespread belief among Mormon women, then as now, that so long as a mother nursed her baby she could not become pregnant again. There is considerable indirect evidence that in monogamous and polygamous families alike many mothers prolonged the nursing of their babies as a means of avoiding another pregnancy.

Toilet training likewise followed the middle class European and American tradition. The child was taught regularity of elimination toward the end of the first year and definitely during the second year. The Mormons had a strong feeling about cleanliness which they often said was "next to godliness." Hence, in general, a child's toilet training was viewed as an important phase of a larger context of religiously sanctioned personal hygiene. Deviations from the habit of regularity were likely to be punished, sometimes severely, sometimes mildly.

The sex training of a child fell into the aforesaid tradition. Personal expressions of sexuality such as examining the sexual organs or masturbation were punished either by scolding or by physical means. In fact, any overt interest of sexuality on the part of children was severely tabooed. As indicated elsewhere in this book, official Mormondom regarded sexuality in much the same manner as the more rigid and puritanical

Christians everywhere. It was not to be indulged in except for procreational purposes. Sexual continence was expected alike of both sexes before and outside of marriage.

At about the age of six or so the child began to take a definite role in the economy of the household. The girls were trained to help in the house, the boys to care for the livestock and to aid in the larger farm operations. "Doing chores" was universal. Boys were early put to milking and herding cows, driving teams, and doing other such work. By the time a boy reached puberty he had usually developed sound work habits and had assumed considerable responsibility in economic matters.

In addition to training a boy in economic skills and duties, he was given responsibilities in reference to his place in the community, especially the Church. There was a strong stress on the religious-moral values of the Latter-day Saint. Among other things these included a deep conviction in the divine mission of the Mormon system and one's place in it, expressed through participation in the priesthood and in marriage and family life. There was much stress on obedience, loyalty, and conformity. In the matter of personal habits there was heavy stress upon the "Word of Wisdom." This "temporal" code forbade the drinking of tea, coffee, and alcoholic beverages. It also tabooed the use of tobacco.

As the child grew up, the church institutions assumed more and more importance in his life. At about the age of four years a child began going to Sunday School. By eight or nine he was sent to Primary and Religion classes on prescribed weekdays. As he came into adolescence he was eligible for the "Mutual" organizations designed for Mormon youth, but divided on sex lines. Of most importance for the male youth was their induction and progress in the lower or Aaronic priesthood, the first steps in their official role as full members of God's Kingdom.

It was into this kind of world—both inside and outside the scope of the family—that plural marriage was introduced. Let us look at the general setting of the polygamous family as it related to child training. For example, what factors having to do with child rearing were changed when a man entered into plural marriage? Among other things, we shall want to know about the interplay of love and discipline as applied to the children and about the respective roles played by the mother and the father therein. We shall deal first with the early training and then with that of adolescence.

As is true among monogamous families there was much variation in the nature and amount of discipline which the parents exercised over their children. Their control ranged all the way from severe physical punishment, usually in the form of slapping, spanking or birching, through various kinds of deprivations or verbal threats to mild scoldings and mere requests not to do this or that. Although the patriarchal pattern was the expected norm, it was much modified by conditions of pioneer life, family and nationality backgrounds of individuals, and by the circumstances of multiple families and household arrangements. As might be expected the wives took over most of the early training and control, especially when the father was not at home. However, for the most part the image of the dominant and controlling father remained in the background.

Yet, as in monogamy, there were shifts in the disposition of authority as the child grew older. During his earlier years the mother was rather generally the child's chief disciplinarian as well as caretaker. It was usually she who provided the first combination of indulgent care with imposed controls. She was responsible for the nursing, weaning, and toilet training and in these matters plural families resembled monogamous ones within the limits of customary or permissive variability. As the child passed into middle childhood—say at about eight or nine years of age—the father came to take a more prominent place in his training. In matters of basic discipline the father figure usually became increasingly evident, either in actuality or imagery, no matter how varied the everyday practice might be.

The coming of puberty marked a definite forward step in growing up. The physiological changes of that period were usually overlaid with heavy puritanic taboos, especially with regard to female periodicity and the sexual maturation of boys. There was a combination of folklore and some common-sense practices with regard to menstruation, but no such frank recognition of the changes as are common today. For the boy, there was a certain masculine-oriented belief about the coming of sexual potency. There were strong taboos on mastur-bation with the then-current notion that so-called "self abuse" would lead to insanity and other dire consequences.

Perhaps the most striking contrast, however, between the experiences of the adolescent then and now is that both boys and girls in these days moved rather quickly into mature re-sponsibilities. By the age of 16 most boys would be carrying a man's share of work on the farm or elsewhere.

During the parallel years the girls were expected to take on increasing duties in the house or outside chores, such as, gardening, and caring for chickens and the livestock that was allotted to the particular household. By the age of 16 many girls were being courted, and certainly a girl beyond her 20th year who was not wed was already likely to be regarded as a potential spinster.

Before proceeding, one further matter must be mentioned. Most of the material in this chapter presents a picture and interpretation of child training under what might be con-sidered the most favorable circumstances. That is, it deals with the period when persecution and legal pressure against the system had little or no place. Certainly the increased federal efforts during the late 1880's to stop polygamy had various and widespread effects upon plural families, including the children. Some of the more striking of these effects will be treated in Chapter 18. So, too, after the Manifesto the climate of opinion regarding polygamy tended to change even among the Mormons themselves, and some modifications in plural family life and hence in the handling of children took place. Certain aspects of this matter will be presented in Chapter 19.

Some of the inter-spousal factors which would influence child rearing were discussed in Chapter 8 and need only be noted briefly here. In many instances the first wife maintained her top status throughout and thus set the stage for certain controls of child training by all the wives. Sometimes a fair degree of equality of status would emerge—a kind of sister-sister pattern. In these families child training might be quite different from those where sharp status differences were in evidence. Occasionally the contacts of the first and older wife to the new and younger one took on the quality of a mother-daughter relationship. Less often, but not entirely absent, were those instances where the plural wife was treated as a domestic by the older and dominant wife. Under such circumstances the children of a plural wife would, in general, reflect the inferior status of their mother. Similar to this would be a plural marriage in which the second family was regarded as a mere appendage of the first.

In a similar way, the housing arrangements, which usually reflected the economic circumstances, made for some variation. Surely bringing up children in a household where several families operated a single ménage would be different from those conditions where a mother had her own apartment or better still her own house separated by distance, no matter how small, from the other wives. In the latter circumstances, while a dominant first and/or favorite wife might exercise a good deal of direction, she could not, if not under the same roof, control the minutiae of the day-by-day relations of a mother and her children.

The husband's plan of rotation of time among his families might well affect child rearing. For example, if a man with two wives operated on an every-other-day schedule, he would ordinarily be in closer contact with his children than if he had four, five, or more wives and spent a week with each in turn. And where families were widely scattered or where occupation or church duties meant long absences from one's families, a man might scarcely know his children as they grew up.

This was somewhat the situation with the Charles Johnsons. Charles was in the freighting business and his families were located in widely scattered communities. He had no regular time schedule for staying with them. Weeks might go by and then without any prior notice he would appear to spend anything from a day or two to some weeks with a particular family. In one of his plural families is the legend that he appeared only often enough to keep his wife Mary Jane pregnant or with a young baby in arms. The family had a hard time making out financially. The story tells how on one occasion Charles returned unexpectedly after weeks of absence. That evening when he prepared to retire with Mary Jane, the oldest daughter, Ethel—then 16 years of age—stood in the doorway leading to the bedroom and said, "No father, you can't sleep with mother; you'll have to sleep in the barn. There are enough mouths to feed in this family without having any more." And, so the yarn goes, Charles slept in the barn, at least for that night.

Against the possible effects of status and age differences among the wives and in view of the variations in economic conditions and household arrangements, it must be noted that considerable modifications took place in the ideal of complete masculine and patriarchal control of the family. As we have already noted there is much evidence that polygamy tended, on the whole, to enhance the place of the mother in matters of child rearing and in family controls generally. The father, although officially head man, was often prevented by circumstances from becoming closely involved in the training and disciplining of his children. Morever, the existence of another family or other families functioning under the father's name meant that the struggle for status of wives and their children might make for anxiety, hostility, and other disturbing reactions.

Before taking up some concrete aspects of training and discipline, let us attempt a short over-view of the division of labor between husbands and wives in the matter of major responsibility for discipline. To get a picture of the relative importance of father or mother in discipline, six categories were set up: (1) father completely in charge and executed the controls personally; (2) father set the basic patterns with the wife more or less carrying out his orders, but for exceptional circumstances; (3) father dominant in all basic matters, yet the mothers with considerable authority especially in routine control of younger children of their own; (4) relatively equal distribution of discipline; (5) wives practically in full control, except in most unusual situations; and (6) wives absolutely dominant in all basic matters.

Of the 42 families on which sufficient information is available to make a judgment on this matter, none showed up under category 1: the father in complete control in the sense of both establishing the pattern and seeing personally that all aspects of it were carried out; however, three families classified in category 2 did approach this extreme.

Thirteen or 31 per cent fell into category 2. The Robert McDougall family represents a stern control by the husband and father. McDougall was definitely in control though he was not arbitrary. His desires were carried out by both wives. Sarah, the first wife, was a bit more outspoken and seems to have got more concessions while Amanda, the second wife, a rather mild person, took what she got without protest. The discipline was entirely in the father's hands when he was at home. It was strict, systematic, and firm, although there was seldom any resort to physical punishment. The informant in this case remembered only one example of the latter, when the father slapped a three-year-old child at the supper table. "Father was getting old then," remarked the informant, "and old men should never try to bring up children."

McDougall, however, permitted the sons to engage in sports and to go on fishing trips. The home was the center for a baseball game nearly every Sunday afternoon. Yet sports were not permitted to interfere with the serious obligations of work. If the town was to have a celebration or hold a ball game, the father always let his sons know early in the day whether they could attend or had to work. The children, however, were not particularly at ease in their father's presence. He was a somewhat cold and forbidding personality. There was never any spontaneous talk or expression of mutual confidences.

John Vance was another example of this group, a father who set the basic standards and, in part, saw to it that they were enforced. Though he seldom resorted to physical punishment, Vance kept a strong hand on all important disciplinary matters. However, the routine controls were left to the wives. A daughter of one of his plural wives reports: "The wives always sustained father in his wishes for the children. When father was not around, a wife's final word of refusal was 'Now, I don't think your father would like that.'"

Another example of this group is the family of Richard Field. His second wife remarked: "Brother Field was the boss, as he should have been. I think that's where lots of trouble comes in: the man is not man enough to stand at the head." Field organized his entire family in a distinctive way. He planned to make it into a single unit. There were many children and they were more or less under the rule to find their pleasure at home. Musical instruments were provided and an instructor brought in to teach the children to play. A family orchestra was formed. The children also gave plays and recitations in the home and the other family members made up the audience. There was a strong bond of solidarity and anyone seeing the family gatherings would have difficulty in distinguishing among the children of the different mothers.

Twenty-nine per cent fell into category 3. Heber Thomas typifies this program. He laid down the basic expectancies as to conduct, but insisted—on what today would be regarded as sound psychological grounds—that the wives chastise their own children. His argument was that since the wives and children were in close association throughout the day, if a mother punished a child, the latter could later be caressed and comforted by the mother if this appeared necessary to soften the impact of the punishment and to restore the child's self-esteem. If the father chastised the children and then was absent most of the day, the children might brood over the punishment and come to resent it.

Only one family, that of Aaron Strong, seemed to typify category 4 or relative equality of responsibility for discipline, and certainly the *modus operandi* in this family was more a matter of an unconscious accommodation than any deliberate division of responsibility. Aaron was a mild man who left most of the control to his wives.

On the other hand, it is interesting to note that 38 per cent

—the highest single proportion in any group—were classified under category 5. In a society so definitely committed to the patriarchal, authoritarian pattern, this represents a remarkable modification in the direction of the practical demands of the day-by-day situation.

The Charles Cook ménage is a case in point. The two wives were sisters who got along well together. There was one household for all, with a certain division of labor. Discipline was left almost completely in the hands of the wives and little distinction was made as to parenthood when chastising a child. William, a son of the first wife, Josephine, remarks: "Neither of my father's wives had any more authority over me than the other. If Aunt Constance said for me to do anything, I felt it as much my duty to do it as if my mother had said to do it." And as to corporal punishment, "I can well remember my mother saying, 'Connie, give him a cuff!' if Aunt Constance was nearest to me and I needed it. Whichever one was most convenient did the disciplining in our household." While some other families operated on this pattern, most women were very careful not to assume responsibility for even mild discipline of the children of other wives.

In a few instances the role of the husband and father was hardly evident, even in theory. Peter Roberts left discipline entirely to his wives. The children rarely, if ever, paid any attention to anything he said to them. The regulation in the Jacob Voss households was even less ordered. What controls there were were completely in the hands of the women. There was no system of chores; the boys had no duties around the house although occasionally they were sent out on the range with the sheep.

No families fell definitely into category 6 though the Roberts and Voss families approach it. The only actual examples of complete control by the wives were those of widows who had to assume all responsibility for discipline, but such instances were not included in our tabulation.

With respect to the form of discipline, 38 family stories contained specific reference to the kinds of control which were used by the father. Four categories were set up, as follows: (1)

highly indulgent; (2) reasonably mild; (3) reasonably severe; and (4) severe.

Of the cases tabulated, 21 per cent were clearly of the indulgent sort; nearly one third were reasonably mild; 29 per cent were reasonably severe; and the balance, or 18 per cent were listed as severe. Cross tabulations show, on the whole, that the more indulgent forms of discipline were positively correlated with permitting the wives much latitude in handling the problems of control.

Indulgent forms of control are neatly illustrated in the Winslow and Lowman families. In both instances various obligations of the children were well laid out in advance, but the routine controls were relatively mild and friendly. At the other extreme some households were regulated in a very strict fashion.

The eldest daughter of the first wife of Hyrum Stratton says that in his families

> Discipline was terrible and cruel. Father was unjust and unreasonable in his punishment of the children . . . I am sure he never loved his children. He just regarded them as obligations he had to assume in order to carry out the terms of plural marriage. And the children were terrified of him . . . The change when he came into the house was very noticeable. Usually the younger children all sat on the floor around the room afraid to move when he was there; they were silent until he told them to move. The children were never permitted to eat with their father. They either sat at a second table or came and got something to eat, took it outside to eat it, and then came back for something else.

Joseph F. Smith ruled his families by kindness. One of his last efforts at physical punishment—of one of the children of his fourth wife—was laughed at by the child and he evidently felt that he had been defeated in this attempt. He seldom tried whippings after that. For severe breaches of his rules he set up a kind of family court where the culprit was dealt with in the presence of the entire family. An instance of the use of the family court occurred when some of the sons had stolen and eaten chickens belonging to a neighbor. The latter complained to Smith and family court was held in one of the homes, with the entire family and the neighbors present. There was no formal trial procedure but informal questioning and judgment by the father. In this instance the boys were adjudged guilty and sentenced to pay seven times seven the value of the chickens. They worked out their sentences on the neighbor's farm. Smith believed thoroughly in the device of a family court and thought it might well be emulated by others.

As the child, especially the boy, moved through adolescence, his indoctrination in the moral and religious ideas and practices of his culture became increasingly important. In this training the father usually played the chief role. His dominance not only took economic form but as a carrier of the holy priesthood he had a central obligation to see that his family was brought up in the way of the Lord. In this, of course, he did not differ from his monogamous brethren, except that the range of his obligations was extended.

In the early days all good Mormon households had family prayer at least once a day, usually more often. Remarked one person reared in polygamy, "There was family prayer at home twice a day. It was usually before meals, and we would kneel around the table." A daughter of a second wife relates: "Every morning, if father was staying at his first wife's house, he would lead the family in prayer there and then come over to our house and lead family prayer there, too. And in the evenings he always led family prayers in both houses the same way."

In the matter of spiritual teachings, the report of the Edward Quinn family is typical: "Father's few evenings at home were spent in his reading the Bible and explaining it to mother. He could understand it better than she could. He also sang a lot to us . . ." And in another family—that of John Taylor: "In the evenings father often told stories of his experiences to his children and gave them fatherly advice. He was not dogmatic, however. He almost never read the Bible to the children . . ."

Then, too, attendance at Sunday School, other Sunday services, and at the various weekday meetings was expected as evidence of faithfulness to the gospel. Parents not only instructed their children to go to these meetings, but their own example was considered important. Alice Reynolds, daughter of George remarked: "Another factor in successful discipline I think is good religion. We always went to Sunday School, and that was important. Father's example was the very best, and we tried to follow it."

There was, and still is, heavy emphasis on following the Word of Wisdom. The main methods of teaching were oral exhortation and example. While a few immigrant Mormons found difficulty in giving up tea and/or coffee, and while some of the brethren did use tobacco—chiefly in the form of chewing—and a few tippled a little, the church officials were constantly harping on the evils of narcotics and alcohol and on the need to obey this "temporal law." One son of John Thomas told how his father taught him the importance of the Word of Wisdom by commenting on several notorious town drunkards. His father contended that one beer or one cigar might not injure a person, but that habits had a way of growing. If his son wanted beer or tobacco, it was all right for him to take them but he must first make sure that he would not become like the town sots. Yet one could never be sure since people reacted differently to such things, and one could not tell at the outset whether one would not end up like the town drunkards. This line of argument kept the informant from using liquor and tobacco.

In keeping with the puritanic theory and in common with pioneer needs and attitudes, great emphasis was placed on the sacredness of work. Almost every record which has any data on the economic life under polygamy, makes clear the high emphasis placed upon the young learning to work. Ample evidence of how plural households were organized for productive labor was given in Chapter 7.

Before going on to discuss inter-family contacts, a brief comment must be made regarding the education of children under polygamy. One of the most prized tenets of Mormonism is the aphorism, "The glory of God is intelligence." From the outset the leaders of the movement put heavy stress upon the importance of education. Wherever they settled provision was soon made for the schooling of the children. In fact during the first five decades in Utah the Church provided practically the only elementary and secondary education available.

The faith in formal schooling was practically universal. The social status and the economic condition of the particular family, however, would make some difference. With few exceptions, all those plural families in our sample which represented the elite of Mormon society, furnished at least a modicum of formal education for their children. In families like that of Brigham Young and John Taylor formal educational programs were set up for the children; but these were clearly exceptions. As a rule schooling was provided in tuition schools run by the Church, usually under the local ward organization. School terms were short and the teachers frequently were ill-prepared to carry their pupils beyond the most elementary aspects of the traditional three R's.

In some families, like the Earl Vernon's, poverty prevented anything but the most rudimentary schooling. Of more serious importance were those families where the children of one wife might be given a better education than those of another. In the Henry Roper family—one which had a good deal of conflict and trouble—the children of wife number two had little or no schooling beyond the lower grades. On the other hand, at least two sons of the first wife had some college training. So, too, in the Edward Quinn family, some of the first wife's sons had professional training and have become well regarded in their respective fields.

It is already clear from what has gone before that the training and disciplining of children in a given family might well have some bearing on what went on in another. Such matters as the status relations among the wives, household arrangements—separated or together—economic conditions of the families, including division of labor among wives and children, and timing with reference to establishment of plural families have been noted.

Friendly relations with Aunts is evident from the remark of a daughter of Hans Olson: "We were taught to respect the wishes of our Aunts just as much as the wishes of our own mothers, and we did, too." Evidently during the time when the families were all housed together, the wives assigned chores to any of the children, regardless of actual parenthood.

While the name "Aunt" was almost universally applied to the wife and mother of another than one's own family, negative attitudes sometimes emerged. Thus, the first wife of Jonathan Baker and her children, greatly resented his marrying a second time, 18 years after his first marriage. Eliza, the second wife, under 20 at the time of her marriage, was never called Aunt, just Eliza. It was a none too subtle symbol of the resentment felt by members of the first family. Yet Eliza was of a mild and even disposition and never seemed to have minded. In short, where a monogamous family had been long established and the children were already of age or approaching it, such resentment at a father's entering the Principle was not uncommon. This was true of the older children of Henry Knight, Samuel Baxter, Jr., and of Joseph Adamson, to mention only three other examples. Very often in these families there were children of the first wife who were as old as the new bride. But despite wide age differentials and considerable negative feelings about plural marriages, on the whole, the relations of the children with their Aunts was quite satisfactory.

In remarking on the way in which the children came to the other wives for permission to do or have things, the fourth wife of "Heartbreak" Stratton, went on to say, "But I guess they went to their Aunts for more things than they did to their own mothers, because their Aunts indulged them more. That was the way most of the polygamous families did." There is much evidence in our comments to support the fact that women were often more kindly to the half-siblings than to their own children. Psychologically it is quite possible that indulgence in such cases might be rather freely given because it did not have to be followed by, or linked to, punishment or deprivation in other situations. Here both Aunt and child, in a manner of speaking, were getting something for nothing!

In the matter of attempted cross-family discipline, however, it sometimes happened that rather sharp differences appeared when one wife would try to correct the child of another. In fact, in most of our families the wives were most careful to avoid inter-family difficulties which might stem from one wife trying to discipline a child of another.

The relations of the half-brothers and half-sisters varied with other circumstances surrounding a given family. They reflected more basic adjustments of the total family including inter-wife relations, especially matters of relative status of wives and families, distribution of income, household arrangements, and so on. Moreover, it is my impression that direct inquiry into these matters often resulted in somewhat idealized or defensive pictures being given. The actualities may have been somewhat less rosy. Thus, Mary Becker Duke, one of a family of 25 children, remarked: "Our home was united and I loved my half-brothers and sisters just like my own." Then, too, information from families of the Mormon elite, in particular, are likely to be a combination of idealization and rationalization. In such families there was public expectation that they would live up to the Principle more adequately than the ordinary run of Saints and set good examples.

In the highly conflictive Roberts family—where the husband took a second and young wife after 20 years of monogamy—the children of the two families, at least those of somewhat comparable ages, got along together much better than did the two wives. Number one was a dominating woman who never forgave her husband for accepting the Principle in practice. Some of our other records likewise report that the half-siblings got along much better than did the various wives.

Yet, in contrast, all the Edward Gilbert families got on very well. After 20 years of monogamy, Edward took a second wife and shortly after that a third, a sister of number two. In fact an informant, the oldest daughter of the third wife, was named Lucille after the first wife. While many of the children of wife number one were already grown up, those in about the same age group, especially of wives two and three, got on famously. "When we were little children," says this daughter, "we didn't know which was which. If my Aunt gave cookies to her children, she always gave some to us too. We were always in and out of each other's houses." What occasional difficulties there were were always quickly patched up, often under the firm but friendly guidance of the father.

Time tended to modify many of these earlier patterns of relationship. In some instances where there had been some friction among the children of plural wives, the later years saw the half brothers and sisters in congenial relations. In other instances, the friendly relations of childhood and adolescence disappeared and avoidance, or at times, open conflict emerged.

An important feature of child rearing was to make sure that the children understood and appreciated the Principle under which plural marriage operated. The broader aspects of rationalization and idealization of the Principle were described and analyzed in Chapter 5. Here we shall note them briefly as they related to the inculcation of attitudes and values favorable to polygamy.

In discussing the Joseph F. Smith family, we noted how the elite of the Church were supposed to set an example for satisfactory settling of problems in plural families. A daughter of Edward Gilbert said, "With few exceptions the best men among the Saints went into polygamy," inferring that under such conditions one might expect good results. Moreover, where the general consensus of the community supported the practice, we should expect little or no personal problems to arise regarding status as children of plural marriages. Two daughters of Aaron Strong remarked that nearly all their childhood friends were from polygamous families and that they never believed "they were cheated by it." A son of Henry Roper by the first wife said it never occurred to him as a child that anybody would consider polygamy wicked. This same attitude was voiced by a daughter of Howard Keith. A daughter of Joseph Adamson by his second wife expressed a view which was very common, at least when the Principle was not only widely accepted but carried out in practice: "We children were all brought up to feel that 'we had something' by being born into polygamous families. We were superior to other children, and enjoyed an inestimable privilege in living as we did."

Yet as the climate of opinion changed to somewhat less enthusiastic support of the Principle, as the federal pressure on the Saints in the late 1880's was intensified, and particularly in the post-Manifesto days, negative attitudes were more in evidence. For example, the realization that children of plural wives were, by law, really illegitimate struck many a growing boy or girl with great force. As a daughter of the second wife of Russell Bradley once bitterly remarked to a friend: "We've always been like a family of illegitimate children turned loose." Her half-brother, Lee, often cruelly reminded her that they, the children of wife number two, had no legal rights. Or, to be told in the presence of others, as one daughter was, that "she was the cause of my being sent to jail" tended to arouse guilt feelings not easy to bear.

In closing, one psychological aspect of the relations of parents to children must be noted. While there were many variations in the nature of the inter-personal relations of the fathers to their children by plural wives, it is my impression that on the whole these children had much closer ties to their mothers than to their fathers. While strong attachment of children to their mothers is a part of our larger American culture, such bonds were probably increased in plural families. First of all, the father was less likely to be in evidence than in a monogamous household. Here we have something of the parallel enhancement of mother-child affections in homes broken by periodic desertion or even by death or divorce. In other words love for children was partly a compensation for the transfer of love by the husband to other wives.

The disappearance of affection for the husband and its increased concentration on the children is neatly brought out in Daisy Yates Barclay's story. In describing the final break with her husband, Daisy relates:

One Sunday morning as my husband and I stood on the front porch of our home together, he informed me that he would not

come to Bountiful to see us any more. There had been no previous
differences between us except the children's education to which no
reference had recently been made, so the statement was a great
shock to me at the time. Inwardly I felt impelled to persuade him
otherwise, and I am sure he expected me to. I nevertheless controlled myself and made no response to his far-reaching decision.
My silence at the moment was not an easy thing. Yet, I am aware
now that the years of the preceding struggle to live polygamy had
all helped to steel me for whatever may come. I thought in those
few moments before he departed: "I'll be equal to whatever must
come," though I did not for a moment suppose that he intended
to contribute no more to our support.

As he stepped from the porch to the walk, he turned to add:
"You must look to your brothers for help . . ."

The separation was final. No further comment was made.

Neither of us, while he lived, ever referred to our separation,
so we were both true to his desire that no unpleasant affair be
discussed . . .

This plural marriage which had begun on a highly romantic note ended up in separation. In the years that followed
Daisy and her children supported themselves. The more immediate basis of the trouble between Mrs. Barclay and her
husband was over a matter of whether her sons should remain
on a ranch in Canada to work for him or go to school. In discussing this matter, Daisy remarked: "I had the attitude of
many Mormon women in polygamy. I felt the responsibility
of my family, and I developed an independence that women
in monogamy never know. A woman in polygamy is compelled
by her lone position to make a confidant of her children. How
much more is this true when that woman is left entirely alone."
Her displacement to the children had become complete.

*President Daniel H. Wells spoke about the brethren making their wills, especially those in polygamy, and thought that it was a matter that should be attended to.—* From a diary entry of a convert, September 11, 1871.

# 13   INHERITANCE AND DIVISION OF PROPERTY

FROM THE OUTSET the Mormons knew that neither in common nor statute law were plural marriages recognized. Yet they soon realized that some kind of provision should be made for the protection of plural wives and their children in the matter of inheriting property. With this in mind the Mormon leaders who then dominated the territorial legislature of Utah sponsored various acts making it possible for the children of plural marriages to inherit, in full share, the estate of their fathers. Obviously if a father made a will he could dispose of his property as he saw fit. However, many Mormons who accepted the Principle neglected to make wills or were even opposed to doing so. It therefore became necessary to make legal provisions, if possible, to regulate inheritance.

The present chapter will deal, first, with the formal and legal aspects of inheritance of property, second, with the manner in which inheritance was handled practically by the Mormons with plural families, and finally, with the various difficulties which grew out of attempts to meet the basic issue of inheritance.

The first law dealing with the inheritance of property of plural families was passed by the territorial legislature of Utah in 1852. Among other things it provided that if a father died without a will, the children and the wives (both the legal first wife and the plural wives) should inherit his property in equal shares. The act specifically states, "Illegitimate children and their mothers inherit in like manner from the father, whether acknowledged by him or not, provided it shall be made to appear to the satisfaction of the court that he was the father of such illegitimate child or children." This is clear acknowledgment on the part of the Mormons that they well knew that the children of plural marriages were in law illegitimate. While this act made no mention of the dower right of the first wife, it did not definitely abolish it. In 1872, however, a law was passed which specifically provided that "no right of dower shall exist or be allowed in this territory." From 1876 until the passage of the Edmunds-Tucker bill in 1887 various other acts were proposed and some passed to make certain that plural wives and their children would have equal rights with first wives and their offspring in matters of inheritance.

Those opposed to polygamy, both in Utah and outside, realized that if the right of dower could be restored to lawful wives, it would serve to deprive the plural wives of at least one third of their husband's estates. The abolition of dower, provided in the law of 1872, remained on the statute books until 1887.

The Edmunds-Tucker Act of that year restored the dower right in Section 18 which reads: "A widow shall be endowed of the third part of all the lands whereof her husband was seized of an estate of inheritance at any time during the marriage, unless she shall have lawfully released her right thereto." The next section goes on to provide the same rights to the widow of any alien who shall at the time of his death be living in the territory of Utah.

Even more drastic was Section 11 which "disapproved and annulled" all earlier laws of the territory of Utah which gave "illegitimate children" a share of a father's estate. Rather it provided that "no illegitimate child shall hereafter be entitled to inherit from his or her father or to receive any distributive share in the estate of his or her father."

A further step in regard to the inheritance of property as it affected polygamy took place after Utah became a state on January 4, 1896. As a state, of course, Utah could now make her own laws of inheritance. One of the first acts of the legislature was to abolish the dower right of the widow but it did provide a substitute by giving the widow one third of her husband's real estate and also for the first time restricted the husband's testatory capacity by a section containing the clause: "Provided, that a married man shall not devise away from his wife more than two-thirds of value of his legal or equitable estates in real estate without her consent in writing." But the right to inherit under their father's wills was restored to illegitimate children. The Act further provided that the mother of an illegitimate child who died intestate without heirs should succeed to his property. Moreover, the same law legitimatized the children of plural marriages born after the passage of the Edmunds-Tucker bill and before January 4, 1896.

The first Utah state legislature made even further efforts in favor of the children of polygamy. One law provided that children who had suffered adverse decisions in court proceedings in estate matters could reopen the same under certain conditions. However, this law was soon declared unconstitutional by the State Supreme Court on the grounds that it destroyed the finality of judicial decisions and that the legislature had assumed a control of the judiciary not warranted by the constitution.

The situation with regard to both wives and children may be summarized as follows: Children of plural marriages could always inherit shares in their father's estate under a will, except for the years 1887–96. The plural wives likewise could inherit any share the husband wanted to give them up to 1887. After 1887 the legal wife had a dower right to the estate. This portion was often so large that after providing for the children, little was left to bequeath to the plural wife or wives. If the husband died intestate, the lawful wife retained her dower right, and the legitimate and acknowledged illegitimate children succeeded to the remaining. Plural wives, lawfully the heirs of their children, might receive their children's share. Yet, in any case, the first wife generally received the largest part of the estate. A legal wife might give up her dower right for distribution to the other wives. This act of generosity seldom occurred, if our family records are at all representative. It is true, as will be seen later, that many estates were divided informally without recourse to the probate courts, the resulting ownership pattern being ratified by the necessary legal sanctions. The uncertainties of such procedure were well enough known, however, to inspire many a plural wife to make certain of her economic future during her husband's lifetime.

On the death of the father a plural family might be confronted with any one of three different situations. In the first case the property might already have been distributed in some way or other prior to the father's death. Second, there may have been a will or other testamentary arrangement, either formal or informal, for the distribution of the property. In the third instance, there might be no will or other provision, the man dying intestate. The whole property division would then have to go into the courts unless the family could agree on some sort of satisfactory arrangement among themselves.

The fourth wife of wealthy Hyrum Stratton described the settlement of his property in approximately these words. When he was 80 years of age Hyrum divided up his property and gave it equally to his two remaining wives and to all the children. Sister Stratton said that there was a considerable amount of personal property which he retained and which was to be sold when he died. However, she went on to say that "She knew how children and wives sometimes fought over these things" so she asked her husband to give her and her children all that was coming to them when he made the original distribution. She said she did not want to be involved in any conflict after his death. Hyrum agreed to this and the whole estate of the fourth wife and children was settled at that time. There was no difficulty in this division and upon his death the balance of the property was distributed among the remaining children and the other surviving wife.

Joseph Adamson whose story has been of interest to us throughout also divided his property before his death. At the time this was done Joseph was having difficulty with the law over polygamy and he felt that it would be wise to get the property settled before he might be driven into hiding or otherwise got into more trouble with the courts. The first wife got the family homestead which included both houses although she did not take possession of Louise's house until the latter voluntarily moved out. The 160-acre farm was left to Louise, the first wife signing the deed jointly with the husband. Apparently Joseph and his first wife talked the whole thing over and decided upon this procedure. It was not entirely satisfactory to the second family but it was about the best they could do under the circumstances. Joseph died at Louise's house and when she asked what to do with his watch, chain and other things, she was told to keep them and to give them to her little boys. This showed some friendly feeling although the Adamsons had had considerable trouble.

Regarding the property settlement of the Isaac Lambert estate, the second wife had this to say:

> No, I have no property whatever. This house I'm living in belonged to Lucille, the first wife, and her daughters have fixed it so I can live here until I die . . .
>
> Yes, the first family got everything. When Louise died and I moved here to live with Lambert, the property had already been deeded away and there wasn't anything left. Well, I could have gone to court to get something for my children, but there wasn't anything left to get. Lambert did give my four children that city lot that wasn't worth anything. When he died the first family had got everything fixed up.
>
> I never let my children run my affairs, but Isaac did. Lucille's son James ran things for Lambert and I guess he did it. I haven't got a thing against him. Let the Lord judge.

It was a rather common practice for a polygamous husband to marry legally the next wife in line after the death of his first wife. Lambert, however, did not do this. When asked about this matter the second wife said that he never believed in going before the law for anything if it could possibly be avoided. She said, "No, we couldn't go to court for anything. It wasn't legal . . . There was no legal marriage between him and me. He kicked about it like heck, and said he didn't believe in anything but a temple marriage anyhow." But some effort was made in the mother's behalf. A daughter and son of the second wife put up a real battle to try to get a more equable settlement for their mother at the time of the property settlement.

The general authorities of the Church were quite aware of the difficulties involved in probate proceedings in the matter of property for plural wives and their children. They frequently urged the Saints to make wills to avoid such difficulties.

The case of a more formal will is neatly illustrated in the John Vance family. The first two wives of John Vance predeceased him. Both these women had accumulated a considerable amount of personal property and this was distributed to their own children on his death. When Vance died his will provided that the estate was to be held in trust for the use of his third wife as long as she lived. It was provided that she should have whatever she needed for living in comfort. This was to be paid out of the interest on the estate but if the interest should not prove sufficient the principal might be used. On her death the residue of the estate was to be distributed among the children.

The executor of the estate, a son of the third wife, who tells this story, visited his mother in company with two of his half-brothers to find out how much money she needed to live in comfort. She made an offhand estimate, whereupon the other two boys—not her sons—insisted upon increasing the amount by one-third. The informant told this as an example of the good feeling that prevailed among the members of his family.

When the third wife died she had saved something like $750.00 from her maintenance money which she put back into the estate instead of spending it on herself and her children as she had a right. The estate was then divided among the children of all the wives.

The unhappy events in the life of Oscar Dahlman which we have described elsewhere led to a somewhat interesting provision for his family. You will recall that there has been a great deal of trouble in this family, including a divorce and, later, the legal marriage to the third wife instead of to the second as was customary. Wife number two was disturbed by this action. Finally, his two adult sons had so mismanaged his business while Dahlman was on a mission that a good many members of the family felt that these boys had taken money for their own benefit at the expense of others in the family.

These circumstances gave rise to the peculiar will disposing of his property. It provided that one boy got a dollar and it canceled the debt of another. Just before his death Oscar had given these boys some property so he felt justified in cutting them off in this way.

His two surviving wives had homes in their own names and certain income from some property. The bulk of the remaining property went to the third or legal wife. Her view, however, was expressed thus: "And I think I didn't get too much property, either, marrying as young as I did and having such a hard time. Besides, he left me land poor. When my husband died he had not a nickel in cash money."

One provision of the will prevented disposal of the business property for 20 years after his death. However, this property became so involved in taxes and paving assessments that the wife obtained permission from the court to sell it before the 20 years were up, thus in effect, breaking the will. When this occurred, "The boys thought they could break the will, too, and hired a lawyer to do it so they could get more property. They failed in that, however."

The division of Hans Olson's estate took place in this fashion: Each wife had been deeded her own home before Olson died. He also made a will which provided that each woman's children should have an equal share in the property. When the children came home from the funeral they met in their father's house and within two hours had divided all the property. The oldest son took charge and there was no dissension whatsoever. The personal property was divided by giving to each child his choice, various ones asking for his horse, his watch, knife, saddle, and so forth. One of the daughters owed her father $100.00 and she asked that it be canceled as her share in the personal property and it was allowed her.

Sometimes the procedure was considerably less formal though it had the effect of a will so far as the action was concerned. John Taylor who died in 1887 had made a will consisting merely of the statement: "These are my wives and children," and then appending a list of them and with his name signed at the bottom. The procedure of division followed is described by a son of the fifth wife in approximately these words: The family meeting was called and the property was distributed in a pro rata fashion. Each wife and each child received an equal share of the property and the children then turned their shares over to their mothers to use until their deaths. The use of the farm was given to the seventh wife because she had the youngest family and needed more income. One of the daughters, who was a mental case, received a double share of the property to support her. The informant was firm in his statement, "There was absolutely no disagreement over the distribution of the property."

Where a husband died intestate families met the crisis in various ways. In some instances there was no difficulty at all. If the families remained friendly, arrangements satisfactory to everybody were made. In some other cases, however, there was trouble deciding who should get what property and why.

How failure to make a will led to difficulty is neatly shown in the Benjamin Wolfe estate. A daughter of the first wife said that her father had deeded the home to his plural wife on the grounds that she would be left no home if he died first. However, he had given nothing to Gertrude, the first wife, on the assumption that she would share in the estate when he died.

The failure to provide for the first wife prior to his death led some of the children of Gertrude to urge their father to deed her home to her, but this only aroused his anger. Moreover, when Gertrude died, Wolfe legally married the second wife, Christine. On his death a real battle ensued over the estate, the two families forming hostile camps. A daughter of Gertrude related:

Before father died Christine had been busy building up her bank account. One of the boys said if father had lived a week longer we wouldn't have got anything. Besides that, all of father's friends around Brigham City had supposed that father was worth about a hundred thousand dollars when he died, but when Christine had the inventory made out and turned it over to the court it totalled only twenty-five thousand.

There are some members of the family, in fact, who think that she had held out the balance of the estate in some easily concealed form, cash or stocks and bonds. But the family didn't protest this short inventory because they did not want "to disgrace father's name by protest."

The worst blow to Gertrude's children came when her home was included in the inventory and Christine's was not, because she owned it separately. The result was that Christine got a widow's share of the farm and Gertrude's home and was able to keep her own home also.

The account of the property division given by the surviving wife differs somewhat from that of Gertrude's daughter. Christine said that Wolfe married her in 1931, soon after the first wife's death "just so I could have my rights in the property. Wolfe never made a will. I guess he thought if he made a will, the family might have more jealousy about that . . . I got a third, and the other two-thirds of the property was divided among the children equally, mine and hers; there were nineteen children. Yes, I guess there were some disagreements, but it was all settled by law and what could they do. What I mean is, a lot of the children would have liked to have had more."

George Mackay left no will but the estate was settled amicably by all concerned. When Mackay died the family was advised by legal counsel not to take the estate into the court because then all the wives except the first would be cut off. At any rate, the first wife would be likely to get a larger share than might otherwise be the case. So the wives and children got together and decided to divide up the property. The first wife said that she would not take any more than any other wife got. It was finally decided that each wife should get twice what each child got. The range land was apportioned, each child getting 750 acres. The horses and cows were selected one at a time by the beneficiaries in rotation. The wives kept the houses in which they lived although there was some buying and selling of shares among the family afterwards.

It will be recalled that the Winslow households were highly systematized effective economic organizations. On Winslow's death it was discovered that he was in the process of dividing up his estate. He had already deeded his farms to the sons of the second wife and the wives' homes to them. He had also given a $1000.00 share in the business to the oldest unmarried son of Mary, the first wife, and had the papers all drawn up to give an equal share to the oldest unmarried son of Norah, the second wife, but had not completed this arrangement.

When Winslow died the estate was thrown into the courts. The probate court gave the whole property to the legal wife, leaving the daughters of the third wife with nothing. Several people made suggestions that Rebecca's children could get the court to upset this decision but their mother would not permit it. Apparently the first wife and her children felt completely complacent about the possession of the property and had no intention of sharing any of it with the others. Public sentiment in their community, however, seemed to support the idea that the third wife had a bad deal in the division of the estate although she never tried to do anything about it. She got some comfort from the statement of Winslow "on his deathbed" that he knew he should have given her a better estate but that there was "no time for it now."

After 1887 the legal wives were assured of a dower right in the property. On the other hand, the plural wives had no standing in the law at all except as heirs of their own children. It was almost imperative, therefore, for the husband to make special provisions for the plural wives in the forms of gifts of property.

A plural wife without title to her home or other property could easily develop a sense of insecurity and might be expected to make some effort to acquire such title from her husband. The children, too, would likewise be anxious for the mother to be given a home of her own. This whole question is tied up with the status factor and the mother's status was reflected in the children. Moreover, according to Mormon

folkways the children would become responsible for the
mother's support if their father should die without providing
for her. We have little or no information as to how the husbands were persuaded to convey title. In all probability it was
usually a voluntary and spontaneous act. Certainly there is no
evidence in our materials or other historical sources to indicate any wish on the part of the husbands to leave their plural
wives destitute.

An example of the consequences of failure to convey title
to a wife of any property at all, home or otherwise, occurred
in the Mathew Hale family. As one informant puts it, "Because the wives weren't recognized by law and father had
made no will," the children of two of the wives took the matter into court and there was litigation over a long period of
years. The conflict was chiefly between the children of the
second wife and those of the first. The third wife, Martha, and
her young children took no part in this struggle. She had some
years previously moved to another community and had more
or less cut herself off from the family except for polite visits.
Sometime later when the case was beginning to be settled
Martha was given a "legal paper" by one of the children of
another wife and asked to sign it and have the children sign it
so as to give up their interest in the estate. Martha signed the
paper without any legal advice and when the estate was finally
settled she and her children got nothing whatsoever.

One daughter of Martha who was acting as informant thinks
that her mother later regretted signing this paper because her
children had as much right to a part of the estate as any other
although she as a plural wife had no such rights. Apparently
there was no bitter feeling on her part at this turn of events.

The whole matter of provision for the plural wives was
tied up with the question of whether, on the death of the
first and legal wife, a man should or should not then lawfully marry the next succeeding wife. Certainly there was a
general feeling among the authorities of the Church that the
brethren should follow this practice. However, a good many
did not do so. For the plural wives to outlive the first wife

and her dower right was really a convenient outcome of the
situation if the husband thereafter did not marry one of the
survivors legally.

It is worth noting that sometimes a man thought it hazardous to give his wives independent property before his death.
For example, Howard Keith confided to a friend that his wives
were to have their homes but that they were not to know it
until after his death. "They weren't going to be able to tell
me to get." Sister Dahlman number three, who was 19 years
younger than her husband, once remarked, "I have known
some women who when their husbands would get cross and
unreasonable would say 'You get out of this house. This is my
house.' But I didn't."

These accounts of the husbands' methods of distributing
their property show considerable variation. It is clear that a
husband might experience difficulty in trying to decide which
one of these methods to use. After years of efforts to avoid undue conflict within the family, this last act of control bulked
large and important. People generally were aware of the experience of other families in these matters. Many times
families disintegrated almost immediately on the death of the
father into separate groups of conflicting personalities regardless of how well the man had directed the disposition of
his property. As a result to many men who recognized the
symptoms of disintegration within their own family, it may
have seemed wholly unnecessary to leave any directions or
hardly worthwhile to do so. Again we have a good illustration
of the fact that under Mormon polygamy workable patterns
of action did not develop in the relatively short time the system was in operation.

In about 50 per cent of the 35 families on which we have
data on property division, informants said that the members
of the family were on the whole satisfied with the outcome.
The other half of the records contain accounts of disagreement and conflict ranging all the way from rather trivial and
easily healed breaches to serious and disruptive quarrels. In
few of these families has the disorganization gone so far as to
prevent a certain amount of polite intercourse between mem-

bers of the various families and in many cases time has healed the earlier wounds.

There is little doubt that the factor of social status looms large in the whole relationship of one family to another under polygamy. We have already explored various aspects of this and need but to indicate briefly the relationship of status to property division.

We have pointed out that no matter how much the Principle might be adhered to by the Mormons, there remained a realization that after all only the first wife and her children were really legally entitled to status and property. While there was no attempt on the part of the Mormons to set down formal rules or practices which made the first wife automatically the chief wife—as is true among some other peoples who practice polygamy—nevertheless the factor of legitimacy and the factor of expected consent of the first wife frequently left her in a position of power over the other wives which could not be gainsaid. In the second place, it will be recalled that after 1887 the dower rights of the first wife were firmly established by the Edmunds-Tucker Act. This left the first wife's children in a highly favorable position knowing well that their mother stood to receive at least a third of the estate. If she owned her own home in addition so much the better. However, such an expectation might be considerably disrupted were the first wife and their mother to predecease the father. Especially hazardous for them was the situation when the father then proceeded to marry legally one of the plural wives. While superior status in the form of legitimacy remained to them, this was hardly a satisfactory substitute for the loss of one-third of the man's estate through his marrying a plural wife. If a man married his plural wife on the death of his first, her children then would finally come into possession of the dower third of the estate. We have already noted some of the difficulties involved in this kind of situation in presenting the settlement of the Wolfe estate.

In many ways the status factor was a somewhat unstable and fragile element in polygamous families. The evidence for this statement is clearly brought out in discussion of the property division. Anxiety about status might remain covert for years in a family to break out when these last collective acts of the family were about to occur. The distribution of property with all its legal trappings is generally an occurrence that happens once and for all. Moreover the dominant personality, the patriarch of the family, had by his death abdicated his previous arbitrary authority. While it was in theory a function for the oldest son to take the place of a father in family councils, this rarely went beyond the division of an estate in those families that got along well together. There was absolutely no provision that the oldest son should take over the patriarchal duties and functions from that time on.

The examples already cited give ample evidence of the variety of difficulties or the degree of harmony which might exist in various families. Among the outstanding instances of high satisfaction with the property division which we have discussed, it is interesting to note that these families were from the elite of the Church. As we know, these families were operating under a general public expectancy of performing in a satisfactory fashion.

There is no doubt that these leaders did, at least externally, try to live up to the ideals that were expected of them. Three particular characteristics of the ideal procedure are exhibited in these instances: In the first place, all the surviving wives were treated with equal fairness; that ardent upholders of the Principle did not view their wives as any different whether plurally or legally married is clear enough in our records.

In the second place, all the children received equal shares of the property. Sometimes this was made immediately after the death of the father, sometimes provisions were made for subsequent division of the property following the death of the wives and mothers.

In the third type special needs of individual members were always to be taken into account. Sometimes this might be a provision for the wife with the set of young children. In other instances it might be a matter of a mental case in the family, or a cripple, or perhaps some girl who was unmarried and whose chances of matrimony were slight.

One of the most tragic examples of family disruption over property is that of the Albert Procter ménage. Procter became incompetent some years before his death and a guardian was appointed to look after his property. In time the third wife, Carrie, and her children began to believe that the estate was being mismanaged and started considerable dissension which resulted in an investigation by the High Council of the Stake. A committee was appointed and in general their findings supported the conduct of the estate under the guardianship. The final paragraph of this interesting document runs:

From the investigation made by us, we feel it our duty to state that we find that Joseph Procter as manager of the company has given evidence of managing the affairs of the company with ability, and to the best interests of same in our opinion; the difficulties and troubles in this case have been complicated by reason of the unfortunate illness of the head, Brother Procter. We desire also to assure the accusers that we find no evidence of any attempt on the part of the accused to take any advantage of the accusers, and we advise that every effort be made to promote peace and harmony in the family by all members thereof, and that each one carry out in the spirit thereof the suggestions herein made.

However, Procter lived only a few years after this and on his death the third family again appealed to the Stake High Council to break the will. The High Council appointed arbitrators. In general the arbitrators came to about the same conclusions as had the previous investigators. The award of arbitration declared that Carrie had received from Procter about all that was coming to her and that the estate should be divided among the other heirs, except that some of the sons who had already taken their share would get a lesser share under the provisions of the will.

An examination of the full report on Procter seems to indicate that in his later years he spent much of his time with the third wife. He had already given her a good deal of property but nothing to the other two wives. The first two wives were sisters and got along reasonably well; neither of them particularly cared for Carrie. There was already a certain foundation for the difficulties in this family that came to a more severe crisis when it was time for the property settlement.

Other features in these disagreements may be noted. First of all, those who were favored in the distribution seldom seemed disposed to make such arrangements as would lessen the conflict. Yet, often enough, for those who were dissatisfied, the distribution was not regarded as final. Efforts were made through the courts—either governmental or ecclesiastical or in some other way—to reopen or alter the decisions on distribution.

In summary, there is no better illustration of the difficulties which plagued polygamous families than their attempts to adapt themselves to a system of inheritance which was linked to monogamy. In societies where polygamy is well recognized in law and the mores, there are various kinds of more or less standard ways of handling the matter. Nothing of this kind was developed among the Mormons although it will be recalled that during the territorial days the Mormon leaders tried to legislate so as to provide equality for all wives and all children. They did away with the dower right so long established in British and American law. Had they been able to continue on their own without interference from the federal authorities, they might have been able to make this arrangement permanent. But the Edmunds-Tucker law definitely restored the dower right and since the people were under territorial rule, they could do nothing about it. It will be remembered, however, that some effort was made to rectify this situation after Utah obtained statehood.

In this whole matter the status factor is also crucial. The legitimacy of the first and legal wife and her children was never in doubt before the courts. Clearly the division of property aside from the sheer financial aspect became a symbol of status and a mark of the degree of remaining solidarity or disunion which might hold for any given family.

*I am proud to follow an Adam into the celestial kingdom.*—One of Brigham's wives.

*Polygamy furnishes every woman who wishes to marry, a husband and a home, and gives every man an opportunity of expending his superabundant vitality in an honest way.*—*From* History and Philosophy of Marriage; or Polygamy and Monogamy Compared, *by* Christian Philanthropist, 1869.

# 14 THE PSYCHOLOGY OF WOMEN AND MEN UNDER POLYGAMY

In the nine previous chapters we have discussed some of the problems of inter-personal adjustment among the Mormons who took up the practice of polygamy. In particular these involved the relation of husband and wives, the accommodation of the wives to each other, and changes in the customary parent-child contacts due to living under the multiple-family plan. The present chapter will give a summary over-view of the effects of polygamy upon the attitudes, values, and habits of the men and women who participated in it. The balance of the chapters will deal chiefly with the wider public controversy which arose between the Mormons and the non-Mormons over the plurality system.

As we observed in Chapter 4, the plural system began in secrecy and ended in secrecy with only a short interlude between these periods when there was anything like an open acknowledgment of it even among the Mormons themselves. Yet the wide acceptance of polygamy by the Mormons was not enough to offset completely a number of forces which impinged on all those who tried to practice it. Among other things it upset the romantic ideal of monogamy, it confused individuals as to their roles and statuses, and in many other ways ran strongly counter to some of the deepest values of the Christian world from which Mormon members were for the most part recruited. Before taking up these matters, a comment on the significance of secrecy is in order.

To live in the world without contact with other human beings is impossible. Communication is the basic law of social life. Yet there is often some element in knowledge and activity which sets one man off from another, or one group from another. In situations fraught with danger, or with great promise, it is easy to develop a kind of response which takes on the character of secretiveness. We all know people who get a great lift by being "in the know." For example, men who are engaged in secret intelligence work for military and other governmental agencies often derive much personal satisfaction from the realization that they know things that other people do not. There is here a combination of thrill and threat: one gets a thrill out of knowing something which someone else does not, and yet there may be a certain threat if the knowledge itself is considered dangerous.

Living in polygamy was just such a combination of thrill and threat: one had a thrill or emotional reward from living for the Principle, and yet one was constantly under a threat of exposure for doing so. And while the principle of polygamy was accepted as divinely established, the requirements were that one had to keep the facts of its practice from the American public. Then, too, the secrecy of the Mormon temple rituals has long been the subject of a great deal of gossip and rumor. There is no doubt that people who indulged in these rituals got all the thrills that individuals get in any secret society. Moreover, in the endowment ceremony, at least, the women were able to participate with the men. This was one secret event that Mormon men and women could and did share. As for the masculine head of the plural household, his holding a secret priesthood provided an important support to his ego.

The basic difficulty of living in polygamy so far as personality adaptability is concerned grew out of the conflict between the acceptance of the Principle verbally and its day-by-day operation in one's family. The practice of polygamy may be viewed in terms of role and status, which are but types of behavior carried on vis-à-vis people in a given group. A role is always an activity with regard to some particular social situation. We begin as children with certain roles laid down for us by others and finally move on through a series of roles in adolescence to those of our adult years. Accompanying such functions are certain statuses. Status is one's position in a scale of values or power. Status is largely determined by how other people regard one's roles. In fact, role and status are intimately bound together.

The subjective or internal aspects of role and status may be examined in terms of one's self-image. This would include one's sense of self-esteem, self-reliance, and one's ideals. Then, too, one's sense of security is a central feature of the human personality. This rests not only upon one's image of oneself but also as to how one is accepted by others. Whether one is considered to be good, bad, or indifferent in terms of moral behavior is correlated closely with the judgment of one's actions by others. One's self-image, moreover, is compounded, in part, by the expectancies and demands of others and certain kinds of images of an ideal sort which one builds up from one's contact with friends, relatives, and enemies. These give one the basis of organizing these images into something of a unity.

What has been called the ego ideal is such an element in the personality. It is a self-image projected from our needs or desires into what we would like to be. Both as children and as adults we build our ego ideals on the basis of what is sometimes called the ego model. These ego models may be real personalities or they may be composite or imaginary ones, but they serve as the blueprint which we each want to follow. This is neatly illustrated in the small boy who wants to be a Babe Ruth, a Lindbergh, or a General Eisenhower; or in the young girl who sees in the glamorous women of the screen or television the ego models of her own wishful thinking.

To understand the role and status and the accompanying self-images of men and women in polygamy, we must recall that Mormondom was a male-dominated society. The priesthood—which only men could hold—was in complete control and celestial marriage, either monogamous or polygamous, exemplified the higher status of men. Women were viewed as of lesser worth, to be saved only through men holding the priesthood.

The self-image of the woman reflected her inferior status. Alice Johnson Read, after hearing a sermon by Brigham Young, put the matter in her journal thus: "The Principle is that a woman, be she ever so smart, cannot know more than her husband if he magnifies his priesthood . . . God never in any age of the world endowed woman with knowledge above the man." And Daisy Barclay, herself brought up in a plural family, remarks: "Polygamy is predicated on the assumption that a man is superior to a woman . . . [The] Mormon tradition follows that of the early Hebrews. It teaches woman to honor and obey her husband and look upon him as her lord and master." As a daughter of the second wife of Isaac Lambert once complained, "Mother figures you are supposed to spend your life taking care of a man, and he is God."

That this masculine principle went deep, and far more fantastically than the Saints could comprehend, is shown in a sermon by Brigham Young, reported by John Read. In a letter to one of his wives Read said that Brigham referred to some future time "when *men* would be sealed to men in the priesthood in a more solemn ordinance than that by which women were sealed to man, and in a room over that in which women were sealed to man in the temple of the Lord."

Here is evidence of deep, psychological *Brüderschaft*. There are obviously latent homosexual features in this idea and its cultural aspect has many familiar parallels in other religions. Most Saints, including Brigham himself, would have been much shocked by such an interpretation. Yet the Mormon system, with all its ecclesiastical trappings and military controls, like other organizations of this sort, had strong homosexual components. This is true of armies; it is true of priestly orders in all religions; and certainly in many aspects of the occupational guilds of the Middle Ages. Moreover, it is evidenced in our own society in the masculine, fraternal orders so prevalent.

Still, for many Mormon men, plural marriage was no "bed of roses," popular mythology to the contrary. As one of the daughters of Edward Gilbert put it, "I've heard my mother say that father knew polygamy was a trial to his wives, but that it was a greater trial to him." This was partly an explanation that her father had married "for the Principle," not for personal and sexual interests. In commenting on a husband's role with respect to conflict between two wives, the second spouse of Oliver Owens had this to say, ". . . For all their talk, polygamy is harder on the man. He has to put up with two women, and when he does anything he has two pairs of eyes watching him and two people to account to."

While the ego ideal of a man and a woman bound together under monogamy may represent something short of what they had previously daydreamed about in terms of romantic love, nevertheless life is relatively simple for them compared to what it might be under the plurality system.

In our society monogamy is associated with the belief that romantic love is the basis of marriage and family life. The fundamental ideas of romantic love are obvious: it is a kind of predestination; it is love at first sight or at least of sudden blossoming; and there is a great deal of idealization coupled with inaccessibility with regard to the prospective mate. Pioneer life among the Mormons facilitated some aspects of romanticism, in particular with reference to free choice of partners in contrast to marriages arranged by the respective families.

Yet the romantic ideal, no matter how temporary it might prove to be under monogamy, was definitely a disturbing factor in most polygamous adjustments. The use of jealous behavior when one's love relations were threatened was likely to lead to more rather than less difficulty in the plural family. As we have seen, the official Church provided no ego model for women in these matters, hence wives were obliged to try to make the best adaptation they could.

A husband might have had a romantic attachment in his monogamous marriage, to be followed by quite other motivations with regard to polygamy. We found, however, that sometimes a man married in polygamy thinking that he was following the Principle and having little of the romantic idea in his head, only later to find himself very much in love with various plural wives, or a particular plural wife, as the case might be. Then, too, the combination of Mormon theory of bringing spirits to the world and giving them bodies and the need for a large labor force provided a convenient motivation for plural families; while the race for babies must have had some beneficial effects upon the man since the producing of more children enhanced his glory. On the other hand, it sometimes produced an anxiety if he felt he could not support such a large brood.

For these reasons a man might have some inner conflict as to whether he should enter the Principle or not. Furthermore, if he did make up his mind to do so, he faced competition with other men, either single or married, in seeking the hand of a given girl. While some Mormon women seemed to prefer an older man of material substance to the risks of marrying a younger one with nothing but promises for the future, sometimes older men felt a sense of guilt in entering a contest to court and marry a young woman already pursued by younger and normally more eligible men. However, despite some sense of guilt in the matter, many older men got a thrill out of courting a younger woman.

Coming from a monogamous background, the self-image of a man must have been considerably altered by facing a plural household. Willy-nilly he found himself emotionally involved with two or more women. Since the wider culture demanded adherence to monogamous fidelity to one woman, to have plural wives was a patent source of conflict. In other words, no matter how fair and just a man tried to be with respect to division of income, of time spent with each wife, and in other day-by-day matters, he might find himself confronted with problems of competition, jealousy, and anxiety which disturbed the expected plural way of life.

A wide variety of methods was used in the control of families. Some men went into the matter in great detail, and others left much of the day-by-day operations to the women. As a matter of fact, many men found it simpler to let the wives work out their own *modus operandi* on routine matters rather than to interfere. Again temperamental differences in the man himself would play some part. If a man as patriarchal head of a family persisted in putting his fingers into every pie, he was bound to invite trouble.

The difficulties which a man faced in his family were of three kinds. First, there might be trouble among the wives which he would have to help settle. Second, there was always the possibility of his own conflict with the given wife or wives. And third, there was the problem of possible difficulties with the children. Any of these three conflict situations might range all the way from the mild to the severe. The milder difficulties would become a strain only because of their possible frequency or because they involved many more individuals than would be the case in a monogamous family in like difficulties. Certainly the first type of conflict would not appear in monogamy, but troubles of the second and third kind were common enough. Conflicts of the first type must have had repercussions of various sorts upon the man.

One of the most widespread and gravest problems in practicing polygamy had to do with the status of the first wife and her children. Certainly the psychology of the first wife is different from that of a plural one. In the case of the first wife and her family, there was over and over again evidence of the feeling of infringement on their rights with the coming of a plural family. This was particularly acute when the family had been established for years as a monogamous one only to break out into the polygamous pattern when a man was middle-aged or older.

The most important single factor supporting the high status of the first wife was the legality of her marriage and the legitimacy of her children. No matter how much preaching there might be from the pulpit or how much people in private conversation made a point that all children in polygamy were

the same, everyone knew that this was not actually so in terms
of American law and wider public sentiment. Moreover,
since property loomed large in the matter of status, it should
not be forgotten that the legal rights to property were a factor of considerable importance all down the line. As we saw
in Chapter 13, this often became a serious problem after the
death of the head of the family. In other words, psychologically
the first wife might accept the principle of plurality of wives
rather easily when she knew that after all she was still the
*only* legal wife. Moreover, in periods of enforced secrecy, as
at the beginning and end of the system, this sense of security
would be even greater than during the period when Mormon
polygamy flourished more or less without outside interference.

Where the first wife was very dominant, a plural wife might
accept the role and status of a domestic or other inferior position. In some families there is almost a hint of the emergence
of the kind of relationship which existed between the first
wife and concubines in some of the other societies that practiced polygamy. This was true in the Old Testament days and
is true in some illiterate and civilized peoples of today. In
other words, the plural wife and her children were regarded
as second-class members of the family.

We have ample evidence that a first wife was not always
completely secure. She did, on occasion, lose out in favor
of a younger wife. This kind of difficulty was particularly
likely to arise where a monogamous family had long been established only later to be confronted with a plural wife or
wives.

Obviously the coming of a plural wife altered a great many
of the situations in the family. One of the basic problems
was neatly put by Sister Gilmore, wife number three, in the
remark that it was "the constant pressure of adjusting yourself to another woman" that caused the "trouble." There were
many ways in which a new wife might be introduced into a
family. Certainly during the early period of secrecy it frequently happened that the other wives knew nothing about
the taking of another spouse. This was also true during the
late 1880's and subsequently after the Manifesto.

During the period when polygamy was more or less openly and publicly recognized by the Mormons in Utah, men used different devices for introducing their new spouses. If they followed the accepted pattern, of course, they would have secured the consent at least of the first wife for the new marriage. This sometimes did not occur, however, but usually the first wife had to put up with the new arrangement anyway.

Other factors influenced the attitudes of the women toward each other and toward their role and status. While plural families often began by living in the same house, most men believed that their marriages would be more successful if each wife had her own home. It was all too easy for the first wife to continue to dominate the household when the second wife was brought to live under the same roof. The second wife's attitude toward herself and her role and her feeling of status improved as she got her own place with her garden and other accoutrements for a separate household. Some of the psychological problems faced by a plural wife are neatly shown in the journal of Belle Thompson, a third wife. Belle was a person of high spirit and sense of independence.

In adopting the rules and regulations of my husband's family already established, I had to submit to an almost entire reversal of my nature and habits. The greatest difficulty I had to meet was the hot Irish temper that had always swayed me when occasion aroused it. Many times the words of my Uncle McCorkle were brought to mind, "Remember in your plural home speak no words when angry." When I disobeyed that injunction, it brought me sorrow.

To adopt an early hour for arising and retiring worked rather a hardship upon me. When at the stroke of five in the morning I was obliged to drag my drowsy head from my pillow, I would bless my mother for having let me enjoy so many late morning naps when I was at home. And when the clock at nine in the evening sounded the curfew and I had to retire to bed to toss sleeplessly there until near the middle of the night, I felt that order and method were hard masters . . . Again my uncle's admonition to me to, "Conform to all the established rules of the home to which you are going, and be careful of how you try to set up your own government."

The difference in the attitude of one plural wife toward another in contrast to the attitude toward the first wife is neatly brought out in the Daisy Barclay story. To quote:

Margaret [the third wife] and I had much in common. Toward Aunt Harriet [the first wife] I seemed to feel an obligation. I could not get away from the idea that she had made a great sacrifice for me. I am sure that women would never have accepted polygamy if it had not been for their religion. A woman never consented to its practice without great sacrifice on her part. There is something so sacred about the relationship of husband and wife that a third party in the family is sure to disturb the confidence and security that formerly existed. As far as Aunt Harriet was concerned, I felt like an intruder. Margaret, on the other hand, came into the family after I did. It was a great relief to feel that we were on the same level. She and I really enjoyed each other's company.

This well illustrates a certain carry-over of attitudes from monogamy. Despite Daisy's conviction that polygamy was a sacred privilege and despite the fact that she had been raised in a plural family, she could not quite bring herself to feel on an equal basis with the first and legal wife. Then, too, she had romanticized marriage a great deal and apparently projected into the first wife a good many of her own feelings about romantic love. It should be noted too that the time when she was writing, her ardor for Barclay had somewhat begun to dim. Later, as we saw in Chapter 12, it disappeared altogether.

Sometimes the deferential attitude toward the first wife did not take any such subjective turn. Faced with poverty or near-poverty, many plural wives just accepted unequal treatment as inevitable; yet they did not completely abandon their deference toward the first wife. As one wife said, "I always had to take what he gave me and shut up. Anyhow, she was the first wife and his first duty was to her. My husband had quite a responsibility. He done pretty good anyhow."

There is ample evidence that frequently a wife's loss of affection for a husband was associated with a decline in the acceptance of the Principle. In some instances this went so far as to lead to an ultimate rejection of the whole system. For example, the second wife of Russell Bradley was so bitter that she said she did not want to see her husband in the hereafter. This was, in effect, a complete rejection of the belief in the eternity of the marriage covenant.

Occasionally the suppressed attitudes of hostility came out only after the husband's death. In Chapter 13 we saw that sometimes there was a quite definite reversal of feeling toward the husband as well as toward the Principle when inequities appeared in settling an estate. So too at a time of property settlement a first wife might show strong hostility to her dead spouse and to the Principle by insistence on inheriting the major if not a full share of the estate.

Then too there was always the threat of displacement by another wife which may well have dogged the lives of many of the first wives or of a plural wife who had become a favorite. The defenses against such a contingency have been noted: use of overt affection, doing special favors, performing household and wifely duties to a high degree of satisfaction for the husband, the father, and others. Also, in some instances, there was, in effect, a kind of psychological rejection as when the woman's love for the man grew cold or was transferred to her children. In any case, some kind of inner reorganization had to be made if a wife was to make a reasonable outward adjustment to the other wives.

Again, wives might cooperate to withstand certain kinds of pressures or controls from the husband. Heber Thomas had four wives, but Susan, wife number two, and Anne, number three, had been married previously to men who had predeceased them. Under the celestial law these first marriages were for time and eternity. On their husbands' death they were permitted to marry again under Mormon practice, but theoretically they would belong to their first spouses in the hereafter. A son of the first wife reports that while the second and third wives were cooperative enough, they gave in to Thomas' demands only when they felt they had to, because all their lives they considered themselves the wives of Oliver and Johnson, respectively, and hence not completely under the authority of Thomas, except "for time only." Moreover, they had brought some property into the family along with four children apiece by their prior marriages. Therefore in certain matters of property they felt that they had some rights with which Heber should not interfere.

The kind of concern which men had for their families is nicely brought out in letters which they wrote while they were on missions or otherwise engaged away from home in either church duties or in their own business. Charles C. Rich, one of the Mormon leaders who was often absent from home attending to church matters, wrote his three wives periodically giving them advice and directions. For example, in a letter to all three of them, he remarks:

> I am glad and thankful as far as I know that there is a kind and friendly feeling amongst you. I hope and pray that this spirit and feeling may increase among you till you will be one, as the Church of God is one . . . I feel thankful to the Bishop and all the brethren and sisters that take an interest in your welfare.

The interplay of the plural wife and her husband is evident in the journals and letters of John Read and his wife Alice. Alice Read was an independent-minded person who had some difficulty adapting herself to plural family life. She was deeply in love with Read, but saw little of him over the years. His families were widely scattered and, moreover, he was occupied for a long time as United States Marshal in the Territory of Utah. Still later he was engaged in business for Brigham Young. In a letter of October 9, 1854, Read wrote among other things to his wife, "Hope you will learn by experience not to take up branches of business without my first directing you." This in reference to Alice's starting a business of her own. Later in the same letter he says, "I feel anxious about your health, and can see that you are quite unable to take boarders, and I wish you and every other member of the family to know that I do not want them to prepare another meal of vittles to sell unless it is to board someone who is employed by me." The letter closes, "This is from your affectionate husband, John."

Alice's journal and his letters provide an interesting picture of the manner in which one man tried to manage his families even though he did not see them for months on end. From time to time Alice had serious doubts about her entrance into polygamy and she was particularly upset by the death of her small daughter, Mary. In 1856 John wrote Alice from Washington, D.C.:

My dear Alice:

I thank you for your letter as it came at a time when it was a consolation to me. I do hope that you are learning the right way to be happy.

I presume if you analyze your feelings in years that are past, and recall your prayers, that the desires of your heart have been more fully realized than you now suppose; and if you will only put in practice the wholesome truths that have been taught you from time by the servants of the Lord, that you will overcome and the Devil will let you measurably alone, or when you do have him to oppose you, it will be on some general principle wherein your glory will be augmented.

I hope you will be wise in relation to your health, guard against fatigue, either of body or mind, but gain an equilibrium. I wish also that you will watch George [a son] closely while you let him go out and play often, do not let him play too long, even if it is a cross to him. Make him take a nap in the middle of the day, go to bed early, and be sure to get up early in the morning whether you do or not.

I hope you are wise in relation to your health, and cease to mourn or write mourning poetry for our dear little Mary, who is no doubt better off than when with us, and we have treasures in a safe place . . .

One of the most obvious ways to avoid trouble in plural families was to treat them all alike. As we have seen, sometimes this was carried to such lengths that a husband would take to buying or furnishing the same things for each wife, be they furniture, foodstuffs, or dresses.

Another, though not common device, was that used by John Taylor. While he rotated his time among his wives, he built himself a special room, with bed and other equipment, in each house, and retired there whenever he was staying with a particular family. This represented a kind of avoidance, if not escape, from the routine of the family. Taylor was a busy man, and doubtless felt he needed relaxation and quiet. Not every Mormon could afford such luxury.

If men could not make adequate provision for their wives or otherwise provide some isolation for themselves, at least they could daydream a little about an ideal situation. Samuel Baxter, Sr., once gave his idea of what would be the happiest day of his life: It would be to see his three wives coming downstairs in the morning pleasantly saying "Good morning" to each other.

While never officially or openly admitted, two other means of avoiding trouble with one's plural families was to go for a year or more on a mission, or to manage to be "called" to colonize some remote territory yet to be taken over by the Mormons. In the former instance, one might be forced to leave one's families behind, and often without much financial support; but at the same time a man was relieved of the need to listen to difficulties and settling them on the ground. When sent on a colonization project, a man might be "counseled" to take but one family with him, at least during the early years of such new community developments. This would mean escaping from other families, at least for a time. Of course, escape in this manner was sometimes short-lived as when an ardent missionary converted some young woman with an eye to later taking her as a plural wife or where a man called to colonize might meet a comely daughter of one of his co-workers and subsequently marry her as another plural mate.

While the Gentile world may have viewed Mormon polygamy as illustrating the lechery and debauchery of the human male, there is no doubt that for the most part the Mormon men were as puritanical a lot as could be found anywhere. M. R. Werner's characterization of the system as "puritan polygamy" is in point. In common with other followers of the Christian moral code, the Mormons believed, in theory at least, that sexual intercourse should be for purposes of procreation only. Certainly so far as the wife was concerned, there was to be no fun connected with it. However, in every-day life there doubtless were sex relations that had little or nothing to do with desire for procreation.

The interest of older men in young girls has been noted previously. Many men concerned with practicing the Principle did not overlook the possible hedonistic delights associated with marrying young women. Yet too obvious concern of this sort might lead not only to family conflict but to community pressure in the form of gossip.

At the close of Chapter 1, note was made of sexual variationism under the plural system. That is, under polygamy men had approved access to more than one woman. Just what physiological and psychological effects this variation in intercourse had on masculine personality is hard to say. As for the wives the chances are that few of them enjoyed an orgasm. Under the general puritanical patterns, women were not supposed to have any need for sexual gratification. The male was the dominant member of the family in theory and in practice, and the wife was expected to be ready to serve him biologically as well as otherwise at any time.

Yet for the man an opportunity to have sex relations with various women in turn may have had some stimulating effects. Certainly there is every reason to believe that a man would come to look forward to intercourse with one wife in preference to another. This would be qualified not only in terms of direct sexual appeal, but in terms of friendliness and expectancy.

On the other hand, the wife had no chance to look for another man to satisfy needs, sexual or otherwise, which her husband could not give. Given its puritanic foundations, a mixture of polyandry with plurality of wives would probably have wrecked the Mormon system completely.

While the variety of marital relationships may have provided some change and sense of release, Mormon men could not escape their puritan consciences. No matter how well adjusted to polygamy a man might be in terms of conscious adherence to the Principle, his unconscious sense of guilt and shame might well induce conflict. Neither he nor his wives could quite avoid the pressures of their own consciences and the conviction of the outside world that they were living in sin.

Although the Church tried to provide certain historical supports for polygamy and though they certainly twisted the generally accepted story of the life of Jesus by contending that Martha and Mary were his plural wives, nevertheless centuries of Christian monogamous marriage and especially the strong puritanical taboos upon any expression of sex outside of monogamy were the foundation stones upon which most Mormons must have organized their basic values about matrimony. Certainly when Smith first introduced plural marriage, he had to face up to the fact that he and the leaders had been avowing publicly that polygamy was not approved. And even during the four decades after 1852, when plurality was openly preached and practiced, people coming out of Protestant homes must have had difficulty in accepting this doctrine. Even those children who were brought up in plural families frequently had sufficient day-by-day experience with the system to know something of its limitations.

One of the common psychological devices to escape or cover over one's own guilt is to project such guilt feelings upon other people. The Mormons were full of this reaction. They continually referred to the sinfulness of the monogamous world. While the Gentiles were making much of the so-called harems of the leaders of the Church, and while they were continually making public appeals to abolish the evils of polygamy, the Mormons, in turn, were pointing out the continued presence of prostitution among the Gentiles and that the officials who came to the territory as federal appointees frequently brought along their mistresses. Apparently these contentions were, in part, projections of the Mormons' own uneasiness about polygamy.

Another important factor was the frustration, hostility, and anxiety linked to trying to satisfy a self-image or given role with regard to the husband and the plural family system. As we have seen, first wives and their families frequently developed a good deal of fear because they felt threatened with the loss of their rights and statuses with the appearance of another wife and her family. In contrast, the plural wife or wives experienced frustrations and anxiety because they did not have the status they expected and had to fight for it, often against considerable odds. Thus arose a social situation likely to induce frustration and anxiety on the part of all the wives.

How the challenge was met varied widely. In some instances individuals retreated and took a secondary place. In other instances they were highly hostile and competitive. And in still others they tried to work out some kind of cooperative compromise. In any event these people not only had a sense of guilt and shame but also revealed considerable confusion as to just what role and status they should play vis-à-vis each other.

These two sets of factors, guilt and shame on the one hand, and frustrations and anxieties on the other, really laid the foundation for a split personality. While we have no illustrations of serious personal dissociation, we have plenty of evidence that there was a real problem of reconciling the theoretically exclusive aspects of the monogamous role-taking in such matters as child bearing, child care, housekeeping, supplying the husband's needs, and full rights to property with the nonexclusive elements of polygamy, such as sharing the husband, the children, and the property. We have already noted that this conflict of roles often produced overt conflict among the wives and, at other times, cooperation. This condition is not unknown in monogamous families but probably was enhanced in polygamy by the continual pressure for adjustment.

There is some evidence of compensatory and neurotic responses on the part of men to certain of their difficulties. An earlier chapter reported a few cases of neurotic invalidism on the part of some women. A good illustration of a nervous and ill husband who exploited this is Adam Winthrop. Though Adam was a silversmith by trade, he became private secretary to Brigham Young shortly after arriving in Utah. Later he was sent to help colonize in southern Utah and became an important leader there. He was never robust and always felt physically incompetent. As one who knew the family well remarked, "Brother Winthrop didn't do any physical work, [and] was always waited on hand and foot by his wife. She could do anything, but not him. I have seen Mrs. Helen Winthrop hitch up the horses, drive to the temple gate, drive him home, then unharness the horses." Winthrop had three wives and they all accepted his ill health and even competed among themselves to see who could treat him best.

A few men among our families developed psychosomatic symptoms. Such an one was Edward Gilbert, a successful businessman and prominent in the Church. The informant was a daughter of the third wife. During the days of the federal raids her brother had been sent to the penitentiary for a year for concealing a polygamist in his store. Gilbert, also in hiding at the time, was finally caught. He was fined $300.00 and sentenced to six months in the penitentiary. He went into prison just as his son was coming out. The informant continues:

They [the prison officials] liked my brother, and he asked them to be good to father, because father had such bad headaches—he had been a business man all his life and I guess the head work made him have those headaches. The prison officials did not shave his beard or make him wear stripes. He made the soap for all the prisoners and supervised the laundry—the others did the work, he just supervised it. He did not have many headaches because he was out in the open so much. They let him send home for his own mattress and bedding. He got a good rest. He felt as if he were with the best people while he was there.

While externally this family seems to have been reasonably harmonious, there is some evidence of occasional stresses. Apparently Gilbert's headaches were not unrelated to his trying to resolve these difficulties. It is interesting that the headaches were far less frequent and severe during the time he was serving his sentence. This period provided an escape from the day-by-day routine worries, especially those connected with being on the Underground.

George Reynolds was afflicted with migraine headaches.

While he was indulgent with his children and used to play with them, on the other hand, his headaches restricted his work as well as his recreation. During these periods, the children had to keep quiet. Because of his prominence, Reynolds, like many other leaders, felt a strong pressure to maintain the appearance of a successful plural household. The informant tells a little episode which illustrates some of the difficulties in this matter:

He didn't often appear in public with two wives, except at church parties where he might take all three. He took his wives to concerts and plays by turns. These turns might not coincide with the time of his visits, but they worked out very well. For example, he would announce to Polly, the first wife, that he was taking Amelia, the second wife to the concert this evening. This routine was broken at times because of his headaches. One time Amelia had to be disappointed because one of his headaches came on before he could take her to the concert. He was greatly worried over this, and sorry about having to disappoint her.

All through the Reynolds' record runs an undertone of a certain anxiety on his part to make the plurality system work. He was firmly converted to it, yet sensitive on the subject. While he was serving as clerk in the church headquarters, he had the job of signing the papers in church divorce cases. On one such occasion where the evidence against the husband for mistreatment of his wife was clear, as the husband signed the papers he mumbled something about how he would still have the woman in heaven. On hearing this Reynolds remarked that he would like nothing better than to have the privilege of kicking him out of heaven.

Henry Roper had a lot of difficulty in handling his families. He developed a number of psychosomatic and other evidences of compensatory response. Henry was not an aggressive man and seems to have suffered from the pressure of other people. In fact, his first marriage to Myra Grant was more or less engineered by her sister.

After 10 years of monogamy during which there had been some economic difficulties, Roper began courting Elizabeth Brown, a new arrival in the community. But it was not long before Myra shipped them off to Salt Lake to get sealed so as to cut short the courtship. After the second marriage the first wife gradually rejected Roper because of his attention to the other wife and because of his financial incompetence.

About this time Roper was made Bishop of a difficult and chaotic Ward in one of the outlying communities. Matters in the Ward became more chaotic and Roper developed a "pig-leg —his leg got as big as a post and he had a terrible time." Because of this illness the authorities of the Church released him from the bishopric. The doctor advised him to go to a lower altitude, whereupon he and Myra moved to California. This was in 1900. But he soon decided that he did not like California and began to visit back and forth between there and Utah, using money which Myra made on her farm for his expenses as well as to maintain the other wife. During this period Roper was at loose ends; he completely lost the domination of his family, he was unable to work and make any money, and he became quite thoroughly disorganized.

Later he regained his health and returned home. He was made the Bishop of a much more peaceful Ward in a small town. Here he lived with his second wife until she died. He then returned to his first wife, as she said, "with empty hands," and lived with her until 1933 when he passed away.

In psychosomatic cases there is a combination of physiological with psychological features and the latter are clearly evident in Roper. Both marriages came about through the interference of others. His first wife became rather cold to him although she bore him 15 children.

It is quite possible that Roper was not greatly inclined to a second marriage and probably would not have married again had he not been more or less pushed into it by his first wife's anxiety. Moreover, Roper was never successful in business. Then, too, his efforts to handle affairs as a Bishop worried him a great deal. He must have been somewhat laden with guilt because he could not manage his family and because he was not certain of himself in his role as a church official.

In concluding this chapter let us summarize briefly the outstanding features of the psychology of men under the plural system. Later on we shall make a few final comments regarding the women. In the first place, in keeping with the Church expectancies, a plural family provided high status for men. The more wives and the more children a man had the greater his glory would be here and in the hereafter. Such status, of course, had to be backed up by good church performance. This would include paying tithing, keeping the Word of Wisdom, going on a mission, and serving in various capacities in the priesthood. A man's progress up the hierarchy of ecclesiastical authority was another evidence of successful membership. Then, too, a man should be able to provide amply for his family in material matters. Yet there were many plural families which were really poverty-stricken. The church authorities often regarded such marriages with a certain disfavor. In fact, sometimes a man got quite distressed because the Church tended to disregard him because he was so poor. Then, too, a man's status had to be backed up by evidence of a well-managed family.

The psychology of authoritarian operations is well demonstrated in the story of Joseph Adamson. You will recall that Joseph had for a time been disfellowshiped. Later he repented and was accepted back into the Church. So far as his church work was concerned, his rebelliousness seems to have been completely suppressed. He became thoroughly docile and submissive to the authorities above him in the Church. On the other hand, he was very severe on his family and on those under his control. He is a neat example of what is found in military organizations, in priestly orders and elsewhere where there is a high degree of centralization of power at the top and a downward gradation of this power. In such situations one looks up with great deference to those above one and is severe and rigid in one's attitudes to those below. This is a kind of sacred "pecking order" of power, to borrow a phrase from psychology.

Such authoritarianism, however, was likely to lead to difficulties in managing a family, as it did with the Adamsons. The more adaptable and more flexible men left a good deal to their wives which probably made for greater success. Adamson is an

instance where complete conformity to the Church did not
pay off in terms of a successful family life.

There was another factor which might give rise to some
anxiety and distress. The church officials provided no settled
way to handle marital strife between the husband and his
wives or among the wives themselves. A man was faced with a
good deal of trouble in trying to work out the pattern of exclusiveness that goes with monogamous marriages when such
controls and affections had to be shared with other people.
This was really one of the great difficulties of both men and
women in polygamy.

For the women, first of all, the system of plurality sowed the
seeds of doubt and threat in many monogamous families. Because the Church authorities openly encouraged men to enter
polygamy, a great many wives must have had moments of
real anxiety.

Surely the expectation of a man's taking a plural wife was
a threat which made for instability in all Mormon families.
It certainly would be true in those monogamous establishments even where the first wife had promised that she would
tolerate or permit plural wives subsequently. A monogamous
family in this situation must have been different from one
where plurality was never anticipated.

For those who entered the system, however, some help might
be had by the development of emotionalized rationalization
of the Principle. This was certainly an aid in face saving and
in some ways in inducing stability. In their efforts to adjust to
other wives and to avoid conflict, the more faithful members
resorted, at the conscious level at least, to their adherence to
the Principle. Yet over and over again they admitted that
this verbal rationalization was bought at a good deal of emotional expense.

That Mormon women, both single and plural, in their marriage relations developed a certain cynicism about polygamy
is evident enough. Brigham Young, Heber C. Kimball, and
other leaders frequently inveighed against this cynicism from
the pulpit. Alice Johnson Read, a plural wife, records in her
diary of April 27, 1851, some evidence of the shock she had

at finding a certain negative attitude among her women friends:

> I made a call on Mrs. Joseph Young and had a smart discussion on the merits of my choosing a man who had a wife and how much more the first wife had to endure than those who voluntarily took the man afterwards. This I would not allow. My doctrine is that both have their trials, not alike but one just as much as the other.
>
> Spent Thursday afternoon with Sarah Lawrence where I had another battle with a Mrs. Butterfield, one of the neighbors, on the same subject that arose from the remark that she made among others that she would not consider permitting her husband to have another wife. It seems to me a strange thing to believe in Mormonism and not believe or receive the doctrine of plurality of wives as coming from the one source of authority, and when the subjects of this Principle are not respected on its account then the Principle is not valid . . .

Finally there were the limiting instances where there was open opposition to the Principle. This, of course, was often rationalized in terms of the hardships people suffered. We have mentioned certain bitter remarks about polygamy made by people who had lived in it. Not quite so severe as these views, however, are those who said that the system was all right at the time but that they hoped it would never again be reinstated. I was impressed in many of my records by the fact that though these people were rather open in discussing the whole system and were fairly frank about its difficulties, many of them did not hesitate to admit considerable doubt about the practice of polygamy. This view was often rationalized as saying that the people were not good enough to practice it. In fact, the disappearance of polygamy itself has been officially justified by their preachers saying that the Mormons had not yet become sufficiently saintly to practice the sacred Principle.

Against the background of our descriptive analysis of important psychological aspects of the plurality system, we now turn to examine the nature and course of the violent public controversy set in motion by this revolutionary change in the marriage and family system, long regarded as sacred in the Western world.

# 15 GENTILE AGITATION AND REACTION: EARLY PHASES

THE PERIOD in which Joseph Smith grew up was a time of religious uncertainty and unrest and he, like others, was caught up in the whole period of revivalism. When he began to reveal his own program, it offered much to some but to others it was revolting. Almost from the start he was accused by the latter of being lazy, given to seeking hidden treasures including those of Captain Kidd, of falsehood, of drunkenness, and of licentious conduct. But these accusations aside, he was a dreamer of dreams and a teller of tall yarns and these facts were soon used against him and his followers.

This chapter will undertake to present the reactions of the American public to polygamy. It will deal with the first of these reactions against plural marriages, especially during the Nauvoo period.

There was considerable conflict between the Saints and their neighbors almost from the outset. It was intense in both Ohio and in Missouri. And after a few years of peace it broke out with even more vigor in Nauvoo, Illinois. In the latter locality, the increasing talk about a new and secret system of marriage which flew in the face of strong Christian mores produced an additional foundation for increased violent reactions against the Mormons. Here was ample evidence, it was alleged, of their viciousness and immorality. There were, of course, the deeper problems of economic and political conflict against which the plural system must be examined. Polygamy simply added more fuel to this already growing conflagration.

Before taking up some of the historical details of the Gentile agitation and reaction against plural marriage, I want to make a few introductory comments; first, as to the chief sources of these attacks, and then something about the psychology of the apostate and the reformer—the two important types of persons with whom we will be concerned.

The attacks on polygamy had their roots in three particular groups: (a) There were the Christian moral reformers headed by preachers and others who saw in polygamy a threat to the sacredness of the home and family. (b) There were the Gentile politicians of the day who recognized in the Mormons a strong political force which could be manipulated or which might be opposed to them as the case might be; to them the plural marriage system was only incidental as a charge to use against the power of the Church in civil affairs. (c) Then they were the Gentile business elements who found in the Mormons strong competition and a threat to their own economic success.

The ammunition used by the Gentiles ranges all the way from newspaper stories, editorials, and pamphlets to books both of alleged factual sort to those definitely on the fictional side. The line between myth and legend, on the one hand, and historical fact, on the other, is a difficult one to draw. What people believe will largely determine what they will do and the sources of such beliefs and such activities do not necessarily have to be solid as to fact. Put in other ways, a social fact may be compounded of imagination as well as sound evidence. While we shall draw chiefly upon newspapers, pamphlets, and books of alleged factual kind, we will have some occasion to look at what the writers of fiction had to say about the Mormons as a part of the attack on polygamy.

While the political and economic factors were highly important, the center of our interest at the moment are the Gentile reformers and a word must be said about the personality of such people. Modern psychology has shown us rather clearly that, for the most part, the "do-gooders" are anxiety-ridden individuals who are worried about the condition of the world on the basis of their own wishful thinking. This, in turn, derives largely from their sense of guilt and shame. Consciously or unconsciously these people project on others their own wishes, accusing them of immorality and sinfulness. In Christian countries sin is closely associated with sex. Sex is always attractive and yet the impulse to follow its promptings is tabooed by the dictates of our moral code. From the standpoint of Christian dogma sexual expression is never proper unless it takes place within the family life as necessary to procreation. Certainly polygamy was viewed by the Gentile preachers as a horrible return to barbarism and savagery in a would-be Christian country.

Reformers, furthermore, in their efforts to clean up morals, do so largely on the basis of certain psychological factors. At the conscious level they rationalize such movements as a device to save others, but actually the reform is itself a protective device to save themselves from their own unconscious sense of guilt. In other words, the fixed moral order which they advocate is a kind of external device to provide a control for their own wishes as well as those of others.

In the attempts to abate plural marriage the Gentiles had a strong ally in the Mormons themselves. Despite any theological rationalizations the Saints may have produced, they were all brought up in the same culture as the reformers—a culture which was strongly opposed to infractions of the monogamous code. Therefore, whatever the Mormon leaders might have said in public about the Gentile reformers and their attacks on polygamy, they must themselves have had a considerable amount of guilt and shame. In fact, we have seen evidence of that in some of our family stories.

In all situations involving large inter-group conflict, such as war or as in the struggle between sectarian groups with which we are concerned, the use of information from various apparently reliable sources is always useful in planning the strategy and tactics of a campaign. The use of the spy and the informer is well known in military and other conflict. In the situation we are describing the apostate gave information which the Gentiles could use in their propaganda.

The psychology of the apostate has never been adequately and objectively explored. It is essentially, of course, the same as the psychology of the traitor. While this is not the place to pursue this interesting topic extensively, a few comments about the psychology of the apostate will help us to understand his role in the conflict we are about to describe.

In the first place, as a traitor an apostate is likely to find himself not really trusted by either those from whom he has defected or by those with whom he would presently affiliate himself. Honesty and truthfulness being strong elements in our mores, a man who departs from these and especially one who departs to the extent of telling secrets which the world outside is not supposed to know will naturally be suspect even by those to whom he is giving the information.

In the second place, the apostate is likely to be loaded with feelings of guilt. It is well recognized, for example, that in the trials carried on by the Communists against those who have departed from their party, this guilt factor plays an important part in the alleged confessions of these rebels. The same thing is apparently true in some of the apostates from religious movements. Then, too, there is always the anxiety of these people that someone of their former fellows may do something physically or otherwise to injure them. This anxiety itself probably tends to foster the further guilt feelings, at least in reverse. However much it may make them hostile toward their former associates, it nonetheless induces continuing anxiety and fear.

In the third place, as an informer the apostate tends to make things out to be far worse than they really are. In other words, in reporting on what he has experienced, or what he knows about a given group, he is likely to exaggerate. Therefore, the sophisticated user of such information will discount it in part or, at least, try to get supporting evidence from other sources.

This exaggeration, however, has certain functions for the apostate as a personality: (a) It is a face-saving device; it tends to protect his own ego and to re-establish his worth in his own mind if not in the minds of those to whom he is talking. (b) This provides a possible bridge to rebuild trust and confidence and to make a place for himself in the new group. With regard to this latter, the new group may be more than a little suspect of the traitor because they do not really trust him. If he would betray others, he might betray them.

Despite these psychological difficulties and the whole question of the reliability of his evidence, the apostate provides important information in conflict situations and a good deal of the material which we shall use in this and later chapters comes from individuals who had once been affiliated with the Mormon movement and then later gave it up. Moreover, we must bear in mind that the American public with its tremendous interest in sex was ever eager to get lurid details about the Mormons. Apostates and other writers on the subject, especially those who had an eye to making money, were likely to distort and extend their accounts in order to get attention and to sell their wares in the public market.

Apparently as early as 1831, in Kirtland, Ohio, Joseph Smith intimated interest in the system of plurality of wives. It is said that while making a new translation of the Old Testament he was much impressed by ancient polygamy among the Hebrews and made comments to those close to him that there was some likelihood of this doctrine being practiced again. At least he was toying with the idea. There is even some evidence that he had considered the idea while translating the *Book of Mormon*. (See Chapter 4.) That he may have gone beyond merely thinking about it is shown in the strong rumors in Kirtland that he was practicing plurality of wives. Although he vehemently denied this and issued ample public statements and even revelations against polygamy, the very fact that he protested against these matters so strongly suggests that there may have been something in the rumors after all.

Open accusations about polygamy, however, were really incidental to conflicts of another sort. One of these had to do with the fraudulent land and bank schemes which Smith had initiated as a part of the expanding community around Kirtland. He got himself into difficulties through mismanaging his bank and later with regard to other business schemes. This led to a great deal of local dissension and criticism. The other attack was along doctrinal lines, especially regarding the origin of the *Book of Mormon*. Dr. Philastus Hurlbut had been going about lecturing that the alleged account of the early history of the people of the Americas was nothing but a revised and elaborated story taken from a novel written by one Solomon Spaulding. While this theory has long since been more or less discarded, in the early 1830's in Ohio its telling was regarded as a threat to Smith's power.

Hurlbut had been converted to Mormonism but had been excommunicated in June, 1833, for "un-Christian conduct with the ladies." He became increasingly hostile to the Church and in gathering data on various aspects of its origin and operation, he secured a large number of affidavits, letters, and other documents. While most of these had to do with troubles in Kirtland and Missouri along economic and political lines, there were some references to plurality of wives. One item concerns the plan to convert the "Lamanites," as the American Indians were called by Smith, and take their women as plural wives. In another place there is the assertion that Smith made clear to his close followers that he did not regard adultery as a sin and crime.

The Missouri phase, in part, overlaps with that of Kirtland and, as indicated in Chapter 4, almost from the time of their first arrival in Jackson County the Mormons had trouble with the older settlers in Missouri. An attempt was made to establish an independent community but this was thwarted and the Mormons moved on to Davis and Clay counties. While polygamy was alleged and at times was noted as a factor in the opposition to the Mormons, the Missourians were chiefly afraid of the Mormons on political and economic grounds. It was in Illinois that polygamy became one of the strong charges against the Lord's Anointed.

The conflict in Missouri was bitter and the published plans of the Saints to set up a new Zion there were viewed with alarm. The conflict reached its climax in the fall of 1838.

Under orders of the state militia the Mormons were driven out of the state by force. There were a number of serious conflicts. The Saints lost practically all their property, many of their leaders were in jail, and it looked for a time as if the Mormon Church might be broken up. However, plans were made to settle across the river in Illinois.

The initial reception of the Mormons in Illinois was friendly. After their years of conflict in Missouri, it was a pleasant relief to find people in the non-Mormon world willing to say a few kind words about them. At the time of their expulsion from Missouri, the newspapers of Illinois often commented on the plight of the Saints. For example, the *Quincy Whig*, December 22, 1838, writes, "The distresses of these people, without home or shelter of any kind, is said to be truly heartrending." And the *Sangamon Journal* for January 17, 1839, stated, "Hundreds of them driven from their homes are without shelter."

The Mormons reciprocated in the matter and later sent a series of resolutions printed in the *Quincy Whig* for June 13, 1840, in which they thanked the citizens of Illinois and the governor for their kind treatment on their arrival in the state. They also thanked the governor of Iowa for his "sympathy, aid and protection."

Smith and his fellow-leaders began to look around for a new location. West central Illinois was in many ways as much a frontier as were the borders of Missouri nearly two hundred miles to the west. During the latter half of the 1830's there had been a widespread land boom reaching all the way from the Appalachian to the Mississippi. Not long after getting into Illinois Smith met one Dr. Galland who had been a speculator in lands in that area and he offered to sell the Saints a rather substantial piece of property, including the city of Commerce, Illinois. This place was nothing but a few scattered houses, but it seemed to Smith to offer the possibilities of building another Mormon community. Lands in and near Commerce were purchased as well as lands in what was called the "Half-breed Tract" across the river in Iowa. The Saints were hard up for funds but some money was raised for cash payments and the balance was taken in the form of notes signed by the leading Mormons. Galland joined the Church and was made the land commissioner for the organization. Smith undertook to handle all the purchases for the Saints and then to redistribute the property to them under certain arrangements with the individuals concerned. It turned out that Galland was more than a scalawag. He not only did not have clear title to much of the property which he sold to Smith but he absconded with some of the church's money.

Yet, Smith again demonstrated his vigorous leadership. With energy and great encouragement he set the Saints to work. In the settlement in Nauvoo he started what we would call a public works program and every member was supposed to give a certain amount of time to projects such as street-building, drainage, and other community programs. Smith declared Nauvoo to be the new gathering place for the faithful. For the fourth time in less than 10 years the Mormons set out to establish themselves in a new Zion. A large number of missionaries were sent into the Eastern states and to Great Britain to exhort the converts to move to Illinois.

During these early years the press roundabouts made note of the large numbers of Mormon converts who were arriving both overland and by river boat at Nauvoo. On February 9, 1841, the *Sangamon Journal* reports, "Nauvoo is said to have a population of about three thousand inhabitants, some three hundred buildings, several small traders, tavern keepers, physicians, and various kinds of mechanics and laborers and some watercraft, among which is a small steamboat called 'Nauvoo.'" A few years later the *Warsaw Message* was reporting:

Nauvoo, the great emporium of the west, the center of all centers, a city of three years' growth—population of 18,000 souls, congregated from the four quarters of the globe, embracing all the intelligence of all nations, with industry, frugality, economy, virtue, and brotherly love; unsurpassed in any age in the world— a suitable home for the Saints.

Among other things it was important for the Mormons to secure a sufficiently strong charter and other rights which would make it possible for them to build up a community where they could be in complete control.

The Mormons had barely got to work in establishing the new community, when Dr. John C. Bennett, mentioned in Chapter 4, appeared on the scene and became the close associate of the Prophet. It is said that Bennett had once been a professor of midwifery at Willoughby University. At the time he joined the Mormons, however, he was practicing medicine in Springfield and was also the Quartermaster General of the state militia of Illinois. Smith, who felt he needed strong friends from outside, at once took up with Bennett. As it turned out Bennett was probably an even bigger scamp and charlatan than was Galland.

With Bennett's advice and planning Smith was able to obtain an interesting charter from the state legislature at Springfield. This charter made Nauvoo in effect a state within a state. Its courts had complete civil and criminal jurisdiction, could issue writs of habeas corpus, and the mayor was, in effect, the executive, judicial, and legislative head of the city. There was a legislative council but the powers of the mayor were paramount. In addition, the city had the right to a separate and independent military organization to be known as the Nauvoo Legion and Smith was appointed Lieutenant General of this military unit. A charter was granted for a Nauvoo University and elaborate plans were made to set up a center of education.

In the next two or three years there was an increasing awareness in Hancock and surrounding counties that Smith and his followers constituted a serious political threat to whichever party did not favor them. During the early 1840's Stephen A. Douglas, then a judge of the district which included Nauvoo, was head of the Democratic party in that section of the state. Smith entertained Douglas on occasion; but Silas Walker, the Whig leader, also visited Smith in Nauvoo. Then Douglas appointed John C. Bennett Master in Chancery for Hancock County. This aroused the opposition of both parties. Bennett was a newcomer and he was a Mormon. It seemed to the politicians that this good job should have gone to someone who had a longer record of party service.

Bennett became a major general under Smith and practically all the able-bodied men of the community were enlisted in the Nauvoo Legion. As early as September, 1841, its muster roll numbered 1,494. At the time of Smith's death the Legion was nearly 6,000 strong and was probably superior in military skill to all the rest of the Illinois militia.

At this time the leaders of both the Whigs and Democrats were anxious to be friendly to the Mormons in the hopes of securing their support at the elections later. In the local elections of 1839, few of the Mormons had lived long enough in the state—a six months' period—to be able to vote. But in the year 1840 there was a presidential election, and though the Mormons had been aided by the Democrats in getting settled in Illinois, Van Buren's cool treatment of Joseph Smith, who had in 1839 tried unsuccessfully to get some redress for the hardships in Missouri, led the Mormons to favor the Whigs.

At the first election Bennett was chosen mayor and Smith and his brother Hyrum, Sidney Rigdon, Wilson Law, and Don C. Smith were among others elected to the city council.

In the state elections of 1842 Smith more or less directed the Saints to vote for the Democratic candidates for governor and lieutenant governor. The candidate for governor was one Snyder but he died before the election and Judge Ford became the candidate in his place. The *Quincy Whig*, August 13, 1842, remarks, "There can be little doubt of the success of Thomas Ford and John Moore as Governor and Lieutenant Governor. The Mormon influence . . . have all been brought to bear against the Whigs." It was generally agreed that the Saints had helped to elect Ford and for a time he was regarded as friendly to them. Later, at the time of Smith's assassination, the feeling between the Governor and the Prophet had cooled off considerably.

In 1844 we find the culmination of Smith's fantasies regarding political power. Whereas he could definitely affect the politics of Illinois and, in turn, have some effect on national elections, when he announced himself as candidate for President of the United States in 1844 many people regarded this as a serious matter. While there was not the remotest chance that he could be elected, many individuals who had up to this time regarded Smith as something of a religious fanatic and freak, saw in this a threat of the combination of church and state which the Americans had so long eschewed. While the Mormon missionaries acted as political sponsors for Smith, his untimely end on June 27, 1844, meant, of course, that no further campaign was necessary.

On the economic side things were not going too well. While the Mormons had been thrifty and hard-working as farmers and tradesmen, there is no doubt that during the conflict in Missouri depredations on property had been made on both sides. Some Mormons having been ravaged and their property stolen did not hesitate to avenge themselves against their would-be enemies in Missouri. In time rumor began to flourish that the Saints were stealing property in and around Nauvoo. A number of lawsuits seemed to indicate that some of this was doubtless true.

It was against the background of these facts that John C. Bennett's exposé must be seen. After remaining with the Saints for nearly two years, and even though Smith tried to mollify him, in the end there was an open break and Bennett was excommunicated from the Church. However, the whole proceeding was handled quietly and it was some time before the Mormons generally knew that Bennett and Smith had come to a parting of the ways. When Bennett began to publish a series of stories in the *Sangamon Journal*, everybody knew that a battle was on. This newspaper for July 29, 1842, reports that in a sermon, Joseph Smith had said he "wished Bennett was in hell!—He had given him more trouble than any man he had ever had to do with."

One of the most exciting stories which General Bennett gave to the world about Joseph Smith and the Mormons was addressed to the *Louisville Journal* and published on July 30, 1842. It was entitled, "The Mormon Seraglio." This article purported that there were three distinct orders or degrees to a secret society of women in Nauvoo which Smith had set up.

Regarding the first order, the "Cyprian Saints," Bennett said that the females in this group saw to it that those Mormon women who did not accept the spiritual wife doctrine were brought before them and given a trial. The sentence of the guilty members was that they were to be made available for the sexual gratification of any man who wished to have them. The second order, the "Chambered Sisters of Charity," consisted of those women who were permitted sexual indulgence whether they were married or not. All the higher officials of the Church had access to these women, according to the story, but Joseph Smith had the first choice. The third order, the "Cloistered Saints," or "Consecrates of the Cloister," were "set apart and consecrated to the use and benefit of particular individuals as secret spiritual wives."

While there is no external evidence that there was anything to this yarn, it made its impression and furnished the basis of a good deal of subsequent discussion about the infidelity, the licentiousness, and the general debauchery of the Mormons, men and women alike.

Smith did not let this matter rest with the accusations of Bennett. The *Quincy Whig* on July 9, 1842, reported,

Mr. Joseph Smith has quite a long communication addressed to the members of the Church in this part of the community, "exposing the character and conduct of John C. Bennett, while Mayor of the city, Commander of the Nauvoo Legion, Master in Chancery of Hancock County, candidate for the legislature, a distinguished member of the Church, etc., etc. By this publication it appears that Bennett has been guilty of seduction, adultery, slander, lying, etc. . . . He came to Nauvoo, joined the church, and "put on the livery of heaven to show the devil in."

Bennett made much of Smith's adherence to the spiritual wife doctrine charging that Joseph had introduced the whole practice of plural marriage under the guise of spiritual wifism in 1843. He remarks in an affidavit quoted later in the *Nauvoo Expositor*, June 7, 1844:

I hereby certify that Hyrum Smith did in his office read to me a certain written document, which he said was a revelation from

God . . . a revelation (so-called) authorized certain men to have more wives than one at a time, in this world and in the world to come. He said that this was the law and commanded Joseph to enter into the law,—and also that he should administer it to others.

A sample of the kind of accusations which Bennett made appeared in the *Sangamon Journal* for July 7, 1842:

Joseph Smith, the great Mormon seducer, one who has seduced not only hundreds of single and married females, but more than the great Solomon, attempted to seduce Miss Nancy Rigdon, the eldest single daughter of Sidney Rigdon, to submit to his hellish purposes, and become one of his clandestine wives under the new dispensation . . . Joe approached Miss Rigdon "in the name of the Lord and by his authority and permission," as he said. Joe attacked Mr. Rigdon, General Robinson, Colonel Higbee and myself in order to destroy the influence of all of us to prevent the exposition of this case . . . Call upon Miss Martha Brotherton, of Warsaw, and see what she will say as to the base attempt at seduction in her own case . . . Call upon Miss Mitchell, of this city, one of the most chaste and spotless females in the West, and see what she knows as to the prophet's secret wives. Hundreds of cases can be instanced, and if the Danites do not murder me you shall hear a tale of delusion and sorrow. Joe's licentiousness is unparalleled in the annals of time.

Bennett also repeated the gossip of Smith's attempt to induce Mrs. Sarah M. Pratt to become his spiritual wife while her husband Orson was on a mission. In addition Bennett told stories of Smith's extensive land frauds in Iowa and Illinois, and of the doings of the Masonic lodge of Nauvoo. From the day Bennett was cut off from the Church there began a period of charge and countercharge, of slander and counterslander.

In *Times and Seasons,* July 1, 1842, Smith answered the charges made against him. In the editorial Bennett was accused of being "a very mean man," to have a wife and three children in Ohio and notwithstanding this be paying attentions to the young ladies of Nauvoo; that he had been circulating the report "that promiscuous intercourse between the sexes was a doctrine believed in by the Latter-day Saints, and that there was no harm in it"; and of telling the women mem-

bers of the community that Smith himself "not only sanctioned, but practiced" the same. It was stated further that
Bennett attempted to commit suicide and that he had allied
himself with the Missourians for the purpose of betraying
Smith to them.

What a sharp contrast to some of the earlier statements
made by Smith about Bennett! Just 13 months previously
Smith had written an article in the *Warsaw Signal* stating,
"It is obvious, that the intention is to make the community
believe that General Bennett is a mere renegade—hypocrite
—and all that is base in humanity. But General Bennett's
character as a gentleman, an officer, a scholar, and a physi-
cian, stands too high to need defending by us . . ."

In his book, *The History of the Saints; or, an Exposé of Joe
Smith and Mormonism,* 1842, Bennett declares that he joined
the Mormon Church only to expose it and goes on to demonstrate, from a variety of sources, his own good character.

The Whig press in Illinois had at the outset exploited the
Bennett letters with the idea of making political capital. In
time these disclosures became so extreme that the *Quincy
Whig* on July 18, 1842, began to caution its readers not to
put too much reliance upon the statements of Bennett. At
the same time the Democratic press refused to publish any of
Bennett's stories and accused the opposition of descending to
"political pornography." The whole scandal was regarded by
some as a Whig plot to injure the reputation of the Saints.
For a time the Democrats were a little frightened that the
allegations might produce such a reaction that the support
from the Mormons would not be sufficient to put their men in
office. It was during this period that the ticket of the Democratic party for the governorship was headed by Adam Snyder,
who on his death was replaced by Judge Ford.

The situation in Nauvoo was anything but happy. The
*Wasp,* a Mormon newspaper, on July 27, 1842, published a
special pamphlet entitled, "Affidavits and Certificates Disprov-
ing the Statements and Affidavits Contained in John C. Bennett's Letters." Bennett was denounced for seduction, pan-
dering, and abortion. Sarah Pratt and Nancy Rigdon were

accused of having been Bennett's mistresses. Many Saints did
not dare accuse Joseph of plural marriage since it might imply
that they linked him with Bennett. Sidney Rigdon was outraged at the slander against his daughter and this episode was
one of the final ones leading to his complete break with Smith.
Yet Rigdon was honest enough to appreciate the character of
Bennett and the mischief he had set afoot. If Bennett had expected Orson Pratt and Sidney Rigdon to leave the Church
with him he was disappointed. For a time Orson was considerably shaken by the stories regarding his wife, Sarah, and disappeared from Nauvoo. Later he returned to the full bosom of
the Church and became a strong defender of plural marriage.

The spring and summer of 1843 again saw Smith under
heavy fire. He had become the target of the larger national
press and everywhere the Christian ministers were beginning
to accuse him of all kinds of horrible conduct. Moreover, the
coercive pressure of the anti-Mormons around Nauvoo became
more and more apparent. Most serious of all, dissension within
the Church was beginning to be a serious threat. In June,
1843, Smith told an assembly in Nauvoo:

> Before I will bear this unhallowed persecution any longer, be-
> fore I will be dragged away again among my enemies for trial, I
> will spill the last drop of blood in my veins and I will see all of my
> enemies in hell . . . Deny me the writ of *habeas corpus* and I will
> fight with gun, sword, cannon, whirlwind, thunder, until they are
> used up like Kilkenney cats . . .

Soon after the High Council and other leading Mormon
groups had learned of the revelation authorizing plural marriage, it became clear that there was a real split among the
members regarding the new doctrine. A considerable number
refused to obey the revelation and during the fall and winter
of 1843–44 the lines of battle became more and more sharply
drawn. By the spring of 1844 the priesthood of the Church was
openly divided into two contending factions; one supported
Smith and polygamy, the other denounced both.

Certainly, the doctrine of plural marriage was something
which ran strongly against the moral code of even the most

faithful Saints. To accept the system of celestial marriage for time and eternity was easy, but that this included the possibility of polygamous marriages was something else again.

Some of the more immediate circumstances that led to this split in the Church have been related by a number of writers on this period. One of these is the yarn that Joseph Smith attempted to get Mrs. William Law for his spiritual wife. According to Joseph H. Jackson's exposure of the Mormons, published in 1844, "He [meaning Smith] said that he had used every argument in his power, to convince her of the correctness of his doctrine, but could not succeed." Smith told him, so the report goes, that Law was trying to seduce Emma. A little further along in the narrative Jackson alleges that Smith said "That the truth was, Emma wanted Law for a spiritual husband, and that she urged as a reason that as he had so many spiritual wives, she thought it but fair that she should at least have one man's spirit left to her, and that she wanted Law, because he was such a 'sweet little man.' " The account goes on to say that Smith had in mind to get a revelation that Law was to be sealed to Emma and that Law's wife was to be sealed to him. Whether true or false such stories fed the growing rumors of spiritual wifism.

The second case involves one Dr. Foster. He had been out of town for sometime and returned to find Smith in company with his wife at the dinner table in his own home. Later he accused Mrs. Foster of having been approached by Smith with an eye to spiritual wifehood. At first she denied this, then she confessed to the fact that Smith had been teaching her the spiritual wife doctrine. On the basis of this Foster got in touch with Law. Together they began to secure evidence regarding plural marriages in Nauvoo.

Smith and his group got wind of this and on April 18, 1844, there appeared in the *Times and Seasons* a notification that Foster, both Wilson and William Law, and Jane Law, and Howard Smith had been "cut off" from the Church. On the 6th of May following, Francis M. Higbee, another dissenter, sued Smith on the charges of slander and asked for damages in the amount of $5,000.00. The warrant had been issued by the clerk of the Circuit Court of Carthage. Smith, however, hiding behind the charter of Nauvoo and the system of courts there established, secured a writ of habeas corpus and was tried before the municipal court in Nauvoo and discharged.

On May 18, 1844, Higbee, Austin Cowles, and some others were excommunicated on the charges of apostasy. It seems that the dissenters had decided to try to purify the Church by setting up a rival organization. At any rate, that same day in the *Alton Telegraph and Democratic Review* there appears this comment:

. . . A rupture has taken place among the Mormons—a respectable number of the most intelligent members of that body have seceded, under the guidance of William Law, and set up for themselves. It does not appear that the religious views of the seceders have undergone any material change. They profess to believe that Joseph Smith was once a true prophet; but contend that he is now fallen from grace and no longer worthy to remain at the head of the church.

The rebels held frequent meetings to further their cause and to spread their grievances to other Mormons. They charged the Prophet and other leaders with coercion, corruption, financial exploitation of the laymen, adultery and fornication, and especially of the introduction of the spiritual wife doctrine.

Among other efforts they decided to establish a newspaper in Nauvoo to further their cause. On June 7, 1844, the *Nauvoo Expositor* published its first and only issue. Serious accusations were made against the Smiths and a number of affidavits were given to sustain them. The *Expositor* opened with a set of general charges under a preamble and resolution.

First, they would not accept the action of the church court in excommunicating William Law, Wilson Law, Mrs. Law, R. D. Foster and others. Secondly, they opposed the church authorities on the grounds that

Inasmuch as they have introduced false and damnable doctrines into the Church such as the plurality of gods above the God of this universe, and his liability to fall with all his creation; the plurality

of wives, for time and eternity; the doctrine of unconditional sealing up to eternal life, against all crimes except that of shedding
innocent blood by a perversion of their priestly authority . . .
we therefore are constrained to denounce them as apostates from
the pure and holy doctrines of Jesus Christ.

A third resolution indicated their opposition to attempts
to "unite church and state." Other items in the resolution
concerned their willingness to come to terms with Missouri,
that the controversy with the authorities there was contrary
to Christianity, that the authorities of the Church had been
harboring certain individuals from justice, that they coun-
tenanced attendance at houses of revelry, dram shops, dance
halls, and theaters, that they had been using church funds for
speculation as well as organizing secret societies in the interest
of the Church and countenancing the despoiling of the Gentiles.

In addition to a general editorial statement, the newspaper
contains a number of affidavits about polygamy. For example,
one by William Law signed before Robert Foster, justice of
the peace on May 4, 1844, states in effect that Hyrum Smith
read to him

a certain written document which he said was a revelation from
God . . . he afterwards gave me the document to read, and I took
it to my house, and read it, and showed it to my wife, and returned
it the next day. The revelation (so-called) authorized certain men
to have more wives than one at a time, in this world and in the
world to come. It said this was the law, and commanded Joseph
to enter into the law . . .

Jane Law and Austin Cowles likewise made affidavits that they
had heard or read this alleged revelation.

The *Expositor* goes on to say that "harmless, inoffensive,
and unsuspecting" women converts from the Eastern states
and from Europe were, on their arrival in Nauvoo, told of the
privilege of visiting the Prophet. These women believed that
they were going to secure some kind of special blessing but
were ushered in to the Prophet who then proceeded to ask
them to become his spiritual wives. Moreover, they were told

to keep all this very secret. But if they did accept the offer, they would be given great blessings.

The issuance of the *Nauvoo Expositor* kicked up further disturbance. Smith was furious and on the 10th of June the city council, dominated as it was by Smith, declared the *Expositor* to be a nuisance and the mayor was ordered to have it removed in any way he might see fit.

At this time Smith was mayor—Bennett having been removed—and he ordered Marshal John P. Green to proceed with a posse to the office of the *Expositor* and to abate this nuisance. It was abated completely! The posse entered the building, tore out the press, distributed the type, burned the paper and fixtures, and destroyed the remaining copies. Those who had published the newspaper fled from the city and secured a warrant for the arrest of Smith and several of his followers on the charge of riot. When the warrant was served Smith appealed to the local court for a writ of habeas corpus and after a hearing was discharged. But the apostates were not so easily frightened off and the writ for riot was renewed. Joseph and Hyrum fled to Iowa.

How the Saints viewed this thing is neatly illustrated in the autobiography of Alvin Zenger:

> Mob threats and bad men from Missouri were busy stirring up the citizens of Nauvoo and the border county of Hancock, also a few apostates in Nauvoo joined with them, namely, William Law, Dr. Foster, Chauncey Higbee, and others. Their object was to kidnap the Prophet and take him to Missouri under the pretence of law, so that they might kill him. The above named apostates commenced printing a newspaper in Nauvoo called *The Expositor* defaming the character of the prominent men of the city, publishing lies, and traducing their families. The City Council declared it a nuisance, and ordered it to be abated, which was done by the marshal and police of the city. I was there and saw it destroyed. I was an eye witness, and took an active part to protect the city from any attack of the mob.

This episode precipitated even stronger conflict between the Mormons and their Gentile neighbors. The *Lee County*

*Democrat* for June 15, 1844, described the attack upon the *Expositor* as the act of a mob and headed up the description as "Outrage at Nauvoo." There was tremendous excitement throughout the county and the Mormons prepared for open warfare. There were not only charges and countercharges on both sides but acts of violence were committed including a considerable destruction of property.

After he fled from Nauvoo, Dr. Foster had written the *Warsaw Signal* a detailed account in which he told of the destruction of the press. In addition he listed a large number of crimes of which Joseph was supposed to be guilty. This led the editor, Thomas Sharp, to bring out an extra in which he stated among other things, "War and extermination is inevitable! Citizens arise, one and all!!! Can you stand by and suffer such infernal devils to rob men of their property and rights, without avenging them? We have no time for comments; every man will make his own. Let it be made with powder and balls!!!"

Smith wrote a long letter to Governor Ford justifying the destruction of the *Expositor* on legal grounds. He ordered the Twelve Apostles to return home at once but advised them to pack their rifles and ammunition neatly in their luggage. Further, he alerted the Nauvoo Legion to prepare to defend the city. He read the Legion the inflammatory editorial of Sharp and replied in part as follows:

We are American citizens. We live upon a soil for the liberties of which our fathers periled their lives and spilt their blood upon the battlefield. Those rights so dearly purchased shall not be disgracefully trodden underfoot by lawless marauders without at least a noble effort on our part to sustain our liberties. Will you stand by me to the death? [Members shouted a thunderous "Aye" to this and Joseph went on to say] It is well. If you had not done it, I would have gone out there [pointing his arm to the West] and would have raised up a mightier people . . . I call God and angels to witness that I have unsheathed my sword with a firm and unalterable determination that this people shall have their legal rights, and be protected from mob violence, or my blood shall be spilt on the ground like water, and my body consigned to the silent tomb!

Events moved rapidly. Governor Ford went to Carthage to make an investigation and discovered that the members of the Illinois militia in nearby localities, without his orders, were beginning to gather and prepare for open conflict with the Mormons. Ford interviewed the Laws, Fosters, and Higbee, after which he wrote the Prophet demanding that he and everyone else implicated in the *Expositor* case submit to the authorities at Carthage and come to that city to stand trial.

Smith, in fact, had already offered to do just this provided he had an escort of the Nauvoo Legion. Ford fearing an open break between the Legion and the state militia if they should meet in Carthage, denied Smith this protection. Ford concluded his letter as follows: "If you by refusing to submit, shall make it necessary to call out the militia, I have great fears that your city will be destroyed, and your people many of them exterminated. You know the excitement of the public mind. Do not tempt it too far."

The climax came soon. Joseph and Hyrum were hiding in a secret room in the Mansion House in Nauvoo and with certain of their close friends discussed the whole matter of what to do. At the close of the meeting Joseph told Stephan Markham ". . . if Hyrum and I were ever taken again, we should be massacred, or I am not a prophet of God. I want Hyrum to live to avenge my blood, but he is determined not to leave me."

The two men had decided to go to Iowa by crossing the river at night in a rowboat. Porter Rockwell accompanied them. It had been raining and the river was swollen over its banks. Once across the river, they found a trustworthy Saint's home where they dried out their clothes and dispatched messages back to Emma to get horses and to prepare to move their families out of Nauvoo. Smith advised the Nauvoo Legion to scatter and not cause any further difficulties by preparing to defend Nauvoo. Rockwell took the message to Nauvoo. On arrival he discovered that a posse had been there to arrest Joseph but that on finding that he had escaped, it had rushed back to Carthage with the news. Rumors were rife and everybody was excited over the prospect of another move to the West. It is said that Emma took Rockwell aside and begged him to get the Prophet to return.

Years later in recounting that Emma had refused to give Rockwell the keys to the barn so that he could get the horses, Brigham Young is reported to have said that if it had been he who was doing this, he would have well seen to it that the horses were procured, implying that he would not tolerate any nonsense from Emma. In this same account Brigham implies that Smith showed considerable cowardice and bad management in handling the whole situation. The implication is that Smith should have laid more adequate plans to escape. It must be borne in mind that Brigham Young was not in Nauvoo at this time but on a mission, as were the other Apostles.

Joseph and Hyrum did return to Nauvoo under cover of darkness and further plans were made. Governor Ford continued to bungle the situation. He ordered the disbandment of the Nauvoo Legion and the surrender of its arms. At noon on June 24, 1844, Joseph and Hyrum and a small group of men started for Carthage. They were escorted by a company of militia from MacDonald County who met them en route. These men were not hostile and served as a security measure. But when the party arrived in Cathage, the Warsaw and Carthage militiamen ordered the MacDonald troops away and said that they were going to do Smith in at once.

A preliminary hearing was held before a justice of the peace in Carthage on the charge of riot, but the case was deferred and the Smiths were remanded to jail. Ford was well aware of the flimsy procedure but lacked sufficient courage to take matters firmly in hand. He visited Joseph in prison and they argued for some time about the whole question of freedom of speech and conduct but Ford made no effort to do anything to protect Smith really. Smith asked Ford to take him back to Nauvoo but he refused to do this and while he was away in Nauvoo the end came. In the afternoon of June 27 a mob of militiamen gathered around the jail and Joseph and Hyrum were shot to death.

For a time the killing of their two leaders unnerved the

Saints. There were more depredations but most Mormons had
no stomach for another civil war. The return of Brigham
Young and the other members of the Twelve Apostles raised
the question of who would be Joseph's successor. Apparently
Smith had planned to have Hyrum succeed him as President
of the Church but since he, too, had been killed, Brigham took
charge in the name of the Twelve Apostles. Rigdon was unable to secure support for his contention that he should be
the successor. In the presence of further disaster and the threat
of expulsion from Illinois, the whole matter of polygamy for
the time being dropped into the background. Yet the conflict
between the Mormons and the non-Mormons became even
more intensified.

The press reports on the affair at Carthage varied somewhat.
For the most part the newspapers which had been violent in
their accusations against Smith and the Mormons did not con-
done this outrage. The *Burlington Hawkeye* in its issue of
July 11, 1844, remarked:

> Peace and quiet reign once more in the city of the Latter-day
> Saints. The calm is of that peculiar nature that is experienced by
> a people dismayed by a dreadful calamity . . . On Friday the
> 28th ult., the bodies of Joseph and Hyrum Smith were brought to
> Nauvoo . . . They were placed at the Mansion House and ex-
> hibited to about twenty thousand people. They were interred the
> next morning.

That the Gentile forces were afraid of what might happen
is indicated by a report in the *Sangamon Journal* for July 11,
1844, which says, "Many of the inhabitants of Carthage have
fled with their families. Others were preparing to go . . . In
Warsaw . . . everything was placed in an attitude for defense,
and the inhabitants of the surrounding country were requested to come to our aid . . ." Further in the same issue:
"It was expected that as soon as the news of the death of the
Smiths reached Nauvoo, the Mormons would take vengeance
on Carthage and Warsaw . . ."

On the other hand, the *Lee County Democrat* remarked,
June 29, 1844, "The Mormons have no disposition to avenge

their wrongs, further than to ferret out the persons who murdered their prophet and his brother, and bring them to justice."

The efforts to bring at least the ringleaders of the mob to
justice were not successful. The *Burlington Hawkeye,* June 5,
1845, reports as follows, ". . . The trial of the five persons
indicted in Hancock County for the murder of Joseph Smith,
nearly one year since, was brought to a close on the afternoon
of the 30th ult., by a general verdict of not guilty." In the
same issue the newspaper goes on to say, "The whole appeared
more like a farce than a solemn trial involving the lives of
five men."

There followed a series of additional events which were the
prelude to the expulsion of the Mormons from Illinois. The
charter was repealed and other special legislation regarding
Nauvoo was stricken from the statutes of Illinois.

The tension between the Mormons and non-Mormons increased in bitterness and violence. The accusations of the
Gentiles against the Mormons for thievery and depredations
against property continued. Murders of non-Mormons were
laid at the door of the Mormons and, in turn, a number of
Mormons were killed during the Hancock County disturbances. The Mormons, of course, were quick to accuse the
Gentiles of these crimes.

The attitudes of the citizens are exampled in the meetings
held in Bureau County in the autumn of 1845. Among other
resolutions, the following are reported, "Resolve, that from
the knowledge we have of the Mormons, we believe that they
cannot reside in the same community in peace with their
neighbors, and that their doctrines, so far as we are acquainted
with them, are subversive to our free institutions."

The *Alton Telegraph and Democratic Review,* October 4,
1845, suggested:

Resolve, that we call upon the citizens of this county to raise a
force of three hundred men, or more, to be in readiness at a moment's notice, to march to any part of Hancock County, to cooperate with the neighboring counties, should it become necessary, in order to suppress Mormon depredation.

In October an anti-Mormon convention met at Carthage with delegates from nine neighboring counties. The *Alton Telegraph,* October 11, 1845, reports: "They are determined that the Mormons must and should leave the state, and they gave them until spring to remove peaceably."

There was little else the Mormons could do. In October, 1845, the Mormon leaders addressed a letter to General John J. Hardon stating "That one thousand families, including the twelve, the high council, the trustees and general authorities of the church are fully determined to remove in the spring, independent of the contingency of selling our property, and that this company will comprise from five to six thousand souls."

Once more the Mormons had to sell their property at great loss. But they finally did get out of the state and across to Iowa where they remained temporarily on the banks of the Missouri, opposite what is now the city of Omaha. Even in the final days of the expulsion blood was spilled in Nauvoo, and Ford finally did send a body of troops to Hancock County to quell the disorders. The military force remained there for several weeks, but much of the city had already been destroyed, including the Temple.

Surely the whole episode in Illinois served to make Mormonism more and more a national rather than a purely local issue. In this struggle the practice of polygamy had become one of the important symbols of this new and growing church. As we shall see in the next chapter, the conflict became more intense soon after the settlement in Utah.

*It is never wise to attempt by legislation and arms, reforms which time and social forces are sure to bring about . . . If our government will exercise a little foresight, if it will practice a wise and masterly maturity, the Mormon problem will solve itself.*—Editorial in New York World, 1867.

# 16 UTAH AND THE FULL-BLOWN ATTACK AND COUNTERATTACK

THE YEARS 1850 through 1890 were exciting ones for Mormon and Gentile alike. On the one side were arrayed the strong forces of Mormonism under the able leadership of Brigham Young and his successors. Brigham Young was a man to give no quarter nor ask for any. Yet soon after the settlement in Utah, an ever-increasing number of non-Mormons began to put up a fight against his rule. As a minority group among people who had for nearly three decades themselves suffered as a minority, the Gentiles took on all the truculence and violence of the abused everywhere. With the support of anti-Mormon sentiment from outside and abetted by the federal officials in Utah and Washington, the Gentiles stepped up the vigor of their campaign to a point which at times almost led to open violence. Their efforts to cripple the Mormon Church and destroy polygamy were met by equal opposition on the part of the Mormons themselves.

In this chapter and the next we shall examine the strategy and tactics involved in the Gentile versus Mormon conflict regarding Utah and polygamy.

The struggle between the Mormons and the Gentiles may be stated in terms of the concepts of "in-group" and "out-group." On the one hand the in-group is one in which the members are motivated by a strong sense of solidarity of sentiment, mutual participation, tendencies to conformity, acceptance of the group controls and of the group aims; on the other stands the out-group toward which the members of the in-group have attitudes of avoidance and/or hostility. Members of the out-group are viewed as enemies, members of one's in-group are viewed as friends.

The Mormons were a strong and well-knit in-group. They had a deep sense of internal solidarity, they had great pride in their distinctive traditions, and they had complete belief in a divine mission. This was the spirit of the ancient Hebrews and the early Christians who were instructed to come out of the wicked world and gather with other faithful. Relations to the out-group—here the world outside—are marked by a sense of distance. This distance is not necessarily physical in nature but psychological. When the Mormons settled in Utah they tried to make their isolation physical as well as psychological. But they had hardly got away from their troubles in Illinois and settled in the remote West when they were again thrust face-to-face with a hostile Gentile world.

Now, we can reverse this whole picture. If one were a Gentile in the period of which we are writing, he could be regarded as a member of a strong though somewhat loosely organized in-group in opposition to a much stronger out-group, the Mormons. As we shall see, actually the Gentile opposition was never a completely solid unit, but rather a co-operation of various non-Mormon groups which finally liquidated, at least on the statute books, the practice of plural marriage.

In addition to the use of public opinion and mass force in conflict, we have the use of legal means. This method was essentially the one employed by the Gentile world in an effort to subdue the Mormons. In the early aspects of this struggle, as we shall see, the Mormons themselves attempted to so formulate their local laws as to protect the practice of polygamy.

Yet the central theme of the struggle between the Mormons and the non-Mormons in Utah was not entirely a moral or religious issue. An examination of the historical facts shows that there were three important elements in this conflict:

The first of these concerned the political organization of Utah territory. Soon after their arrival in the Great Basin, the Mormons had set up their own government of Deseret and began applying for statehood. Had they obtained statehood at an early date, they would have been able to dominate the local operations. It took nearly 50 years to secure statehood. During this long period there was a struggle in Utah between the Mormons who were in the numerical majority and the Gentile minority abetted by the political appointees who were sent to Utah to carry out the law.

The second is the economic or business element. Almost from the outset a few non-Mormons settled in Utah, mostly in the merchandising business. In time their numbers became greater and especially after the opening up of mining properties in the territory, the Gentiles tried to break the hold of the Mormons over the economic order. There was often a linkage between the political operators and the business forces in the struggle with the Mormons, which struggle, however, was often rationalized as an effort to abolish polygamy.

The third is the religious and moral aspects concerned— as indicated, the plural marriage system. This got much attention but it also provided a wonderful stereotype and symbol for the larger conflict. It was a red flag of danger which the Gentiles in Utah waved to their friends over the Rocky Mountains as they called for help. To the Mormons it was a sacred doctrine and practice and they were not going to give it up without a fight.

That trouble soon began to brew between the Saints and the federal officials in Utah is evident from Alice Johnson Read's journal. For February 23, 1851, she remarks, regarding the services on that day, "Brigham dished up a certain judge who had been laying his plans about going to the President of the United States to make report that the governor of Utah territory has so many wives . . ."

The reactions of the run-of-the-mill Saints toward the federal appointees in the Territory of Utah is neatly illustrated in the Joel Mason journal. In October, 1853, and while living in Nephi, he wrote:

On Saturday court adjourned and left. Our streets are once more clean of Gentiles and thank the Lord. Beware of the leaven of the

Gentiles, their atmosphere is poisonous to Mormonism. It is commonly reported that General Holman and Mr. Kaufman, the latter Judge Kinney's clerk, visited Ammon's camp and lay with his squaws and caught the clap and then were not willing to pay their fare to friend Ammon. This is Gentilism. These are the men sent to execute justice and they are the first to break the law. A. W. Babbitt drunk . . . an apostate spirit; Colonel Steptoe drunk and acting very foolish / . . Oh, Lord, open the eyes of the people that they may see and understand the signs of the time.

A few years later John Taylor remarked upon the spoils system as it was operating with regard to Utah. He pointed out that when a president was elected the henchmen came around and wanted jobs. And went on to say:

. . . And, finally, after worryings and teasings, and whining and begging, some of those little men, mean, contemptible pups, doggery men, broken-down lawyers, or common, dirty, political hacks, bring up the rear, swelled up like swill barrels; they come to the table for the fragments, and with a hungry maw and not very delicate stomach, whine out "Won't you give me a place, if it is only in Utah?" In order to stop the howling, the President says, "Throw a bone to that dog, and let him go out"; and he comes out a great big "United States" officer, dressed in a lion's garb, it is true, but with the bray of an ass. He comes out here, carrying out his groggery and whoring operations, seeking to introduce among us Eastern civilization.

When they left Nauvoo the Mormons thought they could find a haven in Mexican territory where they would be free from the interference of the United States. Shortly after they had arrived in the valley of Salt Lake they discovered that Mexico had ceded the whole western area to the United States. True to their patriotism or for other reasons, they are reported to have planted an American flag on Ensign Peak upon the news of this event. In March, 1849, the Mormons made their first bid for statehood to the federal Congress. The petition lingered in various committees and no action was taken. But on December 31, 1849, a memorial against admission of Deseret was presented in Congress by a faction of Gentiles some of whom later became leaders in the Josephite Church (to be discussed later in this chapter). In this memorial they stated that 1,500 immigrants from Nauvoo to Salt Lake had taken the following oath:

You do solemnly swear, in the presence of Almighty God, his holy angels, and these witnesses, that you will avenge the blood of Joseph Smith upon this nation, and so teach your children; and that you will from this day henceforth and forever begin and carry out hostility against this nation, and keep the same a profound secret now and ever. So help you God.

This same document alleged that the Mormons in Utah were openly practicing polygamy. The Church was accused of treason and its control was said to be essentially such that free state government would be impossible because it would be sure to fall under Mormon dominance.

That the leaders of the Mormons were not too hopeful of attaining statehood at this early date, is indicated in the fact that in the petition in which they asked for the state of Deseret to be organized, they said that they would, in effect, settle to be made a territory. On September 9, 1850, Utah was made a territory and Brigham Young was appointed her first governor.

The development of the struggle in the 1850's must be seen against the background of certain events. Some of these derived from the Mormons, and some from the outside world. Certain of the Mormon items had to do with their doctrines, others had to do with overt events in which they were involved.

If the Mormons had been secretive about the open acknowledgment of plural marriage in Illinois, after the settlement in Utah they became less and less worried that the world outside should see evidences of the patriarchal system of marriage. Captain John W. Gunnison, who lived in Salt Lake during the winter of 1849–50, relates in his book, *The Mormons*, 1852:

That many have a large number of wives in Deseret is perfectly manifest to anyone residing long among them, and, indeed, the subject begins to be more openly discussed than formerly, and it is announced that a treatise is in preparation, to prove by the Scriptures the right of plurality by all Christians, if not to declare their own practice of the same.

Thus, while the Mormon missionaries in the Eastern states and in Europe were publicly denying the practice of polygamy in Utah, the Saints were being prepared for a public announcement of the same. This came on August 29, 1852, when the revelation given to Joseph Smith in 1843 was read to the assembled Saints in Salt Lake City. It was followed, you recall, by a long defense of the practice by Orson Pratt. This is exactly what Gunnison had foreseen.

The first item, then, which was bound to shock the Gentile world was the plural wife system. The second was the preaching of what was known as "blood atonement." This was essentially the doctrine that enemies of the Church or members who apostatized or otherwise committed unpardonable sins would be better off if their souls were atoned by blood sacrifice, that is, by the taking of their lives. Brigham explained the doctrine by saying:

There are sins that can be atoned for by an offering upon an altar, as in ancient days . . . but there are sins that the blood of a lamb, or a calf, or a turtledove, cannot remit, but they must be atoned for by the blood of the man. Any of you who understand the principles of eternity, if you have sinned a sin requiring the shedding of blood, except the sin under death, would not be satisfied nor rest until your blood should be spilled, that you might even gain that salvation you desire. That is the way to love mankind.

While later the Mormon Church more or less completely repudiated the doctrine of blood atonement, at the time it served as an additional incendiary force to arouse the Saints. It not only created terror in the consciences of the members but it no doubt stimulated a good deal of violence among the Saints themselves. For example, stories got around that Mormons had been known to slay their unfaithful wives, under the doctrine of blood atonement. From the Gentile standpoint it was a frightening dogma which but went to prove the complete barbarity of the Mormons.

The third item which involved both doctrine and action was the so-called "Reformation." In the late 1850's the Church leaders began revivalist preaching that the Saints should repent from their sins, be rebaptized, renew their "covenants," and otherwise prove to their neighbors and the world outside that they were faithful members of the Church. This religious excitement swept through the Church and especially the southern communities just prior to an event of greatest importance at this time, namely, the Mountain Meadows massacre. We give here but the barest details.

In September, 1857, a company of migrants from Arkansas en route to California encamped in a small valley in southern Utah known as the Mountain Meadows. On the morning of September 7 the company was attacked by a band of Indians. There followed a three-day siege during which there were casualties on both sides. On September 11, a body of Mormon militia under the leadership of John D. Lee appeared on the scene and a truce was arranged through their intervention. On the pretext of escorting the immigrants to safety, the entire company, with the exception of a few children, was brutally massacred.

This horrible event further stimulated the growing conflict between the Mormons and the Gentiles. Many of the latter accused the Church of complicity in this butchery. This was promptly and strongly denied by the Mormon leaders who contended this was the work of certain bands of Indians who were wreaking revenge for the killing of their tribesmen and the committing of other depredations by other white parties.

There seems little doubt but that the massacre was planned and carried out under the leadership of certain fanatical Mormons in that section of Utah. Rumors had spread rapidly, prior to this time, that members of this immigrant train had abused the Saints as they passed through the Mormon communities and that they had boasted that they would return from California with reinforcements and drive the Mormons

out of the country. On the other side, the event was regarded
by a large section of the Gentile world as further evidence of
the violence and treachery of the Mormons.

Finally, there was the "Mormon War." In 1857 President
Buchanan dispatched a considerable number of troops under
Colonel Albert Sidney Johnston to Utah to quell an alleged
rebellion. "Buchanan's Blunder," as it was called, came to
nothing except that it produced further friction between the
Saints and the Gentiles.

In addition to these events the Gold Rush brought the
Gentile world closer to Utah, at least in the sense that Utah
was on the road to the California gold fields. Many Mormon
communities were again in the main stream of American west-
ward movement and they could not escape the effects of this
fact.

The publication of the revelation on polygamy, the preaching of blood atonement, and the overt events mentioned,
could not but stimulate the development of strong in-group
and out-group attitudes on the part of Mormons and non-
Mormons. The solidarity of the Mormons became increasingly evident.

While Brigham Young was made the first territorial governor of Utah, most of the other chief officials were non-
Mormons and from the outside. Almost from the outset
trouble ensued between the Saints and the Gentile federal
officials. It was often the personal lives of these federal appointees rather than their official acts that irritated the Mormons. In any case, the initial hostility began to be evident in
the speeches and actions of Associate Justice Perry C.
Brocchus.

In September, 1851, a meeting was held in the Bowery in
Salt Lake City to discuss the matter of sending a block of
Utah marble as a contribution to the Washington Monument,
then under construction. Judge Brocchus who had been in
Utah about two months was given permission to speak at this
meeting. Among other things he cautioned the Saints about
their loyalty to the government, mentioning a speech of
Daniel H. Wells made on July 24, 1851, as well as Brigham

Young's critical remarks about Zachary Taylor. The Judge went on to say that unless the Mormons could send their block of marble in sincerity and good patriotism they ought not to do it.

He then turned to the women of the audience and advised them, "to become virtuous." The implication was clear enough that they should abandon polygamy. At once the congregation was in an uproar and several men volunteered to answer the judge but Brigham Young arose and tried to calm the disturbance. Brigham, moreover, told the judge that if he had but crooked his finger the audience would probably have torn the judge limb from limb, and especially that the women would have taken a hand in this in view of his remarks about them. The whole story was carried in the Eastern press which from then on found news from Utah "good copy."

During the following winter Lemuel H. Brandenberry, Brocchus, and B. D. Harris, three federal officials in Utah, reported to Washington, D.C., that they had been "compelled to withdraw from the territory, and our official duties" because of "lawless acts, and the hostile and seditious sentiments of Brigham Young, the executive of the territory, and the great body of the residents there . . ." This report was later sent as part of a special message to both houses of Congress on January 9, 1852, by President Millard Fillmore. This was the first official recognition of the conflict by a President of the United States. Many other presidential messages on the topic were to follow in the years ahead.

At this time, however, polygamy was not the central issue. It was the alleged autocratic powers of Brigham Young and the contention that the Church, under his leadership was actually treasonable toward the United States.

Brigham Young's appointment as governor of the territory was to expire in 1854. But various men appointed to the governorship declined to serve. One of these was Colonel E. J. Steptoe who was in Utah on orders to find the murderers of Captain Gunnison. It was not until 1857 when Alfred Cumming accepted that Brigham finally relinquished the office. At about this time Judge J. F. Kinney was appointed to the

territorial supreme court. At first Young and the other leading Mormons were rather friendly with these two men. Later,
however, strained relations developed between Steptoe, Kinney, and their associates and the Church leaders. The general
attitude toward such officials is indicated in the quotation
above from Joel Mason.

On September 12, 1855, W. W. Drummond was appointed
an associate justice of Utah. This man shocked the Mormons
more than any other Gentile because of his personal habits.
Here was a man who came to the territory with the idea of
dispensing justice but who, in the minds of the Saints, was an
immoral character of the first order. Judge Drummond arrived in Utah with a mistress after abandoning his wife and
children. Stories were told that he permitted his mistress to sit
on the bench with him, and that she used her time there to
write billets-doux to the judge while he was conducting court.

In addition to expressing strong views regarding the Mormons in Utah, Drummond wrote vigorous letters to the Eastern newspapers against them. He was most unpopular. Heber
C. Kimball once said of him in a sermon: "There is a poor
curse who has written the bigger part of those lies which have
been printed in the States; and I curse him, in the name of
Israel's God, and by the priesthood and authority of Jesus
Christ . . ."

Brigham was equally strong in his denunciations of the
federal officials and their attempts to seduce the women of
Zion. He warned the women to be cautious of these men who
might try to get them to go out socially with them. Clearly
the leader of the Church was putting pressure upon his followers to sharpen the lines of distinction between them and
the outsiders. Speaking of the federal appointees in a sermon
on February 18, 1855, Brigham said,

Why, from most of the high-minded gentlemen, you can hear,
"God damn the Mormons, they are opposed to the federal government, because they will not let us sleep with their wives and
daughters." I am opposed to such men, and answer them with
the barbed arrows of the Almighty. To what extent? Let them in-

trude upon the chastity of my family, and, so help me God, I
will use them up . . .

All this was but a prelude to the growing issue of polygamy
in national politics. In 1856 the Republican national convention inserted a plank in its platform which declared that
the Constitution gave Congress sovereign power over the territory and that it was both the "right and duty of Congress"
to abate "those twin relics of barbarism—polygamy and slavery."

Under Buchanan the Democratic party hardly dared risk
the danger of losing Southern votes by stressing the slavery
question, but they stole the most effective thunder of the Republican platform by taking a strong position against polygamy. Certainly polygamy in Utah was not more important
than the issue of slavery, but it was an exciting symbol and one
which would be used repeatedly to arouse hostility among the
Gentile voters.

Such events as the conflict between the Mormons and the
Gentile officials which led to sending of troops to quell an
alleged rebellion and the treacherous Mountain Meadows
massacre served to place polygamy in the forefront of public
problems. Republicans and Democrats alike advocated legislation to destroy the system. Even Senator Stephen A. Douglas,
who at one time had defended the Mormons, on June 12,
1857, made some strong comments about the "loathsome ulcer
of polygamy." But it was clear that there was not sufficient
general public sentiment nor sufficient power in Congress to
push very far on this matter. Mr. Hall in the House of Representatives in June, 1856, had introduced a resolution "to inquire into the propriety of enacting against polygamy," but
nothing had come of this. During this time Buchanan and
other leaders in Washington were more concerned that the
Mormons had shown disrespect for the dignity and authority
of the federal government. After the so-called Mormon War
was over, however, the Saints had some fear that the federal
troops might be used by the new territorial officials in an as-
sault upon polygamy.

On February 15, 1860, in the first session of the 36th Congress, Representative J. S. Morrill of Vermont introduced a bill "to punish and prevent the practice of polygamy in the territories of the United States." The proposed legislation contained clauses which annulled some of the acts of the legislature of Utah, including the one incorporating the Church of Jesus Christ of Latter-day Saints. This bill passed the House of Representatives by a vote of 149 to 60 and was sent on to the Senate where it was referred to the committee on judiciary. Nothing came of this and the bill died in committee.

On March 4, 1861, Lincoln became President. His policy toward the Mormons was not quite in line with that of his party. He was inclined to leave them alone. Yet early in the Civil War various moral zealots and people who had been associated with the political operations in Utah became increasingly concerned about the sins of polygamy. Morrill again introduced a bill in the House of Representatives on April 8, 1862. It passed the House of Representatives and was sent on to the Senate where the committee on judiciary proposed various amendments as a substitute for part of the bill. The new bill passed the Senate, with certain further changes, 37 to 2. It was then sent back to the House of Representatives for their concurrence where it was finally passed. It was signed by President Abraham Lincoln in July, 1862.

In the meantime there were certain events inside the Mormon Church which needed attention. I refer to the schisms and apostasies which threatened the organization from the inside.

During the time of which we are writing there were three serious splits within the Mormon Church. The first of these was the Gladdenite secession in 1852, the second was the rise of the Josephite branch in the same year, and, third, the Morrisite movement in 1861. Later the Godbe defection was significant but it will be taken up subsequently.

Apostasy against the true church has always been regarded by those in power as a serious threat. As a rule such defection is treated severely, but if the individuals so inclined repent they are usually permitted to return to the fold. It is clear that not all Mormons agreed with the plural marriage doctrine, as we saw in the story of William Law and his associates.

When the doctrine of polygamy was openly announced in 1852, a number of people banded together in protest under the leadership of one Gladden Bishop. Bishop had already had considerable experience in disaffection, having gone through a series of 13 apostasies, repentances, and readmissions. Brigham Young aimed some sharp remarks at this group in an address of March 27, 1853:

We have known Gladden Bishop for more than twenty years, and know him to be a poor, dirty curse . . . I say to you Bishops, do not allow them [the Gladdenites] to preach in your Wards. Who broke the roads to these valleys? . . . We broke the roads to this country. Now you, you Gladdenites, keep your tongues still, lest sudden destruction come upon you . . .

I say, rather than that apostates should flourish here, I will unsheath my bowie knife, and conquer or die . . . Now, you nasty apostates, clear out, or a judgment will be put to the line, and righteousness to the plummet . . .

The Josephites, so-called in distinction to the Brighamites, represented another schism. The people who formulated this group had refused to acknowledge Brigham Young as their leader. They maintained that the son of Joseph Smith should be the successor as head of the Church. Moreover, they had not approved polygamy. The Josephite movement had its beginning in a meeting held in Beloit, Wisconsin, in June, 1852. At this time resolutions were adopted disclaiming the leadership of Young. At a conference held in Plano, Illinois, in 1860, the group established itself as "The Reorganized Church of Jesus Christ of Latter-day Saints," under the leadership of Joseph Smith's son. Some of the founders of this organization, notably William Smith, had sent the memorial to Congress referred to earlier. For years the Josephites provided the non-Mormon religious and political factions with ammunition against the Utah Mormons.

The Morrisite schism was a more effective item in the publicity of the Gentiles against the Mormons. In November, 1860, Joseph Morris claimed to have received a revelation which told him to reform the Mormon Church and prepare for the coming of Christ. He gained support of about 500 followers most of whom settled at Kingston Fort, near the mouth of the Weber River.

The little colony, however, was riven by strife. Morris tried forcibly to detain some of those who wished to leave the colony. As a result a posse was sent to the fort to liberate the prisoners. A siege was laid which lasted 14 days and then was terminated by a truce. In arranging for the surrender of Morris, he and several of his followers were killed. The Mormon and Gentile stories of the event differ considerably, as they do about the Mountain Meadows tragedy. The Mormon accounts make the arrest legal and the killing of Morris and his followers as a justifiable act on the part of officers of the law. The Gentile story claims cold-blooded murder. In any event the incident was fruitful for the building of further legends about the horrors of Mormonism.

In some ways the actions of individual apostates were more important than these small schisms. Certainly the defection of John D. Lee, of Bill Hickman, the Stenhouses, and Ann Eliza Young provided lots of ammunition for the Gentile reformers. Their writings and speeches helped to give the Gentiles stereotypes of the Mormons, to promote the stories of murder and lechery, and otherwise to justify the prosecution and persecution visited upon the Mormon Church.

For nearly a decade following the passage of the Morrill Act the American people were too occupied with the Civil War and the Reconstruction to attend fully to Mormon problems. However, there were certain continuing struggles inside of Utah between the Mormons themselves and the federal officials. Three matters in particular are important from the point of view of the Gentiles: The first was the quartering of troops in Salt Lake City at Camp Douglas. The second was the completion of the transcontinental railroad in 1868. The third was the continuing influx of Gentiles into Utah, particularly as mining properties were developed.

Just prior to the Civil War the troops which had been

sent under Johnston to Utah were recalled to the States. During this time, however, the Utah militia remained an effective potential military force for the protection of the Mormons against the Indians.

Although Lincoln had assumed a hands-off policy, in 1862 his Secretary of War ordered to Salt Lake City a company of volunteers from California under Colonel Patrick E. Connor. They arrived in October, 1862, and encamped three miles east of the city. The Mormons were disturbed by this "insult to the citizenry" and were in no mood to welcome the return of federal troops to Utah.

For years there was a good deal of strong feeling between the officers and men of Camp Douglas and the Mormons. One of the first journalistic attacks on polygamy was stimulated by Connor and his group. On the other hand, their presence made for some contact and necessary accommodation. Moreover, there was an opportunity to provide supplies for the military and this was not to be overlooked by the Mormon merchants.

Another and in some ways more important and direct influence in breaking down isolation was the coming of the railroads. Although the transcontinental lines were not completed until 1868, Brigham Young and the legislature of Utah had memorialized Congress as early as March, 1852, asking that a national railroad be built to the Pacific coast. Long before the railroad was completed there was a network of telegraph lines which connected Utah with the outside world. When the railroad was finally finished across the country, Brigham and the Mormons began building local railroads to connect up the valleys of Utah and Idaho.

Outside of Salt Lake and Ogden, the Mormons had a complete monopoly on the business interests of the territory. Brigham Young had spread the cooperative movement. He had a woolen mill built in Provo, a cotton mill in St. George, and a smelter in Iron county.

From the outset Brigham believed that solid community life could be built only around agriculture and economic self-sufficiency. During the early settlement period Brigham ad-

vised his followers not to go into the mining business. However, in the 1860's, the rich mineral deposits of Utah began
to be opened up and a considerable amount of Gentile capital was introduced to develop the properties.

George Alfred Townsend's letters to the *Cincinnati In-
quirer,* written in 1871, give an excellent picture of the situation in Utah at that time. In one letter entitled, "The Federal
Enemies of the Saints," he tells of the anti-Mormon ring as it
had developed among the politicians and certain non-Mormon businessmen. The Gentile centers of activity were the
Wasatch Club and the United States district court room
"over a livery stable." The Wasatch Club—otherwise known
as "the jumper's club" in allusion to the tendency of the
judges and their satellites to jump or possess without right
and by force valuable mining claims—was the social and political headquarters of the federal appointees. The group was
particularly active while Judge James B. McKean was on the
bench.

McKean and another federal judge, O. F. Strickland, got
mixed up in a variety of mining schemes and by transference
of titles back and forth were able to secure certain valuable
mines. In one lawsuit involving their claims, McKean himself sat as the judge. This judicial irregularity caused a lot of
local comment among Mormons and Gentiles alike. It is quite
possible that his conduct in this case was as effective in getting him removed from the bench later as was his mishandling
of the much-publicized divorce case of Ann Eliza Webb against
Brigham Young.

In time the ring dwindled to a small group of bitter federal
appointees. Most of the other Gentiles in the community abandoned them or became indifferent. Townsend cites a number
of prominent Protestant and Catholic leaders as well as various army officers as believing that the ring had done the
Gentile cause a distinct disservice. As a matter of fact, most of
the Senators and Representatives in Congress from west of
the Rocky Mountains were thoroughly disgusted with the behavior of such political appointees in Utah.

Many of the federal ring perpetually bombarded the Eastern press with letters and stories about the horrors of Mormon polygamy and the treasonous conduct of the Church. Townsend is quite correct in pointing out that these attacks were really a cover-up for their own activities as well as a device to secure Gentile support from outside.

To return to the problems of polygamy more directly, though the 1860's were a time of relative quiet, there were some irritating situations. For example, in July, 1862, Governor Harding was welcomed by the leading officials of the Church who at first thought he would be satisfactory to them. Later in his December message to the legislature, he had something to say about polygamy, mentioning that many Mormons doubted the constitutionality of the Morrill Act. Then he went on to say, "I take this occasion to warn the people of this territory against such dangerous and disloyal counsel."

Such remarks were not likely to endear a man to the Saints. A little later Judge Charles B. Waite got a good deal of abuse from the Mormons because he tried to get Congress to change the judicial system in Utah. He, like other judges, had found that in any lawsuit involving the interests of Gentiles as against those of the Mormons, juries made up of Mormons would almost always bring in verdicts favorable to their fellow churchmen. At first this had nothing to do with polygamy but the idea that this invariably occurred became a stereotype of the judicial officials in Utah.

When General Connor founded Fort Douglas in 1863, he began the publication of what was called the *Union Vedette*. This was one of the first anti-Mormon newspapers in Utah. A little later T. B. H. Stenhouse, under stimulation of the leaders of the Church, established the *Daily Telegraph* the first issue of which appeared on July 4, 1864. For some time there was a battle of public opinion between these two newspapers.

The first issue of the *Union Vedette* appeared on November 20, 1863. Vedette means a sentinel stationed on the outpost of an army to watch an enemy and give notice of impending danger. The whole life of this newspaper is exactly in this tradition. It concentrated its hostile attacks at once upon the hierarchical authority of the Church and on polygamy. It contended that Utah would never become a state until it had abolished polygamy and had severed the relationships of Church and state.

A sample of the editorials of the *Vedette* will show the vigor of its style and the nature of its attacks. These foreshadow the kind of material to appear later in the *Salt Lake Tribune*. In the January 3, 1864, issue the *Daily Union Vedette* remarks:

Wherefore this antagonism [to the Mormons]? Because the propagandists of polygamy openly advocate, and persistently practice, in defiance of public opinion, a system of licensed prostitution, obnoxious to decency and virtue, and totally subversive to the fundamental principles of civilization; thus, not only offending the known laws of the land, but outraging the common sentiment of Christianity on which rests the foundations of all good government . . .

In 1868–69 occurred the defection from the Church of William S. Godbe, E. L. Harrison, E. W. Tullidge, Eli B. Kelsey, and others. This group began the publication of the *Utah Magazine* on January 16, 1868, a journal, which they said, was devoted to the interests of "intellectual, social, political, and theological" issues. This was the official organ of the so-called Godbeites. While there was never any formal organization of this group in the sense of a new sect, it did represent a rather sharp dissension from the official body of the Church. These men often maintained that they had not abandoned Mormonism, but rather that the Church had gone off into economic and political matters which had nothing to do with religion. They even continued to believe in the doctrines of polygamy as illustrated by the fact that Godbe married a plural wife— certainly against Church dogma—*after* he was excommunicated.

After their excommunication, Godbe and Tullidge issued a statement in defense of their action. In part they said:

For some years past we have felt that a great encroachment of power is being made by the ruling Priesthood of our Church, beyond that allowed by the spirit and genius of the Gospel. We also have perceived that a steady and constant decline was taking place in the manifestations of the spiritual gifts, as well as in the spirituality of our system as a whole, and that as a church we were fast moving into a state of the most complete materialism . . .

. . . For daring, mildly, and respectfully, to reason upon the inconsistencies of some of his [Brigham's] propositions, he has deprived us of our fellowship and standing in the Church, and thus with his own hand has dissolved our allegiance to him. He has declared that his will is surpreme and omnipotent in the Church, and that it shall be unquestionedly obeyed, and that to oppose any of his measures will be deemed apostasy and punished by excommunication.

They then go on to mention Brigham's orders that the Mormons should not trade or have social relations with the Gentiles as further illustration of his high-handed methods. The *Union Vedette* for December 24, 1866, says that in a sermon in the tabernacle, Brigham Young

alluded extensively to the subject of the patronage of Gentile merchants by Mormons, and counseled them to pass by the stores of those who, he said, were here for no other purpose but to destroy the Saints. He argued that there was in this community a class of men who were striving to deprive the Mormons of their houses, lands, and money, and that all who patronized that class would be cut off from the Church.

Previous to 1870 there had been no division in Utah along the lines of the traditional political parties. In the local elections the churchmen dominated matters anyway. As to the delegate to Congress, the Gentiles had from time to time put up their own candidate, but the Mormons always overwhelmed them in voting power. During the winter of 1869–70 many of the Gentiles had become increasingly interested in organizing a political party of their own. The non-Mormon population had been growing steadily; the railroads made possible transport and travel to both East and West coasts; there had been a considerable amount of agitation for additional federal legislation with regard to the Mormons; and there was always the possibility of further military action within the territory. Against the background of these factors the Gentiles thought the time ripe to take advantage of apostatizing Mormons and their own group and move toward some kind of political control. This led to the organization of the Liberal party at Corinne, Utah, an all-Gentile town in northern Utah, on February 9, 1870.

This was just prior to the biennial elections in Salt Lake City and the group made an attempt to put a ticket into the field, called the Independent's ticket. On this were the names of some faithful Mormons, the Gentiles thus hoping to split the Mormon vote. Of approximately 2,300 votes cast at that election, only 300 went to Liberal candidates. The *Salt Lake Tribune*, which had begun publication on February 19, 1870, said that one reason for the small Liberal vote was because the territorial laws compelled "the numbering and identifying of each vote, a system practically robbing every citizen of his freedom of ballot . . ." The *Tribune* regarded this party as the beginning of a "great work of vindicating the rights of free speech, free thought, and free press in this territory . . ."

The Liberal party's fundamental platform, as established in its July convention, centered around the following principles: (1) the supremacy of the Constitution and laws of the United States; (2) the separation of church and state in the territory of Utah; (3) the use of a free and untrammeled ballot; (4) the passing of adequate and proper legislation for full protection of the mining interests and the miners in the state; and (5) that all public officials be required to render a complete and full account to the public of all revenues received and dispersed by them.

There was no mention of polygamy. The truth is that there was a good deal of division in the group itself over this very issue. As noted above, most of the Godbe faction had no serious quarrel with polygamy. On the other hand, one Gentile, D. J. Toohy, went so far as to say, "Here in Utah sensuality and crime found a congenial home; here immorality has been lifted up where virtue ought to reign." These words led to a strong reply by Tullidge who remarked that he himself was a polygamist. In fact, Toohy's comment caused a considerable furor at the convention.

This effort on the part of the Liberal party to bring the Godbeites into their fold is a nice illustration of the difficulty of the apostate in situations of this kind. Here was a marginal group brought up under one culture attempting to accommodate itself to the ways of another. Though estranged and excommunicated from the Mormon in-group, the Godbeites were nevertheless still sufficiently attached to its traditions that it was difficult for them to adopt the conflicting standards of the out-group to which they were now trying to join. Such a dilemma must have caused considerable frustration to the apostates.

However, judging by the comments of the *Salt Lake Tribune,* an effort was made to play down the difficulties over polygamy and center the attention upon the so-called priestly rule of Utah. In its issue of August 27, 1871, the *Tribune* remarked:

We can oppose the union of church and state without stopping to quarrel about church doctrines. Polygamy is a social if not a religious institution of the territory, and it is established in such a manner that it can not be suddenly extirpated. Neither is there any necessity for any such violent measures. It is an institution which, if let alone, will die of itself, for the simple reason that it is not in harmony with its present surroundings. It needs no opposition. On the contrary, persecution will only serve to prolong its life.

As we shall see, the *Salt Lake Tribune* later took a very different tone regarding polygamy. The attempt, at this time, to bring the apostate Mormon group into the Liberal party more or less failed. On the other hand, certain leaders, both Gentile and Mormon, tried in the spring of 1872 to get the people of the territory to divide along traditional party lines; and although both parties held conventions, nothing came of the effort. The split between the Liberal party and the Mormon group, known as the People's party, continued.

The Liberals kept up their agitation, and though small in

numbers, they became increasingly anti-Mormon and anti-polygamy. They tried to organize the Gentile elements in the mining communities, and they appealed to the women of the Gentile groups to join them in strong strictures against polygamy. A little later they were active in opposing efforts to secure statehood. Whitney, the Mormon historian, remarks, "the Liberal Party secured the defeat of the statehood movement, and by continued malicious assaults upon the Mormons compelled the perpetuation of the People's Party as a measure of self-defense . . ."

About this time the Gentile League of Utah was organized. This group, sponsored by certain of the federal appointees to Utah, was apparently ready for more direct action. At one point 100 men planned to invade the city council of Salt Lake City and drive the members out of their place of operations. Word got around that if any trouble ensued, they would shoot the leaders, particularly Brigham Young, if he were present. This threat was an effort to incite open conflict with the Mormons prior to an election; but calmer heads among the opposition prevented an open break. Yet ever since the Gentiles had first begun to oppose the Mormons in Utah on political or economic grounds, the hotheads among the former group were anxious for an open fight which would bring the federal government into the picture on a military basis. At the same time, there were Mormons with itchy fingers and there is no doubt that part of the difficulties derived from them as well. Certainly the Mountain Meadows massacre was an illustration of the fanatical violence of which certain Mormons were capable and the Gentiles never tired of recalling that unhappy event.

By the beginning of the 1870's, although no active legislation had been proposed against the Mormons, the conflict began to shape up along more definite lines, both inside and outside of Utah. The *Salt Lake Tribune* had begun to exploit the country's feelings regarding polygamy as a part of its local campaign against the Mormons.

After the Civil War Congress again paid some attention to Utah. In 1865 and again in 1866 efforts were made to strengthen the Morrill Act and otherwise to put legal pressure on polygamy. Gradually the two basic issues, statehood and polygamy, began to emerge. In January, 1867, the Utah territorial legislature petitioned Congress for repeal of the Morrill Act. At the same time they petitioned for admission into the Union as a state. The House Judiciary Committee in reporting on the latter said in effect that this was practically a request for the sanction of polygamy.

At the time these petitions were before Congress regarding statehood, Senator Jacob M. Howard of Michigan was proposing legislation which would extirpate Mormonism and polygamy by force. This proposal was so severe, however, that it aroused a considerable amount of opposition in the Eastern press.

Many of the Gentiles in Utah were not satisfied and kept needling the authorities in Washington. R. N. Baskin, a Gentile attorney in Salt Lake City, claimed a considerable amount of credit for having kept up this activity. In 1869 two drastic bills were introduced into Congress, one by Senator Aaron H. Cragin of New Hampshire in the Senate and the other by Shelley N. Cullom in the House. The Cullom Bill passed the House by the decisive vote of 94 to 32. It was accepted in the Senate by Cragin as a substitute for his own bill, and became the first effective anti-polygamous legislation.

The news that the House had passed the Cullom Bill aroused a great deal of excitement in Utah. It was definite evidence of the growing anti-polygamous feeling in Washington. The Mormons had no intention of relinquishing their practice of polygamy and began a strong resistance against the bill. Mormon women were particularly aggressive in their protests. They called a "great indignation meeting" in Salt Lake City and passed resolutions against the Cullom Bill. On March 5, 1870, the *Mormon Tribune* (not to be confused with the *Salt Lake Tribune*) remarked:

While we think that the United States desires to destroy our institutions, the people of the United States believe that we are wanting to overturn theirs, and of course there must be difficulty until this point is settled. We best prove to the United States that the government need fear no political rebellion from us . . . Polygamy, as some of the highest officials of the government have declared, is not the point aimed at, it is simply a convenient question upon which to test the point as to whether we intend to be an independent kingdom or a territory of the United States.

The Cullom Bill was attacked in the Eastern papers as altogether too severe. It practically destroyed self-government in Utah and removed the safeguard of trial by jury. The public conscience of the time was not quite ready for such strong measures. Yet the exhaustive discussion of the Cullom Bill meant that gradually the whole issue of Utah, Mormonism, and polygamy was coming to be recognized a serious problem that must be dealt with at the national level.

In his message to Congress in December, 1871, President Grant, stimulated by John P. Newman—then chaplain of the Senate—and Baskin, stated among other things:

In Utah there still remains a remnant of barbarism, repugnant to civilization, decency, and to the law of the United States . . . Neither polygamy nor any other violation of existing statutes will be permitted in the territory of the United States. It is not with the religion of self-styled saints that we are now dealing, but their practices. They will be protected in the worship of God according to the dictates of their consciences, but they will not be permitted to violate laws under the cloak of religion . . .

This concern at the national level became the factor which in the end undid polygamy in Utah. We shall take up the matter of the new statutes in the next chapter as well as the court cases which were involved.

# 17 INTENSIFICATION OF CONFLICT AND OFFICIAL LIQUIDATION OF POLYGAMY

THE YEARS from 1870 to the Manifesto in 1890 were marked by an intensification of the conflict between the Mormons and the Gentiles. What had started out as a local and somewhat tangential issue had become a central problem for the entire American public. Millions of words were poured out in public discussion. Strong emotions were evoked by the federal judges as well as by the reformers who wished to get rid of the cancer of polygamy. This whole period provides an excellent illustration of the interplay of public sentiment and judicial action. Moreover, among the Mormons there is evidence of a gradual decline of enthusiasm for the Principle and a good deal of readiness to compromise so that they might obtain certain other benefits, especially that of statehood. This chapter will discuss the interplay of public opinion, legislative action, and judicial decision as they operated in the last two decades of the plurality system.

The first definite legislation against polygamy, the Morrill Act of 1862, had not been effective. While the bill was directed against the practice of polygamy, it had been so framed as not to interfere with the dictates of conscience. Nevertheless, the bill was viewed by the Mormons as put by the *Deseret News*, April 26, 1866, as a means of getting them to deny their "faith" and in particular as a method of "bastardizing our children," and "making shipwreck of our salvation for disobeying an unconstitutional stretch of the law-making department."

349

The first serious attempt to put teeth into the anti-polygamy laws came during the administration of President U. S. Grant. Various proposals were advanced to disfranchise the Mormons, disincorporate the Church, and take away its property.

The Gentiles in Utah were generally in favor of any bills which would cut down the local power of the Mormons. On the other hand, some of the Gentile press outside of Utah regarded these bills as aimed at the deprivation of civil rights. The *California Alta,* December 4, 1872, commented on the proposed legislation in Congress as follows:

It [polygamy] would no doubt have been arrested years ago, if it had not furnished material for demagogues to bring themselves notoriety. They were opposed to a simple disposal of the question, but wanted to rob the Mormons of their property, deprive them of the protection of the courts, and drive them into banishment or rebellion. Their purpose was not order but revenge . . .

One of the basic difficulties with the administration of justice in Utah, particularly in reference to polygamy, arose from the fact that there was really a dual set of courts: (a) Probate courts which also had civil and criminal jurisdictions at the local levels; these courts were with few exceptions manned by Mormons. (b) In addition there were the federal district courts—three in number—and the territorial supreme court. The three federal judges, appointed from Washington, were without exception Gentiles. These men served as the supreme court, consisting of a chief justice and two associate justices. But the same men were respectively assigned to the three district courts as sole judge in each. This produced the anomalous situation in which appeals from the district courts to the territorial supreme court were adjudicated by at least one man who had handed down the original decision while serving on the district bench.

The conflict between local and federal authorities was further complicated by the fact that the territorial marshals and the territorial attorney general were appointed by Washington. These officials frequently were at odds with the local police and territorial attorneys.

The re-election of Grant in 1872 was viewed by the Gentile forces as indicative of more severe measures to come. In his annual message to Congress, December 1, 1873, he requested legislation for Utah which would modify the system of obtaining jurors and sharply limit the power of the probate courts. Most of Grant's recommendations were embodied in a bill by Representative Luke P. Poland of Vermont introduced on January 5, 1874, and finally passed in the early summer of that year.

The "Poland law," as it was called, took from the probate courts in Utah all civil, chancery, and criminal jurisdictions. These were now allotted to the district and supreme courts of the territory. It provided further that when a woman filed a bill to declare void a marriage because of a previous marriage, the court could grant alimony. Furthermore, in any prosecution for adultery, bigamy, or polygamy, a juror could be challenged for belief in, or practice of, plural marriage. In short, this law removed the power of the Mormon Church to control the territorial courts. The probate courts had only to do with matters of inheritance and guardianship.

The *Salt Lake Tribune* for June 24, 1874, was happy over the passage of the Poland Bill and its headline screamed out in such phrases as: "Polygamy and murder no longer justified"; "Human slavery abolished forever and priesthood rule killed"; and "The last rites of barbarism extirpated from the earth."

The official church view, as expressed in the *Deseret News* was that the law "takes from the people and their legislative representatives powers and rights enjoyed by them for a quarter of a century . . . a thing entirely foreign to constitutional and republican principles."

Then, as later, the Mormons argued that polygamy was not the basic issue in the attack but a camouflage under which the Gentiles would destroy their Church. In truth, this view was freely admitted by some non-Mormons who continually harped on the stranglehold, both economically and politically, of the Mormon Church. Yet, as the issue became more and more nationally recognized, the reform groups came to view polygamy as the central feature of the entire conflict.

The Gentiles in Utah were particularly anxious to abolish the marked ballot. This was a device by which it was possible to identify the voter after he had voted by assigning a number to his ballot and keeping this with the voting lists. There was also a good deal of agitation to abolish women's suffrage which had been early introduced into Utah. The grounds for this latter agitation was that the Mormon polygamists were "voting" their plural wives to the detriment of the non-Mormon contingent in the community. Some Gentiles went so far as to advocate the outright disfranchisement not only of all polygamists but of all Mormons.

Late in 1881 Senator George F. Edmunds introduced a measure to amend the anti-polygamy law of 1862. There was some opposition to the bill in both houses of Congress. Representative A. S. Hewitt remarked, "Polygamy can be stamped out without resorting to a remedy, which, if generally applied would vitiate our whole political system . . ." and Senator L. Q. C. Lamar of Mississippi arose from his sickbed to attend a session of the Senate where he protested vigorously: "In my opinion, sir, it is a cruel measure, and will inflict unspeakable sufferings upon large masses, many of them the innocent victims of a system."

In certain organs of the public press as well as in Congress, the view was expressed that this measure was in effect "a bill of attainder and obnoxious to the Constitution." The opposition, however, was unable to stem the public pressure on Congress to put force into the anti-polygamy legislation. With some modifications the bill became law in March, 1882.

The important features of the new law were: It defined polygamy as a crime but left the penalty the same as in the law of 1862. It defined living with a plural wife as "unlawful cohabitation," a crime punishable by not more than $300.00 fine or imprisonment not to exceed six months, or both, at the discretion of the court. It provided further that the offenses of polygamy and unlawful cohabitation could be joined in the same information or indictment. It provided that all persons guilty of polygamy, bigamy, or unlawful cohabitation were excluded from voting, or from holding any public office, or from serving on juries in cases concerned with polygamy. The law further declared all registration and election officers in Utah vacant; and until other provisions could be made by the legislative assembly, the work of these registration and election officers was to be performed by a board of five commissioners appointed by the President with the consent and advice of the Senate; also that not more than three of these were to be of the same political party. The bill did humanely provide that all the children born of polygamous marriages before the date of January 1, 1883, would be legitimatized. Finally, the President of the United States was empowered to grant amnesty to such persons guilty of polygamy prior to the enactment of this act under such limitations and upon whatever conditions he should deem proper.

The view of the Mormons on this law is neatly summed up in an entry by Wilford Woodruff in his journal of March 14, 1882:

It is entirely a breach of the Constitution of the United States; condemns men before trial or conviction by court or jury; takes away the right of trial by jury of their peers; makes an *ex post facto* law and a bill of attainder; takes away from the Latter-day Saints, because of their religious convictions, the franchise, and deprives them of sitting on juries because of their opinions; but if the nation can stand it, we can. It is taking a stand against God, against Christ and his Kingdom and against his people.

While the Mormons declared that they would test the constitutionality of the Edmunds Act, for the first time many of the authorities of the Church felt that this was the most serious threat to polygamy which they so far had faced. Most Mormons were sure of this when the act *was* declared constitutional.

Yet, the enemies of the Church were not satisfied. There was further agitation to strengthen the new law. In 1884 Senator Edmunds sponsored legislation—called the "Utah bill"—which would have meant the setting up of martial law in the territory, the disfranchisement of all Mormons, the confiscation of the property of the Church, and the strengthening of sanctions against plural marriage.

In short, it sought to crush the political and ecclesiastical power of the Church and at the same time put down polygamy with a strong hand. To facilitate the latter objective it provided that the lawful husband or wife could be compelled to testify in prosecutions for bigamy, polygamy, or unlawful cohabitation. It is clear that although the legal machinery to enforce the Edmunds Act of 1882 was operating reasonably effectively, many Utah Gentiles felt that they had not as yet accomplished their true mission.

It is amply clear that the anti-Mormons in Utah were not disinterested moral crusaders striving for purity in the American home. They really sought to secure political and economic power by completely dismantling the Mormon Church. While the national interests against polygamy outside of Utah did not all share this view, they were nevertheless willing to go along with additional severe measures against the "twin relic."

During these years there had been periodic proposals for a constitutional amendment which would forbid polygamy. The Mormon leaders were quite unwilling to see the struggle go so far as to lead to such a drastic measure. They knew that if such an amendment were passed, it would forever put the quietus on polygamy.

After remaining dormant for nearly two years the "Utah bill" was reintroduced in December, 1885, as the Edmunds-Tucker bill. There was considerable opposition on various grounds. Senator George G. Vest of Missouri, said among other things:

. . . I am well aware of what the public sentiment of this country is, but . . . I cannot vote for this bill because in my judgment it violates the fundamental principles of the Constitution of the United States and the rights of property . . .

It is a naked, sinful confiscation, nothing else . . . It is no answer to tell me that this is the Mormon Church and that the great vice or crime of polygamy is in existence there. This bigotry may go to the extent of saying that the Baptist Church, or the Presbyterian, or the Catholic Church is amenable to just such legislation.

He further pointed out that the test oath would mean abso-lutely nothing if the contention of the non-Mormon element was correct that the Saints would not worry about perjury in such matters.

The Edmunds-Tucker bill finally passed both houses late in February, 1887, and became a law without the signature of the President. The new act provided that the legal husband or wife might testify against the other, if they so wished, in trials involving polygamy and unlawful cohabitation. All marriages were to be made matters of public record and information should state the nature of the ceremony and give the name of the priest or other person performing the ceremony. Complaints regarding adultery and other sex offenses could be entered by others than the alleged abused husband or wife. The probate judges of the territory were to be appointed by the President of the United States. Of particular significance was the provision which escheated all of the property of the Mormon Church except burial grounds, places of worship, parsonages, and surrounding plots of ground. The Perpetual Emigrating Fund Company was dissolved, its property taken by the government to be used for the common schools of the territory, and, most important of all, the Mormon Church was disincorporated.

The act provided further that a commissioner of schools was to be appointed by the Supreme Court and that sectarian teaching of any sort in the common schools was forbidden. Women suffrage was abolished as was the Nauvoo Legion. As a prerequisite to voting, to holding public office, or to serving on juries in Utah, a test oath was required in addition to the usual regulations. In this oath the individual pledged obedience to the federal law regarding polygamy and swore that he would not encourage, aid, or teach anything contrary to the laws of the United States. Finally, all persons were to be disfranchised if they were found guilty of polygamy or unlawful cohabitation; and illegitimate children, with certain exception, were disinherited.

This was by far the most serious legislation yet passed against the Mormons. They carried their first cases to the

Supreme Court, but the latter, in May, 1890, affirmed the
constitutionality of the law.

Still another bill proposed to disfranchise all Latter-day
Saints. Moreover, the courts had ruled that alien Mormons,
could not become citizens because of their membership in
the Church.

These legislative and judicial developments show clearly
the rising tide of Gentile agitation both in Utah and outside.
The extreme proposals, which in some quarters were regarded
as destructive of certain fundamentals of democracy, show
clearly the power of mass reactions. The Gentiles would stop
at nothing in putting an end to polygamy. In fact, the severe
enforcement of the law had much to do with eliminating the
system.

Although the Saints made every effort to preserve their
civil rights, the campaign was on. On October 2, 1871,
Brigham Young, along with George Q. Cannon and others,
was arrested for lascivious cohabitation under the law of
1852. This act had been drawn against adultery by the Mormons themselves and was never intended to apply to plural
marriages. Young was released on $5,000.00 bail and allowed
to stay in his own home under guard.

On October 9, 1871, the case was called before Judge Mc-
Kean. The defense first raised the question as to the legal
competence of the Grand Jury to indict but this motion was
denied by the judge. McKean then went on to indicate clearly
his emotional involvement in this whole matter. He rendered
an opinion from the bench in which he said, among other
things, ". . . while the case at bar is called 'The people versus
Brigham Young,' its other and real title is, 'Federal authority
versus polygamic theocracy' . . . A system is on trial in the
person of Brigham Young."

In his pamphlet entitled "The Mormon Trials," Alfred
Townsend relates that the general authorities of the Church
held a serious discussion as to whether Brigham Young should
have submitted himself to trial. He was seventy years old and
in failing health. Many advised that it would be better for the

Saints to destroy their communities and move to Mexico than to endure further indignities at the hands of the courts. But Brigham would have none of this and remarked: "God is in courts as well as in battles and miracles. There will be no resistance. I shall obey the summons."

Young went to court and pled not guilty. In the courtroom he was so dignified that he impressed everybody. Even Judge McKean, who on other occasions had been quick to snap and cackle at the Mormons, refrained from his usual tirades.

The Eastern press continued to be supplied with inflammatory messages charging the Mormons with outright treason. However, some of the Gentile press by no means approved the conduct of the federal courts in these cases. For example, the *Montana Herald* in October, 1871, commented editorially, "The conduct of Judge McKean does not look to us like that of a democratic judge in a free country, but more like that of Judge Jeffreys in the most gloomy and despotic era of English history."

The anti-Mormon zealots were not satisfied but indicted Brigham Young on charges of having ordered the notorious Bill Hickman—said to be one of his Destroying Angels—to murder certain Gentiles. Young was committed to jail but allowed once more to remain in his own home under guard. Subsequently nothing came of these charges.

Another important test case was that of Thomas Hawkins who was arrested in October, 1871, on charges of adultery and lewd and licentious conduct with his plural wife. The importance of this case is that Judge McKean permitted the first wife to testify against her husband. The principle of a wife not testifying against her husband is one of the oldest in common law. Here we have an illustration not only of an overzealous judge who wanted to see the victims convicted but one who permitted a type of testimony which had long since been regarded in British and American jurisprudence as contra the best rules of evidence.

Perhaps the most famous case which received much public attention was that of Ann Eliza Webb Young against Brigham, filed July 28, 1873. We noted in Chapter 11 that McKean's granting her alimony practically gave judicial sanction to plural marriages.

That Judge McKean viewed himself as a crusader against Mormonism is neatly illustrated in his charge to the grand and petit juries on one occasion. He said: "I apologize to nobody for being here . . . I know . . . that the day is not far in the future, when the disloyal high priesthood of the so-called 'Church of Jesus Christ of Latter-day Saints,' shall bow to and obey the laws that are elsewhere respected, or else those laws will grind them into powder."

McKean was not alone in his judicial zealotry against the Saints. Other judges took frequent opportunities to berate the Saints for their lack of patriotism and their breaking of the law regarding polygamy. For example, after the passage of the Poland law Judge Jacob S. Boreman openly admitted that he had no intention of permitting any person who believed in or practiced polygamy to serve on any juries over which he presided.

Finally, there was an unofficial and informal agreement between the federal officials and the leaders of the Church to produce a test case. The man chosen for this trial was George Reynolds, then secretary to Brigham Young. Reynolds had but recently taken a second wife. He was found guilty and given a fine of $500.00 and sentenced to two years in the penitentiary.

The territorial supreme court upheld the action of the lower court and two and a half years later on January 6, 1876, the United States Supreme Court concurred in the action of the lower court and declared the law of 1862 to be constitutional.

The significance of the Reynolds case cannot be overlooked. While Reynolds served out his full time, the whole episode represented a definite shift in judicial action. It was a precedent for the convictions that followed. Moreover, it foreshadowed the increasing hostility of the government toward the Mormons. It was a sanction of the Gentile crusade and certainly facilitated the passage of more proscriptive legislation regarding polygamy.

We have already indicated that one of the serious problems

confronting the prosecution was the difficulty of securing adequate evidence of the plurality of wives. Because the federal officials could not get at the Mormon records, it was often hard to discover whether a man really was married in polygamy or not. Then, too, the refusal of wives to testify against their husbands and husbands against their wives was an added barrier. There were a number of cases in which courts applied rather severe coercion upon Mormon women in order to get such evidence. Upon several occasions these women were sent to the penitentiary, some for days and others for months, for their contempt of court in refusing to give information concerning their marital or sexual relations. These women were celebrated as heroines of the Church. Their refusals often delayed and in a few cases helped frustrate the prosecutions in progress. Nonetheless, a great number of the individuals were found guilty and were convicted. After the Edmunds-Tucker law the work of the courts was facilitated by the provision that wives might testify against their husbands.

One of the first Mormon women to be sent to prison for contempt of court was Annie Gallifant. She was sentenced on November 17, 1882, by Chief Justice John A. Hunter for refusing to tell the name of the man to whom she was married. She was obviously pregnant at the time of the trial and served only one day at the penitentiary. A few days after her release she gave birth to her baby. The reaction to this episode on the part of the Mormons was one of disgust and horror. For the moment Annie Gallifant was a real martyr to the cause.

An even more noteworthy case was that of Belle Harris which we described in Chapter 11. Other instances were those of Nellie White and Lucy Deborah both of whom served short terms for refusing to tell of their alleged marriages to certain Mormon men.

The federal crusade against polygamy is illustrated further in some of the judicial rulings of the court. For example, Angus M. Cannon, was tried on the charge of unlawful cohabitation before Judge Charles S. Zane. The crucial question was how to define "unlawful cohabitation." Judge Zane, in rendering his decision remarked on May 9, 1885:

I am of the opinion that it is not essential to constitute an offense against this law to show sexual intercourse. It is sufficient to show that a man lives with more than one woman, cohabits with them, and holds them out to the world as his wives. That being so, that he did not have sexual intercourse with them or occupy the same bed with either of them, is no defense and is immaterial so far as the jury is concerned.

In December, 1885 the Supreme Court of the United States upheld Zane's contention that it was unnecessary to prove actual sexual relations in cases charging unlawful cohabitation. Two justices dissented from the majority decision and maintained that Zane's ruling put "a strained construction on a highly penal statute."

By the mid-1880's certain breaks in Mormon solidarity began to appear. In April, 1885, O. P. Arnold pled guilty to the charge of unlawful cohabitation and, moreover, promised to obey the law in the future "to cease to treat his second wife as a wife more than to support her." Judge Zane approved this promise and inflicted only a moderate fine of $300.00. The reaction of the church officials to Arnold's promise was expressed in the *Deseret News*, April 14, 1885, as follows: "That Mr. Arnold could consistently plead guilty of having violated the Edmunds Act no one can question, but that he could agree to no longer recognize the sacred relationship into which he entered with his second wife is at variance with his profession of faith as a Latter-day Saint . . ."

Such rifts in the solid front could not be stopped. A number of others followed Arnold's example. But the best known of these agreements was that of Bishop John Sharp, a prominent Mormon, who told the court:

I expect to remain under the political disabilities placed upon me, but I have so arranged my family relations as to conform to the requirements of the law, and I am now living in harmony with its provisions in relation to cohabitation as construed by this court and the supreme court of the territory, and it is my intention to do so in the future until an overruling Providence shall decree greater religious toleration in the land.

Sharp got off with a light fine of $300.00 and the *Salt Lake Tribune,* the archenemy of the Church, was quick to praise the Bishop's action. The *Deseret News,* on the other hand, put forth what was essentially the official view of the Church when it commented: "No matter what position any single man or number of men may take in regard to what God has given, the truth must be sustained and vindicated at all hazards."

For a time after this, Sharp was at odds with the general authorities but his importance to the Church, especially in the field of finance, was such that he did not suffer any serious ostracism. The more prevalent attitude of the time was exemplified in the statement Hiram B. Clawson made September 29, 1885, as he was about to be sentenced for unlawful cohabitation, "If I make any promises, so far as regards the future, I am ostracized, and looked down upon, I am dishonored in this community among my brethren—those that I respect and honor—and among all men."

The *Deseret News* reflected both official and lay opinion by remarking that Clawson chose imprisonment and honor while others had chosen "liberty and dishonor in promising to obey."

A year later, on October 6, 1886, an epistle from the Presidency of the Church exhorted the brethren against promising future obedience. At that time both John Taylor and George Q. Cannon were hiding to avoid imprisonment, but they advised the Saints:

. . . According to the latest ruling, a promise to obey the law signifies an agreement to violate the most solemn convenants of marital fidelity that mortals can make with each other and their God. It means the utter repudiation of loving wives and the separation with either of the father or of the mother and her children. It is a promise not to visit, go to the same place of worship or amusement, or recognize, associate with or even call on when sick or dying, or when her child is sick or dying, the plural wife who had been faithful in all things. It means dishonor, treachery, cruelty, and cowardice . . . It is a promise that no true Latter-day Saint can make and that no human being would demand.

The zealots who were out to crush polygamy were not finished, however. In 1885 they introduced a practice known as

"segregation." This was based on the idea that unlawful cohabitation was not a single, continuous event, but that it
might be broken up into any smaller unit such as a period of
years, half-years, months, weeks, or even a shorter period of
time. Each fragment thus broken off or "segregated" could be
covered by a separate indictment. This provided the court
with an opportunity to increase greatly the severity of punishment. The first conviction under this new ruling was that of
Hugh S. Gowans, who was found guilty under three indict-
ments in February, 1886. The following year, in the Lorenzo
Snow case, the United States Supreme Court killed the theory
of segregation by ruling that unlawful cohabitation was a
continuous offense and therefore only one indictment could
be found.

While the Mormons were rather happy at this decision, it
was clear enough that they were in for even more severe treatment. The passage of the Edmunds-Tucker bill was just
around the corner. In fact, the sense of pressure which
mounted with the additional anti-polygamy legislation led
to some modification of enthusiasm for the Principle on the
part of the Saints. At the same time, there was a lessening of
the vigor of pursuit on the part of the federal judges. The
penalties they afflicted were less severe than they had been in
the days of McKean and Zane and the particularly obnoxious
practice of denying naturalization to Mormon converts because they believed in polygamy was abandoned. At the same
time among the rank and file of the Mormons, the notion was
growing up that the practice of polygamy was more a matter
of permissiveness than of outright obligation. The severe
prosecutions had begun to pay dividends in weakening the
Saints' faith in the Principle.

In this connection, note must be made again of the manner
in which the judges took occasion over and over again to express strong value judgments regarding plural marriage. For
example, in September, 1874, Judge Boreman remarked about
the effect of polygamy on children: "The children of such
marriages are generally growing up like wild animals, without training, instruction, or parental care. The consequences

are seen all through the territory that polygamy in every phase of its character is degrading and beastly . . ." A year later Chief Justice Michael Shaeffer commented on the effects on the family in this vein:

The dissension, the degeneracy of the domestic circle by the introduction of practices and relations which are tolerated only among barbarians and semi-barbarous peoples, not only creates a disregard for law and good order, but unfits a people for their highest civilization which Americans so justly boast.

All this is clear evidence that public sentiment was willing to override the legal procedures and support officials who would go far beyond what the law, be it constitutional or statutory, really permitted. The modification of the system of choosing juries, the introduction of the permission for a wife to testify against her husband, the weird not to say wild interpretation of the term "cohabitation," the attempt at segregation, and others are all indications of the fact that when an aroused public is in pursuit of a minority group, as it was after the Mormons, they will stop at practically nothing.

Let us now look at the manner in which public sentiment was whipped up to support particular overt action. Obviously the central theme was polygamy and the relationship of this problem to the obtaining of statehood. Additional themes were the "vicious power of the Mormon hierarchy," charges of disloyalty, and the Mountain Meadows massacre as a symbol of Mormon savagery.

The chief sources in the attack were editorials, stories, and cartoons from newspapers, pamphlets, sermons, and memorials passed by various mass meetings. The press of the country outside Utah drew largely upon the materials furnished by the two organs of local opinion, the official Mormon *Deseret News* and the pro-Gentile *Salt Lake Tribune*.

While the use of pamphlets in public discussion had declined after the Civil War, hundreds of pamphlets circulated over the country dealing with the Mormon issue and, in particular, with polygamy. Sermons and other public speeches were a source of an enormous amount of agitation and discussion of this whole issue. Yet changes took place in the content and tone of these public addresses. In the non-Mormon religious circles the sermons often became more violent as we move from the beginning of this period to the passage of the Edmunds Act in 1882. On the other hand, there is a considerable shift in the tone of the Mormon sermons. Fiery and often violent remarks of Brigham Young, Heber C. Kimball, and others were replaced by rather milder statements by their successors. Seen against the background of events, the shift to more violent public sentiment on the part of the Gentiles and the shift to more moderate sentiment on the part of the Mormons symbolizes an increasing confidence on the part of the former and a sense of impending defeat on the part of the latter.

Of various devices used in public discussion and propaganda none is more universal or effective than name-calling. This practice was indulged in freely by both sides of the controversy.

The psychology of name-calling is clear enough. It means for the individual that he has some word or symbol in his mind which is a means of identification with his own group and likewise with counteridentification or avoidance and opposition to the out-group.

The Mountain Meadows massacre came to symbolize to the outside world that the Mormons were "blood-stained murderers." In August, 1875, in discussing the trial of John D. Lee, the *Salt Lake Tribune* wrote, "Brigham Young is the biggest murderer known to the 19th century," and shortly thereafter referred to him as "the real murderer at Mountain Meadows." It was not at all uncommon after the Lee trials to call the Church "the Mountain Meadows Church." In the same year when the Gentiles were conducting a campaign against Governor Axtel whom they regarded as pro-Mormon, the leaders of the Church were referred to as "these traitors and blood-stained priests." "Polygamy" was designated "a blot upon our civilization" and as "a filthy practice," one "which drags the family relations down to the barnyard level."

In addition to such name calling the *Tribune* frequently used spicy headlines to attract attention. For example, on February 10, 1874, when Cannon had a hearing before the Utah Commission, this newspaper carried a headline reading:

CANNON DENIES THAT HE IS A
POLYGAMIST AND TRAITOR
*Thus Making Prostitutes of his*
*Wives and Bastards of his Children*

While the *Deseret News* was less colorful, it too took to name calling. This newspaper did not hesitate to refer to the "bigot like McKean," who conducted a "mob court" using "trumped-up charges" and "packed juries," nor to talk about "ring tactics and ring-tailed organ," the latter referring to the *Salt Lake Tribune*. And in discussing the "anti-Mormon ravings" of Attorney P. T. Van Zile, the *News* remarked:

We notice . . . that the vilest debauchers, the most corrupt and libidinous scoundrels, the lowest drabs, the most shameless Cyprians, as well as the sleek and unctuous male libertine and the sly and artful female voluptuary, are the bitterest opponents and denouncers of the plural marriage of the Mormons and the most anxious for the enactment of laws to suppress and break it up as a family arrangement . . .

Ridicule and satire not only pleased and supported the solidarity of each side in the fight, but served to undermine the self-esteem of those toward whom it was addressed. In 1875 when the Church was putting on a strong campaign for economic self-sufficiency, the *Salt Lake Tribune* printed the following doggerel:

The Mormons are excited,
And Brigham he is wroth
To find that some refuse
To wear his home-made cloth.

While apostles, too, are angry,
When they think that some refuse
To join the holy order
And wear the wooden shoes.

Cartoons likewise provided a means of ridicule and satire. During the 1875's the *Salt Lake Tribune* began running a series of cartoons poking fun at Brigham Young, the Mormons generally, and various officials whom they disliked. For example, Governor S. B. Axtel was under attack by the *Tribune* and a number of cartoons were directed against him. He was said to be under Brigham's control.

In the decade under question, the issue became more sharply drawn. The Gentile forces were more carefully organized and public pressure was exerted upon both the courts and Congress to strengthen the hands of those who opposed the plural marriage system. In an editorial of October 4, 1871, the *Deseret News* stated the Mormons' fundamental charge against the Gentiles:

You went into a community which had established itself in the howling desert and presented a picture of unequalled peace and good order for a quarter of a century, and you introduced disorder, confusion, anarchy, fire and the sword; you destroyed the results of a quarter of a century of heroic, peaceful, well-directed industry; you found a country full of smiling farms and orchards and gardens and houses and mills and factories and productive industries of all kinds redeemed from the desert, and you reduced it again to its desert state; you found capital flowing from a distance into the territory, and you drove that capital back again; you found a sober and virtuous people, and you introduced, encouraged, and protected drunkenness, gambling and whoredom and all manner of licentiousness and abominations of every kind; you found a peaceful and law abiding community, and you left it full of violence and blood and rapine; you let out the waters of strife in the mountain and lo! they have run down to the plains and the sea and spread over the whole nation, till peace is taken from the land, and violence and destruction prevail everywhere . . .

In the early days of Salt Lake City there was practically no liquor and no prostitution. But as the number of Gentiles increased and as the court officials encouraged liquor dealing and prostitution, the *Salt Lake Tribune,* in order to answer some of the claims of the Mormons that polygamy was one way to erase prostitution completely, maintained that prostitution and polygamy were practically the same. In an editorial for August 31, 1872, entitled "Prostitution and polygamy compared," it stated: "Now, then, suppose a man, under whatever pretext you please, religious or otherwise, indulges in sexuality to the same extent with a like number of women, does he not equally commit the crime of prostitution?" It goes on to say, the only differences are in one case the plurality of women and in the other case the plurality of men.

The Gentile press had taken the position that a realistic recognition of the function of prostitution and "the impossibility of crushing it out" were only practical views. Since the Mormons were always infuriated by any statement that polygamy and prostitution were identical, these comments of the opposition newspaper further stimulated the conflict. Yet, one cannot overlook a certain illogic in the position of the *Tribune*.

The brave words of Apostle Woodruff uttered in a sermon in June, 1879, must have given many of the Saints real emotional support in their struggle with their enemies. He stated bluntly, "I will not desert my wives and my children and disobey the commandments of God for the sake of accommodating the public clamor of a nation steeped in sin and ripened for the damnation of hell. I would rather go to prison and to death."

In general, the non-Mormon press outside of Utah tended to reflect the rising opposition to polygamy. From time to time, however, certain non-Mormon organs of opinion pointed out that the continuing attacks upon Mormonism and especially upon polygamy rather served to solidify the Mormons than otherwise. This was the view frequently taken by the *New York Herald* during the early 1870's. Again the non-Mormon press occasionally pointed out, as did the *New York Graphic,* December 9, 1873, that "the licentiousness and vice and crime against domestic purity in our great cities hardly justify us in making a national raid against a community which, with all its sins and shortcomings, has abolished the social evil from its borders and provides every woman with at least the semblance of a home."

The views of women might well be considered as an important item in any public discussion of plural marriage. Those brought up in the strong traditions of Christian monogamy were amazed to find that many Mormon women defended the system of polygamy. Many of these Gentile women regarded such statements as evidence either of complete degradation or of outright hypocrisy.

In October, 1871, a petition to Congress, signed by 2,500 Mormon women, expressed belief in the sacredness of polygamy and asked that congressional attacks on the system be stopped. After the passage of the Poland bill Mormon women sent another memorial, signed by nearly 30,000 members, asking the repeal of the laws of 1862 and 1873. In 1873 Gentile women in Utah sent their memorial to Congress regarding the need to correct "the evils and abuses" of civil rights by the Mormon authorities.

Later the women members of the Liberal party sent petitions to Washington which, in turn, were countered by petitions favorable to the Saints. Regarding one of these latter protests, signed by 1,200 Mormon women, the *Salt Lake Tribune* said it was a case of "twelve hundred polygamous women proclaiming their shame."

All during this time the Mormon forces were defending their course in terms of freedom of conscience and the divinity of polygamy as witnessed by Joseph Smith's revelation and by the Old Testament practices of the same. But there was a growing view of both judges and federal legislators that plural marriage could not be defended or excused in terms of any "constitutional guarantee of religious freedom," as Justice Waite put it in the opinion of the Supreme Court which upheld the Morrill Act. And, in his message to Congress in December, 1880, President Hayes remarked: "It is the duty and purpose of the people of the United States, to suppress polygamy where it now exists in one territory and prevent its extension . . ." In the year following President Arthur asked for strong legislation to abolish "this odious crime." He advocated further that a wife be permitted to testify against her husband and that full records be kept of marriage ceremonies.

Fortunately for them, the Mormons had a strong delegate in Congress as well as other help there. In fact, the Gentile press accused them of conducting an expensive lobby. In 1880 Delegate George Q. Cannon, much against the wishes of the opposition elements since he was a polygamist, was quite outspoken in his criticism of President Hayes' attitude toward Utah. He said that the President was misinformed and that the Gentiles had really made no serious effort to enforce the laws of Utah but had used the issue as a shield to protect their political and economic campaign against the Mormons. He said that as far as the Church influencing a man's actions on a jury, such an accusation was sheer nonsense.

The increasing aggressiveness of the Gentiles began to crystallize in the passage of the Edmunds Act in 1882. In contrast, Mormon officialdom expressed continuing belief that the opposition would be unable seriously to damage their cause. The concrete facts hardly supported their optimism. There was a constant trickle of apostasy which provided the Gentiles with arguments against polygamy, and there was a growing restlessness among the run-of-the-mill Mormons over the prosecutions for polygamy.

During his term of office Governor E. H. Murray started a strong campaign in Utah to uproot polygamy. In commenting on his message to the territorial legislature in January 13, 1886, the *Salt Lake Tribune* remarked that "either the church will have to surrender or the government will . . ."

Although Murray was removed from office a few months later, his successor, Caleb West, continued the firm stand regarding the enforcement of anti-polygamy measures. In his message in July, 1886, he pointed out that the Church was bringing in an increasing number of immigrants, was continuing to teach against the Christian marriage laws, that the First Presidency was in hiding, that many members were in the penitentiary, and that the trials were proving very expensive. Therefore, he was going to see if they could not really enforce the law and get this whole business cleaned up. He warned all and sundry to avoid entering into "any marriage relation other than that allowed and sanctioned by law, or to aid and abet others in so doing."

While the official Church had persisted in saying that it would not capitulate to non-Mormon pressure against polygamy, it is clear that both the general authorities and the bulk of Mormons realized more and more that the system could not continue without some compromise. It is interesting that eight years before the Manifesto itself, the *New York Tribune* on January 24, 1882, had this to say, "If public opinion rises, the Mormon conspiracy will pretend to yield, will possibly go through the form of abolishing polygamy, and will do what it can to break the force of the attack . . ."

During the mid-1880's the *Salt Lake Tribune* recurrently suggested that the Mormon leaders should provide a revelation to abolish polygamy as one way to save face. But to such suggestions the *Deseret News* remarked that the Church would not yield "a divine law on account of human pressure." However, as we shall see, many Mormons viewed the Manifesto— promulgated less than four years later—as, in effect, a divine revelation.

In June of 1885 the *Deseret News* was saying that the Mormons would not even consider a temporary suspension of the law. Yet little more than a year later Heber J. Grant remarked, "We never believed polygamy was wrong and never will, but one of the cardinal rules of the Church is to obey the law. So long as polygamy is illegal we ourselves will strictly enforce the law." This is a clear evidence of giving way; and toward the end of that decade the Church officially discontinued permitting men to take plural wives. However, some plural marriages were performed in secret during these years.

As it became more and more evident that the Edmunds-Tucker bill would pass Congress the *Salt Lake Tribune* for January 13, 1887, commented: "In this hour so long prayed for; in this morning watch in which tired eyes have been strained so long for the dawn, one of the things happiest to think of is that in ten thousand Mormon homes there will be quiet thanksgiving that Utah is to be Americanized, and that the next generation—their grandchildren—will never know by contact, the horrors of polygamy." And the next day, this newspaper printed the following ditty:

> All hail the power of Brigham's name,
> Let Danites prostrate fall;
> Bring forth the *cohab diadem*
> And crown him Lord (goose) of all!

One of the most exciting charges was that the Mormons were practicing incest. The *Salt Lake Tribune* for July 22, 1885, carried a headline:

### A REVOLTING CASE

*Thomas Porcher's Polygamous Love Unveiled*
*An Incestuous Alliance With His Own Niece*
*With Death to the Progeny and Misery to the Mother*

In the story occurs among other tidbits the following, "Eliza the niece and polygamous wife of Thomas Porcher is 34 years of age; has borne him ten children in nine years, and not one remains alive; is suffering now from dropsy, and goes out nursing for a livelihood. Of such is polygamy!"

The crucial issue in the controversy between the Mormons and the Gentiles was statehood. At the very time when the federal government became increasingly interested in the suppression of polygamy, the agitation for admission of Utah as a state was accelerated. As early as December, 1871, the *Deseret News* indicated that some kind of compromise might be affected regarding polygamy in order to obtain statehood. But the *Salt Lake Tribune,* in keeping with its general policy, came out strongly against granting of statehood at that time. In January of 1872, the Governor of the territory, George L. Woods, had a few things to say about this matter:

To become a state in the Union is not a *right* but a privilege. Good judgment would, therefore, require that before any convention should be called, Utah should place herself in harmonious relations with the general government . . . All violations of the laws of Congress should cease; polygamy should be abandoned and laws should be enacted by you in accordance with the laws of Congress on that subject.

During the early months of 1872 the *Tribune* pointed out that if the Mormons should concede polygamy in order to obtain statehood, such a move might undermine the faith of the Saints in the divinity of the plural system; but that some such plan would have to be worked out was made clear to the Church authorities by a friendly non-Mormon, Thomas Fitch, who was acting as their attorney and lobbyist. At this juncture the Church leaders were not ready to make such a concession through any official pronouncement. However, they did assemble a group of representative citizens and adopted a state constitution, which provided for the abolishment of polygamy. The Liberal party opposed this move and instead memorialized Congress to the effect that the promise to abolish polygamy through the state constitution was a mere trick. They contended that once statehood was obtained, the Mormons would control the state and put into effect any laws they wished.

Again in 1882 an effort was made to write a state constitution in advance and submit the same to Congress. As a matter of fact, this proposed constitution was submitted to popular vote in Utah in 1882. There were 28,000 votes for it and less than 5,000 against it. The constitution was regarded as very liberal in its provisions but nothing came of this proposal. Public sentiment and congressional action alike were moving in quite other channels as witnessed by the passage of the Edmunds Act at about this time. All during the 1880's whenever the matter of statehood was proposed, the Gentile forces were quick to argue that although various proposed constitutions contained articles to suppress polygamy such proposals were mere subterfuges.

In midsummer of 1887, the *Salt Lake Tribune* approvingly quoted the *New York Times:* "Utah should not be admitted to the Union until the Mormon Church formally renounces the doctrine of polygamy and the people have abandoned the practice for a period sufficient to guarantee that both the doctrine and practice had been absolutely given up."

After the passage of the Edmunds-Tucker law and as the prosecutions for polygamy became increasingly effective, a fifth attempt was made to obtain statehood. Regarding this effort the *Salt Lake Tribune* frankly admitted that the Church lobby would "leave no stone unturned to influence public opinion and congressional votes."

To indicate the determination to support Gentile efforts to suppress plural marriages, President Cleveland in 1885, acting under reformist pressure, stationed a detachment of troops in Salt Lake City. The idea behind this was that, if necessary, they could be used to enforce the federal law against polgyamy.

This was but one further step in the direction of ever severer measures toward Utah and the Mormons. The refusal to use Mormons as jurors, the development of a system of segregation, the practical disfranchisement of thousands of members, and the general unrest that occasionally led to individual violence were continuing factors in forcing the Mormons to capitulate. And the periodic threat to use military force only added more weight. The Mormons had had a good deal of difficulty with the military in the past and had no stomach for another war. As a matter of fact a new generation was on the scene and the older leaders who suffered in Nauvoo and the early days in Utah were on the way out.

Among a variety of basic causes for the abandonment of polygamy may be noted the following: First, the escheat of church property under the Edmunds-Tucker Act as well as the confiscation of the funds of the Perpetual Emigrating Fund had seriously effected the economic strength of the Church. Second, the strong desire for statehood was countered by the persistent contention of the Gentile world that polygamy would have to be suppressed before statehood would be granted. Bound up in this whole desire for statehood was the fundamental loyalty of the Mormons to their country. While they viewed the prosecutions for polygamy as downright persecution nevertheless they suffered a considerable sense of guilt and shame at breaking the law.

In the third instance the young men in the Church were becoming increasingly restless under the competition for wives which they faced. All too often Mormon women seemed to prefer plural marriage to men of substance to the risk of a monogamous marriage with a young man whose economic success was still in the future. Finally, it must not be forgotten that the great bulk of marriages among the Mormons were monogamous and that the one-wife system was far and away the usual practice.

Symptomatic of the shift in opinion among the Mormons was the modification of the official stand after the death, in exile, of President John Taylor on July 25, 1887. Taylor had been in hiding for two and a half years and during this time the leadership of the Church had suffered in prestige in some quarters. It will be recalled that Taylor had long been an ardent defender of the principle and practice of plural marriage both on religious and constitutional grounds. It was he who at the April conference in 1882 had said, "We cannot sacrifice every principle of human right at the behest of corrupt, unreasoning and unprincipled men . . . We will contend inch by inch, legally and constitutionally, for our rights as American citizens."

No successor to Taylor was named immediately and the Twelve Apostles as the next ruling body took over the control of the Church. In April, 1889, the First Presidency was reorganized and Wilford Woodruff, the senior member of the Twelve, became the head of the Church.

In view of Taylor's firm stand for the retention of polygamy, there is no doubt that after his death there was a freer opportunity for discontented young Mormons to express their opposing views regarding the practice. More and more people got the idea, at least began to talk about the idea, that the system was never meant to be rigidly imposed upon the members.

As we have noted, the federal authorities in Utah stepped up the prosecutions for unlawful cohabitation. For example, in the year 1887 alone nearly 200 Mormons from Utah and Idaho were sent to penitentiaries.

Another threatening situation was the judicial support given the test oath legislation in Idaho. In the case of Davis versus Beason in which it was charged that a man was not to be allowed to vote because he was a member of a church which taught and practiced polygamy, the Supreme Court found the lower court correct. The Idaho test oath law had disfranchised a good many Saints and like legislation was about to be applied in Utah.

Although the prosecutions for polygamy continued to be vigorous, there were occasional indications of leniency on the part of certain federal officials. Some offers of amnesty for Mormons serving sentences were made and in the latter part of the 1880's a good many of the convictions for plural marriage were followed by relatively light sentences and light fines. While the more extreme Gentiles were furious at such actions, it is clear that a certain spirit of compromise was emerging.

This is particularly evident in the fact that in 1888 for the first time the report of the Utah Commission indicated a split in the views of its members. While the majority were against any "surrender of the great advantage" which had accrued to their efforts of suppression of polygamy, the minority had this to say:

We are thoroughly satisfied that the work of reformation in Utah is progressing rapidly and that it will soon result in a successful issue, without a resort to legislation that is proscriptive of religious opinion. Our view may be epitomized in a few words—punish criminal action, but religious creeds, never.

In 1889, while the majority recommended even harsher legislation, the minority members remarked in part: "We decline to advise Congress to inflict punishment by disfranchising any portion of the people of Utah on account of their religious or irreligious opinions."

On the side of the Mormons, changing attitudes suggested strongly that official abandonment of polygamy was in the offing. In August, 1888, the territorial delegate, John T. Caine, pointed out in Congress that the Church no longer gave official permission for plural marriage. Yet, the years 1889 and 1890 were marked by a continuation of claim and counter-

claim. Thus, Governor A. L. Thomas in 1889 strongly urged
that the Saints be disfranchised and that the territorial government be given over to the Gentile minority. At the same time
Caine, aided by Frank J. Cannon and others, was busy in Washington maintaining that polygamy was a dead issue in Utah.
There is some evidence that the Mormon lobby made promises to leading members of both parties in Washington that
the Church would do something specific and official about
polygamy if they could get ahead with their program for statehood. At home their leaders were giving ever more serious
thought to develop some formula which would save face as
far as polygamy was concerned and at the same time facilitate
the steps toward statehood.

Perhaps one of the more immediate causes of the Manifesto
was the report of the Utah Commission in 1890. In this report
it was charged that plural marriages were still being solemnized by Mormon Church officials and that 40 or more such
marriages had been contracted in the year just past. Moreover, the report went on to say that the leaders of the Church
were continuing to preach, encourage, and urge the practice
of polygamy. This allegation on the heels of public announcement that the Church was no longer sanctioning or solemniz-
ing plural marriages and certainly was no longer preaching
it openly, led to a public denial and an official church declara-
tion abandoning the practice.

On September 24, 1890, Wilford Woodruff, President of
the Mormon Church, issued what has been termed the "Manifesto." He said that the charges of the Utah Commission regarding recent plural marriages were "false." "We are not
teaching polygamy or plural marriage, nor permitting any
person to enter into its practice, and I deny that either 40 or
any other number of plural marriages have, during that period, been solemnized in our temples or in any other place
in the territory."

He then goes on to say:

In as much as laws have been enacted by Congress forbidding
plural marriages, which laws have been pronounced constitu-

tional by the court of last resource, I hereby declare my intention to submit to those laws and to use my influence with the members of the Church over which I preside to have them do likewise . . .

There is nothing in my teachings to the Church or in those of my associates, during the time specified, which can be reasonably construed to inculcate or encourage polygamy; and when any Elder of the Church has used language which appeared to convey any such teaching, he has been promptly reproved. And I now publicly declare that my advice to the Latter-day Saints is to refrain from contracting any marriage forbidden by the law of the land.

This Manifesto was the product not of Woodruff alone but of the First Presidency and the Apostles as well. At the general conference of the Church on October 6, 1890, Lorenzo Snow, one of the Twelve Apostles, presented a motion to sustain and approve the Manifesto and this was done unanimously by those assembled.

While Woodruff was careful at the time to make no claim that this was a revelation in the sense of the earlier revelations of Joseph Smith, many members of the Church tended to so regard it. About three years later, during the dedication service of the Salt Lake Temple, Woodruff stated that the Lord had shown him a vision of what would happen to the Church if it continued to sanction polygamy. And directly referring to the Manifesto he said that the Lord had commanded him to do what he did.

The *Salt Lake Tribune* kept up its usual policy by maintaining that the Manifesto did not represent any sincere intention to abandon the plurality system. Other reactions to the publication of the Manifesto varied considerably. Judge Zane, who had been vigorous in the prosecutions of cases against the polygamists, quickly accepted the document at face value and remarked: "This alleged revelation I regard as an authoritative expression of the Church of Jesus Christ of Latter-day Saints against the practice of polygamy." So far as Judge Zane was concerned one of the serious threats to the Mormons was removed almost immediately. Governor Thomas was less convinced. In fact, he was in something of a dilemma because he had issued a highly critical annual report early in October after the Manifesto had been published but before it had been ratified by the general conference. He was under the impression that the Mormon Church did not really intend to live up to the Manifesto.

A more or less immediate gain was an amnesty for those who were in prison. In December, 1891, the Mormon leaders sent a petition, endorsed by the territorial governor and the chief justice of the Utah supreme court, pleading for amnesty. This request was addressed to the President of the United States. On January 4, 1893, President Harrison issued a proclamation of amnesty and pardon to all who had obeyed the federal laws since November 1, 1890, upon condition that they would continue to do so. Later, in 1894, President Cleveland issued another proclamation of amnesty and pardon to polygamous offenders.

In October, 1893, the escheated property and money of the Church was returned by order of a joint resolution of Congress and approved by the President. Later all real estate was returned by another joint resolution. On January 4, 1896, Utah became a state.

Yet, the issue of polygamy was by no means dead so far as national affairs were concerned. Brigham H. Roberts, who was elected Congressman from Utah in 1898, was refused a seat in the House of Representatives because he was a polygamist. At a special election a nonpolygamist Mormon, W. H. King, was elected in his place. In 1903 Reed Smoot, an Apostle of the Mormon Church, was elected to the Senate. Strong opposition developed to this and Gentiles in Utah and outside joined in a long petition to keep him from retaining his seat. The Senate Committee on Privileges and Elections conducted extended hearings on Smoot's character and also of the Church to which he belonged. In the end, however, Smoot was permitted to retain his seat in the Senate.

Officially the polygamous system had run its full course. From its beginnings in secrecy it continued through a period of open practice but violent conflict between the Mormons and non-Mormons regarding both its theory and exercise. To many of the devout Saints the Manifesto was a great blow, and we will have something to say about some of their attitudes later. But it was a *fait accompli* as far as the official Church was concerned. Though there was some winking at plural marriages for a few years, after the Smoot investigation the Church issued what was in effect the second Manifesto and began to put strong pressure upon any member who was known to have married in polygamy subsequent to this Manifesto. Even marriages contracted outside the United States where there were no laws against polygamy, as in Mexico, were also frowned upon by the official Church. However, during the 1890's the Mormon colony in Mexico was a place where plural marriages continued to be solemnized. The Church rationalized this on the ground that the Manifesto dealt only with the temporal law and in no way abolished polygamy as a divine Principle. Some aspects of this whole topic will be discussed in more detail in Chapter 19.

*The trials of the Saints in the courts are
not trials of vulgar criminals, but this is
a religious persecution . . . These perse-
cutions are the seeds of conspiracy, composed of ministers, black-legs, pimps and
harlots crowded together on one platform,
with one common thought: that of hatred
of religion . . . While polygamy was the
battle cry, the object was to take away all
forms of political power.*—Message to
Saints, April 5, 1886, from First Presidency, then in hiding.

# 18 THE COHABS IN FLIGHT:
# THE UNDERGROUND AND IMPRISONMENT

To INTRODUCE some of the troubles of plural wives and their
husbands during the final attack upon the system, we relate
the story of Alice Yates. She was the second wife of George
Yates who had converted her to the gospel in England. At his
suggestion she migrated to Utah and not long after her arrival consented to be his wife. They were married on January
28, 1884, less than two years following the passage of the Edmunds Act.

Soon after they were married, the United States deputy
marshals tried to find her. And of her trouble trying to avoid
them she remarked: "I never had a place to lay my head that
I could call my own." In fact, her second baby, Stella, was born
while she was on the Underground. She moved from place to
place and finally she remained for some time in Panguitch,
Utah. The Bishop had offered to have her reside at his home
but she was afraid to do so. She told him, "The officer would
come to your house first." Although the Bishop and his wife
were friendly to her, she had to stay cooped up in the steeple
of the ward meetinghouse, not daring to go out. Before the
officers got on to who she was, she had played the organ during
church services and had been seen about the town. As soon
as they found out that she was there, however, she went into
hiding.

On another occasion, apparently not in Panguitch, she was walking along the street and saw a man who she thought was an officer. She ran into a blacksmith shop, out the back, down a ravine, and across the fields, with the man in pursuit. She "ran and ran" until she was exhausted. The man kept gaining on her. Finally, "I turned to wait and face him. I asked him what he was running for and he said, 'I am being chased by the deputies who want to arrest me.' The town was amused by this episode. The man himself had been in danger since he was a polygamist. He became known as 'I-am-being-chased.' "

Later Alice moved to Salt Lake City and ran a boarding-house about a block and a half from the home of the first wife. Her husband did not support her and she was not known as the plural wife of George Yates. In the middle 1890's the officers finally caught and arrested her husband. He subsequently served six months in the penitentiary for unlawful cohabitation.

Alice Yates had full faith in the principle of polygamy. She said one cannot be saved without it: "It is from God."

While not particularly exciting, this is a rather typical story of what went on during the final years of the prosecution of the Mormons by the federal officials. In the present chapter we shall examine certain efforts of the polygamists to escape legal action.

During the middle 1880's the United States authorities put on real pressure to enforce the Edmunds Act. While trying to build up the faith of the Saints, in a practical sense the general authorities of the Church were quick to see that something had to be done to avoid undue personal persecution, as they viewed this matter. The practical advice of the leaders is nicely illustrated in the diary of Joseph Carey, Jr., who on February 20, 1885, remarks that in the morning,

Brother George Spilsbury said word from the authorities in St. George was for all those who had plural families to get their wives out of the way and then get out of the way themselves, so that the officers of the court could not get hold of them; and that he Spils-

bury was authorized to tell this to the people, and that he was now
going up the river . . . to give the message to the people up there.

As might be expected, the people who believed in this whole
system as a sacred principle were quick in their reactions.
Belle Thompson, in her journal, tells of her husband being
forced to flee to Mexico to avoid arrest and of the deterioration of the homes of those wives who went into hiding. She
writes:

I had bitter hatred in my heart against the officials in Utah, and
against the traitors who exposed the Saints.

Looking back after many years I wonder now that the officers did
not lose their lives at the hands of the LDS, when it is understood
how they meddled with the Mormons' affairs, sneaking into homes
without license and into women's bedrooms. Jane [the fourth wife]
came home to her mother to bear her first child. She had been
hunted by the officials for months without being found. It was
conference time and Susan's house was full of visitors, the beds
were all full and many women were finding beds on quilts on the
floor. Jane was in one of the inner rooms with her ten-day old
baby by her side. [Marshal] McGeary and Armstrong [his deputy]
walked into the habitation at eleven o'clock p.m. without announcement.

The marshal . . . marched through the rooms turning his flash-
light into the faces of the sleepers, until he reached the room where
Jane slept. Turning his light into her face, he wakened her so she
knew him to be only the sheriff and had always expected that she
would be sure to meet him someday. Yet, owing to her weakened
condition, the contact threw her into a chill which was followed
by high fever which placed her life in great danger for some days.
The marshal left Armstrong . . . to guard her while he went to
get her husband sleeping with the boys at the barn on the hay.
Armstrong sat in her room until morning which added to her distress.

She and her husband were both put under heavy bond to appear
in the court at Beaver. But Providence proved their aid and it so
happened that when the Beaver courthouse burned their bonds
went up in flames. When I came to St. George and heard that story
my wrath knew no bounds. I knew in referring to McGeary, that
he who had been accustomed to act unfeelingly with the plural
wives, [that I wished that] "every bone in his body should be bro-

ken"; and this was his fate, suffering with a fever he walked off on a high window in an Ogden hotel and the account published in the paper stated that every bone in his body was broken.

Belle's uncle, William McCorkle, who had risen to some prominence as a lawyer, was told by Judge Zane that he would see to it that Belle's mileage was paid to Beaver sometime so as to serve as a witness against her husband. This news "aroused the lion in me." She said to William:

Tell lawyer Zane that if one of his minions ever enters my house as McGeary entered Wilma's here without showing a written warrant for such a thing and tries to enter my daughter's bedroom, I'll kill him where he stands. I'll go prepared to kill him and I'll take the consequences of the act. I'll never forget the look on William's white face and staring eyes, as he held up both hands. After he had composed himself he said, "Aunt, if you ever kill one of the sheriffs under the circumstances you mention, I'll defend you in the court to the last dollar I own."

Auntie was present and was greatly distressed at my murderous threat and with tears begged retraction. After some consideration I did. I said to them all, "What I shall do when assailed by these persecutors will be just what the other poor Mormon women do: snatch up my baby and run to the field, the hills, sleep on the ground, under the bushes anywhere and forget all about my braggadocio . . ."

The faithful felt that the legislation against polygamy was an attempt on the part of their enemies to interfere with the work of God. Jonathan Baker unloaded his mind in his journal during July, 1882, in this vein: "Fools to meddle with the things of God and the holy things of heaven." And again later: "Oh fools, to think that measuring arms with the Lord and debarring us of our constitutional rights can hinder us from keeping the divine requirements of Jehovah."

In a letter from Mexico, July 24, 1885, where he had gone to escape prosecution, Joseph Carey, Sr., writes:

Since writing my last in this record, many strange things have happened. Persecution by our enemies has grew more and more fierce (sic). Many of our brethren are lying in jail in Arizona, Utah, Idaho, and Michigan for practicing polygamy and living with more than one woman at a time. Thus a great howl is set up in the name of morality against the Latter-day Saints while filth and corruption stalk abroad unnoticed all over the world.

A common practice among the Mormons was the free association of certain external events with difficulties of their own. For example, Baker's journals are packed with references to the sins and disasters of the world, and James Powell writes:

About these times the United States officials in Utah acted more like bigoted missionaries than administrators of law and justice . . . But here is an item of history worth remembering. The very day that the arrest of Brigham Young was made for polygamy in Salt Lake City, that great and terrible fire broke out in the city of Chicago which raged furiously before a very strong wind until it consumed four or five miles of the main business part of that great city, with all its vast buildings, stores, banks and great factories, [and] were all beyond the power of man to save; the puny arm of man could not stop the raging flames . . .

So we see when they made the first attack on polygamy the Lord suffered that calamity to come on them; offenses must come, but woe unto them by whom they come. God will not be mocked, they will find out someday, it will not do to fight Him or interfere with His commands.

Yet other members were not so sure but that something was amiss with the Saints themselves, otherwise they should not have been persecuted for obeying the laws of God. Clara, second wife of Isaac Lambert, expressed her views on the difficulties during these times, "I believe if people commit a sin they run into bondage. We were all in bondage during the Underground and the Manifesto freed the people." She felt that the Saints had not lived the Principle as faithfully as they should have done and that God had taken the divine system away from the Saints, at least temporarily.

And Bessie, second wife of Aaron Strong, had this to say:

In the beginning of the movement men took wives because it was a sacred duty, but in later years they were beginning to take them more because they fell in love with younger women. And when they did this, the older wife often suffered. Men abused the Principle and the raids came as a scourge.

The "raids," as the Mormons called them, did in time have considerable effect upon many people. On the one hand, it made for solidarity and there was a continual pressure from the general authorities for the Saints to hold fast. On the other hand, the prosecutions divided and confused many. A daughter of the second wife of John Vance tells of changes which took place in her community where previously the children of plural marriages had been treated "exactly as any other children . . . until the raids began."

Once a young woman came to Paris and began to teach music. My sister was taking lessons and I wanted to also. But the teacher wouldn't take me and I wondered why. I asked my sister [first wife's child] and she said she guessed it was because of our way of living. I began to wonder what it was that made us different then, and later also. The music teacher used to give parties for the children but she would never invite the second wives' children. Once my sister was invited and she told me she wouldn't go unless I was invited too. She didn't go either.

I couldn't understand about the raids either. I didn't know what it was the officers had against us. It was a long time before I realized what they felt about our way of living.

Most Mormons had heard of the Underground system which grew up in the days of slavery before the Civil War and certainly were acquainted with the book, *Uncle Tom's Cabin*. Few, if any, had had any personal experience with this particular type of operation. Yet faced with growing pressure from federal officials the Mormons developed a whole set of institutions to facilitate escape and hiding.

The higher officials of the Church worked out a rather elaborate scheme to protect themselves. The lesser fry frequently had to do the best they could when being sought by the deputies. Edward Wylie's diary tells how John Taylor and other leaders were kept out of sight.

The hideout was at a farm a few miles northwest of Salt

Lake City but one which could be reasonably well guarded. Communication and transportation were maintained between the farm and the church headquarters. It was here that John Taylor died in 1887 after being on the Underground for nearly two and a half years. A few selections from Wylie's diary for 1886 shows how the system operated.

On August 26, he was "all day at D.O."—the secret code name for the hideout. "We spent the day reading and pitching quoits." At night two runners arrived to say that they thought the "deps"—deputy marshals—"were on their track."

The great caution taken is shown by his entry from September 4. At 3:30 A.M. he went on guard. About four o'clock two shots were fired. These were a signal from an outpost on the road that the "deps" were coming. All were asleep at the time but Wylie woke them up and got the President and the rest of the party out of the way. However, this proved to be a false alarm.

His entry for September 13 describes his own narrow escape from the deputy marshals at his own home. At about 10:30 A.M. a boy came and asked one of the children if they had any "fat calves" there, and if they had, to keep them and Bishop Holden would come down and see them. A little later the son who was hauling a load of coal met a neighbor who asked him if he understood what the boy had meant. He said that he did. The "fat calf" was Wylie himself. When this was made clear to the family, they were frightened and they urged Wylie to get out of the way.

So I put on my coat and buckled on my big pistol and started to Samuel Jenkins'. I got there all right. Just after I got there my brother came to my house and said the deps were coming . . . He came down to where I was. The deps did not come. I gave my wife ten dollars that the President gave me for them to buy the children Christmas presents . . . I got back to my exile home at one o'clock. Found all well.

At one point Wylie describes some entertainment on the Underground. Dances were occasionally held for people "that could be trusted." Once he took President Cannon and some

others to a remote schoolhouse for a dance. About 30 Saints
were present. The President spoke in encouraging tones for a
few moments, and then the dance was held, with the music
furnished by Brother Beasley. The calling was done by Joseph
E. Taylor and Wylie. "At ten o'clock President Cannon's family passed around sandwiches, pie and cake, and lemonade. We
all enjoyed ourselves splendidly and I must say that we had a
good time. The dance was dismissed at twelve o'clock. I then
took the President and his wife back to the farm . . ."

One device to keep out of the way was to leave the country
on a mission for the Church. One of the younger leaders, Joseph F. Smith, spent five years and eight months in exile,
mostly on missions. In a letter of March 4, 1890, to a friend, he
comments among other things:

I have grieved in my spirit at the fiendish hate and damnable
intolerance and bigotry which have haled men and women and
infants to prison for conscience sake, but have joyed at the manhood and womanhood of most of those who have thus bravely suffered for their religious convictions and obedience to the dictates
of conscience.

Still other techniques were used. Some men sent their families into different localities. In other instances the husband
would move about from place to place as did George Mackay
who had his wives scattered on several of his ranches. In several of the families of which we have records the second wife
was in hiding for more than ten years.

To send a plural wife into another community was made
possible by the fact that almost all of the small towns were
solidly Mormon and hence, with few exceptions, people were
perfectly willing to protect those on the Underground. Of
course, if individuals in such a place were at outs with the
Church or had some grievance against a given plural family,
they might turn informer.

Sometimes a given community became known as a place
of successful hiding. This was true of Franklin, Idaho, where
a great many plural wives from other places located. Daisy
Barclay who spent some time on the Underground writes:

"Dozens of polygamist women, under assumed names, had temporary homes there while their husbands were employed elsewhere. No one asked questions."

In other circumstances plural wives were sent back to their own folks. This happened in at least four of the families studied in this work.

Of course, all kinds of personal arrangements had to be made. Hannibal Lowman took two of his wives to Idaho and left the children of the fifth wife in the care of the fourth. In the Strong family wife number two was in hiding for years and two of her children were brought up by number one.

Occasionally the church authorities provided a remote hiding place for plural wives and their children. Such a place was a large ranch at Pipe Springs, otherwise known as Winsor Castle, in northern Arizona. The sixth and last wife of Alexander Todd relates, "Pipe Springs was a haven for polygamy women and many polygamy children were born there." Many of the cattlemen who had been located there had to make other provision for housing. Mr. Loren Little, foreman of the ranch, says that,

The plural wives, particularly the ones about to bear children, came there. It was called by the cattlemen, "The Lambing Ground." Once the women got across the line into Arizona, they were comparatively safe for the Utah marshals could not touch them and the Arizona marshals could not get there without crossing the prairie and making an almost impossible trip.

He went on to say that the Utah marshals had to cross that way when returning from Kanab but they could do nothing. The women would hide when word was sent that they were coming. There was a midwife at Winsor Castle. There was nothing for the women to do except tend to the housework, care for the children, and go on top of the castle as lookouts. They got very lonely and tired.

Peter Rowe, who had been a school teacher, married a second wife just prior to the Manifesto. Finding himself under indictment, he and his second wife took a job peddling school supplies. They traveled by buggy and made a good living at it. In this way Mrs. Rowe number two easily passed herself off as number one.

Men of property could provide for their plural wives in much better ways. The second and third wives of Henry Zeller traveled constantly: Canada, Europe, and elsewhere. In British Columbia the two women passed as daughters of Zeller. In Norway, on one trip, the third wife pretended to be the nursemaid of the children of the first wife. Actually the children were her own.

Sometimes the first wives put themselves to a lot of trouble to protect the husband and the plural wife. On one occasion, Angelina, first wife of Samuel Baxter, Jr., drove all night to a farm where her husband and his second wife were living to warn them both of impending trouble with the deputies. They got away to Mexico. Angelina was never happy about Baxter's plural marriage, but she was loyal to him and to what the Church sanctioned.

An interesting twist to courtship and marriage is found in the story of the fourth wife of Hyrum Stratton. She got to know him well because he stayed at her parents' home several times when he was on the Underground. This acquaintance blossomed into love and marriage. Mrs. Stratton shrewdly observed: "The officers thought they were destroying polygamy, but they were increasing it by scattering the men around in different houses."

Hiding places might be anywhere thought safe. While barns, attics, and even haystacks were used, the officers would be pretty certain to look in such places. Hence elaborate precautions were often taken. A home in Paris, Idaho, is described in these words by one of our informants:

Bishop Westfall had a triangular trap door cut in the corner of the living room floor. The light carpet which completely covered the floor was nailed to it. The door led into a large dirt cellar about ten by twelve feet in size with shelves for provisions, rooms for beds, and a pump for water. It could accommodate several men. The Bishop always retreated to the cellar at the approach of any person, causing considerable amusement when the approach of a friend forced him to hide. The bishop's cellar was a sort of gathering place when things got hot.

The Temple in St. George was a popular hideout. The third wife of Adam Winthrop "used to cook for some of the men hiding in the Temple." This was necessary because as another informant, the third wife of Roger Knight, said, "They would stay in there for days."

Life on the Underground was hard on women and men alike. There are many stories of difficulties of childbirth and other episodes that are quite pathetic. The family of Emory Fairchild lost five babies at different times when the wives were forced to go into hiding. The second wife of Samuel Spaulding remarks:

We had to be secret. When my children come the first wife was the only one I had. She was no midwife, but she was my only doctor for fear people would find out. Never a doctor or nurse did I have for my ten children and her the only one to do for me. It was a miracle that I lived and that the children lived, though all my life I'm suffering from not having proper care. When my babies was young I couldn't live like a normal human being. I had to hide in the granary out there all day long and when my baby cried, I had to feed it and try to cover its head. At night I had to lie in that little bedroom and stifle my baby's cries while the Lord's teachers called. And that was a Mormon community and all was supposed to believe that polygamy was a holy principle. There was no one you could trust in them days (*sic*).

Wars are always exciting. Even those who take part in the battles and participate under great sacrifice enjoy telling their experiences afterwards. Certainly the period of which we are speaking represented a war for the Saints. Our materials contain many accounts of arrests and difficulties with the federal police in which the participants played exciting parts. These, in turn, as they were told and retold laid the basis of many legends still extant in Mormon folklore.

The story of the arrest of Roger Knight and the part his second wife played in the family drama is rather typical of what went on in plural families. Mrs. Knight relates:

I couldn't go to Pa's because the marshals were always coming there. And where could I go? I couldn't take my baby and impose on people like that. One day I'd been hiding away from home and when I came back about dark I saw the two marshals, McGeary and Armstrong, out by the gate. I couldn't turn back because they had already seen me, so I went inside. I hung quilts over the windows and doors to keep the light out but not the transom. I didn't light the lamp but I had only a little bit of coal oil and I didn't want the light to be seen, only just enough to see to give the baby something to eat, but the moment I lit it there was a knock. I can remember how my knees shook together. I had to go to the door and there were the two marshals. They thought that I was one of Allen Tucker's wives because my house then was so close to his. They asked me who I was and I couldn't think of any other name to tell them but Knight . . . McGeary says, "You'll enjoy a trip to Beaver. It would be a nice summer trip." It was April then and I had to get in a wagon and spent four days going to Beaver. I didn't tell them everything, but I had to tell a lot and they had the evidence against Roger.

Knight got away and began peddling books in other communities, but was finally identified by McGeary, arrested, and sent to prison for six months.

Although Aaron Strong was never captured, the second wife was obliged to testify before a grand jury. She describes her experience as follows:

The deputy came to my house. My baby wasn't quite two years old, but she was very large for her age, and when he pulled the covers over her bed aside, I told him she was three years old and he believed me. But I had to go to court. I asked if I might give my children something to eat and he said yes. Then I asked him to eat with us and he did. He was a man who had lived in Utah for some time. We got to talking and I said, "We people have come to this desert country and worked and suffered to make it possible for you to come and have the plums and the honey of our labors. Out in the world adultery is so common it is not noticed. Sometimes the women suffer but the men are shielded. Here it is a part of our religion for a man to take other wives. He works and sacrifices for them and raises his children to be good men and women, and for that you come and hound us and put our men to prison. I think it is a dirty deal we get." "I, too, think it is a dirty deal," he replied. "I hate to do this, but I haven't any other way of making a living. And other men are making money from it, so I have to."

In court, however, Sister Strong was so evasive in her answers that finally the judge in exasperation dismissed the case. And, as an aftermath to the case, an apostate Mormon who had known Strong on a mission promised to "warn him if there was any danger of arrest."

There are many stories of escape as well as of arrests. Asa Kendall tells a number of his experiences. One of these was so serious that he was sent on a mission in 1886 to get him out of the country. He and a friend had taken to carrying pistols in order to have some protection from the deputies. Kendall was arrested one night but escaped by drawing his revolver. A large reward was put on his head and only the help of his father prevented what might have been a serious brush with the law. After Asa had left on his mission, a lawyer friend of his had the indictment quashed. On his return from his mission, Kendall paid his friend $25.00 for his services.

In view of the bitterness engendered by the raids, both in Mormons and in some of the more zealous officers, it is remarkable that there were so few serious brushes between the two factions. For the most part the officers were cautious and tried to avoid the use of firearms. The Asa Kendall episode could easily have ended differently if the deputies had not been sensible. The killing of Edward M. Dalton at Parowan on December 16, 1886, was the most exciting instance of more or less deliberate use of firearms on the part of an irritated officer.

Dalton had twice escaped arrest on warrants charging him with unlawful cohabitation—at that time only a misdemeanor. But Deputy William Thompson, Jr., was determined to "get his man" and with some other officers, both local and federal, plotted to shoot Dalton next time he was found. After some months in hiding, Dalton returned to Parowan to see his family and the officers laid an ambush for him. Although Thompson called out for him to halt, he scarcely gave Dalton a chance to stop when he opened fire. Dalton died within the hour.

Only cooler heads on both sides prevented a lynching if not more serious trouble. A daughter of William Arnold, who was a child in school at the time, tells of the event:

Someone saw the shot and rushed into the school to tell us. I didn't wait for anything. I ran for home and told father that Dalton had been shot. He started to run and mother begged him to stay. She said it would mean either his death or arrest but he said for all of us to stay in the house. "I'm afraid," he told us, "that this will mean more deaths than one." He got to Dalton just as he was breathing his last. Father was one of the men who helped to carry him to Page's house where he died. Uncle Hugh Adams was sheriff then and if it had not been for him there would have been much bloodshed. Uncle Collie Clark had been with Dalton and, when the latter was shot, Clark rushed to his home to get his gun. He swore he would kill Thompson. The sheriff sent me to keep Uncle Collie from coming back and he managed to get the town calmed down so that there was no more bloodshed.

The shooting of Dalton became another *cause célèbre* on Mormon and Gentile sides alike, but with different interpretations, one that he was a desperate criminal in flight, the other that the officers deliberately murdered him. As might have been expected Thompson and others charged with the deed were found not guilty.

No matter how strong a Saint might be in the faith and how much effort he might put into trying to escape arrest, many men grew tired of this hare-and-hounds game. The perpetual running and hiding interfered with their occupation as well as with their family and community obligations.

Richard Field had been on the Underground for four years and finally felt he "couldn't go on like this," and voluntarily surrendered. He said later that if he had to do it over again he would have given himself up "right away rather than go on the Underground." His farm had been allowed to run down during the time. His house which was his pride suffered badly from his four-year absence. "He was just losing everything he had. Besides, he was thinking about his family." He took his first wife and several of her children and went to Ogden where he was tried and fined. After that he was not molested but he was watched to see that he had nothing to do with his second and third wives. Other of our families report similar final decisions to give up the struggle to avoid being harassed.

Such escapades were bound to attract attention in the public press, particularly if the persons involved were prominent. On November 25, 1886, the *Salt Lake Tribune* had a headline story about Angus Cannon, an Apostle, whom they dubbed "Anguish":

### ANGUISH CAN AGAIN

*He Was Picked Up on the Road by the Marshals*

### HE AND HIS SON HEAVILY ARMED

*An Exciting Race—The Old Man and Boy Threatened With Their Guns But Are Disarmed*

### HELD IN TEN THOUSAND DOLLAR BONDS

During the heyday of the prosecutions it became increasingly difficult to carry on courtship and marriage in any normal fashion. We have example after example where the plural wife was courted secretly and where the marriage was frequently not known even to the most intimate members of the family. For example, Herbert Winslow's third wife said that Mary, the first wife, did not witness the ceremony because of the fear that she might later be called upon to testify. In the courtship of Adam Winthrop and his fourth wife the whole matter was kept under cover. This was relatively easy since the prospective bride· was a hired girl. Winthrop courted her in the home of his third wife where she worked.

Daisy Barclay tells how her husband spent three and a half years away on a mission as a device to keep out of sight; that she taught school and sent him most of her earnings. During this period she passed herself off under her maiden name as Miss Yates and taught school in communities where she was not known. After her husband returned they had a few months together, but when she became pregnant, it was evident that she would have to go into hiding, at least until after her baby was born. After the baby came in September, 1888, she "was continually on the move . . . Once more I dreaded the future, hating as I did a roving life."

How well she could keep her secret is illustrated by the fact that, on one occasion, she refused to tell even President Woodruff who was the father of her child. George Q. Cannon reflected the current view in mildly rebuking his chief in these words: "That is hardly a fair question, is it, Brother Woodruff?"

Isaac Lambert married a young servant in his wife's employ. The new bride lived in an upper room of the house. "I stayed right there," she said, "and continued to do the housework just like before, but [later] I went on the Underground." Her first baby was born while in hiding. Altogether she spent five years in hiding. "In one year Lambert made me move seven times. I did exactly as he said, and lived in some awful shacks in Cache Junction, Hyde Park, and Franklin. I was packed and practically ready to move all the time. I would pity a dog when he had to move around so much."

The taking of a false name was an easy aid to secrecy. The second wife of Oliver Andrews was on the Underground for years under another name. She resided in Salt Lake City and her husband in Beaver. She lived with her parents but helped support herself by sewing. However, her husband escaped arrest. The second wife of Amasa Lang went by the name of Lamb and few people except those close to the family knew that she was his second wife. The second family of Stanley Winters was on the Underground for a long time under the name of Winslow. Physical disguises of various sorts were used on occasion. Cutting off mustache or beard, or coloring the hair or mustache were tried.

Of ruses Alfred Zabriskie tells in his diary that word came to him that certain men who were supposed to be officers had come to Beaver and taken Brother Wilford Woodruff off into the brush and hid him until after dark. He was then told that he was to go after him and bring him to town, which he did.

Such an event as this might start a counterrumor that Wood-ruff had already been arrested and therefore mislead informers and officers alike.

In addition to false names, disguises, and ruses, a whole system of information gathering, signaling, and spotting informers was developed. For example, the church authorities would pass the word down to the smaller communities of movements of federal deputies out of Salt Lake City in the direction of any particular town. There are a variety of stories about the lookouts and warning systems. John Read tells that elaborate systems had been established along the border of Idaho and Utah and relates one instance. There was but one possible approach which the marshals could use to a certain town. A watch would be stationed on the road with a shotgun which he was to fire three times when he saw the officers coming. After a long period of waiting, strangers appeared whom he thought to be deputies. He fired the gun and shortly the church bells started to ring. The alarm was successful and the police returned empty-handed.

The Alexander Todd story is interesting in this connection. When the raids became serious, various of his wives moved out of the large house on one of the ranches leaving his first wife to occupy it. Todd made his headquarters there whenever he could. The account continues:

One of the boys, Henry, who was more quiet than the others, used to stand up on the dugway by the farm. The dugway was the only way a person could get down in the valley, and he'd stay up there and when he saw a stranger or a man on horseback, he would wave a red flag and Todd and a Mr. Covington would run and hide. Once Henry waved a flag and it was the deps all right. The two men went down in the creek by the bushes and the deps came up to the field and of course none of the men knew anything about Todd. So the deps hunted everywhere. They even went down to the bushes where the men were. When they had gone Todd sent word to them that they had stepped on his toes.

In telling of the activities of the deputies, Loren Tiffany says: "The marshals always came in buggies and as that was a luxury not dreamed of by any of the local residents, the appearance of a buggy was a sure sign that the marshals were here. At the appearance of these vehicles, the appointed runners hastily spread the news."

The role of an innocent and naive child is neatly portrayed in one of Tiffany's adventures. Word had come by messenger that the deputies were looking for Tiffany. Two of his children, Charlotte and Maggie, were at home alone when a stranger appeared at the gate in a buggy. The elder child, sensing the situation, solemnly warned the younger not to say a word but let her do the talking. When the deputy entered the house and asked for the mother, Charlotte replied:

"She's gone away."

"No, she's down at the mill," said Maggie.

"Where is your father?"

Again the older sister replied that he, too, had gone away, only to have the younger one pipe up, "No, he's down at the cove."

To the question as to the identity of a baby which the deputy saw on a bed, the older girl said it was a "neighbor's," only to be disputed by her sister's, "That baby belongs to Ma." At this the marshal returned to the buggy and took off as Charlotte raced across a field to warn her mother and others who were hiding in a mill. Maggie was left with the baby but curiosity got the better of her and off she ran to the mill. Her sister pulled her into the mill just as the deputy reappeared and asked for the miller. When told by Charlotte there was none, he replied:

"This is a funny mill to be run without a miller." Maggie again insisted, "She is in the willows by the ditch." Then came the rebuke never to be forgotten. "Now they will get Pa and put him in prison because you told about him and Ma."

But the scout had given the signal through the valley and on to the cove went the marshal, but returned without seeing man or woman. As he returned he wondered how successful farming could be carried on without the directing power of man or woman, and meals prepared and babies tended without women.

In some cases apostates or people bitter toward some particular individual gave the authorities information leading to arrests. Obviously such people were unpopular and occasionally in some personal danger. The third wife of John Webber told how someone had informed the officers that he "always came home at daylight to water his mules."

That was when I was living by myself, so the officers laid in wait for him. Just after I went to bed they broke in my kitchen. I called from the bedroom, "Who is there?" No one answered, but I heard one say, "She isn't far away, because she has mixed bread." Then they went out and across the road and waited in the Relief Society hall till about daylight. They arrested Brother Webber just as he was finishing watering the mules while he was still in the corral.

The *Salt Lake Tribune* and other newspapers often carried stories of the Underground, the spy system, informers, and the like. On March 16, 1883, it remarks:

If a Mormon is indicted for polygamy, there is always a spy in camp to warn him so that he can avoid arrest by getting out of the way of the officers for a while . . . Nobody knows where he is until after the grand jury are discharged, then he comes home and preaches that the United States government will never put down polygamy.

And in a story of April 16, 1885, the same newspaper stated that:

The Mormon priesthood has organized a "Bureau of Information" and it has been in operation some six weeks. The objects of the concern are manifold. One is to collect information and report the same to the church authorities touching on the prosecution of polygamists, and to enter the names of all informers on polygamists in a black book, to spot such grand jurors and witnesses as in any way aid in the prosecution of saints, that they may be tabooed and boycotted . . .

Just how well organized any central intelligence service might have been, we do not know. However, there is little doubt that some kind of information was passed around including the names of those who could and could not be trusted.

In the year 1885 there occurred a little episode which brought about an interesting interplay between the *Deseret News* and the *Salt Lake Tribune*. In its issue for November 24, 1885, the *Tribune* carried a story with a headline as follows:

THE MORMON THOUGHT
INFAMOUS INTRIGUES IN THE INTEREST OF THE VILE CHURCH

*Harlots, Spotters and Enticers Hired to Entrap Good Citizens*

DESPERATE ATTEMPT TO PROVE POLYGAMY
*No Worse Than Prostitution*

*Arrest Ordinance Pronounced Invalid by Mr. Rawlins*

To this the *Deseret News* the next day replied under the title, "The Latest Libel":

The organ of the prostitutes and the apologists for lechery, "one of the common vices of humanity," is working hard to divert attention from the official and private persons who are charged with beastly crimes, by reckless and wholecloth lying—its usual tactics.
It is a story that the Mormon Church has hired prostitutes to lead away the poor, innocent deputy marshals, *Tribune* supporters, merchants, ex-U.S. commissioners, and other persons addicted to, "one of the common vices of humanity."

In the issue of December 5, 1885, the *Tribune* published a letter under the date line of July 25, 1885, which it contended had been used as bait. The letter runs as follows:

Dear Sir:
If convenient, I would be pleased to have you call this afternoon or about dusk this evening. I want to see you on a particular business. Please send answer by messenger boy when you will call.
Respectfully.

The lady involved in this was one Fanny Davenport, a prostitute, who was brought before Commissioner William McKay on December 8, 1885.

More than considerable bitterness developed between the Mormon brethren and the federal officials who tried to enforce the law. One device was to harass the latter while they were trying to perform their official duties. For example, the young men of Clarkston, who were openly hostile, would band together and in buggies, on horseback, or in sleighs follow the deputies around town, jeer at them, and otherwise annoy them. In fact, the young men of Clarkston became so hotheaded that President Woodruff took official notice of the situation and sent urgent word to them to cool off and not interfere with the officers.

Some political corruption was bound to occur in the course of trying to enforce the anti-polygamy laws. Our record of Aaron Montgomery tells how his Stake president told him that arrangements could be made to buy off a number of the polygamists who were in hiding if they would surrender. After some negotiations as to how much the bribe should be, Montgomery gave the arresting officer $200.00. He relates that "They took my first wife, and son, and a couple of other witnesses down to Ogden and had a mock trial. I wasn't even there, and the witnesses told a couple of white lies and the case against me was dismissed." Our materials cite a number of instances of bribing officers to avoid arrest.

On the other side, the federals made use of paid informers and only complained that they had insufficient funds for such operations. On July 11, 1879, federal attorney P. T. Van Zile wrote a letter to the Attorney General of the United States stating that if he had the money to bribe "some apostate Mormons," he could get evidence to convict under the law of 1862.

At the height of the campaign in the middle 1880's some funds were secured from the federal government for detective work. On November 2, 1885, Marshal Edwin Ireland wrote to the Attorney General in Washington calling attention to the Mormon system of counterintelligence and the difficulties in making arrests and in securing convictions. He complained among other things, ". . . People along the road [railroad] are advised of the presence of a deputy marshal on board any train always in advance, the county sheriffs and deputies and entire police of the towns are employed to watch the movements of officers and to secretly aid the criminal witnesses to escape." He reports that his deputies were dogged by spies, refused room and board by Mormons, and had to go in pairs in order to be safe from molestation.

The local press took account of these matters and the *Salt Lake Tribune,* May 4, 1884, in replying to the stand of the *Deseret News* on the question remarked:

When it is proposed to ferret out violations of the bigamy laws by the use of money, they [the Mormons] retort that they will raise a fund to do like work for prostitutes and all who consort with them. All this shows that the claim of religious dogma or revelation under which polygamy is sometimes defended is a mere sham . . . the Mormons know and feel in their hearts that one form of the social vice is no more divine than the other; that both belong in the same category; so that whenever the polygamy shoe pinches, they demand that its mate, the prostitution shoe, shall also be made to pinch.

A critical situation arose where someone in the family itself either acted as an informant or threatened to do so. This was true in the Bach family. Bach was afraid that the mother of his plural wife would betray him to the officers. She had been bitter about her daughter going into polygamy and when the latter had to go on the Underground and later escaped to Mexico, the mother-in-law was enraged. Such interference from a dominant and aggressive woman did not often occur under the patriarchal system.

The long conflict in the Joseph M. Carey family was complicated by the fact that the first wife turned over information to the officers in Arizona which forced Carey to flee to Mexico. Moreover, some of the neighbors were drawn in.

In his journal for May 7, 1888, Carey reports, "I hear that Mrs. Burke says that Marshal McGeary told her to watch me and tell him if I went on to my place where the girls live. He would arrest me. I and my wife Anne moved into Roselle Nagley's house." And on the 6th of June he reports, "The folks are fearful that I will be seen on the lot." Carey had already been in prison and was afraid to be arrested and indicted again.

The local police—town constables, marshals, and deputy

marshals—sometimes acted as informers for the Saints. They were often asked to go along with the federal police in making arrests, but being Mormons and often closely tied up with polygamous families, these men were not averse to double-crossing their federal colleagues.

Although Chapter 12 discussed the whole impact of polygamy on children, we shall deal here more particularly with the effect of the raids and prosecutions upon the children's attitudes at that time. Certainly such activities were not found in the usual democratic and frontier life.

At very early ages children were introduced into conspiratorial operations. Not talking to strangers, being part of a warning system, and being taught outright falsification were all elements in their training during those years which would certainly not be considered normal today. The stress on secrecy, isolation, and the avoidance of strangers is but an example of the general indoctrination for membership in a strong in-group. A daughter of the second wife of Stanley Winters remarks of this period:

We moved from place to place; as soon as people learned who we were, mother moved on. We went to school and church, but we weren't allowed to associate with other children for fear we would give ourselves away. Mother took in washings and did everything she could to help. Father used to come to see us whenever he could. We thought his name was Winslow and that he was away all the time because his work called him. He did his best to support us but he couldn't do everything. Sometimes my half-brothers and sisters came to see us, and we loved to have them come. We thought they were our cousins.

It is an interesting fact that after serving six months in the penitentiary and paying a fine, Winters decided to live openly with both wives and apparently was not molested thereafter.

Of this period, a daughter of Edward Gilbert says:

I had a very happy childhood except for the years of the Underground. That was terrible. The officers sometimes came at three in the morning to search the house. At night if we opened the

door, people would go scurrying—people who had been looking
in the windows to see if father was there. I wouldn't go out at night
alone. We never knew where father was so if the officers asked us,
we couldn't tell them.

In Chapter 12 we made note of the possible social effects
upon children of plural wives when they came to realize that
in law they were not legitimate. Whether anxiety over this
matter of legitimacy was more acute during the raids is hard
to say. It probably was. For one thing there was an increase in
the resentment against polygamy among Mormons themselves.
It was getting them into lots of trouble and many did not
like it. The topic of legitimacy was bound to be discussed and
under the crises people doubtless made some use of the knowledge of this fact although in most polygamous families there
was no external evidence of any such feeling. The *Salt Lake
Tribune* on one occasion showed a good deal of insight as to
the possible effects of this upon the personality:

The boys and girls that grow up here are going to be Americans,
they are not going to abide by a system that keeps half the mothers
in this territory in shame, because they are not first wives, and half
the children with blushes on their faces because they are not first
wives' children.

For the most part the Mormons took it for granted that
children of plural wives were legitimate. On the other hand,
some informants would agree with the second wife of Erastus
Bacon when she said that she had been more or less looked
down upon because of being a plural wife and that her children suffered something of this same sense of inferiority.

It goes without saying that anxieties and hostilities would
surely be enhanced under the strain and stress of the period
of which we are writing. Our records reveal a good many
instances where the children expressed resentment at their
fathers' having gone into polygamy. It is quite likely that such
negative feelings grew as the federal efforts to suppress the
system became more severe. The *Tribune* caught something
of this whole idea in its editorial for January 13, 1872, when it
said:

The implacable enemy of polygamy, because the most intelligent—so far as the miseries which the practice engenders are concerned—is its most secret one. In nearly every thrifty polygamous household this enemy lies in wait . . . I allude to the intense hatred of the system which exists deep down in the heart of every son and daughter born of a polygamous union. The system has no more inveterate, no more powerful enemy than that born of the system itself. The husband of many wives may manifest indifference to any one of them; but to the support and protection of the mothers there comes the strong and willing hand of the son, and in sympathy with her sorrows, such consolation as a daughter may give is not withheld. A bond of union and of suffering to which the paternal head is not a part, may be said to exist in every polygamous family. Mother and children talk matters over and settle them among themselves. The decision may not be announced but it is reached nevertheless. It is unfavorable to polygamy every time. Here is the yeast which shall leaven the whole lump of Mormon immorality.

That there was a strong bond between the polygamous mother and her children has been amply brought out in this book. It cut across the whole patriarchal order which was theoretically in control. There is even an implication of a certain hostility toward the father and the system in this strong emotional alliance.

Evidences of personal sacrifice have already been given. While the Saints were continually urged to make no show of violence, they were equally strongly urged to stand on their civil rights. The *Deseret News*, January 21, 1885, in commenting on what it calls "Unwarrantable Intrusions," goes on to say:

We advise the people of this city to stand upon their rights. We counsel no violence, but we do not want to see peaceable people abused and insulted. No person claiming to be an officer has any more right than a private citizen to enter anyone's dwelling without the consent of the owner, unless he has a warrant in proper form authorizing him to make a search. People are not required by law to answer the impertinent questions of any man claiming to be an officer either of the United States or of the territory.

Mistreatment of individuals was the subject of some comments of Sarah M. Kimball at a mass meeting held in March 1886: "Pure women are brought before the courts by lewd and debauched men, insulted with indecent questions, and threatened with imprisonment if they do not answer them."

Of the hundreds of cases brought before the courts in Utah where convictions were found, the great bulk of them led to inflictment of both fines and imprisonment. However, there was a small minority of this total number who got away with fines only.

As to the length of prison sentences, this too varied as did the treatment while incarcerated. Joseph Carey, Jr., kept a day-by-day diary while in the prison. Some sample notations give a taste of routine life there:

Thursday, December 1, 1887. This is visiting day, and there were a good number of the brethren in the penitentiary called to the gate, and had an interview with their families and friends for a half hour. Also received any little comforts their friends had to give them.

The journal goes on to remark on the importance of getting mail and a good deal of disappointment when mail did not arrive. The entry for Christmas Day follows:

The friends and relatives of the prisoners here brought in their dainties liberally and the tables were all well supplied, and all the prisoners, here, without regard to caste, creed, or color, were allowed to enjoy a sumptuous repast. One that had been here a long time said that today was the first day he had spent here that did not seem like prison. He had really enjoyed himself today . . .

Reminiscences of life in the penitentiary were not unlike the reminiscences of soldiers who fought in wars or had otherwise made sacrifices for a cause. Merlin York's journal reveals something of this:

My experience in Utah penitentiary was fraught with much enjoyment. Liberty to go to my home and family and associate with the people at Cedar was the only drawback. The good men I met in the pen, our associations, walks and talks and a good many visits paid me by friends, their kind contributions to my temporal requirements, everything tended to while away the hours and days of my confinement . . . I generally made myself very attractive and homey looking as I was alone in the occupancy of [the] cell . . . I was awarded the cognomen of having the neatest looking cell in the prison . . . I spent many pleasant hours in the pen, always slept well and had a good appetite.

Brother York was something of a local poet and addressed verse to fellow cohabs, members of his family, and others. I quote but one example:

> Elder Jno C. Harper
> Dear Brother
> Two months to day I met you here
> In Utahs "Pen" for love—not fear
> Our cause the same—'tis persecution
> Because we love God's revelation
> And took of Eve's fair daughters those
> That lov'd us and who were disposed
> To keep God's laws and love each other
> And be united all together
> Trials tho hard will soon pass by
> And then how great the victory
> If to our covenants we've been true
> To God, our wives and children too

The spirit of martyrdom was prevalent enough under these circumstances. The whole Principle was at stake and many men felt great pride in having to suffer for the Principle. One Mormon friend commenting on the situation said:

I remember one man who had been imprisoned three times and when the third time came people asked him if he would go home and put away his other wife and he said, "No, sir, they are the women God gave me. They are my wives and my children. When you put me in jail again, I'll go back to them." So they did not imprison him again.

We have already noted that the prosecutions were the basis for a certain sense of guilt and shame. First of all, were the attitudes toward the civil authorities. Most of the Saints were loyal and patriotic Americans, yet they were forced into hiding and obliged to lie and engage in all kinds of deceit in order to protect themselves in the name of their religion. In the second place, there was a certain ambivalence between their Christian conscience regarding monogamy and their loyalty to the principle of plural marriage. These are deep sources of inner conflict. These conflicts probably operated chiefly at an unconscious level and yet some of our records give indication that people were aware of these difficulties. Susan, the second wife of Samuel Spaulding, remarks:

When I came back to Pleasant Grove I had to ride lying down in the wagon and covered like a load of freight. And that was what life was like before the Manifesto. And it was not so much better since. He [the husband] was not supposed to have another wife and there was nothing to do with me but to keep me here, and I went on living in secret, like I was living a life of sin. I couldn't go to church with them and he was always afraid someone would tell.

Such a hardship was a real test of a woman's willingness to put up with the difficulties. This must have given secret satisfaction to some of the first or older plural wives. Such reactions would probably not appear on the surface or if they did, they would be suppressed. Some of the overattention which the first wives gave to the plural wives on the Underground was perhaps compensatory response to their own sense of guilt and shame in the whole matter.

The men were likewise caught up in various dilemmas. Jonathan Baker, who had a number of narrow escapes from the marshals before he was captured, tells in his journal that on one occasion in June, 1888, he barely escaped.

After an absence of seven days I visited my home by stealth in the night not daring to be seen in daylight. Found all things well. While absent the deputies paid me another visit. It don't feel very good to be hunted like a beast or a criminal. They have also served papers on President Knight's family . . . and are sneaking and prying around to arrest others and this is a Christian (?) country.

It is clear from this and other evidence that while his conscious reaction was one of hostility toward the pressure, there was perhaps a sense of shame and guilt.

Some children showed a combination of guilt and hostility. A successful medical man in Utah contends that his entire life had been seriously affected by virtue of the fact that he was raised in a plural family. He bitterly remarked that there was nothing but "unhappiness in my family because of polygamy" and that he has "nothing to do with my half-brothers and sisters." He believes that Brigham Young not Joseph Smith started polygamy. He cites his wife's father who had a number of wives all living together and that they had poverty, bitterness, and unhappiness. He mentions an instance of eight wives living in one tiny house. He recalls many examples of family strife over property and many other disagreeable episodes.

On the whole this seems to be an exaggerated reaction of a child of polygamy. Apparently this person is not too well adjusted emotionally and has used polygamy as a symbol upon which he has projected a good many of his deep-lying difficulties which may have nothing much to do with it.

We must not overlook the fact that there was a great deal of thrill in all the undercover activity which we have been describing. Even imprisonment was not entirely a negative experience as indicated in the York and the Baker diaries. These men like old soldiers enjoyed retelling their experiences.

On the whole, then, there was an increase in the group solidarity as witnessed in the secrecy, the mutual help in hiding people, and refusal to give satisfactory evidence in court. On the other hand, there were hardships, imprisonment, breaking up of families, and threats to property which caused real fear and suffering. Such experiences may have served to loosen some of the solidarity. Moreover, the Mormons' basic loyalty as law-abiding citizens as well as their loyalty to the Church produced inner conflicts not easy to solve. As we shall see in the next chapter, the Manifesto produced an enormous amount of relief on the part of many Saints. But it also increased the conflict in some quarters because people turned their backs on their neighbors where formerly they had helped them in times of distress. As we shall see, members of plural families sometimes felt even more keenly the sense of difference in status after the Manifesto than they had before it was made the basis of abandoning the patriarchal order of marriage.

*The only remarkable thing that occurred this year is the suppression of the revelation on celestial marriage by the heads of the church. And for how long I do not know.*—Jonathan Baker's journal, December 31, 1890.

# 19    POST-MANIFESTO
## ADJUSTMENTS

MOST MORMONS living in Utah at the close of 1890 would have agreed with the entry of Jonathan Baker in his journal quoted above. This chapter will discuss the way in which the Mormons reacted to the Manifesto, what adjustments were made in plural families, what modifications in attitudes occurred, and the gradual relinquishment of the prosecutions by the federal government. Attention will also be given to the increasing pressure on the part of the official Mormon leaders to suppress the continuation of the practice of the Principle among their own members. In particular, after the well-known investigation of Reed Smoot on the charges that he was not entitled to hold his seat in the Senate because of his membership in the Church, the latter issued what has often been called the Second Manifesto. Then, too, we shall take up briefly the undercover continuation of plural marriage by certain dissident groups of Mormons.

By the late 1880's the more alert Mormons were aware that the increasing pressure of the federal government would sooner or later force the Church to abandon polygamy. The number of plural marriages had been declining in the late eighties and the Church announced that it would no longer approve of men entering into polygamy. Nonetheless, the reaction of the plural wife of Samuel Spaulding regarding the announcement of the Manifesto was common to many faithful Saints. She writes:

I was there in the tabernacle the day of the Manifesto, and I tell you it was an awful feeling. There President Woodruff read the Manifesto that made me no longer a wife and might make me homeless. I sat there by my mother and she looked at me and said, "How can you stand this?" But I voted for it because it was the only thing to do. I raised my hand and voted a thing that would make me an unlawful wife.

And the daughter of Edward Gilbert, whose mother was his third wife, when asked about the Manifesto—she was 17 years old at the time—said she guessed that the church authorities could not go far wrong. If they had to stop, then people ought to stop. She admitted that there were some marriages after the Manifesto and that it seemed to be all right with the Church until the "second warning" in 1904. The Manifesto shocked a great many of the Saints and left many in considerable confusion and doubt. James Powell has this to say: "The church and people have to do away with polygamy, one of the best laws that God ever gave to his children, if the Saints had lived up to it, our government could not have passed the law to prohibit the laws of God." This rationalization in terms of their own sinfulness has been mentioned in the previous chapter. Another of the faithful remarks:

I will say that when polygamy was done away with it was a great blow to me, not that I expected to ever take more wives yet I might have done if ever I thought I was good enough as the law was only for good men and women. But the thing that bothered me was that the Lord had said to the Prophet Joseph that it should be a standing law and now it was done away. (sic)

Could it be that the Lord has made a mistake? This question bothered me for a long time but it came to me all at once. That it is still a standing law and will be so forever, but we are not allowed to practice it for a while. I can now rest easy about it.

Further evidence of the distress of the Saints over this action is brought out in the October 20, 1890, entry of the Baker journal:

This announcement by the President of the Church caused an uneasy feeling among the people, and some think he has gone back on the revelation on plural marriage and its covenants and obligations. Some faint-hearted men who have entered into plural marriage have taken advantage of these sayings in the lawyers' courts and put away their plural wives that were given them of the Lord, and deserted them to shift for themselves, taking President Woodruff's statement as a good excuse for so doing.

Men and women married in polygamy at this time faced two serious questions. The first had to do with their own faith in the Principle which was much shaken by the Manifesto. The second problem was the practical one of what to do on the domestic front? Should a man go on living with his plural wives, having more children? Should he support them but no longer live with the plural spouses? Should he try to get a church divorce from his excess wives? Certainly he could not get a divorce by law. And what about the matter of desertion?

There were doubtless varied motivations behind personal decisions on how to solve the problems of plural family life after the Manifesto. One way to meet the new situation was expressed by an informant who lived in Parowan, Utah, and knew a good many polygamous families. She recalled that her father said of one of their neighbors: "Oliver Andrews should have obeyed the Manifesto and the law; he should have supported his second wife equal to the first, but he should never have lived with her after the Manifesto." Many men put away their polygamous wives after 1890 and our informant thinks chiefly for three reasons: cowardice, respect for the law, and the desire to be rid of the burden of supporting the plural families.

Another informant remarks about the Allen Tiffin family: "It was after the Manifesto that all the trouble started. People were more critical. The neighbors would say, 'Well, it looks as if the other wife were getting the best of the bargain. Look at what she's got and how the children are dressed.' " A neighbor of the second wife persuaded her to leave Mr. Tiffin. He was reluctant to see her take this step but he finally consented. He divided his farm with her. She later married again, but whether she bothered to get a church divorce is unknown.

The breakup of this family brought on a lot of public attention. Tiffin lost his position in the presidency of one of the quorums of Seventies and was not recommended to be promoted to the High Priest's quorum. This almost broke his heart. Although he had always been an active worker in the Church, right to the end of his life officials of the Ward did not permit him to participate in any official way in church affairs.

After the Manifesto Paul Lamb's second wife left at the insistence of the first. There was a fairly equal division of the property but after 1890 Lamb did not live with the plural wife. This family was interesting because the wives were sisters. However, the first wife predeceased Lamb and not long before his own death, he married this plural wife before the law. The informant remarks, "Lamb would have lived with both women, except that he had an old-country respect for the law and his first wife was determined that he give the second one up."

The Isaiah Morton family had a difficult time. In the late 1880's Morton spent some months in the penitentiary as a cohab and for a long time his second wife was on the Underground. After the Manifesto, Morton and another Mormon decided that they would desert their plural wives. They felt this to be the correct thing to do. The second wife was much upset by this decision and Morton relented and permitted her to stay. But from then on there was a distinct coolness between them although the plural wife bore Morton two more children in the middle 1890's. Then she decided that she would have no more children. She believed it wrong not to have children but felt that she was justified in stopping.

The Mortons lived in Monroe, Utah, where some of the residents, though Mormons, had long made life miserable for the plural families there by informing on them to the police. Moreover, when Morton would come to visit the second wife or even if he but stopped to talk to her over the fence, the neighbors would watch them, and, on occasion, threatened to report them to the deputies. When he came to chop wood or do other chores, he had to do so after dark and wear her bonnet and shawl as disguises.

As to the general community reaction, a daughter of the second wife said: "I was never made to feel slighted because I was a polygamous child but I know in many instances after the Manifesto when children were. At school the other children would jeer at them."

These reactions of the neighbors represent a certain release of tension that had formerly kept them from making too open criticism about plural marriage. Such reactions were rather common. Once the official position of the Church had changed, people were much freer in their negative comments. This, in turn, probably reflected some loss in status on the part of certain of these plural families.

Somewhat special circumstances surrounded those Mormons who had gone to Mexico so as to continue in the Principle, but who were later forced to return to the States. The third wife of Howard Wilson tells her story in approximately these words:

In 1912 when the exodus from Mexico came, I was pregnant with my last child. We went to El Paso and the baby was born there . . . I realized then that I had no protection and I didn't know what to do. I had no thought of leaving Brother Wilson then. In Utah it was very different and there were times when he tried to hide the fact that I was his wife. One time his brother was in town and he told me that he would not be back that night. He didn't want his brother to know about me. I told him that he need never come back to me and he used vulgar language for the first time in my presence. I heard that in later years he was hard with everyone, but with me until then he had always been kind. But that night he came back and apologized for things he had done. I realized, however, that I could not live that way and I wanted no more children who would be illegal. I finally decided to leave him and it is easy to get a church divorce. I had a hard time of it but I have always been glad that I left him . . . I went to school and taught and reared my children without his assistance.

Walter Whitehead, another Mormon colonist in Mexico, had a variety of troubles when he returned. At the time of the Exodus, as it was called, he had four wives. They were settled in different towns in the Southwest. Later he moved with his fourth wife to Provo, Utah, at a time when the church officials were seriously trying to stop further plural marriages.

Whitehead says that while he was residing in the Fourth Ward, two prominent members called on him to inquire as to when he had married his fourth wife. They had been commissioned, they said, by the High Council of Utah Stake to make this investigation. The question of the possible disfellowship of Whitehead had been discussed by the Council.

Whitehead was irritated at what seemed to him interference in his private affairs. He felt that his fourth marital venture, like the others, had had official approval although this last marriage had taken place after the general authorities had pronounced officially against the continuation of the practice, even in Mexico. He told his visitors, "Well, if you want to know about my fourth marriage, you had best talk to Anthony W. Ivins about it." According to Whitehead's story the two brethren asked no more and departed. Ivins was an Apostle who apparently earlier as Stake President in Mexico had approved plural marriages, even after 1904. While nothing further came of this investigation by the High Council, trouble was brewing in certain other quarters for Brother Whitehead.

His second wife, apparently anxious to get some of his property, began to agitate for a church divorce and also threatened him with legal action. Her story to the federal officials led to the issuance of a warrant for his arrest but he escaped and got to El Paso where shortly he crossed over into Mexico. Later he joined other Saints in returning to the old colony in Chihuahua.

Despite the continuation of prosecution after 1890 the position of the Mormon authorities was that plural families should not be broken up. Baker reports in his journal for November 7, 1891, that President Woodruff at the Box Elder Stake conference said that no man with a plurality of wives was required to break his covenants. He should provide properly for

his wives and the children. As a son of the second wife of
Joseph Adamson remarked:

After many years of practicing polygamy, it was unreasonable
to expect the thing to cease immediately with the Manifesto. Of
course, it was never intended that plural wives should stop having
children, but that only that no more marriages should be contracted.

To many families the Manifesto made little or no differ-
ence; the household arrangements continued as previously.
On the other hand, some plural wives like the second wife of
George Yates had to remain on the Underground for years.

Many of the Saints followed the pattern of Joseph F. Smith.
After 1890, he had only one official residence although he
continued to live with his plural wives. For years each of
these women was listed in the telephone directory of Salt Lake
City as "Mrs. Joseph F. Smith." During the Smoot hearings,
Smith admitted to having had 13 children born after the
Manifesto.

Joseph Adamson went on living in polygamy for years and
wife number two bore him 10 of her 12 children after 1890.
However, from 1902 on he resided only with his first wife.
The Idaho authorities were on the alert and Adamson had a
good deal of trouble keeping out of their hands. To avoid
suspicion at the time she was about to have another baby, the
second wife left the state for a few months. For years the officials in Idaho were more persistent in their efforts against
polygamy than was true of the police and judges in Utah.
The Mormons were only a small minority in Idaho and there
was greater public pressure on them.

While some of the Mormons who were driven out of Mexico
by the Revolution took the opportunity to break up their
plural families, most of them did not. Many had a severe time
of it, however. Jerome Sweet, for example, had three wives
whom he located in different communities. He had lost all
his property in Mexico and had a hard time financially. The
three wives had to get help from their children or do what
they could to supplement Sweet's meager income.

Ross Gilmore, on the other hand, brought both his wives to Provo and was soon well integrated into the community. But by this time the official church agitation against polygamy had somewhat slackened. Moreover, there was a lot of public sympathy for the Mormons who had been forced out of Mexico.

The rather common practice for men in polygamy to marry the plural wife when the first or legal wife predeceased him continued after the Manifesto. In general the community reaction to taking this step was favorable. It served as a kind of emotional as well as legal cover for polygamy.

On the other hand, there were exceptions to this practice. Thus Aaron Montgomery lived with his second wife in his later years after his first wife died but the bank regarded him as a widower in his business dealings. Aaron was quite irritated at one point when, in order to sell a piece of property, he had to secure his plural wife's signature to the conveyance. Legally she was not his wife, but in a sense she was his common-law spouse since she had long been acknowledged as his wife.

Prosecutions under the Edmunds-Tucker law continued to be rather frequent for the first years after the Manifesto. By the middle 1890's these had begun to slack off, at least in Utah. This shift in federal concern is bound up with the general amnesty to polygamists granted by Presidents Harrison and Cleveland. Moreover, the Manifesto was considered one of the prices for Utah being made a state. Apparently only the more flagrant cases were brought to federal attention or those which derived from some vengeful woman who wished to get her husband in trouble.

However, the Underground continued in operation, especially for those people who were under indictment prior to 1890 but who had escaped arrest. One of these was Jonathan Baker whose journal entry for August 6, 1892, reads:

This morning while eating breakfast, U. S. Deputy Marshal James McGeary arrested me and left a warrant charging me with unlawful cohabitation . . . and demanded me to appear before the Commissioner at Silver Reef . . . This is the first time in my life that I have been arrested and this is for choosing to obey the commandments of God.

In September, Baker was tried before the court in Beaver on a charge of unlawful cohabitation and thus describes his experience:

My name was called and I stood up before the judge devoid of all fear or tremor. The clerk read the indictment charging me with the crime of unlawful cohabitation against the dignity of the people of the United States, etc. I pled guilty to the charge and the judge asked me if I was willing to obey the law and the Manifesto as issued by President Woodruff. I told him I was willing to obey the law. Many received counsel as to that matter from those who knew best.

He then said, "Mr. Baker, I shall dismiss your case with costs." I told him I was in embarrassed circumstances and that I could not pay the costs which were $173.00. He then said he would consider my case and give sentence in the morning.

[The day following] Went down to court and was called again before the judge . . . As I stood before the judge I detected a roughish twinkle in his eye, which I bode as an omen of good. He said in a very pleasant manner, "Mr. Baker, I have considered your case and I shall dismiss you with a fine of 6 cents."

One of the devices in these towns was for the undercover informers of the federal deputies or others to keep an eye on men who came out of prison to see whether they had gone back to their wives or not. Joseph Carey, Jr., tells of the anxieties which arose as he tried to keep away from the marshals. Finally on August 9, 1892, he was arrested again for unlawful cohabitation. Marshal McGeary told Carey that "a prominent Mormon" had tipped off the authorities. For some months Carey tried to discover the identity of the informer. He finally found out that it was a well-known local Saint who had for years been at outs with him. Moreover, the informer —himself a polygamist—said he resented Carey's openly living with his plural wives when he and others had stopped doing so. Carey went to court at Beaver, but the case was dismissed for want of evidence.

The Mormon colony in Mexico was set up as a refuge for plural families. But it became more than that. Many Saints saw no reason why they should not continue to marry additional plural wives or take their first plural wives so long as the latter lived outside of the United States. Certainly for the first 15 years after the founding of the colony in Mexico, the official Church did nothing to disabuse the Mormons on this matter. Later, after the second Manifesto, the general authorities became more and more skeptical and finally stopped sanctioning plural marriages even outside the United States.

The story of Stephan Workman and his second wife is interesting in this connection. He became one of the leaders of the Mexican colony. His case must have been somewhat typical of a number of others at the time. In 1890 just prior to the Manifesto he had became engaged to Joan Williams. She was the cousin of his first wife who had, in fact, recommended her cousin as the plural wife.

Workman had trouble in getting permission to marry Joan, although she came from a fine family. Arrangements had been made to marry her in late 1890 but before they could do so, Woodruff had issued the Manifesto. When Workman finally got to see President Woodruff, the latter simply said, "You know about the Manifesto." Workman pointed out that he was engaged, that all arrangements had been made, and that he felt that his was a special case. He was told to wait. Woodruff retired into his inner office and Workman never saw him again.

A little later George Q. Cannon came out of the inner office and talked over the situation, telling him how distressed Woodruff was, that the Church stood to lose all its property by confiscation, and that Woodruff had issued the Manifesto to save the Church for the people. Workman still persisted in his plea but got no decision, neither approval nor disapproval. He then said he would go to Mexico where he could live openly. He did not want to be a lawbreaker.

Workman later got verbal approval from a particular Apostle, so he told the interviewer, and was told it was all right. He was married in the St. George Temple and he left shortly thereafter for Mexico.

Alexander Todd with five wives in his entourage was not satisfied and moved to Mexico for a few years in order to take a sixth and final wife. This marriage was kept secret for a long time because Todd was one of the most prominent people in southern Utah.

Mention has already been made of Walter Whitehead's marriage to his fourth wife in Mexico by Anthony A. Ivins and of later trouble he had on his return to Utah. Whitehead married a fifth wife some time after the return of the Mormons to the Mexican colony. He would not tell me who performed this final ceremony but he lived openly with his wife during his last years.

As time went on there was less and less general approval of clandestine plural marriages, but it was difficult to control some of the leading authorities. For example, the Smoot testimony before the Senate brought out the case of Benjamin Cluff, then president of the Brigham Young Academy in Provo and his polygamous marriage to Florence Reynolds. Florence was the daughter of George Reynolds who had been the first test case under the Edmunds law.

Benjamin Cluff, leader of an expedition which had set out from Utah to investigate the ruins of the alleged Nephite communities in Mexico and Central America, had taken time out to marry Florence Reynolds in Arizona. She then accompanied the group into the northern part of Mexico. Although this whole thing was done in secret and while the Church did nothing at the time to punish Cluff, the episode caused a considerable amount of gossip. In fact, this case symbolizes the rising pressure in the Church to make some more definite attempts to break up the practice. A few years later Cluff was obliged to resign his position as head of the Academy.

John Barclay who took Daisy Yates as his second wife married three more women after the Manifesto. During these years he was not only practicing polygamy but preaching it rather openly. Finally, in the spring of 1906 he was dismissed from an important church position.

The Frederick James story illustrates the efforts on the part of the Church to stamp out plural marriages. James had moved to Mexico with his families to escape prosecution. Some time after the second Manifesto, however, he married a third time one Sarah Brown. On January 29, 1910, he was brought before the High Council of Jaurez Stake because of this marriage in the Manti Temple in November, 1909. The Council records state that he came to the Temple just before closing time, that it was already dusk outside and said his surname was James, but with another given name than his own. He was duly married, but the clerk later suspected fraud and reported the same to the church authorities.

The case against James was handled by Apostle Anthony W. Ivins for the general authorities of the Church. There was some defense of James and some strong sentiment against him. Ivins told the High Council that President Joseph F. Smith felt strongly about this case and was insistent that James be severely disciplined. Ivins said he considered it a most unpleasant but nevertheless a necessary duty. As a result of this hearing James was stripped of his church offices and disfellowshipped. He never took any part in the Church after that but was active in general community affairs.

Just why James was not excommunicated but only disfellowshipped will never be known but in all likelihood the prominence of his family was an important factor. It is well to note that Harry Nixon, whom we mention later, expressed great bitterness that men like James were not cut off from the Church when those of lesser status were.

We have just seen that although the Church officially withdrew its approval of plural marriages in 1890, there were sporadic instances of polygamous marriages later. Apparently in most instances the ceremony was performed secretly by some high official, usually an Apostle who was sympathetic to the continuance of the practice. These marriages were regarded as sacred and secure although they were not in accordance with the official dogma of the Church. As a rule a man who had married a plural wife under these circumstances would take her later to a Mormon temple and have her "properly sealed" to him. In a few instances, as in that of Frederick James mentioned above, the couple were married in a temple but only on the basis of false identity.

No matter how the official Church rationalized the matter later, the Reed Smoot hearings made public the fact of such plural marriages after the Manifesto and that at least many of them took place with the connivance of prominent members of the church hierarchy. This led to the issuance of what was popularly known as the "second Manifesto." On Sunday, April 3, 1904, in the final session of the 74th annual conference of the Church, President Joseph F. Smith, declared in a written statement that no plural "marriages had been solemnized with the sanction, consent or knowledge of the church" since the Manifesto was issued by President Wilford Woodruff, September 24, 1890. President Smith went on to announce further that all plural marriages "are prohibited" and that anyone who would assume to "solemnize or enter into such a marriage" was subject to excommunication from the Church.

Yet despite this second official taboo agitation in favor of polygamy has continued among a small minority of Mormons. Certainly at the time of the Manifesto a good many Apostles opposed what they regarded as a surrender of a sacred principle. Among others, Owen Woodruff, John W. Taylor, and Mathias F. Cowley, all Apostles, did much to encourage the continuance of the practice in Mexico, in Canada, and even in the United States. They all took additional wives during the 1890's or early 1900's. It was in these same years that Workman, Tyler, and other prominent men in the Mexican colony took plural wives for the first time or added to those they already had. So far as the official Church was concerned the activities of John W. Taylor and Mathias F. Cowley came to an end when it was announced on April 8, 1906, that they had resigned their positions as Apostles. Actually they were forced out and to say that they had "resigned" was but a face-saving device of the general authorities.

In addition to the stimulation of polygamy by certain high

officials, there were many others of local prominence who followed their lead. Gradually little coteries of zealots for polygamy began to form in and around Salt Lake, and later in Juab County, Utah, and in the Short Creek country of northern Arizona. These people often refer to themselves as "Fundamentalists."

The Salt Lake group, led by J. W. Musser, J. L. Broadbent, and others based its defense for the continuation of plurality of wives on two grounds: one might be called the scriptural; the other, historical. The former was much the same as had been the official defense during the period when polygamy was openly approved. The historical defense is rather interesting. This group contends, through its publications, that on September 27, 1886, while on the Underground in Centerville, Utah, President John Taylor received a divine revelation to the effect that plural marriage should *not* be given up. The pertinent passages are:

My son John: You have asked me concerning the New and Everlasting Covenant and how far it is binding upon my people. Thus said the Lord: All commandments that I give must be obeyed by those calling themselves by my name, unless they are revoked by me or by my authority, and how can I revoke an everlasting covenant, for I, the Lord, am everlasting and my everlasting covenants cannot be abrogated nor done away with; BUT THEY STAND FOREVER.

Have I not given my word in great plainness on this subject? . . . Nevertheless, I, the Lord, do not change . . . and as I heretofore said to my servant, Joseph: "All those who should enter into my glory MUST AND SHALL obey my law," and have I not commanded men that if they were Abraham's seed and would enter into my glory, they must do the works of Abraham. I HAVE NOT REVOKED THIS LAW, NOR WILL I, for it is everlasting, and those who will enter into my glory must obey the conditions thereof. Even so, Amen.

It is further reported that various copies of the revelation were made and that one was deposited in the "archives of the Church" although later, it is alleged, the officials of the Church denied this. At the time of this revelation Taylor is said to have predicted that some of those then with him in hiding and who had heard the revelation "will be handled and ostracized and be cast out from the Church by your brethren because of your faithfulness and integrity in this principle [plural marriage] . . ." As it turned out, at least three of those present with Taylor were later excommunicated.

In addition to this alleged revelation the Salt Lake coterie contended that the Church merely issued the Manifesto as a sop to the Gentiles. In the January, 1939, issue of their publication, *Truth,* an article claims that Charles W. Penrose, one of the leaders of the Church, made the following statement at an Elders' Conference in London in 1908:

> I, Charles Penrose, wrote the Manifesto, with the assistance of Frank J. Cannon and John White, and it is no revelation from God, for I wrote it, and Wilford Woodruff signed it to beat the devil at its own game. Brethren, God has not withdrawn this everlasting principle, or revoked it, for how can he revoke or withdraw an everlasting principle?

That this idea had wide credence is brought out in the testimony of Walter W. Wolfe in the Reed Smoot hearings. Wolfe testified that in the late 1890's this was made clear to him by certain prominent leaders. In direct testimony Wolfe related:

> Yes, sir; it was after the Manifesto. On my way home I walked several blocks with B. F. Grant and Apostle John Henry Smith, and on the way we were talking about the conditions existing, and President Smith used these words to me: "Brother Wolfe, don't you know that the Manifesto is only a trick to beat the devil at his own game?"

While later in the Smoot hearings this statement of Wolfe's was emphatically denied by Apostle Smith and others, there is little doubt that for a decade or more after the Manifesto many Saints, both high and low, continued to practice as well as advocate plural marriage.

While the church officials tried to put an end to plural marriages in Mexico after 1904, there have been scattered instances of the practice there since. The community reactions to such disobedience are clear in the stories of Harry Nixon and Axel Hansen.

In the middle 1920's, Nixon and Hansen were cut off from the Church for having married plural wives. While they continued to live in one of the Mormon towns there, both families suffered from official and community ostracism.

On one occasion at a ward dance, Nixon brought his two wives. Various men asked the second wife to dance and after refusing several, she finally consented to dance with one of them. Soon after the dance began, a counselor of the Bishop asked Mrs. Nixon number two to stop dancing but she refused. The counselor became angry and threatened to call in the local police. But the Mexican officers refused to get entangled in any such episode, and at the end of that particular dance Nixon and his wives left for home.

The significant point is that it was a common practice in this very community for a man to bring his plural wives to such community functions. In fact, if Nixon had been married in polygamy prior to the second Manifesto, no objection would have been raised to his bringing his plural entourage to the dance. Apparently a good many ward members were rather sympathetic toward the Nixons in this situation, but the ward officials took the stand of the general authorities.

But the ostracism extended further. The Nixon and Hansen children were refused baptism, and, of course, could not be ordained into the priesthood. However, the children were allowed to attend Sunday School and other auxiliary organizations. Yet their activities were limited. For instance, one of the Nixon girls was denied a part in the grade school play. Later this girl became an elementary school teacher in the community and though permitted to teach—the Mormon Church had its own elementary school system—she was not allowed to entertain her fellow teachers in her parents' home. She was permitted, however, to give the party in the home of a friend who was in good standing in the Church.

The local church officials rationalized their treatment of these families in an interesting way. They said that if the children became members and the boys ordained to the priesthood, it would provide the Nixons and the Hansens an opportunity to use their children to spread the doctrine of plurality of wives among the young people of the community. They knew, too, that both families kept in touch with the Musser group in Salt Lake City. Various publications of the latter group were always in ample supply in the Nixon and Hansen households.

The defense of these dissenters was interesting. They pointed out the inconsistency of the official Church. They noted that Amos Tyler, Stephan Workman, and other leaders in the Mexican colony took plural wives after the second Manifesto and yet they were never disciplined. And Walter Whitehead though once threatened with church action while living in Provo, later returned to Mexico as a highly respected member of the community. Even Frederick James, though disfellowshiped for taking another plural wife through falsification of his identity, continued to live in the community and while not active in church affairs was well regarded. There is little doubt that those of higher social status in the Church escaped the censure and punishments inflicted on those of less importance in the hierarchy.

In addition to these sporadic instances, there are two examples of community settlement, centering, in part, around polygamy, in the United States itself. One of these was the colony founded by Moses Gudmundson in Utah. The other is the Short Creek settlement in northern Arizona.

The Gudmundson colony was founded in 1918 in the western part of Juab County, Utah, and at its best never had more than 60 residents. A cooperative system of farming was set up as well as a system of "wife sacrifice"—a particular form of spiritual wifehood. The founder and religious leader was Moses Gudmundson, erstwhile professor of music at the Brigham Young University.

Deviant groups are a common thing in such religious movements as Mormonism. Almost from the outset there had been little bands of members of the Church who were overzealous or who thought that the general authorities were not functioning properly. Sometimes men claimed to have received divine revelations that they were to lead the Saints. There are a number of episodes of this kind, and when such people became a real threat to the authorities they were usually cut off from the Church. This happened in the days of Joseph Smith and it happened in the regime of Brigham Young, and later. The Morrisite and Godbe defections have been mentioned earlier.

Gudmundson seems to have gained some of his ideas and most of his followers from a group that have been dubbed the Springville "Separatists." This little group in Springville, Utah, met periodically for prayer, bearing of their testimonies, and mutual counsel. The group was not insurgent so much as overzealous.

Among the Separatists certain persons had special gifts, such as communing with the spirits, speaking in tongues, and providing guidance to others. In addition, one central doctrine was that of the "true mates." They believed that certain individuals were spiritually meant for each other. One informant says that his sister and a follower of Mrs. Hannah Sorenson, one of the leaders, were spiritually mated according to the inspiration of the group and hence free to live together. This was before the colony was founded.

Gudmundson, a combination of talented violinist and mystic, was introduced to the Springville circle through his mother-in-law, Mrs. N. E. Crandall. At this time, during the fall and winter of 1917, he began to view himself as a person ready to speak the word of God. He felt called upon to inform others that the end of the world was near. He regarded the first World War as a foretaste of greater calamities to come. Moreover, he showed increasing and absorbing interest in portents and omens.

Among other schemes which Gudmundson proposed to the Springville group was the setting up of a cooperative community in Juab County where land could be obtained through homesteading. He argued the economic advantages of his cooperative plan. Here, too, they would be able to escape the temptations of the world. He seriously impressed the listeners on the necessity for preparing for the last days of the world.

Horrible catastrophes to come were predicted. However, Moses promised security and spiritual salvation if his listeners would live the right kind of life. On his urging a colony was established. About this time, one May Houtz, wife of Melvin Houtz, began to demonstrate special spiritual gifts, and while Gudmundson would tolerate no serious threats to his leadership, she became more or less his chief lieutenant.

Up to this point nothing had been done overtly which could cause any direct action to be taken against any of these individuals by the church officials. As a matter of fact, a Branch was organized in the colony in December, 1919, by the Stake president who resided in nearby Eureka. Gudmundson was made the presiding Elder. Life in the colony began to be organized in a fairly systematic way. There was a common fund of money, a common storehouse for provisions, and mutual use of tools and equipment. A little later, by the spring of 1920, communism was in full bloom, centering around a central cook-house and a dining hall. A planned division of labor was set up among the women as well as among the men.

Gudmundson, however, was becoming increasingly obsessed with his special mission. He warned his followers that their most important job was to get into a higher spiritual condition so as to escape the impending disasters. He put less stress on economic cooperation and more on what had become a true millennial movement. He began to call meetings regularly twice a day and in addition at other and often unexpected times. While at the outset these sessions were given over to bearing of testimonies by the members and clarification of doctrine by various individuals, toward the end Gudmundson's exhortations and revelations were the chief concern. He began to show signs of serious mental disorganization. His remarks became endless and rambling. On one occasion he talked for eight solid hours. Yet if anyone dared remark that what was said was difficult to understand, Gudmundson would reply that the person was not in tune and that he was not living correctly, otherwise they could communicate spiritually.

The leader put more and more emphasis upon direct communication with God and held that this was superior to the conduct of affairs through the priesthood. This marked a definite departure from the long-established practice of the Mormon Church. The followers were urged to seek spiritual guidance in all things. They were requested to record their inspirations and their dreams; but he and May Houtz usually reserved the right to interpret the same.

To become spiritually attuned, however, a member must eat a proper diet, which did not include meat. Excess of any kind was denounced. People were to cooperate unselfishly. Brotherly love was correlated with the idea of common property.

Gudmundson and May Houtz had long been close friends before each had married someone else. May and her husband had been active in the Springville Separatists and were among the most ardent members of the new colony. She was a good-looking and popular person and had a great gift of inspiration. Yet she subordinated her talents to Moses as the leading spirit. Their ideas of loving their fellowmen and of sacrificing for the higher spirituality both felt were great achievements and would prepare them for even greater heights of spirituality.

In the autumn of 1920, Moses and May, probably chaperoned by Mrs. Crandall, his mother-in-law, drove to Moss River Valley, Idaho, in an attempt to convert certain of their relatives. This missionary tour was not successful so far as securing additional converts.

Shortly after they had returned from their Idaho journey, according to a number of informants, the members saw Moses coming out of Mrs. Houtz's cabin early one morning. There were demands for explanations. Moses replied that he would explain fully. Indeed he had a grave and strange disclosure to make to his followers; but they were not yet prepared to receive the communication. They must first fast, which all did for several days. Then he disclosed the *Principle of Wife Sacrifice*.

True mates were persons of the same spiritual plane. As Gudmundson, who often used musical metaphors, expressed it, they were in tune, in complete harmony. Love between true mates was simply a manifestation of their spiritual harmony. If a person lived the proper kind of life he could have his true mate revealed to him. Union of man and wife contracted formerly might be set aside. Thus a man might have to sacrifice his wife for the Principle. Gudmundson, moreover, believed that anyone who disobeyed the dictates of the spirit in these matters would be condemned and lose contact with the spirit. It was the person's religious duty to accept the "spiritual wife." To live with the wrong mate would bring discord as well as interfere with the development of the person's spiritual qualities. Moreover, children of an ideal spiritual union were considered to be superior.

According to one informant it was not long after this announcement that a revelation to one of the members was interpreted to mean that Mrs. Gudmundson should become the spiritual mate of a certain man in the colony. This caused Mrs. Gudmundson a great deal of anguish and she became so ill she returned to her mother's home in Springville. She was pregnant at the time and on December 4, 1920, a girl was born to her. A few days later Moses accompanied by May Houtz called to see the baby. Moses told his wife that through revelation he had been instructed to take May as his spiritual wife. He and Mrs. Houtz then returned to the colony. It was not long before others were having revelations designating particular individuals to be their true mates.

Yet there was no promiscuity or free love in the popular sense of the word. When two persons were revealed as true mates, they entered into a spiritual union which seems to have been regarded as sacred and binding as any sect regards its marriage vows. This, of course, is exactly the rationale the Mormons had used at the outset of polygamy, when spiritual wifehood was regarded as one of the factors in the development of polygamy. The members of the colony, however, felt that they had advanced beyond the temple ordinances in the marriages. It is true that there was a building in which the union was solemnized, apparently furnished only with a stove and some chairs and benches. Precisely what these rituals were is unknown to the writer.

In terms of the doctrine, these people believed they had progressed beyond the traditional scriptures of the Mormons: the Bible, the *Book of Mormon,* and *The Doctrines and Covenants.* In the fall and winter of 1920 Gudmundson had written a record of his revelations. This book became the sacred word of the new cult and ranked above all other scriptures. These people were convinced of their spiritual exaltation and superiority. Gudmundson and others were accustomed to say, when questioned or opposed, "You would not understand. You haven't gone through the cleansing we have."

Following these disclosures about the colony, the Mormon Church took official action in the spring of 1921, although it tried to avoid undue publicity in this matter. Moreover, in keeping with its usual practice the records of the trials of the Saints were kept confidential. But the findings were made public. The *Provo Herald,* March 17, 1921, announced that five members, including Gudmundson, were excommunicated, and seven others disfellowshiped.

It was only after the church trials that the civil authorities became active. The sheriff of Juab County, T. H. Burton, conducted an investigation of the colony on April 19, 1921. As is common with the Mormons generally and under these conditions, the adults in the settlement had been cautioned against telling any of the new beliefs to people who, being on a lower spiritual plane, would misunderstand. Yet one of the oldest members of the colony, Grandma White, apparently had not received instructions and when cross-examined by the sheriff told some of the conditions of life there with rather childlike candor. Finally other members of the colony were able to catch her attention and motion her to prudence. But enough had come out to convince the district attorney. Later he ruled that since there appeared to be no criminal motive, he could institute no legal action provided the cult was dissolved.

The colony did break up temporarily. Gudmundson departed for California. Others returned to Idaho or to Springville. Only J. Leo Hafen and his family remained in the colony. Four months later, in August, Gudmundson suddenly reappeared. He dropped off an east-bound train at Jericho, Utah, and trudged across the desert 15 miles to the abandoned colony. He told Hafen that the day of destruction was upon them. It was a matter of days, perhaps of hours. He sent Hafen in a truck speeding to Springville to gather the elect to their former sanctuary. Hafen apparently had no trouble persuading the members who frantically gathered bedding and some food and left the doomed town in the night.

Shortly, however, trouble ensued. The district attorney got word from the conductor of the train on which Moses had come from California that the prophet had returned. The district attorney issued a complaint, charging Gudmundson with adultery. Similar complaints were issued against David White and Eldon Houtz. They were arraigned before a justice of the peace in Eureka and held under bond. White was shortly released as it appeared he had not contracted a "spiritual union." But Gerald Lowry was said to have taken a spiritual wife and a complaint was entered against him. He stood trial with Gudmundson and Houtz. Gudmundson was acquitted but the other two were convicted. The inconsistency of locking up two followers and letting the leader go free led to a petition pleading for the liberation of White and Houtz. The effort was successful.

These criminal trials marked the disruption of the community. Gudmundson returned to Los Angeles and while most of the others returned to Springville and Idaho, a few zealous ones followed their prophet to California. Whether the spiritual unions continued after this breakup is unknown, but it is certain that individuals connected with the Gudmundson ventures continued to advocate, if not practice, polygamy.

There has been recurrent national publicity about the Short Creek settlement of polygamists since the first serious trial of certain members held there on September 28, 1936. Short Creek, Arizona, lies just over the Utah line about 15 miles due south of Zion National Park. It is one of the most isolated and inaccessible places in Arizona. The only road from Utah is from Hurricane. From Kingman, the county seat of Mohave County, it is only 135 miles by airline, but was, until recently, 425 miles by highway. In the period of which we are writing, to get from Kingman to Short Creek one had to go to California, across southern Nevada, and through a corner of Utah.

For years there were a few scattered homesteads in the area and an occasional cattle ranch. The town itself was founded about 1913 by the Lauritzen family. Lauritzen got hold of all the water available and began a successful farm. Gradually other families moved to the town. Most of these people were on public or private relief. All were Mormons except a few cowhands from the nearby ranches.

Plural marriage in Short Creek had its inception at Lee's Ferry, about 65 miles to the east. Here resided a few Mormon families some of whom had continued to live in polygamy. But neither the Church nor the civil authorities had ever bothered them.

One of the early settlers in Short Creek was Isaac Carling, a cousin of the Johnson brothers of Lee's Ferry, both of whom had plural wives. One of the brothers, Price Johnson, was a good talker, had served on a mission, and ardently believed that polygamy should never have been abolished. He had been preaching this to Isaac Carling for years and by 1929 had the latter practically convinced.

The church authorities in Salt Lake City, however, had become aware of increasing public talk about the Mormons who were practicing polygamy at Lee's Ferry. When the latter heard that the Church might take steps against them, practically the whole group of polygamists at Lee's Ferry decamped to Short Creek. Price and Elmer Johnson, Carling Spencer, and Edner Allred, each with two wives, were the new colonists at Short Creek. Isaac Carling was delighted.

There had been a considerable amount of hostility between

the few Gentiles in Short Creek and the Mormons. Isaac, who was the spiritual head of the community, would not let the Gentiles smoke within 50 feet of the schoolhouse, warned them not to drink or create any disturbance, and was always prowling around trying to catch them in some kind of sin. The coming of the polygamists from Lee's Ferry solidified those members of the community who believed that they should practice plural marriage as the true gospel in spite of the laws of the land and of the Church. This tended, in turn, to arouse the antagonism of the non-Mormons and of those Mormons who did not go along with this doctrine.

A little later the church authorities at Hurricane summoned Isaac Carling and Price Johnson with his two wives to answer to certain charges about polygamy. Isaac and Price challenged the priesthood to deny the revelation of the Prophet Joseph Smith. Without trying to meet this challenge, the authorities proceeded to excommunicate the Short Creek members for practicing polygamy. The Branch there was reorganized under Charles Hansen, a monogamist and the village schoolteacher.

Isaac and Price would not be hushed up and began a campaign in favor of plural marriage. By 1935 they had practically taken over the community. Joseph W. Musser and John White Barlow of the Salt Lake coterie of pluralists visited the colony and a rich fantasy developed that this would be the first city of the Millennium, where a large number of the faithful plural families would settle to await the coming of the Lord. Although Musser returned to Salt Lake and soon afterwards lost interest in the colony, Barlow remained and for a time became a kind of spiritual leader. He was well advanced in age and had been on public or private relief for years.

A few additional polygamists did drift in. Barlow's younger brother with two wives came from Salt Lake City. His third wife was left behind so that she could draw a relief check and forward the money to him. Lyman Jessop, Carl Jentsche, and Cleveland LeBarron used the colony as a place in which to hide their second wives. Edmond Barlow brought two wives and finally John Barlow brought in his two plural spouses and the daughters of his first wife, then dead. One Jack Fish arrived from Los Angeles with a wife and "two widows" who were living with the Fishes.

Funds were donated to the colony by ardent polygamists in Salt Lake City and Los Angeles. The town simply bulged with people. It was a small area and had limited resources. The attempts to found a communistic order were not successful. A corporation called the United Trust was set up. Everyone was supposed to donate his property to this. Some members, like Fish, refused to join the United Trust and this made for trouble. Others failed to do their allotted share of work in the cooperative; still others would not follow the counsel of Barlow. Some crops were attempted but, on the whole, the colony was not motivated along economic lines. Later, in 1942, legal papers were filed for the establishment of a tax-free cooperative association to be known as "United Effort Plan."

During this time rumors began to grow in Kingman and elsewhere in Arizona that relief checks were being drawn to several wives but with the same man's name on the document as the legal husband. So, too, the political bosses of Mohave County were disturbed by Barlow's publicized claim that 500 polygamist families would soon settle in Short Creek. Such an event would be sure to upset the voting balance in the county.

In the summer of 1936 Sheriff Graham accompanied by the county attorney, Bollinger, made their way from Kingman to Short Creek. They looked around the community but had trouble getting complaints. While polygamy was admitted, people were reluctant to make formal complaints or agree to serve as witnesses. It was difficult to get direct evidence of the times, places, and circumstances. Finally Jack Childers, a homesteader, signed complaints against several families based on "information and belief." Mr. Childers' "information and belief" were not very satisfactory; some of the families mentioned in the complaint did not even exist. However, charges were made against Price Johnson and Carling Spencer and their respective second wives.

On September 6 the accused parties were brought before the justice of the peace, Lauritzen. Although Lauritzen had been at outs with the polygamists for a long time, he was a man with a sense of fair play. When it was pointed out by J. W. Musser, that the complaints rested only on "information and belief" and were thus invalid, the judge sustained him and turned the accused loose. That afternoon, however, Bollinger thought he had valid evidence, but when the court reconvened, the prisoners were not to be found.

A few weeks later, however, the four accused decided to stand trial and on September 28 the case began. The town was jammed with newspaper men and motion picture photographers and a great deal was expected of the trial. The evidence had to do with a relief check signed by Helen Hull, second wife of Price Johnson, and a birth certificate of one of her children born in 1931.

The proceedings at Short Creek came to a quick end when the attorney for the prosecution said he would dismiss the complaints and have the sheriff arrest the prisoners over again and take them to Kingman for trial. There was also a request for change of venue. In Kingman, Johnson and Spencer were convicted and sentenced to two years each in the penitentiary.

While the outside world soon forgot the Short Creek episode, 10 years later the whole story became prominent again. In the early 1940's charges were brought against six members of the colony for violation of the Mann Act. As everyone knows, the Mann Act was a legal measure to prevent the interstate commerce in prostitutes. It was never regarded as a law bearing on bigamy or polygamy. However, these six men were convicted in the lower courts under this law.

The case was appealed to the Supreme Court of the United States, where a new wrinkle in an old story emerged. On November 18, 1946, the Supreme Court affirmed by a vote of six to three the conviction of these six men on charges that their practice of plural marriage had violated the Mann Act. Justice William O. Douglas, who wrote the majority opinion said among other things, "Polygamous practices are not excluded" from the federal law against interstate white slave traffic. The Mann Act made it an offense to take any woman or girl across a state line "for purposes of prostitution or debauchery, or for any other immoral purpose." Douglas declared that polygamous practice constituted an "immoral purpose" since it had "long been outlawed in our society." He went on to say, "The establishment or maintenance of polygamous households is a notorious example of promiscuity."

Douglas sounded much like the justices on the bench in the days of the polygamous trials of the 1880's when he said, "Polygamous practices have long been branded as immoral in the law. Though they have different ramifications, they are in the same genus as the other immoral practices covered by the act." He added that to defend polygamy in terms of religious belief, "would place beyond the law any act done under the claim of religious sanction." This last point, of course, is one of the oldest defenses made by the courts in rulings on the earlier polygamous cases.

Justices Black, Jackson, and Murphy issued a dissent. Justice Murphy contended that the court was continuing "its failure to recognize that the white slave traffic act is aimed solely at the diabolical interstate and international trade in white slavery." He went on to say that the act as specifically read was not directed to "immorality in general." He also argued that the differences between monogamy and polygamy did not place the latter in the same category with prostitution or debauchery. "Marriage, even when it occurs in a form of which we disapprove is not to be compared with prostitution or debauchery or other immoralities of that character."

Once more Short Creek dropped into obscurity, but the Fundamentalists persisted in their practice of plural marriage. Trouble broke out again on July 26, 1953, when, on orders from Governor Howard Pyle, a police force of over 100 men swept into the community at dawn and arrested 36 men and 86 women. Since Arizona has no law forbidding polygamy, the state officials had to trump up other charges. On July 1 the Governor had, without publicity, declared that "a state of insurrection" existed in Short Creek. Under this blanket charge of conspiracy a variety of specific counts was

used ranging from rape and adultery to misappropriation of
school funds, falsification of public records, and failure to
comply with the corporation laws of the state. The raid had
been secretly planned and was carried out in imitation of a
military foray. However, the people of Short Creek knew
about the plan in advance and the leaders of the would-be
military contingent were somewhat deflated to find the entire
population quietly awaiting the police in the schoolyard
under the Stars and Stripes and singing "America."

The men were taken to Kingman and placed in jail. On
August 1 they were released on bail and returned home. During the interim, however, the women and their children, the
latter said to be 263 in number, were taken to Phoenix. The
state welfare agencies said they intended to place the children
in foster homes.

The avowed aim of this raid, said the Governor, was to
wipe out the community which he described as "a lawless
commercial undertaking" under the domination of a few
"greedy and licentious men" who used religion as a screen for
"white slavery" and economic exploitation. Most Short Creek-
ers and many others outside saw in this nothing but a publicity stunt of the Governor and his political henchmen who
had their eyes on the next election.

Just what the next scenes in this recurrent human drama
will be are hard to predict. It may well be that the Short Creek
community will be liquidated. Yet it is a reasonable guess that
undercover preaching and practicing of plural marriage will
continue among such dissident Mormon groups. There is
evidence that polygamy is being practiced in Mormon settlements in Canada and Mexico. Moreover, there is more than
mere rumor to the stories that the system is secretly in operation even in Salt Lake City and other cities in Utah. When
the individuals involved are discovered, they are usually excommunicated by the Church. But an institution so fervently
accepted is not to be easily wiped out by a mere edict such as
the Manifesto. Forty years of practice planted this doctrine
deep in the hearts of many Mormons and some of them were

not ready to believe that God would change his mind just so that people would obey the law.

Yet the post-Manifesto period brought many changes in attitude and value. A son of the second wife in the Morton family puts the whole psychology of the matter in these words:

After the Manifesto came the hardest time. Up until then people practiced polygamy because of their religion. No matter what happened they had the consolation that they were doing right and living their religion. The persecution did not matter, but when the Church renounced polygamy all the heroism was gone. The whole thing seemed to be in vain. Family life after that was a sort of extended Underground. The attitude of the people changed and in a way there was a stigma attached to polygamous families that had not been there before.

Two types of situations arose in the post-Manifesto period. The first was the problem of continuity of plural familes set up prior to 1890. Secondly, there was the matter of plural families established after the Manifesto. Difficulties ensued in both instances. During the early 1880's the Church had put a lot of pressure on people to go into polygamy, and for the most part the faithful tended to support this view. Yet, after the Manifesto, these very polygamous families, frequently only a few years old, developed the feeling that the Church had failed them and that the community looked down on them. This point is well brought out by an informant in the Adamson family, son of the first wife and old enough to have made some observations of the situation. It was his belief that almost all the polygamists and their families were a little embarrassed in their practice of the system. Moreover, he felt that the Manifesto had intensified this attitude. "For all the church's permission to continue living in polygamy after the Manifesto, the men and their second families were under a blight. I am completely satisfied of this. Polygamist families were always under a sort of cloud in their communities, or at least the second or third families thought they were."

After the Manifesto, John Thomas believed that it was better to keep quiet about being a polygamist, and so he, like his neighbors who were also married in polygamy, discontinued appearing at public functions with a wife on either arm as he once had done. John, however, did take one wife on one occasion and another at another, but the wives did not show up at the same gathering.

The changes in the James Hunter family, however, were of a somewhat different character. During the years prior to 1890, the Idaho authorities—Hunter lived in Idaho at this time— had been very severe on the Saints. But Idaho became a state in 1892 and the raids cooled down a little. In 1893 James who had been a Bishop in Montpelier was called to Paris to become president of the Stake there. Up to this time Rose, the second wife, had been living pretty much alone at Garden City. Now, however, James brought her to Paris and installed her in a rented house. He was the first man in Paris to live openly with his polygamous wife. The informant continued, "All the people were horrified. Many of them had secretly kept their wives in Paris and had tried to keep from being caught, but they were greatly disturbed when father brought Rose in openly. But he said it was all right and so it was. He was not molested."

The question has often been asked if children of polygamy were better Mormons than others. It is impossible to answer such a query. Although some people felt that such was the effect, others did not. For example, the first wife of Hugo Decker remarks, "It would be my own interpretation that the children have in some ways resented polygamy and that it has kept them, particularly the sons, from being active in the Church. It has been difficult for polygamous families who had lived in Utah; that is, where there had been marriages after the Manifesto a slight stigma is usually attached." The second marriage in this family had taken place after the Manifesto and the husband said that he did not believe that the Manifesto was meant to be taken as final. "But I know Wilford Woodruff meant it," said the first wife.

How a sense of shame comes into play is illustrated by a daughter of the first wife of Benjamin Wolfe. After her mother died, Wolfe legally married the second wife. The family was

shocked at this. They read of the issuance of the license in
the town newspaper and had no advance notice of it. The
grandchildren, in fact, were much more disturbed about it
than were the children. Apparently the whole town had read
of the father's marriage and the grandchildren had to hear a
good deal of the public discussion of the subject.

Shift in public sentiment as related to status and sense of
guilt is neatly brought out by a daughter of Joseph Adamson
and his second wife. She had been brought up with the idea
that the children of polygamy were on a completely equalitarian basis with the others. In fact, she was taught that they
were a little better than children born in monogamous families.

She recalled when she was about 16 years old, at the time
of the Reed Smoot hearings,

. . . how profound was my shock at hearing father say . . .
that we children probably were not recognized by law. I thought
and thought over this matter, because of my earlier bringing up
in the polygamous situation.

The whole generation that was reared in polygamy underwent
a profound shock on getting out into the world and finding that
some people didn't think that our parents were legitimately married. We had to almost reorganize ourselves in changing from
where we had been praised and looked up to, to the outside world
where the attitude was entirely different.

In a highly puritanical and monogamous society the implication of bastardy is not an easy burden to carry. No matter
how much the Principle might have meant before the Manifesto, it became increasingly a less important factor in the
belief system of the Mormons afterward. A number of our
family stories clearly reveal a growing sense of guilt and shame
on the part of plural wives and their children after the church
renunciation. For many the fact of polygamous ancestry became harder and harder to acknowledge.

This brings us to the end of our material dealing with Mormon polygamy as seen in the historical record and in the personal documents which have been so pertinent to our discussion. It is important to realize that the institutional forms

which emerged in Mormon polygamy had no blueprint behind them. Aside from the occasional advice offered the assembled Saints by Brigham Young and other leaders, there was no formal or fixed rules on how to proceed. We have noticed wide variation in the success and failure of these families. Furthermore, generalizations regarding the particular advantage of one form of household management over another is also difficult. Yet, from its inception to its official liquidation a variety of efforts were made to solve difficulties such as those between the wives, between the husbands and wives, between the children, and between and among all of those concerned in any given plural household.

Yet, polygamy, or more technically polygyny, as it is called in anthropology, is widespread. There is no doubt that Orson Pratt was resting his case from a cultural point of view on sound grounds when he maintained in his sermon in 1852 that there were far more societies in the world which permitted polygamy than those which were strictly monogamous. The historian and the cultural anthropologists have given us a vast body of material on polygamy as parts of the larger cultures in which they were imbedded. However, there was no diffusion from other polygamous societies to the Mormons. What the latter did, for the most part, was to invent their institutions *de novo*.

*Polygamy when tried under modern democratic conditions, as by the Mormons, is wrecked by the revolt of the mass of inferior men who are condemned to celibacy by it; for the maternal instinct leads a woman to prefer a tenth share in a first rate man to the exclusive possession of a third rate. Polyandry has not been tried under these conditions.*—George Bernard Shaw in The Revolutionist's Handbook and Pocket Companion, appended to his play, Man and Superman, 1903.

# 20 POLYGAMY, MORMONISM, AND THE LARGER SOCIETY

THIS, THE FINAL CHAPTER, will give an overall evaluation of the place of polygamy in the Mormon system and its possible implications for the wider society outside. While polygamy was not the whole of Mormonism, it became the symbol of the same. Yet, the Mormon movement had certain implications for a democratic society that had nothing to do with plural marriage. It might well be argued that a far more serious threat to democratic society lay in the rigid authoritarianism of Mormon dogma and practice than in the fact that a relatively small fraction of Mormon men had more than one wife. The implications of a growing body of people in our society who were trained in totalitarian beliefs such as are implicit in Mormon doctrine may be regarded as undermining certain tenets long regarded as basic to our way of life. Some of the critics of Mormon operations in Utah clearly indicated that it was not plural marriage so much as the rigid authority of the Church which was the target of their attack. But since polygamy became the symbol for all of Mormondom, it provided an important focus for the attacks upon the entire system.

As a working system, Mormonism rests upon two fundamental assumptions; revelationism and divinely established

443

priesthood. The Church of Jesus Christ of Latter-day Saints was founded by Joseph Smith on the basis of direct revelation from God. This meant the restoration of the true gospel, and in a strict sense the only way to get to the highest heaven was to join the Mormon Church. In other words, the Mormons become the chosen people of the last days. Within the Church itself, power and dominance rest on a priesthood which represents at the same time ecclesiastical control and social prestige. Moreover, the Mormon Church is dominated by a few more or less select families. New families may move into this elite, but the essential control for many decades now has remained in the hands of not more than 15 or 20 families.

The position of women within this patriarchal order makes them more or less dependent upon men. While women are baptized and made members of the Church, they cannot hold the priesthood. As a matter of fact, a woman can reach the highest glory in heaven only when she is married to a male member who will take her with him. In short, women represent a kind of second-class citizenship—an item which the Gentiles were quick to seize upon in their attacks upon Mormonism.

Within this system of female dependence upon the masculine order was introduced the "principle of the patriarchal order of marriage or plurality of wives." Officially this system was begun secretly in Nauvoo. It may have been practiced surreptitiously earlier than this, but at any rate the chief authorities of the Church were not made *au courant* with either the idea or practice until shortly before the death of Joseph Smith. Once the system was openly acknowledged in 1852, it spread rapidly throughout the membership of the Church. Yet, just how extensive plural marriage was is not completely clear, but there is considerable indirect evidence that in some communities it ran as high as 20 to 25 per cent of the male heads of families.

While Mormon women could not enter the priesthood in actuality their position under the plural-wife system was not as submerged as the non-Mormon press and preachers would have us believe. But before going into this topic something needs to be said about a larger matter of the relationship of sex to religion, and its relationship in turn to polygamy.

Most serious students of religion sooner or later come to recognize that sexual attitudes and behavior have close correlation with many aspects of religious experience. For example, the ecstasy of one is easily identified with the ecstasy of the other. Under religious excitement individuals report of "being out of themselves." In the same way, at the height of sexual congress, a sense of mutual identification of the man and woman and orgiastic responses have much in common with that reported from zealots at the height of their religious experience.

Then, too, the close relationship between phallic symbolism and religious symbolism has been noted over and over again. Certainly in our own Christian dogma the relationship of the Virgin Mary to Jesus has many ramifications. So, too, the whole notion of the fatherhood of God, and of men and women of the Church being brothers and sisters of the same father, reveals the procreative idea.

With reference to Mormonism, the interplay of sex and religion became clear in the early appearance of the doctrine of spiritual wifism. The idea that mating takes place in a heavenly state prior to mundane birth is widespread. Whether this was used originally as a rationalization for sexual indiscretion of another order we will never know, but it certainly became a convenient element in the doctrine upon which polygamy was projected.

Then, too, polygamy furnished another kind of sexual satisfaction of a direct sort, that is, sexual variationism. The opportunity for variety in sexual congress, especially in a manmade world, is found chiefly in prostitution, polygamy, and in our system of easy divorce and easy remarriage. In fact our widespread contemporary marriage-divorce-marriage sequence may be called "tandem polygamy."

The Mormon plurality of wives provided a moral sanction for variationism which probably had much to recommend it. Just what this meant to the Mormon men will never be known because but few of them were consciously aware of it. But

some inferences can be drawn from observation and from remarks made by the husbands.

There is still another element. It has long been believed by
men in our society that as one becomes older there is a loss
of sexual potency which, in turn, may be restored by the taking on of a younger and fresher mate. This notion of the restoration of sexual potency is probably not well grounded in
biological fact. Nonetheless, the marrying of younger wives
might provide not only the variationism mentioned but, in
addition, some feeling of regeneration. The symbolism of the
search for the fountain of youth is too obvious to require
elaboration.

Variationism aside, there was a high degree of puritanic
morality associated with the plurality system of the Mormons.
Of all the features which the Gentiles exaggerated and distorted, none is more evident than this. Why they distorted the
puritanism of the Saints is another story. It probably depends
upon their own sexual imagination and their own sense of
frustration and suppression. Be that as it may, Werner's characterization of the whole system as "puritan polygamy" is well
taken. As one of my informants, Calvin Williams, in discussing this matter with me remarked: "The morals were
strict in polygamy days. A man could have many wives but a
woman's virtue was highly regarded and a man was taught
continence. Moral conditions were much better then than
now."

The way of selecting a mate followed traditional American and pioneer courtship patterns. However, one important
modification occurred. This was the lessening of the importance of romantic love. It is pretty clear that although monogamous families might be set up under this motive and interest, the taking on of a second or third or more wives would
be complicated if romance became the central factor. However, in the case of older men and young women, there might
be a certain revival of the romantic impulse. We have some
evidence that in such instances the plural marriages made for
trouble. For the most part few of the courtships of plural wives
were romantic. They were rather brief and to the point.

Certain formal features of courtship, however, were developed. At the outset a man was not supposed to take a plural wife without the consent of the head of the Church as well as his first wife. As the Church grew in size, it was obviously impossible for the President to make the decision in every case, and so the Apostles and other high officials took on some of this responsibility. Yet our records and other materials show that in the early days in Utah Brigham Young was consulted personally in a large number of instances. Moreover, he often gave particular men advice about getting themselves plural wives.

Once the man had the consent of his wife and of those in authority, he could proceed to find himself a prospective mate. Again certain conventions called for his asking the parents of the girl before pursuing her too ardently. Once the parents had given their consent, it was up to the girl to say "yes" or "no" to his proposal. In actual fact, of course, this probably was not the way most courting was done. Usually the girl was picked first and the wife and the girl's parents then consulted. The approval of those in authority often came later after the whole courtship had made considerable progress. Of course, some of the more strict adherents to the gospel proceeded in the ideal fashion.

One brief note may be made on sororal polygamy. How general this was we do not know, but from our own records it is clear that a good many plural families numbered sisters among the wives. It is further my impression that with one or two exceptions these plural marriages worked out satisfactorily. When the wives fell into serious conflict, the matters of being sisters or not may have had far less to do with it than personality divergence, economic problems, and sense of differential treatment by the husband.

Of the many facets of the plural system, none is more important than that of the status of the wives with reference to each other, and with reference, in part, to the wider community. In theory all wives were supposed to be equally well treated and were to be of equal status as far as their position in this world and the next was concerned. We can find no evidence of any official statement that the first wife should be the superior or head wife as is found in a good many other societies where plural marriages are practiced. Though Mormon women were second-class citizens in God's kingdom, they were all to be on an equalitarian basis as regards their own status.

No matter what the ideal was, actually the system did not work out in this way. In family after family the first wife began as, and remained, the chief and principal wife, so far as deference and power over others were concerned. One fundamental basis for this can never be overlooked. The first wife and the other wives all knew that the first wife was the only one who was actually married in the eyes of the law. No matter how much the Mormons rationalized their belief that all the wives were equal before God, that all were married in the celestial order, the plain facts in day-by-day relationships, in political matters, and in inheritance of property were that the first wife was the only legal one. The very anxiety regarding the scheme of seeing to it that the husband married the next plural spouse on the death of the first wife is evidence of the recognition of this fact by Mormons.

Being the first wife with the highest status in the sense of legal rights did not necessarily prevent another wife from becoming the favorite in terms of personal attention by the husband. Here, too, was some basis for variation in status as well as a foundation for competition and conflict.

The status relationships of the wives to each other, of course must also be seen with reference to the treatment by the husband. Fair and just treatment in terms of attention, provision of the income and property, and the handling of children were all factors which tended to alleviate the strain that might come from status differences or attempts of one wife to get ahead of another. Some evidence of the struggle for status is illustrated in the race for babies. In addition, competition among the wives for status was found in such matters as being good housekeepers, maintaining better gardens, and otherwise playing up to the man and getting his attention.

While there was some struggle between the wives, there was likewise a good deal of cooperation. Sometimes the wives worked together to secure something from the husband that they could not get individually. Certainly there was plenty of cooperation in the sharing of difficulties in economic matters, and in the care of each other during childbearing or sickness.

The whole position of women, though secondary to men in theory, was, in fact, relatively high compared to the position of women in other pioneer societies. Mormon women were surely not the slaves pictured by the Gentile reformers. This is illustrated in a number of ways. In the first place, Utah was one of the first territories to provide for complete female suffrage. Only later when the federal government attempted to stamp out polygamy was the provision for women's suffrage removed. Secondly, in terms of economics, there was plenty of evidence that both in theory and practice women worked out of the home at various kinds of jobs. This was not only a matter of financial support for their families but it often represented their emancipation from the traditional position as housekeeper. One of the best evidences of this is found in the occupation of telegraphers. Prior to the building of the railroads, Brigham Young had seen to it that all Mormon settlements were tied together by a telegraph system, and in community after community, the telegraph operators were women. Sometimes they were single women, sometimes they were married.

Of course, women have long been associated with teaching school. And in Utah, as might be expected, there were a large number of married women teachers. Other occupations were that of midwife and store or farm managers. We have referred to a number of families where women became the managers of rather extensive properties of their husbands. Sometimes this began when the husband was on a mission. In other instances the women themselves in taking over such responsibilities proved to their husbands a good deal of capacity and were allowed to continue. In one or two divorces among the families studied the rationale was that the woman could do better in managing her own affairs and property than could the husband.

One other factor comes into play here, namely, the development of the mother's control over the family. No matter how much the patriarchal order might put the husband and father in the top place, in actual fact, the women had a great deal to do with the training of their own children. This control was enhanced where the families lived in separate households. So, too, where a man had several wives, his rotation among them might be such that considerable periods of time elapsed when the husband was not around at all. This tended to place greater responsibility on the mother and served to give her more power than she otherwise might have had. Of course, as the children grew up, the role of the father in their training and discipline would normally become more important, especially as regards the boys.

Practices connected with the inheritance of property reopen the whole matter of status. The Mormons made considerable effort to modify the traditional system. Under early territorial legislation, they removed the dower rights of the first wife, but later this was altered by federal legislative and judicial action. In any event, it became rather common practice for a man to distribute at least some fraction of his property prior to his death so that the plural wives would not be left without any support. Yet, there was a great deal of variation in this. Moreover, we saw that in family after family open conflict arose for the first time over the question of the distribution of property. This was to be expected in view of the whole tradition of private property and inheritance to which these people adhered.

Once more, the Gentile image of the husband and father in polygamy and the actualities were often worlds apart. The popular notion and one still extant was that the husbands and fathers of plural households resembled in some fashion the image of the Turkish or Oriental sultan at the head of a harem. The popular fantasy about the Oriental harem is probably equally fallacious. Nevertheless it provided the basis of some fine imagination on the part of non-Mormons regarding the role of the man in polygamy.

The motivation for entering into the plurality system at the conscious and theological level, was the adherence to the Principle. Both men and women believed thoroughly in this as religious doctrine, and this certainly helped alleviate some of the strain which might have otherwise appeared. A large variety of rationalizations were in evidence and among them the status and the economic factors loom large. Certainly the wives and their children would provide additional labor force for ambitious men. As a matter of fact, the economy of the plural system is basic. It is difficult to get statistics on this matter, but our own records and cross-cultural surveys of polygamy in other societies would seem to indicate that there is a correlation between economic status of a family and the presence or absence of polygamy. In some instances this was obviously a matter of an energetic and ambitious man who was able to make use of his wives and their children in building up his assets. Into this picture, of course, would enter the position of the man with reference to the church hierarchy. Men who were high in the hierarchy would be in a position to colonize better land and to operate more effectively in business. Yet, there are plenty of examples of men who started at the bottom of the economic ladder and by hard work and shrewd dealings built up considerable properties. Often these men were aided in this by the presence of additional wives and their children.

In contrast, it must be recognized that there were some instances where taking a plural wife really added to the economic burden of a man and that a monogamous family that was pretty well off was actually less well off when the man had to care for additional wives and families.

The role of the father in the discipline and control of the children has already been indicated. While he had the basic authority and was the final arbiter in difficulties, there is no doubt that the patriarchal order was modified in practice. In religious and moral training and in the basic controls he still remained the headman. And while occasionally some wife would differ with her husband in matters of discipline, in the serious issues he made the final decisions.

Occasionally such serious conflict in the family would arise that dissolution of marriage would be indicated. Mormon doctrine strongly opposes divorce. Marriage is supposed to be for time and eternity and not to be lightly dissolved. Yet, faced with conflict, the church authorities quickly saw that some provision would have to be made. What were called "church divorces" became officially and generally accepted. Just how frequent they were in comparison with the number of plural marriages we do not know. Certainly they were sufficient in number to warrant comment by our informants and to appear in our various written records. In addition to the church divorces, of course, there were, on occasion, legal divorces of the first wife who could not stand polygamy and moved out.

In addition to the church and civil divorces, however, there were plenty of instances where couples just separated and did not bother to get either a civil or a church divorce. While the records are often rather uncertain, the inference may be drawn that there was a general public acceptance of the idea that if a man and woman could not get along, they were free to break up and seek new mates. Sometimes these people went to other parts of the country. We have a number of examples where women picked up their baggage and left for California and hence were lost to the Mormon communities. Sometimes they stayed right in the community without bothering to secure either church or civil divorce although they might later take on new matrimonial responsibilities.

In addition to the general support which belief in the Principle would give, there are some interesting psychological elements in the day-by-day practice. I refer to the unique or idiosyncratic experiences in relationship to overt behavior. While never very widely practiced or generally accepted as a fundamental aspect of Mormonism, there is plenty of evidence that belief in dreams and their relationship to personal life was widespread among these people. To cite some instances: Emory Fairchild had a dream regarding a young girl becoming his plural wife, and this dream is reported to have become a reality in later years. In the Joseph Wright story the mother of a polygamous family herself had a dream regarding her daughters entering polygamy.

The Heinrich Bauer story is interesting in this connection. He relates that he met a girl who attracted him a great deal, but he prayed to the Lord to find out whether she should be the one or not, and it turned out that she showed little interest in him. He then tried a second time, having met a very attractive girl, but she, he discovered after prayer, was not "appointed to me." A little later he met still a third girl in another town, and he went to visit her parents. He writes in his journal:

Before going I prayed in secret to God that if she was the right person with whom I could live happy through life, and as I was still bashful, I prayed for a sign to be given me, that if she was appointed for me by God that he could cause her parents to make a start and bring us together, and that if she was not the right person for me, that they would not make the start to bring us together.

That evening I went to visit them. Brother Allred asked me how I felt about his daughter as there were so many men asking for their daughter, that they would like to know if I felt she was good enough for me. Thinking of the sign I had prayed for as soon as he began to speak of it, I said, "Yes, sure she is." That I thought her much more than just good enough for me.

Then we were promised each other that evening. We decided on the day when we were to get married.

Another story of the magical influence of prayer is illustrated in the Jesse Aldrich account. Aldrich was living in Snowflake, Arizona, and was married to a fine woman who was a good housekeeper. On one occasion she and the children became ill with diphtheria. Jesse prayed seriously about their recovery and vowed that if his wife were saved, he would show his appreciation by taking a wife in polygamy. Some time after the recovery he married Susan Street, aged 17 years.

When the officers were trying to secure evidence of James Hunter's plural family, the second wife on one occasion dreamed that officers came and caused trouble. The next morning she told her husband this dream and asked him to take her to Wyoming to a hideout there. Shortly thereafter officers arrived but did not find her since she had followed the instructions of what she believed to be a divine message.

We have some evidence of second-generation plural marriages. Unfortunately there are not enough examples of these nor are the data sufficiently complete to make any comparisons with the view to answering a question as to whether people who were reared in polygamy were any more compatible with it than those who were not.

The J. W. Nystad family, in fact, represents three generations of polygamist background. Rose, the second wife, came from a plural family, her father having had two wives, and in turn her grandfather on the mother's side had two wives, though one of them had divorced him. This is the only instance in our records where there are three generations involved in plural marriages. On the other hand, fourteen records indicate that the people involved in polygamous families in one way or another came from plural families. Thus would represent about nine per cent of the complete roster of our records.

Samuel Baxter, Sr., had three wives, his son had two. The two brothers Emmet, who married in polygamy, were both the sons of a father who had two wives. Four children of the polygamist Charles C. Rich went into polygamy. The second wife of Roger Knight has this to say about her entrance into the system: "I was just eighteen when I got married and I did not think of anything much. We'd had polygamy at home, I had seen enough of it, but I thought I could manage all right."

Brief mention should also be made of the possible relationship between the polygamy and colonization. Certainly there are many instances in which going into a new colony provided a man with the stimulus to take a plural wife. In many other families, it provided a manner of escaping from legal prosecution. Certainly the colonies in Mexico and Canada and earlier in Arizona were stimulated and developed by people who went there to escape prosecution at the hands of the federal authorities. It is quite clear that along with going on a mission as a device to escape such prosecution, being sent to a new colony was another and well-accepted one.

What happens to a group of people who feel themselves the subjects of long and severe persecution? Certainly, the Mormon story typifies the strength of in-group solidarity and mutual participation against strong out-groups, viewed as enemies. As regards the individual, paranoia as a personality trait is closely bound up with the feelings of being persecuted. In fact, the persecution complex is one of the core elements in the paranoid individual. The sources of such feelings are varied and need not be examined here. But frequently there is sufficient avoidance or sufficient conflict to provide a person with experiences which makes him feel that he is being persecuted by those around him. Applied to a whole group, will the prolongation of actions viewed as persecutory produce a set of attitudes and values that could be designated as paranoid in quality?

If individual Mormons in their experience with federal officials felt that they were being abused, injured, or threatened, they could easily weave such personal experience into a paranoidal pattern and in turn project it on others. Others might have similar experiences or imagine such experiences so that in time there would emerge a set of attitudes and values in a whole group that might be termed paranoid. Whether we should designate this as group paranoia or as a paranoidal cultural pattern is another question.

This semantic difficulty aside, there is no doubt but that the long years of conflict between the Mormons and the non-Mormons led the former to an increased sense of in-group solidarity, a firm sense of being unique and different, and a definite sense of being persecuted by the outside world. In the early years this hostility was viewed as evidence that the Mormons were different from others and that they had God's blessings despite great hardships. In fact, such difficulties, along with physical ones, were viewed as a toughening-up process to make them become real members of God's Kingdom.

Yet, the severity of the actions of the federal agents in the

1880's plus economic and political hardships led to a breakdown of some of the solidarity of the Mormons. There
emerged a willingness to make some compromise. No matter
how strong the feelings had been in the early years, toward the
end of the period of which we are writing, considerable modification in the attitudes of the Mormons regarding polygamy
was evident.

Today the official Church wants to forget that it is a unique
and different people. It has become more and more secularized
and wants to be known as a group not unlike other religious
bodies. This does not mean that the Mormons have relinquished their theory of divine revelation or the power of the
priesthood, or of being the only true church in the world; but
it does mean that certain factors which formerly stimulated
strong in-group solidarity have disappeared. Among other
items that they want to forget is the plural marriage system.
The general authorities do not like members to talk about
polygamy if they can avoid doing so.

One further point regarding this in-group–out-group conflict must be made. The existence of such oppositional attitudes over a long period provided an outlet for the inner conflicts of the Church itself. Even at the family level a certain
amount of inter-family tension might be projected or de-
flected upon the larger world, or the federal agents who were
trying to catch family members; or the Gentile reformers and
their press might be the target of such displacement. Certainly
there is plenty of evidence from the Jonathan Baker and
other records of this kind that many Mormons viewed the
disasters of the world outside as God's punishment of the Gentiles.

Shaw's comment on polygamy, which is quoted at the opening of this chapter, is sometimes mentioned by Mormons as a
defense of the plural system. It will serve us as a text for a brief
examination of certain theoretical considerations and possible
practical implications of plural marriage in the modern world.

Various writers, some more serious than others, have from
time to time raised the possibility of the revival of polygamy,

especially after World War I and World War II. After the First World War there was a considerable amount of comment in the press and elsewhere that the loss of men due to war had resulted in excess of marriageable females in some of the European countries. A remedy for this would be polygamy. While good Christians would hardly approve of such a measure, there were people with political and other interests who did take up a defense of such an idea. Actually nothing came of this, at least in any official way.

Adolf Hitler and his deputy Martin Bormann toyed with the idea of polygamy for Germany as a means to increase the German population and enhance its military strength. This was reported in the press for August 17, 1945, allegedly for a memorandum which had been found in the Reich Ministry of Justice:

The plan was submitted to Hitler by Bormann in January 1944 and was designed to counteract the effects of German war losses. It was also intended to give Germany an advantage over more rapidly reproducing nationalities to the east . . .

Bormann noted concern at the wartime slump in the German birth rate, and the more rapid increase in Asiatic populations. He estimated that after the war, Germany would have three million to four million unmarried young women who had no prospects of obtaining husbands.

His plan called for all available German males to enter into what he termed "stable conjugal relations" with one or more women and he outlined a propaganda campaign of "enlightenment" to win feminine support for the project . . .

"We cannot order the girls and women to bear children," he said, "but German women must want to bear as many children as they possibly can or else in twenty years the Reich will lack the necessary [military] divisions which we will definitely need if our people shall not perish.

"We bring into line the poets and authors," he said. "We must cleverly and incessantly draw attention to famous scholars, artists, statesmen, economists, and soldiers whose ancestors were born out of wedlock, to women who after this war or another will be married and certainly cannot get their children from the Holy Ghost."

Except where there are sharp differences in the sex ratio

in the childbearing ages, little or no demographic argument could be produced to support polygamy. Shaw's argument, which has some social psychological meaning, would be hardly feasible in a democratic society, and his implication that Mormon society was democratic is based on his ignorance of the facts. Certainly only in a highly authoritarian society under complete control of the kind which Hitler and Bormann envisaged would it be possible to work out such a marriage system. In any case to carry out the Shaw plan would involve, first, the determination of who were the superior males; and one would quickly ask by what criteria does one determine superiority in these matters? In the second place, there would arise the question of what to do with the surplus of inferior males? In addition to this, the system would certainly find no place for romantic mate selection. One could hardly expect on the basis of romance to be able to secure superior matings. In short, the likelihood of such a system under democratic conditions is small indeed. That some society of a highly authoritarian sort might be forced by special conditions to try it is quite another matter. The plan of Herr Bormann shows that he had taken into account the importance of building the necessary background to support such practices.

Finally, and to return to our Mormons, we have shown in this book wide variety of attitudes and practices which were associated with polygamy. It began in secrecy and was rationalized as a divine Principle, and it ended in secrecy and in opposition to the official Church which had once supported it. The individuals who were the day-by-day participants in this story all came from a highly puritanical and monogamously oriented society. That within a few decades a system of this kind could be so thoroughly a matter of doctrine and practice is itself some indication of the way in which institutions can change. It could hardly have been predicted that so many people would come to believe and practice a deviant form of marriage without a considerable amount of motivation and the proper kind of rationalization. We have seen that this was accomplished largely because it was believed to be a *religious principle*.

I believe this latter fact has an important implication. Without some kind of high emotional motivation, without some kind of strong feelings in the matter, rapid and serious modification of deep-lying sentiments and institutions is hardly feasible. We know that in political revolutions, such as advocate communism or anarchism, only the most ardent beliefs will carry the leaders and followers to actual practice of such schemes. In the case of polygamy, of course, there were strong sexual motivations, probably at the unconscious level, which tended to support the system once it was under way. I think this factor along with the prestige and power factors must not be overlooked in accounting for its inception and continuity. In any case, Mormon polygamy was one of the most unique, though short-lived, experiments in attempting to change our marriage system of the Christian world.

# INDEX

*Isn't One Wife Enough?* thoroughly examines one of the most harried institutions of the American past: Mormon polygamy. The author, Kimball Young, who spent many years authenticating available information and collecting fresh material (for this book), presents plural marriage in all its success and in all its sadness. This book covers the practice of plural marriage from Joseph Smith and Brigham Young, including missionary operations abroad and "underground" polygamy, to the Short Creek, Arizona, affair of recent memory.